Individual Differences

COLIN COOPER

School of Psychology, The Queen's University of Belfast

A member of the Hodder Headline Group
LONDON • NEW YORK • SYDNEY • AUCKLAND

First published in Great Britain in 1998 by
Arnold, a member of the Hodder Headline Group
338 Euston Road, London NW1 3BH
175 Fifth Avenue, New York, NY 10010
http:\\www.arnoldpublishers.com

Distributed exclusively in the USA by
St Martin's Press, Inc.
175 Fifth Avenue, New York, NY 10010

British Library Cataloguing in Publication Data
A catalogue record for this book is available from the British Library

Library of Congress Cataloging-in-Publication Data
A catalog record for this book is available from the Library of Congress

ISBN 0 340 66274 3 (pb)
ISBN 0 340 66273 5 (hb)

Publisher: Naomi Meredith
Production Editor: Julie Delf
Production Controller: Sarah Kett
Cover Design: Mouse Mat Design

Composition by Phoenix Photosetting, Chatham, Kent
Printed and bound in Great Britain by J W Arrowsmith Ltd, Bristol

To my mother, and the memory of my father

Contents

Preface

This book is all about individual differences – the branch of psychology that considers how (and equally importantly *why*) people are psychologically very different from one another. It also considers how such individual differences may be measured using psychological tests and other techniques. The book is primarily aimed at undergraduate students in psychology departments who are taking courses such as Individual Differences, Personality, Intelligence and Ability, Psychometrics or the Assessment of Individual Differences. However, students in other disciplines (such as education) and at other levels (e.g. postgraduate courses in occupational psychology) are also likely to find much to interest them – as is anyone else who is interested in the nature, causes and assessment of personality and intelligence.

The book sprang from a course of some 20 lectures that I have taught at Queen's University, Belfast, and it was written largely out of a sense of frustration with existing texts. There are plenty of excellent textbooks covering personality theory, but using one of these in isolation has always seemed to me to be inadequate, since students graduating in psychology should surely also know something about the psychology of abilities, mood, motivation, and so on.

Moreover, most texts do not consider how individual differences can be assessed, or how tests can be evaluated. Given that most readers of this book are likely to use tests in some shape or form (e.g. as a part of their project work, or in their professional careers), this seems to me to be a grave omission. However, this is not a psychometrics textbook, so readers will search in vain for the mathematical formulae that are fundamental to this branch of psychology. Given psychology students' notorious dislike of matters mathematical, I have instead tried to provide a conceptual understanding of the important issues. However, I do explore the topic of factor analysis in some detail because of the fundamental importance of this technique for many theories of personality and ability, with one chapter providing a conceptual understanding of the topic, and another showing readers how to perform (and interpret the results obtained from) such analyses.

The chapters in the book fall into two distinct categories. Chapters 1 to 10 cover the main theories of personality and ability, moods and motivation, whilst Chapters 11 to 20 deal with the *assessment* of individual differences. Readers will probably want to read these alternately (Chapter 1, Chapter 11, Chapter 2, Chapter 12, and so on), since doing so will ensure that any necessary technical issues (e.g. the principles of factor analysis) are understood before the corresponding theoretical chapters are read (e.g. trait theories of personality). Each chapter contains several self-assessment questions to allow readers to check that they have grasped key issues, and answers may be found at the end of each chapter.

My criteria for including theories and methodologies should also be made explicit. I have included theories if they are well supported by empirical evidence, important for historical reasons, or useful in applied psychology. I have not included much information about the development of personality and ability, social learning theory or constructivist models, since these are traditionally taught in other branches of the discipline. In the second half of the book, I consider the usual theoretically and practically important issues (reliability, validity, etc.), but also progress to more advanced topics (e.g. item response theory and the nature and detection of bias in mental tests) which may be important for those who will use, commission or interpret the results of psychological tests during their professional careers.

I must thank many people for their help and support during the preparation of this book. Past and present undergraduates and long-suffering graduate students have given useful feedback on draft chapters. My head of department, colleagues and friends (the distinction is often blurred) at Queen's have been more than supportive. Paul Kline was responsible for sparking my interest in the area, and taught me scepticism. Naomi Meredith, my ever-patient editor, was immensely helpful throughout, and special thanks must go to Wesley Moore, for all his help in so many ways.

I will leave the final words to an anonymous undergraduate who wrote the following kind entry on a recent 'module appraisal form':

> This is exactly the sort of thing that I thought psychology would be about when I started this course . . . it really tackles the important issues and gets to the heart of things . . .

which are my sentiments exactly. If readers feel the same way about the science of individual differences after working their way through this book, I shall be well pleased.

Colin Cooper
Belfast
January 1997

Section A: Theories of Individual Differences

1

Introduction to individual differences

INTRODUCTION

Most branches of psychology are based on broad generalisations about how people behave: they assume that people are all much the same. Thus when developmental psychologists talk about 'stages of development', the tacit assumption is that all children develop in broadly similar ways. Likewise, social psychology produces theories to explain why people *in general* may show obedience to authority, prejudice and other group-related behaviours. Learning theorists demonstrate that the broad principles of classical or operant conditioning apply to all individuals within a species – and in many cases are identical across species. Physiological psychologists generally assume that everyone's nervous system has much the same sort of structure, and will operate in much the same way.

Unfortunately, none of these assertions seems to square well with our everyday experience. Some children develop quicker than others, some individuals seem more obedient to authority than others, whilst others show strong prejudice. Although learning theorists' papers sound amazingly authoritative, it is often found that some individuals (be they rats or people) will condition faster than others, whilst some may never learn a particular task and may have to be quietly dropped from the experiment. Drugs such as caffeine and alcohol seem to have much more of an effect on some individuals than on others, and several psychophysiological measures (such as the sweatiness of the skin and patterns of electrical activity in the brain) show marked variation from person to person.

These 'individual differences' are also important in everyday life. Employers tend not to take on the first person who responds to an advertisement, but may seek out someone who has a certain combination of attitudes, abilities, skills and motives. Most of us do the same sort of thing when making friends and seeking partners – perhaps enduring loud music, boring parties and dating agencies rather than simply marrying the person who lives next door.

Thus I believe that there are four main reasons for studying individual differences.

- *It is of interest in its own right.* The examples given above show that we attach considerable importance to individual differences, and so studying how and why some individuals are different from others is an intriguing issue in its own right.
- *Psychological tests are useful in applied psychology.* The study of individual differences almost invariably leads to the publication of psychological tests. These measure abilities, knowledge, personality, mood and many other characteristics, and are of immense value to educational, occupational and clinical psychologists, teachers, nurses, careers counsellors and others who may want to diagnose learning difficulties, dyslexia or outstanding mental ability, or seek to assess an individual's suitability for promotion, level of depression or suitability for a post which requires enormous attention to detail. The proper use of psychological tests can thus benefit both society and individuals.
- *Tests are useful 'dependent variables' in other branches of psychology.* Psychologists make extensive use of psychological tests when conducting experiments. A clinical psychologist may suspect that feelings of hopelessness often lead to suicide attempts. In order to test this hypothesis, it is obviously necessary to have some way of measuring hopelessness in suicidal and non-suicidal people, and by far the simplest (although not necessarily the best) way of doing so is to look for an appropriate psychological test. Cognitive psychologists studying the link between mood and memory must be able to assess both mood and memory in order to be able to test whether a particular theory is valid, and so they need reliable mood questionnaires.
- *Other branches of psychology can predict behaviour better when they consider individual differences.* We saw above that other branches of psychology rely on broad laws to predict behaviour, e.g. 'behaviour therapy', in which the principles of conditioning are used to break some undesirable habit. The therapist may know that a certain percentage of his or her patients may be 'cured' by this technique, but is unlikely to be able to predict whether any *one individual* is more or less likely than average to benefit from the therapy. However, it might well be found that the effectiveness of a particular type of treatment is affected by the individual's personality and/or ability – a treatment that is successful in some individuals may be much less successful in others. Indeed, some of Hans Eysenck's work on the effectiveness of reward and punishment suggests that one personality trait, namely intraversion, does appear to predict whether an individual will benefit more from positive or negative reinforcement.

Thus there are good intellectual and practical reasons for studying individual differences and their assessment.

MAIN QUESTIONS

Any attempt to understand the nature of individual differences must really address two quite separate questions. The first concerns the *nature* of individual differences – how individual differences should be conceptualised. There is a wide range of answers to this question, as will be seen in the following chapters. Indeed, it has been suggested that personality does not exist, and that how we behave may be determined entirely by the situations in which we find ourselves rather than by anything 'inside us', and the evidence for such claims must be scrutinised carefully.

The second main question concerns how and why individual differences in mood, motivation, ability and personality arise. It should be clear that research into the 'how' of individual differences can really only start once there is general agreement about their structure. It would be a waste of time to perform experiments in order to try to understand how 'sociability' (or 'creativity', 'depression', 'the drive for achievement', etc.) works if there is no good evidence that sociability is an important dimension of personality in the first place. Thus studies of processes must logically follow on from studies of structure. Process models of individual differences address questions such as the following. Why should some children perform much better than others at school? Why should some people be shy and others outgoing? Why do some individuals' moods swing wildly from depression to elation and back again? Why are some individuals apparently motivated by money to the exclusion of all else?

We cannot hope to answer all of these questions in the following chapters, but we shall certainly explore what is known about the biological (and to some extent the social) processes that underlie personality, mood, ability and motivation.

However, there is one problem. Unless it is possible to measure individual differences accurately, it will be completely impossible either to determine the structure of personality, intelligence, etc. or to investigate its underlying processes. The development of good, accurate measures of individual differences (a branch of psychology known as *psychometrics*) is an absolutely *vital* step in developing and testing theories about the nature of individual differences and their underlying processes. For this reason, every chapter in this book that deals with a theory of personality has an accompanying chapter that tackles measurement issues.

HOW CAN WE DISCOVER INDIVIDUAL DIFFERENCES?

What sort of data should we use to discover individual differences? This is not an easy question to answer, for there are several possibilities.

Clinical theories

Several theories have grown out of the experiences of clinical psychologists, who realised that the ways in which they conceptualised 'abnormal behaviour' (particularly conditions such as anxiety, depression and poor self-image) might also prove useful in understanding individual differences in the 'normal' population. Some have probably been rather quick to do this. Freud, for example, saw really rather small samples of upper-middle-class Viennese women (many of whom showed symptoms that are so unusual that they do not appear in modern diagnostic manuals), refused to believe some of what they told him (such as memories of sexual abuse), and built up an enormous and complex theory about the personality structure and functions of humankind *in general*.

Detailed studies of individuals

Many people claim to have a rather good understanding of 'what makes others tick' – for members of their families and close friends, at any rate. For example, we may believe that we know through experience how to calm down (or annoy) others to whom we are close, and may feel that we have a good, intuitive understanding of the types of issues that are important to them, thereby allowing us to 'see the world from their point of view' and predict their behaviour. For example, we all have some intuitive feeling about when to mention difficult issues to those close to us. Perhaps this type of 'gut feeling' should be the mainstay of individual difference research?

There are several difficulties with this approach, even if it can be proved that accurate predictions of behaviour can truly be made, which is unlikely. First, it is enormously impractical to study people in this way because it will (presumably) take a long period of time to know anyone well enough to be able to make accurate predictions. Second, it is not particularly scientific, as it will be difficult to quantify the measurements that are obtained. Third, the vagaries of language will make it very difficult to determine whether different people operate in different ways. Two people could describe the same characteristic in a third individual in two quite different ways, and it would be impossible to be *sure* that they were referring to precisely the same characteristic. However, the greatest problem of all is self-deception. It is very easy to overestimate how well one can predict someone else's behaviour, and there is good evidence that most observers will see and remember the 1 per cent of behaviours that were correctly predicted, and ignore or explain away the 99 per cent of predictions that were incorrect. All of these difficulties also apply to attempts to discover the roots of personality through introspection – there is no guarantee that the theories that emerge from such a process will be true in any scientific sense of the word.

Armchair speculation

If one has made good, unbiased observations of how individuals behave in many situations, it might be reasonable to generate and test some hypotheses about behaviour. For example, someone may notice that some individuals tend to be anxious and jumpy, worry, lose their temper more easily than most, and so on. That is, the observer may notice that a whole bundle of characteristics seem to vary together, and suggest that 'anxiety' (or something similar) might be an interesting aspect of personality. Of course, there are likely to be all sorts of problems associated with such casual observations. The observations may simply be wrong, or they may fail to take account of situations. For example, the people who were perceived as being anxious might all have been in some stressful situation – it may be that the *situation* (rather than the person) determines how they react. Moreover, the ideas may be expressed so vaguely that they are impossible to test, as in Plato's observation that the mind is like a chariot drawn by four horses. Literature contains several testable hypotheses about personality, e.g. when Shakespeare speaks through Julius Caesar as follows:

> Let me have men about me that are fat,
> Sleek-headed men and such as sleep o' nights,
> Yond' Cassius has a lean and hungry look.
> He thinks too much; such men are dangerous.
>
> (Shakespeare: *Julius Caesar* I:ii)

This quotation suggests some rather interesting (and potentially empirically testable) process models of 'dangerousness'.

Scientific assessment of individuals using mental tests

Because of the problems inherent in the other approaches discussed above, many psychologists opt for a more scientific approach to the study of personality and other forms of individual differences. One popular approach involves the use of statistical techniques to discover consistencies in behaviours across situations, and to determine which behaviours tend to occur together in individuals. The raw data of such methods are either ratings of behaviour (obtained by trained raters who note well-defined behaviours, and so very different from the impressionistic approach mentioned above) or scores on questionnaires that are constructed using sound statistical techniques. Much care is taken to ensure that the measurements are both accurate and replicable.

Implicit personality theories

Brief mention must also be made of the so-called *implicit personality theories*, although (for reasons that will become apparent) these seem to fall within the remit of social psychology rather than individual differences. Implicit personality theories reflect our tendency to attribute certain characteristics to other people on the basis of minimal evidence. For example, if a friend told you that their new neighbour was 'surly', you would tend to attribute a whole range of other characteristics to that person as well, e.g. presuming them to be ugly, mean and unsociable – three characteristics that need not necessarily have anything to do with surliness. Variables as diverse as wearing glasses, being attractive or having downcast eyes are reliably associated with certain characteristics of personality and intelligence (Mischel, 1986), showing that we all tend to view others in terms of broad stereotypes, and often attribute to them characteristics for which we have no evidence. The danger of this is that it will lead to a 'self-fulfilling prophecy'. Having attributed all of these negative characteristics to the surly neighbour, you are unlikely to behave very pleasantly towards them when you meet them. This behaviour may be reciprocated, and so the expectations will be confirmed.

This is all very interesting, but it does not really describe what personality (or mood, or ability) actually *is* – rather it just deals with people's *impressions* of what personality *should be*, the formation of stereotypes, the use of cues in person perception and other issues that really lie in the domain of social psychology. For this reason these approaches are not considered in this book.

SUMMARY

This brief chapter has introduced the general area of individual differences, and has suggested that the topic is worth studying because of its inherent interest, the many practical applications of tests designed to measure individual differences, the need to measure individual differences in order to test theories in other branches of psychology, and the ability to make more accurate predictions from theories that consider both individual differences and the impact of experimental interventions on behaviour. We have also considered some methods for studying individual differences, each with its own advantages and drawbacks, and have introduced the distinction between structural models ('how do people differ?') and process models ('why/when/where?') and laid the foundations for discussing the assessment of individual differences.

2

Kelly and Rogers

BACKGROUND

The theories of Carl Rogers and George Kelly are included in this book because they are both simple and influential. They suggest that personality is closely related to the way in which people view themselves and others, and that it is necessary to understand a person's individual ('phenomenological') view of the world. Both theories have had considerable influence on the theory and practice of clinical psychology and counselling psychology.

Recommended prior reading

None.

INTRODUCTION

The theories of George Kelly and Carl Rogers are treated together because they are both *phenomenological* in nature – they assume that a person's conscious experience can reveal their basic personality. More specifically, they suggest that an individual's personality can be understood by knowing how they understand and experience the world, both emotionally and cognitively. Thus both Kelly and Rogers focus on how the *individual* perceives him- or herself and other people. The aim is to understand each individual's unique view of the world, through exploring their thoughts, feelings and beliefs. This technique (known as introspection) is perhaps the most obvious and simple way of investigating personality, which is why we consider these theories first.

As will be shown later, other theorists tend to disagree with the view that asking people to 'look inside' and describe their views and feelings can reveal their basic personality. Freud and his followers suggest that the main determinants of personality lurk in areas of the mind that are usually completely unconscious, and so are not accessible to introspection. Furthermore, since they believe that people have an almost infinite capacity for self-delusion, 'remembering' events that did not happen and forgetting those that did take place, the approach of simply asking people to think about how they feel about themselves or others may be doomed to failure. According to

Freud, only the clear-minded and dispassionate analyst can see the true nature and origins of behaviour and symptoms, and the client has to be persuaded of the veracity of the analyst's interpretations. Thus followers of Freud believe that the types of theory discussed in this chapter are unlikely to prove useful in understanding personality.

Another influential group of theorists also has difficulty with the phenomenological approach. Trait theorists suggest that rather than understanding how *individuals* view the world, it is much more useful to discover the ways in which *large samples* of people differ from each other. They view personality as something 'inside' the individual that determines behaviour, perhaps under the control of biological and genetic factors. They are suspicious of the *meaning* attached to people's responses to items in personality questionnaires, and so perform elaborate statistical analyses of the *patterns* of these responses.

For example, suppose that a personality questionnaire asks people to rate on a five-point scale the extent to which they agree with statements such as 'I am easily irritated', 'honesty is very important to me', and so on. Such self-reports can be treated in two ways. First, they can be accepted at face value – it is possible to infer that someone who strongly agrees with the former statement really does feel irritable, and Rogers and Kelly would take precisely this view. Alternatively, the responses can be regarded as mere 'box-ticking behaviours' that need not reveal anything about how the person 'really is' – all that matters is whether people who answer certain questions in certain ways also tend to answer *other* items in certain ways. Responses to questionnaire items are regarded as mere behaviours to be analysed, rather than as true insights into the person's psyche.

The theories outlined in this chapter take the former view. Indeed, they maintain that our *subjective* view of ourselves, other people and events is of paramount importance. Since we can all choose to view events from a variety of standpoints (e.g. being sacked can be viewed as a personal rejection, a minor inconvenience or a great opportunity to change one's lifestyle), any such theory of personality must focus on how we view and interpret events. Kelly once suggested that 'the individual's views of themselves and other people provides the only sensible basis for understanding how the individual's personality system operates'.

Because of this belief in the ability of the individual to communicate his or her thoughts, feelings and experiences, and potentially to *alter* 'unhelpful' views of the world, the theories described in this chapter have had a substantial impact on counselling and clinical psychology. Rogers' theory, in particular, is almost indistinguishable from the practice of 'client-centred therapy' that is the cornerstone of much modern practice in counselling.

SELF-ASSESSMENT QUESTION 2.1

What is meant by the phenomenological approach to personality study?

AN INTRODUCTION TO GEORGE KELLY'S PERSONAL CONSTRUCT THEORY

After narrowly escaping becoming an aeronautical engineer, George Kelly trained as a clinical psychologist and ran a mobile psychological service in Kansas in the 1920s. He had a background in psychoanalytical theory, but gradually became convinced that his clients were 'paralyzed by prolonged drought, dust-storms and economic concerns, not by overflowing libidinal forces' (Rykman, 1992, p. 338). He felt that what was lacking from traditional theories of personality (which in those days meant psychoanalysis, learning theories and behaviourism) was any account of the way that individuals conceptualised, or tried to make sense of, the world. Indeed, such theories appeared to ignore what seemed obvious to Kelly – that people strive to understand what is happening in their lives, and to predict what will happen next. He noted that:

> A typical afternoon might find me talking to a graduate student at one o'clock, doing all those familiar things that thesis directors have to do – encouraging the student to pinpoint issues, to observe, to become intimate with the problem, to form hypotheses either inductively or deductively, to make some preliminary test runs, to relate his data to his predictions, to control his experiments so that he will know what led to what, to generalise cautiously and revise his thinking in the light of experience.
>
> At two o'clock I might have an appointment with a client (i.e. patient). During that interview I would not be taking the role of scientist but rather helping the distressed person work out some solutions to his life's problems. So what would I do? Why, I would try to get him to pinpoint issues, to observe, to become intimate with the problem, to form hypotheses either inductively or deductively, to make some preliminary test runs, to relate outcomes to anticipations, to control his ventures so that he will know what led to what, to generalise cautiously and to revise his dogma in the light of experience.
>
> (Kelly, 1963, quoted by Bannister and Mair, 1968, p. 3)

Kelly's theory thus suggests that each person operates rather like a scientist – making observations, performing inductive reasoning to try to formulate rules which explain how the world works, applying those rules to new pieces of data and observing whether the results are as expected. If the rules do indeed seem to explain behaviour, the 'model' thus created is useful. If not, it needs to be refined or discarded in favour of an alternative. Thus each person is always looking towards the future, trying to anticipate events on the basis of the mental model. Since people form such an important part of our lives, a lot of time is spent trying to evaluate (or *construe*) other individuals in order to predict their likely behaviour. As Kelly (1955, p. 591) observes, 'it is the future which tantalizes man, not the past. Always he reaches out to the future through the window of the present'.

The people or objects that the individual seeks to understand are known as 'elements', and so the aim of Kelly's theory is to understand how people *construe* various *elements*. That is, the theory attempts to identify how we each choose to construe our uniquely experienced ('phenomenological') world, and to indicate some possible consequences of using one system of constructs rather than another. Different people may build up quite different models to predict how others will behave – a principle that Kelly termed 'constructive alternatism'. The key point about a 'good' mental model is not that it represents things as they 'really' are (which is, in any case, untestable), but that it allows accurate predictions to be made in the types of setting that matter to the person doing the construing.

Why different people develop (or appear to develop) different systems of constructs

Kelly's theory suggests that three basic steps are followed: observing behaviour, trying to *understand* what is going on, and testing whether this 'mental model' actually works – in other words, whether it can predict the behaviour of other elements (people) in other situations. We all have plenty of our own informal theories about how others behave – for example, 'people who laugh a lot are probably sad and unhappy inside', 'antisocial people do better at school', 'bigoted people are not in touch with their own feelings', 'aggressive people can be calmed down if you tell them a joke', and so on. Each of these theories may (or may not) be useful in helping us to understand how certain individuals will react in certain situations, and we are constantly trying to determine the types of people for whom these theories make accurate predictions, and the settings in which the predictions work. For example, we may *try* telling jokes to aggressive people, although in this instance we would probably learn quite quickly and painfully that this theory does not work, and abandon it. However, the crucial point is that different people will tend to notice different characteristics about others in order to interpret and predict their behaviour.

In the above example, I may find it useful to notice whether people laugh a lot, are quiet, are bigoted and (perhaps) are aggressive. Other people may notice quite different characteristics when observing the very same individuals and trying to understand and predict their behaviour. For example, another person may choose to notice whether they are well-mannered, impulsive, surly, stubborn, scary . . . the list of possible terms is almost endless.

So, too, is the range of possible outcomes that we may choose to predict. Some individuals may be very keen to understand how people will behave when poised to make a purchase. A salesperson will probably have some well-developed 'rules of thumb' for deciding who is likely to make a purchase and who is just browsing – after all, their commission depends on their approaching the right individuals. Thus it is probable that sales staff will notice features of people's behaviour that are not at all obvious to the casual observer, and they will have developed ways of construing customers that will help them to decide whether or not they are likely to make a purchase. Non-salespersons

Subsection: Evaluation / different constructs

would simply not be interested in predicting this type of behaviour, and so their construct systems will not have evolved to allow them to do so. This is the first reason why all people do not use the same construct systems – not everyone is interested in predicting the same set of outcomes.

Second, people differ in the way in which they use language – by 'antisocial' I may mean 'quiet and reserved', but someone else may mean 'aggressive or destructive'. So even if it is possible to find out what words people use to categorise others, it does not follow that two individuals who use the same word are actually referring to the same thing (i.e. the same psychological or behavioural characteristic) by using that word. Similarly, it is possible that two people who use two *different* words to describe a characteristic might be referring to precisely the same thing – one person's 'aloof' might refer to exactly the same psychological characteristics as another person's 'shy' – although, of course, it is rather difficult to test this.

Third, people's own backgrounds and values will influence the way in which they construe behaviours. Suppose that two individuals witness someone placing a traffic cone on top of a lamppost. One might construe the person as 'criminal' (as opposed to law-abiding) and another might construe them as 'high-spirited' (as opposed to boring).

SELF-ASSESSMENT QUESTION 2.2

Why do people generally use different constructs to describe the same element(s)?

When construct systems fail to work

Of course, our predictions about people's behaviour do not always turn out to be accurate. Suppose that we believe that the three ideal ingredients for a pleasant night's socialising involve other people whom we construe as talkative, relaxed and generous. We would expect a stranger whom we construed in this manner to be good company. Suppose that the prediction is completely wrong, and the night turns out to be a complete disaster. Faced with a discrepancy between their mental model of what *should* happen and the actual behaviour and feelings of all concerned, the individual doing the construing has several courses of action open to them.

- They can re-evaluate the person with regard to each of the characteristics. Perhaps the stranger was not quite so generous/talkative/relaxed as was first thought. This implies that the model for the kind of person who makes good company may still be correct, as it was the initial construing of the stranger's character that was faulty.
- The model can be expanded. Perhaps the whole ghastly evening shows that some *other* characteristics (such as extreme political views, or a penchant for lechery or practical joking) can *also* determine whether a person makes good company. If so, the model can be extended to take these constructs

into account. The stranger would not have performed well against some of these new criteria, and so this accounts for the unenjoyable evening.

- They may conclude that the model is a failure, and that they need to consider quite different characteristics of people in order to predict their behaviour. Abandoning one's mental model of how people work and having to construct a new one is thought to be associated with feelings of threat and fear, as we shall see.

Ways of construing

The 'elements' in Kelly's theory are usually other people, but can be things as diverse as paintings, political parties or cheeses – anything, in fact, where there are individual differences which the person wants to try to understand and predict. As we have seen, Kelly suggests that we use a number of 'personal constructs' to identify individual differences within the elements. These personal constructs are rather like the rating scales with which you may be familiar from experiments in social psychology. Each consists of two terms, of opposite *psychological* meaning *for the individual*.

Some elaboration is needed here. Whilst constructs such as 'lively/quiet', 'good/bad', 'friendly/unfriendly', 'warm/cold' and 'intelligent/unintelligent' are quite acceptable, so too are constructs like 'warm/hostile' and 'laid-back/boring' and even 'tidy/gringly', in which the two words are not logical opposites or (in the last case) even proper words at all. All that matters is that the *individual* knows what is meant by the terms and uses them consistently. The details of how these constructs are discovered are given in Chapter 12.

[handwritten margin note: Subjective – they know what they mean!]

SELF-ASSESSMENT QUESTION 2.3

Why should constructs be defined by two terms, rather than just one?

Kelly's theory is unusual in that it is stated quite formally in terms of a 'fundamental postulate' and 11 corollaries (or logical consequences) in the 1955 book, rather than being developed piecemeal over time. The fundamental postulate states that 'a person's processes are psychologically channelized by the way in which he anticipates events'. Kelly (1955) defines the precise meaning of each of the words in what he called this 'rather simple' sentence. In essence it means that each individual builds and refines a (possibly idiosyncratic) mental model to help them to anticipate life events. One problem which soon arises is that a person's construct system may yield contradictory predictions about an element. For example, I might construe Barbara as a 'good person' (as opposed to a bad person) and 'pleasant' (as opposed to unpleasant). It is quite possible that following an argument Barbara will be construed as 'good person' and 'unpleasant' – it would take more evidence to convince someone that a person has shifted from being fundamentally good to fundamentally bad than from being 'pleasant' to being 'unpleasant'. Given such discrepancies in the construct system, how can one predict how Barbara 'really is', or how she will act? Kelly believed that these discrepancies could be resolved by viewing the constructs as hierarchically organised, with some constructs being more important than others – these will carry more weight when one is attempting to predict behaviour.

Kelly argued that the development and elaboration of a construct system is a vitally important aspect of mental health. If an individual employs relatively few constructs, then they are unlikely to be able to predict with any great accuracy how others might behave in a particular situation. They will simply not have the cognitive apparatus for perceiving the fine distinctions between people that are necessary to predict their actions. At the other extreme, an individual could have a vast and unwieldy system of constructs that are not organised according to a strict hierarchy, and which can provide conflicting suggestions as to how the other person should behave – one can gather a great deal of information (i.e. employ many constructs) but be unable to make much use of it. Instead, Kelly considered that a system of constructs should be relatively small, but chosen and structured so as to yield the best possible predictions about the behaviour of others. Indeed, he suggested that individuals constantly strive to refine their construct systems, to discard old constructs which do not prove useful in predicting behaviour, and to introduce better ones, and to extend the number of constructs so that the construct system covers an ever wider range of events.

Strangely enough, the ability of individuals to predict others' behaviour on the basis of their construct systems has been the subject of rather less study than one might expect, possibly because it is so much easier to perform some statistical analyses on the relationships between constructs than to examine the overall effectiveness of an individual's construct system in predicting behaviour. In one example, Kelly suggests how we may all have some mental image of the kind of person with whom we eventually want to settle down. This corresponds to a series of constructs which we believe are important for an enjoyable relationship. When we meet someone we evaluate them with regard to these constructs (among others). If they consistently seem to fit our preconceived picture of 'Mr/Ms Right', then we may well decide to enter into a long-term relationship. If they do not, then we can either look for someone else, change our preconceived picture (perhaps 'sense of humour' is not *that* vital) or carefully explore the possibility that we have really construed them correctly – there may be a sense of humour somewhere under that granite façade.

Kelly suggested that constructs can be applied to elements in three ways. *Pre-emptive* construing simply enables us to categorise others without allowing for further elaboration. For example, by applying the construct 'criminal/honest' to someone and deciding that they are at the 'criminal' pole, pre-emptive construing would imply that there is simply nothing more to be said – the only thing that it is necessary to know about that individual is that he or she is a criminal, for all criminals are exactly the same, and they have no

useful personality tool of how we construct

other interesting features. The person is (quite literally) viewed as 'just a criminal'. This form of construing is not helpful in developing and elaborating our system of constructs, since it does not encourage fine analysis of behaviour or of individual differences that manifestly *do* exist between different types of criminal.

A *constellatory* construct is little better. It basically works in terms of crude stereotypes – if an individual is construed in a certain way (e.g. as a criminal), then he or she will automatically be assumed to possess a number of other characteristics. For example, a person perceived as a criminal might automatically be construed as violent (rather than gentle), unintelligent (rather than intelligent), and so on – a description that hardly fits the average City fraudster.

It is much better for the individual to use constructs in a *propositional* manner, in which he or she evaluates the individual along each of their available constructs – some criminals might be viewed as intelligent and others as unintelligent, and some would be construed as violent and others as gentle. In other words, the person tries to construe each element as an *individual* rather than in terms of packages of constructs (as with constellatory construing), or by simply not trying to develop their understanding (as with pre-emptive construing).

SELF-ASSESSMENT QUESTION 2.4

Why are propositional constructs thought to be the most useful?

It should be obvious that not all constructs will apply to all elements. The 'good/bad' construct can be applied to most things, but 'friendly/unfriendly' cannot really be applied to cheeses (except perhaps for the pepper-covered ones that burn your mouth) and 'representational/abstract' cannot really be applied to anything other than visual art. Thus we say that each construct has a 'range of convenience', or a range of elements to which it applies.

Emotion

One very important group of constructs consists of those that are used to describe one's self – constructs that are used to understand what sort of person one is, and to predict one's future actions. These are called *core constructs*, and since it is very important that we should be able to understand and predict our own behaviour, any disruption of these constructs is associated with several unpleasant emotional experiences. *Guilt* is experienced when we construe ourselves as behaving in ways that are inconsistent with our previous self-constructions with regard to these core constructs. For example, if someone who has previously used the construct 'honest/dishonest' as a core construct (rating themselves as 'honest') is forced to construe some of his or her behaviours as 'dishonest' (e.g. stealing from a shop in order to keep in with his or her peer group), then Kelly claimed that such an individual will experience guilt.

Feelings of *threat* may arise when one realises that one's core constructs are about to change radically. For example, anyone would feel threatened when diagnosed with some terrible illness (e.g. AIDS, Alzheimer's or motor neurone disease) which inevitably meant that the 'self' would have to be radically reconstrued. *Fear* is similar, but involves things about which we know less. As a result of reading the papers I know something about the symptoms of AIDS and Alzheimer's disease, but relatively little about the effects of being bitten by an adder or being involved in a car crash – I feel threatened by the former two and fear the latter pair. Children feel *threatened* if they feel that their parents may separate, but they *fear* ghosts.

Hostility arises when one continues to try to use a construct that is manifestly not working – our hostile actions attempt to coerce others into giving us evidence that our construing is, after all, correct. Football supporters whose team has tumbled to the bottom of the league will want to continue to construe their team as 'excellent' (as opposed to useless), and will react with hostility whenever anyone suggests the opposite is the case, with fairly predictable results . . .

Anxiety is felt whenever it is realised that one's construct system is unable to deal with events – that is, that the events which occur fall outside the *range of convenience* of the construct system. Feelings of anxiety may well then be followed by attempts to extend the construct system in order to understand the novel situation. To follow up an earlier example, in which a person has rather few constructs that are useful in helping them to predict how people will behave in groups, it should follow that they experience anxiety in group situations.

Kelly's view of *aggression* is, surprisingly, diametrically opposed to his view of hostility. Whereas hostility is seen to be the result of clinging to constructs that simply fail to predict events, aggression accompanies experiments that are performed to check the validity of one's construct system. For example, we may literally 'play games' with people to see if they react as expected, or test out our construct system in new settings, by performing new activities, or by assuming some other persona. It is not difficult to find examples of this from everyday life. For example, the author Eric Blair ('George Orwell'), an Eton-educated intellectual, lived the life of a tramp for many months, an experience that may well have had something to do with his need to test out the general validity of his construct system. This constant testing of the construct system is a vitally important aspect of personal growth, since it is only through finding the weaknesses of one's construct system that one can usefully develop it.

SELF-ASSESSMENT QUESTION 2.5

Ask yourself *why* an individual would want to expand a certain area of their construct system, and try to work out which emotion an individual might experience before aggressively testing out their construct system in a new area.

ints arising from Kelly's theory

.elly's model of 'man the scientist' is now often described as a 'cognitive' theory, since it involves a rational appraisal of other people, objects and experiences along certain dimensions that have meaning to the individual – although Kelly himself was not at all happy with this description. It assumes that people are generally self-aware and rational, and spend their lives trying to improve their understanding of more and more aspects of their phenomenological world (that is, the world as seen through their unique pattern of constructs) by seeking to extend their construct systems so that they can make ever better predictions about more and more things. As will be shown in Chapter 12, the main problems with this theory arise in communicating the precise *meaning* of one's constructs to others. It would be a brave therapist who could claim that they could view their world through the construct system of another person, whose subtle nuances of meaning may elude them.

It is also not obvious how effective the technique may be for assessing personality for applied purposes. For example, if a company wants to recruit salespersons, then sociability is one obvious requirement – the organisation wants a salesperson who will go and talk to potential customers. Whilst it would be possible to attempt to understand the phenomenal (personal) world of each applicant using the techniques described in Chapter 12, and to deduce from this how each person regards him- or herself, first, there is absolutely no guarantee that the self-reports will be valid. Just because someone views him- or herself as being 'talkative' (as opposed to 'quiet'), this does not guarantee that they actually *are* more talkative than the norm. I can think of several rather dull individuals who are firmly convinced that they have a first-rate sense of humour!

Second, it is quite possible that some individuals will simply not *use* any sort of 'talkative/quiet', 'introvert/extrovert' or 'loud/shy' construct – they may simply not notice such distinctions in others. If such constructs simply fail to appear in an individual's repertoire of constructs, it would be impossible to discover how they viewed themselves on these dimensions. However, just because certain individuals do not find that constructs such as these help them to predict the behaviour of others (which is the ultimate reason why no such distinctions between people are drawn by their construct systems), this does not mean that the characteristics really do not *exist*. It might, for example, merely mean that the person doing the construing makes extremely bad judgements when attempting to assess extraversion, and *this* could be why they do not find the construct helpful.

That said, the theory does allow for plenty of interesting predictions to be made, those relating emotion to certain features of the construct system being particularly fascinating, in that the theory tries to define emotion in terms of what is going on inside the individual (in terms of the way in which they construe, or fail to construe, certain crucial aspects of their environment), rather than in terms of what really seems to be happening to people.

Some interesting work has also been performed on the *structure* of construct systems. 'Cognitive complexity' is a term coined by Bieri (1966) to indicate the extent to which individuals can adopt a complex, multidimensional view of others, rather than using just a few constructs. Some research suggests that cognitive complexity is not closely related to general intelligence, which is a *very* surprising finding that needs further study. I am also slightly concerned that some measures of cognitive complexity may be influenced by the accuracy with which individuals can use their construct system, an issue to which we shall return when discussing the reliability with which constructs can be used, in Chapter 12.

There are also a few interesting areas that are *not* covered by Kelly's theory. There is no good theory of personality development apart from the belief that we all seek to expand and extend our construct systems. How, when and why we learn to construe is something of a mystery. Some may also feel that it is all rather mechanistic – classifying individuals and making coldly logical decisions about how they may behave (with emotions popping up as a sort of by-product) does not sound like a very warm, human characteristic – although this itself is hardly good objective evidence against the theory. However, given that personal experience plays such an important part in this theory, it has always struck me as slightly odd that we rarely seem to perceive ourselves *using* constructs consciously. When I meet a stranger, I am not consciously aware of producing my list of constructs from some recess of my mind and evaluating the person on each of them.

What we *need* in order to evaluate this theory are hard, empirical studies of precisely how ordinary people decide that their construct systems are failing and then revise them – that is, we need to check whether our construct systems are indeed used and revised as Kelly suggested.

THE PERSON-CENTRED THEORY OF CARL ROGERS

Whereas Kelly believed that people form hypotheses and behave analytically in forging a useful construct system, Carl Rogers focused closely on the meanings of the *feelings* experienced by each individual. As we shall see in Chapter 3, a Freudian would dismiss emotional experiences as mere by-products of some more fundamental unconscious conflict, and a personal construct psychologist would regard them as interesting indicators of how well the construct system was working. For Rogers, the subjective experience of reality was by far the most interesting source of data. According to Rogers' view, a psychologically healthly individual is one who is in touch with their own emotional experiences, who 'listens' to their emotions and can express their true feelings openly and without distortion.

Rogers believed that an individual's personality can best be understood through building up an understanding of how they see the world, and that the most useful way of obtaining this understanding was through a careful clinical interview. You will have gathered from the above that Rogers was a clinical psychologist by training – his theories developed gradually from the 1940s to the 1980s, and the basic principles of his approach have been adopted enthusiastically by counsellors and clinical psychologists who believe that a careful, empathic study of what a person thinks and feels is the most valuable way of gaining an insight into their nature.

He was to say that 'in my relationships with persons I have found that it does not help, in the long run, to act as though I were something that I am not' (Rogers, 1967, p. 16). This implied, for example, that one should express emotions, admit to feelings of weakness and uncertainty and avoid assuming social roles, such as being a tyrannical supervisor when at work, a dutiful wife with one's family, and an 'intellectual' with the neighbours. He also believes that open honest communication between individuals is an exceptionally rewarding experience for both parties, and his method of therapy is primarily concerned with creating a safe, supportive environment in which the client feels comfortable enough to remove any barriers and to explore his or her true feelings about him or herself and others. For Rogers, therapy is not about a therapist 'doing things to' a client (as opposed to techniques such as behaviour therapy, in which certain behaviours are rewarded and others punished), but instead about giving the client the space and support to verbalise their thoughts and feelings and eventually to work out their own solutions.

The most important concept in Rogers' theory is the 'self'. This concept sprang from his clinical work, in which clients would use terms such as 'I'm not my usual self today', implying that they had a unified mental picture of themselves which could be consciously examined and evaluated. This is known as the 'self-concept'. Rogers' clinical work further led him to believe that his clients basically wanted to get to know their true self – to stop behaving as they felt they *ought* to behave and just fulfilling the demands of others.

> As I follow the experience of many clients in the therapeutic relationship which we endeavour to create for them, it seems to me that each one is raising the same question. Below the level of the problem situation about which the individual is complaining – behind the trouble with studies or wife or employer, or with his own uncontrollable or bizarre behavior, or with his frightening feelings – lies one central search. It seems to me that at the bottom each person is asking 'Who am I, really? How can I get in touch with this real self, underlying all my surface behavior? How can I become myself?'
>
> (Rogers, 1967, p. 108)

Having done so, individuals become less defensive and more open to their own attitudes and feelings, and can see other people and events as they truly are, and without using stereotypes. The overall picture is similar to Kelly's view of using constructs in a propositional rather than a pre-emptive manner. The individual also gets to *like* him or herself, and to stop fearing his or her emotions.

> Consciousness, instead of being the watchman over a dangerous and unpredictable lot of impulses, of which few can be permitted to see the light of day, becomes the comfortable inhabitant of a society of impulses and feelings and thoughts, which are discovered to be very satisfactorily self-governing when not fearfully guarded.
>
> (Rogers, 1967, p. 119)

When he or she becomes aware of the self, the individual becomes much less dependent on the views and opinions of others. What matters now is to do what seems right for them, rather than looking to others for approval. 'Unconditional positive regard' is thought to be of paramount importance in allowing the individual to explore him- or herself. By this is meant a relationship with another person in which the individual feels that it is they themself who is valued and loved. This love would hold whatever terrible thing they were to do (or admit to in the course of exploring their self-concept) – it is not *conditional* on how they behave.

In addition to the self-image, we can all envisage several other types of 'self', e.g. 'self as I was when I left school', and 'self as I would like to be', and it can sometimes be useful to consider the ways in which these memories and ideals differ from the current view of the self, a topic that is explored further in Chapter 12.

SELF-ASSESSMENT QUESTION 2.6

What is the self-concept? How can it be discovered?

The above suggestions have implications for therapy, and Rogers (1959) listed several conditions that should be met if the therapist is to be able to help the client to explore their self-concept. These requirements are as follows:

- that the client and therapist are in psychological contact – that is, that they are 'on the same wavelength';
- that the client's behaviour is not at odds with his or her self-image (a situation known as 'a state of incongruence'), which results in feelings of anxiety;
- that the therapist is congruent – that is, that the therapist's self-image accurately reflects the way in which he or she behaves;
- that the therapist shows unconditional positive regard for the client;
- that the therapist experiences an empathic understanding of the client's internal frame of reference – that is, that he or she can sense the person's feelings;
- that the client *perceives* the therapist's unconditional positive regard and empathic understanding – the therapist successfully communicates his or her unconditional regard and empathy to the client.

Thus, in Rogerian therapy, the therapist will at times disclose his or her own feelings towards the client, even though these may sometimes be rather negative. However, care will be taken to ensure that the client realises that this is just the therapist's *impression* of the client, and does not indicate that there is anything *wrong* with the client.

Rogers believes that people behave in a manner that is consistent with their self-image. For example, someone who views him or herself as shy and retiring will try to behave in a manner consistent with this view. It is almost as if the individual uses the 'self-concept' as a kind of Delphic oracle – a source to be consulted in times of uncertainty that will tell the individual how they should behave. In other words, the individual tries to ensure that their behaviour is *congruent* with their self-image. Whenever an incongruence does arise (for example, when someone who views himself as mild-mannered initiates a brawl), feelings of tension and anxiety are experienced which are most unpleasant. In fact, these feelings are so unpleasant that the person may try to distort reality (e.g. by telling himself that he was an innocent victim of someone else's aggression), thereby denying any incongruence between his self-image and his behaviour. The problem is that such distortions make it difficult for the person to perceive their true self: it is much better, in the long run, for an individual to recognise and accept his or her behaviour than to use 'defences' such as this.

Rogers suggests that each individual 'has one basic tendency and striving – to actualize, maintain and enhance the experiencing organism' (Rogers, 1951). Self-actualisation is a term that basically describes how we each fulfil our human potential – we learn to know, accept and like our true selves, we can form deep relationships with others, we can be sensitive to others' needs and view others as individuals (rather than in terms of stereotypes), and we can learn to break free from the demands of conformity. The term (coined by Abraham Maslow) is highly abstract, and it is not at all obvious how it can be assessed. However, the idea that we become wiser, more sensitive, more in touch with our true selves and less concerned with convention as we get older does have some intuitive appeal. What is less obvious is that this is a 'basic tendency and striving' – it could, arguably, just be a by-product of having had more experience of other people as one ages.

Evaluation

It is difficult to evaluate Rogers' theory, since it is more of a philosophical view of the person than a formal, concrete psychological theory. This is because it was developed using private (rather than public) knowledge. The theory evolved from Rogers' own experiences as a therapist and as a man, rather than from any formal empirical data that can be independently scrutinised. For example, it would be difficult to show that the self-concept does *not* exist. We all think about work colleagues, family members, mass murderers and cabinet ministers from time to time, and make some attempts to understand why they act in the various bizarre ways that they do (Kelly would say that we attempt to *construe* their behaviour). This being so, it would be something of a miracle if we never thought about ourselves at all, and it comes as little surprise to find that my self-concept is 'integrated' – that is, I see myself as a single individual – since this is what I *am*. Thus it could be argued that we are all *bound* to have an integrated self-concept, much as Rogers described.

A great deal of what Rogers says about the development of self-concept and the search for the true self certainly *feels* true to many people. However, this does not necessarily mean that it is correct. Many people presumably feel convinced that they have a good chance of winning a fortune whenever they buy a lottery ticket or back a horse. More empirical evidence is needed to back up these claims, and we shall consider some of the evidence in Chapter 12.

The next problem is the source of data. In Rogers' theory (along with that of Kelly) there is a total reliance on self-report. Yet we know that people are sometimes rather poor judges of their feelings. When I ask students in a lecture to raise their hand if they believe that they have an above-average sense of humour, at least 80 per cent of them generally do so, instead of the 50 per cent that we would expect if they were able to appraise this characteristic accurately. If a person is unaware of something as basic as this, can we be confident that they can become aware of what their 'true self' is like?

That said, the theory has some great strengths. Like Kelly's personal construct theory, it is very broad in its outlook. It attempts to explain how the whole person functions, rather than concentrating on just one or two aspects of personality. It has also made some very specific suggestions about the necessary conditions for therapeutic change, and empirical studies have shown that the client's experience of warmth, unconditional positive regard and empathy are indeed crucial factors in determining the success of some forms of psychotherapy (Truax and Mitchell, 1971). However, the problem is that many of the concepts are rather vaguely defined – the accurate assessment of 'empathy' and 'genuineness' is a non-trivial problem, and patients cannot agree as to what the terms mean (Bachelor, 1988). Nonetheless, some aspects of the theory can be tested, e.g. the assumption that psychological health is marked by congruence between self and experience.

It has also been found that people who are able to recognise negative features of themselves (rather than distorting them defensively) also tend to accept the foibles of others (e.g. Suinn and Geiger, 1965), a finding that has been interpreted as supporting Rogers' theory. Personally I am not quite so sure about this – it is also necessary to check that the accepting individuals are also the most well-adjusted ones. Otherwise, it is possible to suggest that 'acceptingness' could simply be a personality trait: some individuals are merely more accepting (of self and others) than others – a simple explanation that has no connection at all with Rogers' theory. Thus it would be necessary to check that the more accepting people are also the best adjusted in order to guard against this alternative explanation, and so far as I am aware such a study has not been performed. In summary, Rogers' theory has been highly influential and makes great intuitive sense. However, it is not so obvious that it is necessarily correct, or even that it can be simply tested.

SUGGESTED ADDITIONAL READING

Personal construct theory is developed in the two volumes of Kelly (1955), the first three chapters of which are reprinted as Kelly (1963). Kelly's work was particularly influential in the UK, probably because of the efforts of the late Don Bannister through books such as Bannister and Fransella (1971) and Bannister and Mair (1968), which reproduce and discuss some of Kelly's unpublished writings. More recent sources include Fransella and Thomas (1988) and the work of Neimeyer (Neimeyer and Neimeyer, 1990, 1992), with much of the literature being published in the *Journal of Constructivist Psychology* and the *International Journal of Personal Construct Psychology*. There are also several good personal construct sites on the Internet.

Rogers (1967) provides a humble and very *personal* account of his theory and clinical methods that makes compelling reading. Other useful sources include Rogers *et al.* (1989) and the chapter by Raskin and Rogers (1989). Papers by Bozarth and Brodley (1991) and two reprints of early papers by Rogers (Rogers, 1992a, b) may appeal to those who are interested in the therapeutic implications of these theories. Most introductory personality textbooks also consider the work of Rogers and Kelly.

ANSWERS TO SELF-ASSESSMENT QUESTIONS

SAQ 2.1

The approach that believes that it is important to try to discover and understand each person's unique view and interpretation of the world in which they live. For example, when examining family dynamics, a phenomenologist would be interested in the *implications* of a child's belief that her mother was cruel and unkind, and not particularly interested in whether the mother really *was* unkind.

SAQ 2.2

I suggest three main reasons. First, different observers may be trying to predict different outcomes, and so may pay attention to rather different aspects of people's behaviour. Second, the vagueness of language makes it possible that two observers might use two different phrases when they are actually referring to precisely the same characteristic in another person. Third, all kinds of social values are likely to colour the way in which we interpret behaviour.

SAQ 2.3

Kelly argued that it is impossible to comprehend the meaning of a term unless one knows with what it is being contrasted. The word 'good' is meaningless unless there is another term (e.g. 'bad') that shows what 'good' is not. This means that, in personal construct psychology, it is impossible to deduce the *meaning* of a construct from one term alone.

SAQ 2.4

Propositional constructs are useful because they do not force people to use any of their other constructs in certain stereotyped ways that may not be appropriate for a particular individual. If pre-emptive or constellatory constructs are used (e.g. saying 'Alan is nothing but a student'), this forces the rest of the construct system to attribute certain characteristics to Alan, rather than allowing him to be evaluated *as an individual* on each of the constructs following observations of his behaviour. Thus the construct system is unlikely to be able to predict the individual's behaviour very accurately, with unpleasant emotional consequences, as will be discussed below.

SAQ 2.5

An individual would choose to expand one area of their construct system if they realised that their predictions about some aspects of people's behaviour were less than perfectly accurate, and it was important to them to predict these types of behaviour.

SAQ 2.6

The self-concept is our view of our personality, abilities, background, etc., *as it really is*, and not as it is modified by the demands of society, or our own aspirations. It is a coherent mental image of the type of person that we really are, deep down. It can best be explored in the context of a supportive relationship with another person.

3

Freud's psychoanalytical theory

BACKGROUND

Sigmund Freud's theory has been included in this book for several reasons. It was one of the very first formally stated modern theories of personality, and is still influential in some disciplines (although not, these days, in mainstream psychology). It is one of the very few theories that suggests that unconscious regions of the mind may both exist and be important in our day-to-day functioning, a premise that now receives some support from cognitive psychology. Furthermore, it is a very *broad* theory that attempts to explain a whole range of interesting human behaviours. For all of these reasons it merits serious attention.

Recommended prior reading

None.

INTRODUCTION

Sigmund Freud (1856–1939) is one of the giant figures in personality psychology. Although his theories are a century old, they are still exceptionally controversial and influential in many areas other than psychology. Freud was a pioneer in many ways.

- He saw the need for sound observation of behaviour (although the general consensus is that his own observational practices were flawed).
- He attempted to explain behaviour by means of a small number of psychological processes.
- He developed a model of mental functioning which led naturally to a form of therapy (psychoanalysis).
- He attempted to explain virtually all important aspects of human life, including religion, a love of the arts, childhood development, dreams, jokes, 'slips of the tongue', motivation, anxiety, sexual behaviour, depression and other neuroses, and aggression.

Freud's theories are both controversial and influential, particularly in continental Europe and in areas other than psychology, such as literary criticism. The treatment of these theories is therefore split between two chapters, the first dealing with the development and explanations of some of the more important of Freud's ideas, and the second ascertaining which aspects (if any) of Freud's theories are actually correct. Freudian theory is important because it attempts to account for virtually every important and interesting aspect of human behaviour. It was the first 'grand theory' of psychology, and was (arguably) the first to view the unconscious mind as more than a 'waste-paper basket' for forgotten memories. It is still one of the very few theories which proposes that people may be motivated and influenced by factors of which they are completely unaware.

Almost every psychologist seems to have an opinion about Freud, regardless of whether they have actually read any of his writings. There really is no substitute for reading translations of Freud's original works, especially as several of them were written to educate non-expert readers, such as his medical colleagues, and I would strongly urge readers to explore some of the works listed at the end of this chapter.

Freud never intended to become a psychologist. Indeed, the term had barely been coined when he began to study medicine in Vienna in 1873. After qualifying, he concentrated on physiological and neurological research, including some pioneering work on the effects of cocaine and (appropriately for the man who was to discover sexual symbolism) into the testes of the eel. According to his biographer, Ernest Jones (1953), he told his bride that 'the anatomy of the brain was the only serious rival she had ever had, or was likely to have'. Freud was thus well versed in the scientific method – making observations under controlled conditions which led to the generation of theories that were tested through controlled experiment. However, the quality of the data on which Freud based his own theories is still a controversial topic. Critics such as Eysenck have claimed that Freud's theories are based on faulty observations, and that the theories are so complex that they are incapable of being falsified, as they can claim to 'explain' almost anything. We shall return to this issue in the next chapter.

In the nineteenth century, psychiatry was very much the Cinderella of medical practice. Disorders that had no obvious physiological basis were dismissed out of hand as being impossible. Some patients who claimed to suffer from symptoms as varied as memory failure, paralysis, nervous tics (twitching), tunnel vision, anorexia, blindness, loss of power of speech, convulsions and a whole range of other disquieting conditions were diagnosed as suffering from various forms of *hysteria*. This term was almost synonymous with malingering, and such patients were shunned by the medical establishment.

Freud's interest in psychiatry began in the 1880s, when (according to his translator, James Strachey) he needed to establish himself in order to marry his wealthy fiancée, Martha Bernays. In 1885 he travelled to Paris to study with Charcot, the celebrated neurologist – a decision that was to change the course of psychology.

Charcot was researching hypnotism, and in particular the manner in which hypnotic suggestion could be used to 'implant' an idea in the mind of a normal volunteer. This would then result in some activity being performed or some feeling being experienced even after the volunteer had been released from the hypnotic trance. For example, a hypnotised subject might be told that they should stand up whenever the word 'nine' was subsequently mentioned, or that their left leg would feel cold and numb whenever they saw food. Subjects who had been hypnotised in this way would claim to have no memory of having been asked to behave in such ways or experience these things, and would find it quite difficult to explain to themselves why they felt the urge to perform acts in response to the hypnotic suggestion.

Freud saw some similarity between the behaviour of Charcot's hypnotised subjects and that of patients who suffered from hysteria. First of all, in both cases the behaviour or symptom had no physical cause – the numbing of the leg resulting from a hypnotic suggestion had a purely psychological origin, just like the symptoms of hysterical patients. In addition, subjects who were hypnotised were unaware of the *source* of their behaviour or motivations to perform certain actions, in much the same way that hysterical patients claimed to be completely ignorant of the origins of their symptoms. Thus Freud speculated that both of these phenomena may stem from a forgotten memory. Some kind of precipitating mental event may explain the symptoms of hysterics. As both the hypnotised subject and the hysterical patient seem to have no memory for such an event, it must be located in an area of the mind that is not normally accessible to consciousness, but from where it can nevertheless influence behaviour and bodily and mental symptoms.

If this theory were true, it would follow that hysterical symptoms might be cured through appropriate psychological manipulations in much the same way as a hypnotic suggestion can be annulled (or forcibly forgotten) through the instructions of a hypnotist. On returning to Vienna, Freud set himself up as a specialist in the treatment of 'nervous diseases', using a novel technique called free association. He collaborated with an older physician, Josef Breuer, and they jointly published *Studies in Hysteria* (1893/1964), which is widely regarded as the basis of Freud's theory of psychoanalysis.

This seminal work reported some remarkable cures of hysterical symptoms through the use of hypnosis. Patients were hypnotised, and were then encouraged to believe that their symptoms would disappear, and to speculate about the causes of the symptoms (as in Freud's analysis of Emmy von N). Freud later considered that the careful probing of the patients' reminiscences (rather than hypnotic suggestion) was the ultimate cause of these cures. He claimed that:

> Each individual symptom immediately and permanently disappeared when we had succeeded in bringing clearly to light the memory of the event by which it was produced, and in arousing its accompanying affect [a word that Freud uses synonymously with 'emotion'], and when the patient had described that event in the greatest possible detail and had put the affect into words.

(Freud and Breuer, 1893/1964, p. 57)

This is the first description of the technique known as *free association*. It involved the patient reclining on a couch, whilst the therapist sat out of the patient's field of vision and asked him or her to say the very first thing which came to mind in response to occasional words spoken by the therapist. The patient was particularly urged not to omit any detail, no matter how trivial, unimportant, embarrassing or irrelevant it appeared to be. The therapist paid careful consideration to these reminiscences, and noted in particular those occasions when the patient found it difficult to produce an association in response to a word or phrase. This might indicate that some psychological mechanism, known as a *repression*, was interfering with the patient's ability to respond. As the patient had been urged to say whatever came to mind, no matter how fragmentary, ridiculous or embarrassing it might be, a failure to produce an association was unlikely to be due to self-censorship. Instead, it suggested that the therapist was getting somewhere near to an unpleasant, emotionally charged memory which had been pushed into an unconscious part of the mind and which was likely to be the root cause of the hysterical symptom.

Studies in Hysteria and other works describe several case histories in which Freud's patients were eventually able to recall events (often from childhood) that had been completely forgotten for many years, and which had been associated with some strong and unpleasant emotional experience such as anger, sorrow or guilt. He discovered that when the patient recalled the painful event and (most importantly) re-experienced the emotion that was felt at the time, the physical symptom simply disappeared. Freud claimed to have cured symptoms such as an inability to drink, paralysis, blindness, nervous tics and loss of memory using this technique, which became known as psychoanalysis.

The following are two fairly typical examples reported by Freud. The first describes one of Breuer's early attempts to probe the unconscious mind using hypnosis in an attempt to cure a young woman who used to enter trance-like states, similar to some forms of epilepsy. The second example describes Freud's technique of psychoanalysis.

> It was observed that, when the patient was in her states of '*absence*' [altered personality accompanied by confusion], she was in the habit of muttering a few words to herself which seemed as if they arose from some train of thought that was occupying her mind. The doctor, after getting report of these words, used to put her into a kind of hypnosis and repeat them to her so as to induce her to use them as a starting point. The patient ... in this way reproduced in his presence the mental creations which had been occupying her mind during the '*absences*' and which had betrayed their existence by the fragmentary words which she had uttered. They were profoundly melancholy phantasies – 'daydreams' we should call them – sometimes characterised by poetic beauty, and the starting point was as a rule the position of a girl at her father's sick-bed. When she had related a number of these phantasies, she was as if set free, and she was brought back to normal mental life.... It was impossible to escape the

conclusion that the alteration in her mental state which was expressed in the *'absences'* was a result of the stimulus proceeding from these highly emotional phantasies.

(Freud, 1957, Lecture 1)

Instead of urging the patient to say something upon some particular subject, I now asked him to abandon himself to a process of *free association* – that is, to say whatever came into his head, while ceasing to give any conscious direction to his thoughts. It was essential, however, that he should bind himself to report literally everything that occurred to his self-perception and not to give way to critical objections which sought to put certain associations on one side on the grounds that they were not sufficiently important or that they were irrelevant or that they were altogether meaningless. . . . But if the patient observes that rule and so overcomes his reticences, the resistance will find another means of expression. It will so arrange it that the repressed material will never occur to the patient, but only something which approximates to it in an allusive way; and the greater the resistance, the more remote from the actual idea that the analyst is in search of will be the substitutive association which the patient has to report. If the resistance is slight he [the analyst] will be able from the patient's allusions to infer the unconscious material itself, or if the resistance is stronger he will be able to recognise its character from the associations . . . and will explain it to the patient.

(Freud, 1959, section IV)

There is thus nothing egalitarian about psychoanalysis. In contrast to most other contemporary forms of psychotherapy, in which the counsellor and patient together explore memories and feelings, the Freudian psychoanalyst listens for signs of resistance in the flow of free associations, and may infer some underlying trauma of which the patient is completely unaware. The diagnosis having been made, the patient must be persuaded to recognise – and feel – the truth of the analyst's interpretation, despite all protestations and attempts at defence. Only then should the symptom disappear.

SELF-ASSESSMENT QUESTION 3.1

Try to explain the following terms:

(a) Free association

(b) Resistance

(c) Repression

Freud soon came to believe that the behaviour and symptoms of his hysterical patients were little different from those of 'normal' people. Analyses of dreams, 'slips of the tongue', wit and similar everyday experiences led him to concude that the mental structures that he deduced from the analysis of hysterical patients were universal. Thus his theory sought to become a general theory of personality, rather than an explanation for hysterical behaviour alone.

FREUD'S THEORIES OF THE MIND

The discovery that painful memories and fantasies can be dragged reluctantly back into consciousness has powerful implications for the structure of mind. First of all, it suggests that there are two main areas of the mind – one which is susceptible to conscious scrutiny through introspection, and another whose contents are normally unconscious and not available for examination through introspection. Second, it suggests that it is important to understand the precise mechanisms that determine how the contents of the unconscious region of mind seem to influence behaviour, as in the case of hysterical symptoms. Finally, it shows that it is necessary to understand how memories pass from the conscious to the unconscious regions of the mind, and why memories which have been transferred into the unconscious region usually stay there, except in the case of psychoanalytical treatment.

In order to account for his observations that some memories can be forgotten, yet can still exert an influence on behaviour, Freud suggested that the mind could be divided into two basic sections. One of these, the *ego*, is largely conscious, and is capable of logical, rational thought. He identified another, unconscious area of mind, which he called the *id*. This contains the basic instincts (sex and aggression), satisfaction of which leads to feelings of pleasure, and which therefore motivate behaviour – the 'pleasure principle'. Memories and thoughts which have become associated with these instincts have also been pushed into the id, which is far more than a mere 'waste-paper basket' for forgotten memories, as in some earlier theories (e.g. Herbart, 1824). Instead, the instincts, memories and fantasies in the Freudian id affect day-to-day behaviour and experience, without the individual being aware in any way that they are operating.

The analysis of hysterical patients thus led Freud to a conclusion that shocked Vienna. The unconscious memories and fantasies of Freud's proper, well-to-do female patients were almost invariably sexual in nature. Beneath the urbane veneer of each and every patient lurked a seething cauldron of lusts and urges which influenced and motivated almost every action. Aggression was also identified as a basic instinct of the id following World War I. In addition, Freud suggested a third division of mind, which he called the *superego*. This contains a person's moral values, i.e. their conscience.

Psychoanalysis revealed that the emotional content of a thought or memory (or the emotion which became attached to it through association, a process now known as classical conditioning) determined its destiny. Painful memories or unacceptable thoughts were banished to the darker recesses of the unconscious mind (the id), where they joined the seething lusts and aggressive drives which are found there even in the most proper individuals. The id therefore contains two basic instincts, namely *eros*, also known as the *life instinct*, which is satisfied through sexual activity, and a self-destructive force known as *thanatos* or the *death instinct,* which can also be turned outwards against the world, resulting in aggressive or sadistic behaviour.

Freud believed that organisms always seek to satisfy these deep-seated (but unconscious) drives of sex and aggression – the *pleasure principle*. This means that the satisfaction of these drives leads to feelings of pleasure, and that the frustration, or denial of satisfaction, of these basic drives gives rise to feelings of unpleasure. The id demands immediate and complete satisfaction of the sexual and aggressive instincts by the most direct means possible, no matter how inappropriate, impractical or unreasonable these may be, and without consideration of social mores or other people. The phrase 'I know what I want and I want it now', from a recent popular song, offers a good description of how the id operates. Freud called this principle of direct and immediate satisfaction *primary process* thought, which is also characterised by its illogicality and tolerance of ambiguity. For example, although the id would have no difficulty in simultaneously desiring and wishing to destroy a person, the ego would have to resolve this conflict. Some of Freud's followers, such as Melanie Klein, claim to have identified terrifying destructive and aggressive fantasies in very young infants, which are thought to be typical of the way in which the id operates.

Freud believed that the ego splits off from the id as the child grows older, as a result of its experiences of the outside world through sight, touch, hearing and the other senses. A part of the mind becomes conscious, aware of the outside world, self-aware and capable of rational thought. The basic aim is still the satisfaction of the drives from the id, but these can be assuaged far more effectively through postponement and the use of social conventions. Consider the sexual drive, which (following the analyses of his patients) Freud believed to be the most important of all. The satisfying of this drive immediately and completely with the first person one encountered (as the id would demand) would probably not be a good idea. It would result in a prison sentence (segregated from members of the opposite gender!), and so would fail to lead to a long-term solution. It would also run counter to the moral standards of one's conscience (the superego). It is likely to be far more effective in the long term to plot something cunning in advance (quite possibly involving candlelit dinners, soft music, flattery and gin) than to waylay the first person one meets. Aggressive drives can be satisfied more effectively by watching films or participating in sport, aggressive debate or computer games than by the 'one-off' bludgeoning of strangers. Acting rationally and delaying the satisfaction of the instinct may lead to greater satisfaction in the long term.

There are also other ways in which the drives can be satisfied, such as by reading or other activities (e.g. art, humour, gastronomy), in which basic drives are being satisfied in socially acceptable ways. These are sometimes known as *derivatives* of the original drives, that is, ideas which are connected to the basic instincts of sex and aggression, but whose satisfaction is more acceptable to the ego. As Fenichel (1946) observes, most neurotic symptoms are derivatives of the two basic instincts (p. 143). Behaviours which others regard as abnormal symptoms have, through processes such as classical conditioning or symbolism, come to have a special meaning for the individual. Each such behaviour, according to Freud, develops and continues because it indirectly satisfies one of the two main instincts.

Childhood experiences are thought to be all-important for adult development. According to Freud, childhood is a battleground between the two major instincts and the attempts of parents to ensure that they are satisfied in socially acceptable ways. Derivatives of the sexual and aggressive instincts are formed, and the ego develops mechanisms of defence which continue into adulthood.

SELF-ASSESSMENT QUESTION 3.2

Try to think how aggressive drives might be satisfied by:

(a) the id

(b) the ego

DEFENCE MECHANISMS

Merely supposing that the mind is divided into the ego and the id does not explain the link between symptoms and memories revealed by psychoanalysis. For example, it does not explain how memories which are banished to unconscious regions of the mind can still influence behaviour, as in the case of neurotic symptoms. It is instead necessary to understand why some painful memories are 'forgotten', why they result in a physical symptom, and why the symptom disappears when the memory is relived.

Freud noted with interest that the all-important memories that eventually surfaced during psychoanalysis did not do so easily. Despite the instructions given to the patient, the most important hints about the nature of these memories tended to be dismissed as unimportant by the patient, alluded to very briefly, or otherwise played down in importance. Only as a result of careful listening and prompting by the analyst could they eventually be recalled. Thoughts and memories that were repressed within the unconscious mind did not appear to fade – the memory of a traumatic event does not disappear with time, but continues to exert a powerful influence on behaviour. This explains why hysterical symptoms can apparently be linked to events which occurred many years previously, but which remained unconscious and unresolved.

This suggested that there were some forces (of which the patient was unaware) which tried to keep the painful memory out of consciousness. These were called *defence mechanisms*, and over a dozen of them have been proposed by Freud and his followers. The most well known is called *repression*, and this term is used interchangeably with 'defence mechanism' in Freud's early writings. The conscious mind thus strives to forget – to banish from consciousness – painful memories or wishes. However, the repressed wish or memory does not cease to exist once it reaches unconsciousness. On the contrary, fuelled by libido it constantly tries to re-enter consciousness, with the result that there is a perpetual battle taking place between the wish (which has been repressed into the id) and the defence mechanisms.

The defence mechanisms can identify and deal with attempts by the original wish to re-enter consciousness. Anxiety serves as a sort of 'trip-wire' in this context. When a repressed wish or memory tries to re-enter consciousness, anxiety levels supposedly rise, and this triggers the defence mechanisms into operation. Disguised and unrecognisable substitutes for the original wish may, however, enter consciousness. These may emerge as daydreams, fantasies or as neurotic symptoms.

It follows that the more traumatic events an individual banishes into the id, the stronger the defence mechanisms that are required to keep them there. Thus everyone is to some extent neurotic, because we have all dealt with painful memories by forcing (repressing) them into unconscious regions of the mind, from where they continue to exert a malevolent influence on our feelings and behaviour. For defence mechanisms only operate on ideas or perceptions (see, for example, Freud (1932) lecture 32). Instead of being repressed, the emotional content associated with an idea is transformed into anxiety.

Neurosis is therefore a result of repressing or otherwise defending against emotionally charged memories or thoughts. As all humans use defence mechanisms, and as the repressed material does not wane in intensity with time (assuming that it is never brought to conscious awareness, as in the course of psychoanalysis), it follows that all adults will to some extent be neurotic. Thus Freud believed that the model of personality drawn up from the study of hysterical patients should be able to be generalised to 'normal' people – there is no qualitative difference between the mental processes of hysterical and those of normal individuals. This is one of the first examples of what is now known as the 'continuity hypothesis' (Morris, 1985).

At night the defence mechanisms relax somewhat, and the contents of the id can infiltrate the ego in a disguised form, often as symbols. Bearing in mind the nature of the id, it should come as no surprise to find that many of these symbols are sexual in nature – for example, the penis may be represented by sticks, daggers, telescopes, watering cans, fishing rods, feet, etc. The nature of anxiety dreams should now be clear. These occur when the id contents are too strong or insufficiently disguised, whereupon a surge of anxiety causes the defence mechanisms to clamp down, and we awaken with a start.

Repression is the crudest, most primitive type of defence mechanism. When the ego defends itself against an emotionally charged memory moving from the unconscious to the conscious area of mind, it will simply try to oppose the force which propels the memory into consciousness, and to force it back into the id. Thus repression blocks all memory of the threatening memory or instinct. Other defence mechanisms include *isolation*, in which an instinct or memory may be allowed into consciousness because the all-important emotion associated with the drive is stripped away. For example, aggressive instincts may be neatly satisfied through becoming a surgeon. Carving up living bodies with scalpels, saws and drills may well satisfy myriad aggressive and sadistic urges from the id, and as the whole act is performed with enormous emotional detachment, the true motives for doing this never enter consciousness. Indeed, the ego will stoutly maintain that the profession is being followed for the most altruistic reasons.

Projection involves attributing one's own unacceptable fantasies, impulses, etc. on to other people. For example, an aggressive person may see others as being aggressive, when in fact they are not. *Displacement of object* – 'kicking the cat' – involves the expression of a sexual or aggressive wish, but against a substitute person, animal or object. This could well account for the popularity of sport and video games.

Reaction formation occurs when one's ego reacts as if a threat (from the id) is always present. Thus someone who has strong aggressive urges may devote their life to pacifist causes, in order to counter the aggressive instincts if and when they threaten the ego. Reaction formation against sexual wishes can result in extreme prudery, famously obvious in 'clean-up-television' campaigners. As Paul Kline has observed, if one decides that it is one's duty to monitor the airwaves for all signs of filth and depravity, then one is (reluctantly, of course) exposed to rather a lot of it – which conveniently satisfies the demands of the id, whilst keeping the ego in ignorance of one's *true* motives for campaigning so energetically.

There are more defence mechanisms than those discussed above, several of which were suggested by followers of Freud. Descriptions of some of the more popular ones may be found in Kline (1984), or in any of the other texts mentioned at the end of this chapter. Furthermore, although some examples have been given above, it by no means follows that every surgeon is driven to that occupation by unconscious aggressive drives – nor, without there being any good psychological measure of 'strength of unconscious aggressive drives', could it easily be put to the test. However, these examples may serve to illustrate how the ego may allow satisfaction of various instinctual urges, whilst keeping the individual blissfully unaware of his or her true motives.

SELF-ASSESSMENT QUESTION 3.3

(a) What is a 'defence mechanism'?

(b) Suppose that a patient is able to remember some horrific incidents from her childhood, but is able to talk about the events in a detached, unemotional manner. Which defence mechanism may she be using?

(c) Suppose that a person uses *two* defence mechanisms to keep their sexual instincts at bay, namely projection and reaction formation. Try to work out how this may lead them to feel about someone of the same sex whom they (unconsciously) love, remembering that in Freud's day this feeling would have been unacceptable to the ego.

NEUROTIC SYMPTOMS

Freud identified several different types of neurotic symptoms in his patients. These include *anxiety hysteria*, in which excessive anxiety is attached to certain people or situations, *anxiety neurosis*, in which the feeling of anxiety is powerful but diffuse and not linked to any particular individuals or settings, and *conversion hysteria*, in which unconscious fantasies are acted out as emotional outbursts. Freud believed that physical illnesses such as muscle pains, breathing irregularities and even short-sightedness could sometimes be traced back to psychological causes – the so-called *organ neuroses*. Depression, the choice of unusual sexual objects, compulsive actions, addictions and compulsions (such as shoplifting) are also perceived as having an underlying psychological cause.

Despite the highly varied nature of these symptoms, Freudians believe that they have several features in common. First, as Fenichel (1946) reminds us (p. 18), the patient experiences some unusual symptom – a feeling of anxiety, a compulsion to steal, bodily pains, or whatever – but is unable to determine its cause through introspection. Second, Freudians believe that all of these symptoms have their roots in the id, or, more precisely, in some conflict between the id and the ego which has activated defence mechanisms. They therefore stem from the blocking of one of the powerful instincts by the ego. The exact form that the symptom takes depends on childhood experiences and the techniques which the infant used to deal with threats from the id. Third, the symptom is always thought to have some special sexual or aggressive significance to the individual.

Consider a man who obtains sexual excitement from viewing and touching female footwear. A foot may symbolise a penis, so if the man is (unconsciously) afraid of being castrated, it may prove less threatening to obtain sexual excitement from a woman's shoes than from normal heterosexual relationships. Intercourse will raise fears of castration, as it reminds men that women do not possess a penis – foot-fetishists endow women with a symbolic penis in an attempt to reduce castration anxiety (Fenichel, 1946, p. 341).

Alternatively, castration fears may emerge as a phobia, as in the case of 'Little Hans', who became anxious that a horse would bite him. The 'horse' was, of course, the boy's father, and Freud (1926/1955) claims that biting is a frequent allegory of castration.

According to Freud, all symptoms thus result from some powerful emotion, wish or thought which is repressed or otherwise defended against. For example, one of Breuer's patients who was unable to drink recalled under hypnosis that she had seen a dog drink out of a glass, but that she had not expressed her disgust at the time, out of politeness. The memory of this unpleasant event became repressed, and led to the symptom of being unable to drink. Another patient whose nervous tic resulted in her making loud 'clacking' noises had previously made this noise before when trying (too hard) to remain quiet under difficult emotional circumstances – once when her sick child was asleep, and again when her horses were bolting and she resolved not to frighten them further.

However, the huge majority of symptoms seemed to be traceable to forbidden sexual wishes, particularly childhood seductions. Freud took the conventional view of his time that such events could not be true, and so concluded that the 'memory' of these events instead revealed a fantasy about something for which the child longed.

> Almost all my women patients told me that they had been seduced by their father. I was driven to recognise in the end that these reports were untrue, and so came to understand that hysterical symptoms are derived from phantasies and not from real occurrences.
>
> (Freud, 1932, p. 154)

These 'screen memories' are really fantasies which are superimposed on to our early memories and so become indistinguishable from them. Rather than being accurate memories of real events, they expressed wishes or fantasies about events for which the child longed. This is why Freud formed the view that some form of sexual instinct is present even in children, and that the 'blocking' of this instinct could result in neurotic symptoms later in life.

Psychoanalysis aims to cure neurosis through undoing the defence mechanisms that banish a particular thought or wish into the unconscious. It should therefore be able to remove the symptom which emerged as a derivative of the original impulse. Thus the therapist must first identify and test the link between the symptom and some unconscious mental process, e.g. through noting 'blockages' in the free association process, searching dreams for symbolic content and free associating to dream contents. Once the analyst has a clear picture of the possible source of the neurotic symptom, this underlying fear or wish is explained to the patient, together with examples of the defence mechanisms used and the nature of the derivative(s) of the original impulse. When the ego eventually faces up to these childhood memories and fears and appreciates the nature of the resistance that has been applied (through defence mechanisms), there is no need to defend further, as the ego is fully aware of the 'threat'. Thus all of the derivatives of the threat should disappear, including the troublesome symptoms.

FREUD'S THEORY OF INFANTILE SEXUALITY

Freud believed that, during childhood, the infant develops in two major ways. First, the ego and (later) the superego develop from the id. The young child gradually develops a sense of 'self', and later takes on parental values as the superego. Freud's second main claim was that 'sexual life does not begin at puberty but starts with clear manifestations soon after birth' (Freud, 1939). That is, the young child is not pure and innocent, but is driven by the same sexual and aggressive instincts that propel adults, the only major difference being the manner in which these instincts are satisfied. The two issues are, of course, related. Fenichel (1946, p. 34) reminds us that Freud believed that the new-born infant is essentially id – demanding total and immediate satisfaction of all instinctual demands. Freud (1923/1955) postulated that, in the early years of life, the sexual instinct was satisfied through oral contact with objects – exploring, sucking and later biting the nipple and indeed all other objects that the baby encounters. He and others (notably Abraham, 1952) later divided the oral stage into two phases, one involving oral incorporation, or sucking, and the other involving oral sadism, or biting.

Freud believed that, following the oral phase, the focus of sexual satisfaction shifted to the anus during the process of potty-training. Presenting the parents with 'gifts' (or, alternatively, withholding the faeces) at this stage is the child's first real opportunity to exercise control over his or her environment, and faeces are thought to have strong symbolic links to money, babies and the penis. Phrases such as 'stinking rich', 'filthy lucre', 'rolling in it' and 'where there's muck there's money' do, after all, crave explanation.

The penis and clitoris become the focus of the libido during what is known as the 'phallic' phase, but at the age of about 5 years young boys suffer the 'Oedipus complex' and the 'castration complex' – arguably the most important and traumatic event in one's life. The Oedipus complex is named after the eponymous hero of Sophocles' play who unknowingly kills his father and then commits incest with his mother. It occurs when the young boy seeks to possess his mother sexually and so comes to view his father as a rival for her affections. Young boys will realise through observation that girls do not possess a penis, and eventually each will come to a terrible but inevitable conclusion – that the penis has been cut off by a jealous father in response to these Oedipal thoughts. Anxious to avoid this catastrophic event, the young boy will repress all memory of these feelings for his mother, and will 'identify' with his father. Identification is a form of defence mechanism into which threatening objects are incorporated – in this instance, the father's moral values are adopted to form the 'superego', or moral conscience.

Girls, of course, do not possess a penis and are supposed to blame their mother for this inadequacy – they hate their mother and identify with their father in order to have a penis at their disposal (the 'Electra complex'). Following these traumas, both sexes enter what is known as the 'latency period' in which there is no focus of sexual activity, until normal adult sexuality emerges at puberty (the 'genital phase').

These ideas sound as preposterous now as they did when they were first propounded. However, it is strange how frequently Oedipal themes recur in literature (e.g. in *Hamlet*, *The Brothers Karamazov*, *Oedipus Rex*, etc.).

The degree of satisfaction or frustration which the infant encounters at each of these psychosexual stages is thought to have a profound bearing on his or her adult personality type, and on the severity and nature of any neurotic sympoms that may develop. If a child either obtains too much pleasure from one of these zones, or is not allowed to obtain sufficient pleasure from it (as in 'forbidden fruit'), he or she is supposed to show related characteristics in adult life. Indeed, several phrases for activities which Freudians regard as being intimately related to pre-genital fixation have clear links to the various erogenous zones. Reading 'voraciously', possessing a 'biting wit', and being 'a sucker' hardly provide conclusive evidence for their theory, but are at least suggestive. Kline (1981) has collected together some lists of the adult characteristics which Freud and his followers have linked (sometimes rather tenuously) to over-indulgence or frustration at various stages of psychosexual development. Thus those fixated at the oral incorporation phase would be optimistic, dependent and curious, and would love soft and milky foods. Oral sadists would be bitter, hostile, argumentative and jealous. Those fixated at the anal phase would become obstinate, excessively tidy and stingy. The evidence for these adult personality types and their link with child-rearing practices is considered alongside other attempts to test Freudian theory in Chapter 4.

The model of mind outlined above claims to be able to explain a large number of important phenomena. For example, wit and humour are thought to be rather like dreams in that they allow unacceptable impulses to be 'parcelled' so that they reach the ego without being censored. People who enjoy vicious lampooning of characters are presumably those who show strong but repressed aggressive urges. Great art and literature may depict wonderful forbidden themes, such as Oedipal conflicts, in a formalised manner that is acceptable to the superego. Symbolism may also be important – a glance at science-fiction book-covers (aimed, one assumes, at pubescent boys) reveals that many are composed almost entirely of sexual symbols. However, Freudian theory seems to be unable to differentiate great art (such as the Leonardo cartoons) from hotchpotches of symbols – it dwells on content but has little to say about form.

SELF-ASSESSMENT QUESTION 3.4

(a) What are the main psychosexual stages of childhood?

(b) *Why* should children who are over-indulged or under-indulged at the anal stage be 'obstinate, excessively tidy and stingy', as mentioned above?

SUMMARY

Freud's theory is extremely complex – technical terms abound, and as these often changed their meaning over the years, the more specialised works can make difficult reading. Worse still, it is not obvious that the theory can stand up to detailed scientific scrutiny, much less to empirical verification. This is because many of the concepts used (e.g. 'repression', 'penis envy') cannot easily be quantified, and because the theory can suggest several different 'explanations' for the same event. This is not normal in science. Newton's theories claim that two balls of the same size but different masses will fall at the same rate when dropped. If experiment showed that one of the balls fell faster than the other, the theory would clearly be incorrect. However, Freud's theories seldom allow clear, unambiguous hypotheses such as this to be tested. For example, how might one explain cynicism? According to Freud, either this could be an acceptable way of expressing aggressive feelings about an object, or it could stem from a strong sexual desire which is converted into its opposite through the defence mechanism of reaction formation. A cynical view could indicate unconscious feelings of either love or hatred. How, then, can one possibly test whether the theory is correct? It is analogous to having a theory which could 'predict' that either ball A will fall faster than ball B, ball B will fall faster than ball A, or both will fall at the same rate, but which is unable to predict which will happen on any particular occasion. A theory such as this clearly has little power, since it can 'explain' all possible outcomes, and so it would be almost impossible to demonstrate that the theory was ever incorrect. It therefore becomes necessary to consider carefully the criticisms that have been levelled against psycho-analytical theory, and to consider which parts of the theory, if any, seem to stand up to scientific scrutiny. This is the substance of Chapter 4.

SUGGESTED ADDITIONAL READING

The shortest summary is the *Five Lectures on Psycho-Analysis*, with the *Introductory Lectures on Psychoanalysis* (originally published between 1915 and 1917) (Freud, 1917/1964) offering slightly more detailed treatment, and the *New Introductory Lectures on Psychoanalysis* (Freud, 1932) providing an updated and extended summary of Freud's main theories. All of these are, or have been, published in paperback. There are also some useful summaries of Freud's theories, such as those by Stafford-Clarke (1965), Brown (1964), Kline (1984) and Stevens (1983), but it would be a shame to consult these without first reading some original Freud.

ANSWERS TO SELF-ASSESSMENT QUESTIONS

SAQ 3.1

(a) Free association is one of the main features of psychoanalysis. The patient agrees simply to say whatever comes into his or her mind, no matter how trivial, fleeting or shocking it may be. The analyst speaks a word and observes the patient's response, and in particular notes any difficulty in producing an association. Such difficulties may suggest that the word is linked to some traumatic memory, and so an unconscious mental process (called a 'repression' in Freud's early work) strives to keep all associations with this event out of consciousness.

(b) A resistance is an unconscious force that prevents the patient from producing free associations with words which touch on unresolved conflicts. The resistance prevents these associations from becoming conscious – it is the force which opposes free association.

(c) Repression is one example of a defence mechanism. It is a process by which a memory, wish or impulse (generally sexual in nature) is kept out of conscious awareness.

SAQ 3.2

The id would express the aggression directly against some person or object whilst the ego would ensure that the aggression was expressed in some socially desirable form, e.g. contact sport, fantasy games, giving books unfavourable reviews, or indulging in heated debate (as in parliament).

SAQ 3.3

(a) Any psychological mechanism whose aim is to prevent the contents of the id from reaching the ego.

(b) Isolation.

(c) The feeling of love would be turned to hate (by reaction formation), so that the unconscious feeling 'I love him' becomes 'I hate him'. Projection turns this into 'he hates me'. Freud suggested that these two defence mechanisms occurred in homosexuals, who were supposed to feel paranoid for this reason.

SAQ 3.4

(a) The oral (passive and sadistic) stage, the anal stage and the phallic stage. The latency period and the genital stage follow, but are really completely unconnected with *infant* sexuality.

(b) It is all to do with symbolism and reaction formation. Here money symbolises faeces, and so meanness can be viewed as symbolically withholding the faeces – so too can obstinacy (refusing to 'perform' when requested). Orderliness is supposedly a reaction against the desire to smear the faeces and make a great mess.

4

An evaluation of Freud's theories

BACKGROUND

Many psychologists accepted Freud's theories and insights unquestioningly until the middle of the twentieth century, when concerns grew about the nature of his basic data, the validity of the interpretations that he drew from the data, the fact that the theory could sometimes explain any outcome (and so was not capable of being falsified), and the value of psychoanalysis as a form of therapy. For although the theories outlined in Chapter 3 have a seductive appeal, we examined no hard, empirical evidence that they were actually correct. Whatever went on in Freud's consulting room was not tape-recorded or filmed, and so it is impossible for independent observers to check either the quality of the basic data or Freud's theoretical inferences. The finding that doing *nothing* to the patient supposedly produced a better prospect of a cure than a course of psychoanalysis did not help, and a particularly critical account of psychoanalysis is given by Rachman and Wilson (1980). So it becomes necessary to ask whether there is any scientific truth in Freud's theory, or whether it should be regarded as no more than a monstrous fairy-tale.

Recommended prior reading

Chapters 1, 3 and 11.

INTRODUCTION

Readers of Chapter 3 may well be suffering from some unease at this stage – this should be clear from the brief outline of Freud's theories given there. In fact, Freud's theories have been criticised on several grounds, as follows.

- Psychoanalysis does not appear to be an effective form of therapy.
- Freud's theories were based on a very small, rather strange sample of people a century ago, and so may not have general applicability.
- Freud may have over-generalised. For example, the finding that obsessional

neurosis is linked to the defence mechanism of isolation in just one or two patients does not imply that this is invariably the case.

- What took place during Freud's clinical sessions cannot be verified by independent observers.
- Many of Freud's terms are difficult to 'operationalise' and therefore to test experimentally. For example, it is not obvious how one could go about measuring the strength of defence mechanisms, oral fixation, Oedipal conflict, etc.
- The theories are '*post hoc*' – that is, possible explanations of past events that cannot easily be used to predict future behaviour.
- The theory may be inconsistent – the same phenomenon may be 'explained' by several different processes, or the same psychological process may lead to several different behaviours.
- The theories may be able to 'explain' almost any behaviours, thus making them impossible to disprove.

This chapter therefore has two aims. It examines some of the problems of testing the scientific truth of Freud's theories, and it provides some examples of experiments that have been conducted to test certain aspects of the theory.

TESTING FREUD'S THEORIES

As Farrell (1981) has observed, Freudian theory is not a single, unified and coherent theory, but a collection of loosely linked subtheories. This has important implications for the scientific evaluation of Freud's work. It suggests that even if some aspects of Freud's work can be shown to be completely incorrect, other aspects of his theories may be unaffected. For example, suppose that psychoanalysis could be shown to be ineffective in curing neurosis. This does not necessarily imply that all other aspects of Freud's theory (e.g. the structure of the mind, the theory of child development) are completely untrue. It might just mean that the techniques of free association and dream analysis which form the basis of psychoanalysis are unable to reveal the 'true' nature of the conflict, and this could occur for a whole multitude of reasons. For example, the therapist's interpretations may be erroneous because of poor training, the therapist may project his or her own conflicts on to the patient, or the patient may ignore the cardinal instruction and censor the responses made during free association. The essential point is that even if certain aspects of Freud's theories can be shown to have little or no basis in fact, this does not always imply that the rest of the theory is doomed.

That said, certain aspects of Freud's theories are clearly of central importance, since they are used as explanations in virtually all of the subtheories. If it could be shown that behaviour is completely unaffected by unconscious factors (i.e. that the id is an unnecessary concept), that there is no evidence that defence mechanisms filter memories or perceptions on the basis of their emotional content, or that the Oedipus complex does not exist, then many aspects of Freudian theory would collapse. Hence it makes sense to concentrate on such core aspects when evaluating psychoanalytical theory.

SELF-ASSESSMENT QUESTION 4.1

Which of the following would you view as 'core' components of Freud's theory, and which as relatively peripheral?

Freud's theory of art, the nature of adult psychosexual personality syndromes, repression, the superego, the theory of dreams, the id, the theory of wit and humour, symbolism.

Eysenck has made some incisive criticisms of psychoanalytical theory over the last thirty years, the title of his latest book, *The Decline and Fall of the Freudian Empire* (Eysenck, 1985), giving a hint as to its main conclusions. This work is important, as it subjects Freud's theories to rigorous scientific scrutiny by someone who is outside the psychoanalytical movement, and who is thus unlikely to interpret equivocal evidence in favour of psychoanalytical theory. That said, several of Eysenck's comments seem more relevant to Freud's personality than to his scientific integrity. However, Eysenck offers four pieces of good advice to readers of Freud:

Do not believe anything you see written about Freud or psychoanalysis, particularly when it is written by Freud or other psychoanalysts, without looking at the relevant evidence.

(Eysenck, 1985, p. 26)

and

Do not accept claims of originality, but look at the work of Freud's predecessors.

(Eysenck, 1985, p. 33)

For Eysenck follows Sulloway (1979), who argues convincingly that Freud overplayed the novelty of psychoanalysis, and over-dramatised the opposition which he faced, rather after the model of a heroic saga. Eysenck also observes that others had previously used the word 'unconscious' in some form. Whilst Freud may well have viewed himself as a Wagnerian hero or a Messiah, such immodesty hardly seems relevant to the scientific truth of the theory.

Do not believe anything said by Freud and his followers about the success of psychoanalytic treatment.

(Eysenck, 1985, p. 31)

There is evidence that psychoanalysis is ineffective in treating neurosis, and the dramatic improvements reported in some of Freud's case histories (e.g. the case of Anna O, mentioned in Chapter 3) were not sustained, if indeed they existed at all.

> Be careful about accepting alleged evidence about the correctness of Freudian theories: the evidence often proves exactly the opposite.
>
> (Eysenck, 1985, p. 35)

The previous three issues pale into insignificance when compared to this. Freud's possible immodesty and the questionable efficacy of psychoanalysis are hardly grounds for rejecting all aspects of his theories. Eysenck's crucial point is that Freudian theory is not based on sound, replicable observations of large and representative samples of people, that it may be factually incorrect, and that it may not consider simpler alternative explanations. However, this too may be slightly unfair to Freud.

A hundred years ago scientific rigour was not *de rigueur*, as a glance at early editions of the American or British journals of psychology will reveal. Indeed, the statistical techniques which underpin the modern, scientific approach to the discipline had not been invented. The need for control groups was not appreciated, nor could such information have been sensibly utilised, so it seems churlish to castigate Freud on these grounds. Furthermore, whilst simpler explanations may be possible (with Eysenck suggesting how his own theory of personality may explain certain observations more simply than Freud's – although without performing the necessary experiments!), Freud would have needed to have been clairvoyant to have considered such alternative explanations.

Because psychoanalysis has such broad implications for other areas of study, several criticisms have been made by philosophers, scholars of English, and the like. In contrast to the factual points raised by Eysenck, critics such as Cioffi have raised the following issues.

- They note that certain aspects of the theory seem a priori to be rather unlikely or disgusting, and fly in the face of common sense (e.g. the Oedipus complex).
- By drawing attention to one peripheral and ill-supported aspect of the theory, the rest of it is impugned by association.

It is difficult to take the first objection seriously, since these aspects seem to be untestable. In any case, recent research in the field of particle physics has produced theories that appear at least as fantastic to this author as anything penned by Freud, and it seems naïve to suggest that a theory of personality need necessarily be pleasant. However, the truth is that Freud's theories *were* based on rather unsystematic observations by one man of the behaviour and therapeutic experiences of a rather strange group of people, from whom the results were extrapolated to the general population. So there is obviously a strong case for subjecting his theories to rigorous experimental testing, concentrating particularly on the core aspects of the theory.

The quality of Freud's observations, and the gay abandon with which he extrapolated his theories from small samples of mainly young, middle-class, neurotic females to the population at large, may indeed present severe problems for the theory. Whilst these problems do not *necessarily* invalidate the theory (hard data would be necessary for this), they do indicate that the theory must be rigorously tested before any parts of it can be accepted at face value. The crucial issues are whether aspects of Freudian theory are (1) capable of being tested and (2) actually supported by empirical evidence.

ARE FREUD'S THEORIES TESTABLE IN PRINCIPLE?

It is first necessary to determine what constitutes a valid test of Freud's theory. No one suggests that all aspects of Freud's theories are testable. As Kline (1981) has observed, it is extremely difficult to construct operational definitions of some of Freud's concepts. *Operational definitions* are experimental variables that are assumed to measure some theoretical concept. For example, a person's score on an IQ test is one possible operational definition of their general intelligence. But how can one devise an operational definition of 'thanatos' – the death instinct which Freud (1920) described as the instinct 'which seek[s] to lead what is living to death'? Scores on a test of depressive mood will not be acceptable, since Freud explains depression in other ways, and in any case if this instinct is present to an equal extent in all people (i.e. if it exhibits no individual differences) it is impossible to test for its existence.

However, some aspects of Freudian theory probably can be operationalised. For example, the defence mechanism of repression seems to be very close to the phenomenon of perceptual defence as studied by Bruner and Postman (1947), who observed that individuals find it harder to recognise emotionally threatening words than neutral or positively toned words. There are many problems with the old perceptual defence experiments, but some elegant designs have overcome these, and more sophisticated experiments (e.g. Wallace and Worthington, 1970) show that the effects are genuine. These experiments will be discussed in more detail below.

Other experiments are useless because their operational definitions of (complex) Freudian concepts are naïve or psychometrically flawed. For example, asking a child which parent he or she prefers cannot tell us anything about Oedipal conflicts, since Freud's theory maintains that the Oedipus conflict is *unconscious*, and may have no connection with a conscious preference for one parent over another.

Some studies may use psychological tests as operational definitions of Freudian concepts, but with scant regard for the quality of these tests. Whilst there is no shortage of paper-and-pencil tests to measure Freudian constructs (e.g. the Defense Mechanisms Inventory of Ililivich and Glaser, 1986) as well as a number of projective techniques (e.g. the Rorschach test), there is usually little or no evidence that these tests actually measure what they claim to assess.

Any experiments based upon such tests can clearly reveal nothing about the veracity or otherwise of Freudian theory. They could not be *expected* to do so.

Finally, the experimental design of some studies may be flawed. For example, studies that claim to show that psychoanalysis is an effective form of therapy should use control groups to ensure that the therapy works because of the quality of the therapist's interpretations. If a patient's feeling of well-being is taken as the operational definition of the success of therapy (which superficially sounds like a reasonable suggestion), any study designed to evaluate the efficiency of therapy should include control groups in order to rule out the possibility that the patients improve for the following reasons:

- because the symptoms tend to go away of their own accord (*spontaneous remission*) rather than as a result of psychoanalysis;
- because talking to the therapist (rather than psychoanalytical interpretation of what is said) cures the neurosis; or
- because, since psychoanalysis is very expensive, the patient may claim to feel better as a means of reducing 'cognitive dissonance'. If a patient has paid a lot of money for a treatment that has not made them feel much better, they may be tempted either to overestimate the usefulness of the therapy or to play down their symptoms rather than admit that they have paid large sums of money for something which really does not seem to work very well.

Designing experiments to test aspects of Freudian theory is therefore a perilous operation, demanding three very different skills, namely a good understanding of Freud's work, knowledge of experimental design, and a sound understanding of psychometrics. Very few of the studies in the literature meet these standards. However, some do, and these may yield some interesting insights into the veracity of Freud's theories.

SELF-ASSESSMENT QUESTION 4.2

What three qualities are required in any experiment designed to put one of Freud's theories to experimental test?

EMPIRICAL FINDINGS

Testing the theory of defence mechanisms

We argued in Chapter 3 that defence mechanisms – 'guardians of the ego', as Freud once called them – lie at the heart of Freudian theory, since they are responsible for keeping the contents of the id out of conscious awareness, and this is a fundamental assumption of most other aspects of Freud's theory (e.g. dream theory, developmental theory, neurosis, etc.). For example, if there were no such thing as repression or identification, it is difficult to see how the

Oedipus complex could survive. In this section, we shall look at objective experimental evidence that attempts to test whether these defence mechanisms really exist.

Several psychometric tests have been developed in order to measure defence mechanisms, including the Repression-Sensitisation Scale of Byrne *et al.* (1963) and the Defense Mechanisms Inventory of Ililivich and Glaser (1986). Unfortunately, both suffer from severe psychometric defects and, because of this, it is difficult to see how they can possibly measure what they claim to do. In any case, it is very difficult to see how one could *conceivably* write questionnaire items (whose responses, by definition, require self-insight) to measure unconscious mental processes such as defence mechanisms. It is necessary to look at more subtle ways of examining whether information is filtered on the basis of its emotional content.

Following the seminal work of Bruner and Postman (1947), several hundred studies have examined whether the emotional content of words affects their memorability, the ease with which they can be perceived, and so on. A typical experiment might involve the establishment of 'recognition thresholds' for various words, which are basically the minimum duration for which a word has to be exposed for it to be correctly recognised. The words would be printed on cards and displayed for a very brief period using a piece of equipment called a tachistoscope. The person being tested would say (or make a guess as to) what the word was. If they guessed incorrectly, the word would be shown again for a slightly longer duration, the process being repeated until it was correctly identified.

It was generally found that words with negative associations (e.g. 'whore', 'rape', 'death') actually had to be shown for longer periods of time than other words in order to be correctly recognised. This suggested that some type of psychological mechanism monitored the emotional content of the words as they were being perceived, and could in some way affect the visibility of the words in an attempt to keep threatening words from being consciously perceived. These studies were extremely controversial, and raised a stream of protests and alternative explanations, ranging from philosophical objections to the idea of a homunculus – a 'little man inside the head' who monitors what enters consciousness – to sound methodological criticisms of the early experiments.

EXERCISE

(a) Imagine that you sat one of the early perceptual defence experiments. Your lecturer asked you to read out words that were briefly presented on a screen – and to guess if you were not sure. What would you do if you *thought* that you saw the word 'penis'?

(b) What features of words (apart from their emotional content) may make them easier or harder to recognise? Try to guess what two features might make the word 'asparagus' more difficult to recognise than the word 'man'.

The old perceptual defence experiments were flawed because they failed to control for word length and word frequency, both of which can affect the ease with which words are recognised. Short, common words can be recognised much more rapidly than long, unusual words. It also seems likely that participants in the experiment would need to be very sure what the word was before they risked appearing foolish or perverse by calling out a rude word. One would have to be very certain that the word 'penis' really was present before calling it out, whereas one would guess neutral words quite freely. If any of these guesses were correct, this would result in the 'taboo word' appearing to have a higher recognition threshold than the neutral word. This explanation of the perceptual defence effect is sometimes called 'response suppression'. There are other problems with the design of perceptual defence experiments, some of which are discussed by Brown (1961) and Dixon (1981).

The results of these experiments are not usually analysed in the most interesting ways. Since the paradigms were developed by experimental psychologists, the emphasis has been on proving that the perceptual defence effect exists, rather than on examining its correlates. Thus whilst many studies claim to show (or not to show!) that the emotional meaning of a stimulus is related to its detectability, in some form, hardly any of them examine individual differences. It would be very simple to calculate scores indicating how pronounced the perceptual defence effect is for each individual, e.g. by subtracting the individual's mean threshold for neutral words from their threshold for threatening words. One could then test whether individuals who show a massive difference are anxious, rated by their therapists as 'repressors', and in other ways examine the correlates of perceptual defence. However, such studies are extremely rare.

Experiments based on recognition thresholds therefore pose problems. However, there have been several ingenious approaches which do not require the study participants to read out words. Instead, the effects of the word on the perceptual system can be measured directly. Dixon (1981) describes some of his own experiments in this area. Another, rather simpler experiment was performed by Wallace and Worthington (1970). Their volunteers believed that they were taking part in a simple psychophysical experiment to investigate the speed with which the eyes get used to the dark. These authors tested people individually and first 'light-adapted' the eyes of a volunteer by asking him or her to stare into a brightly lit, featureless sphere known as a *Ganzfeld* for a fixed period of time. All of the lights in the room were switched off, and the volunteer was asked to look at a screen on the wall. Every few seconds a buzzer sounded. Whenever the buzzer sounded the subject was asked to decide whether or not he or she could see a very dimly illuminated cross that was projected on to the screen. The aim of the experiment was to time how quickly the individual's eyes became accustomed to the dark – the number of trials before the cross was correctly identified was recorded as the dependent variable. This experiment was repeated several times for each subject.

Unknown to the subjects, the screen was not blank in between the trials. A word was projected on to it, even more dimly than the cross. This word could either be threatening (e.g. 'death') or neutral (e.g. 'heath' or 'dear'). Since the subjects' eyes had not become sufficiently accustomed to the dark to see the cross, they would be completely unaware of the very *presence* of such words, as the words were much dimmer even than the cross. So can the nature of such words affect the recognition threshold for the cross?

The answer is that they can. Both the original study and a replication of it (Cooper and Kline, 1986) found that threatening words and letters matched for length and frequency (such as 'death' or 'VD') slow down recognition of the neutral stimulus, the cross, relative to neutral words or no words. Since the participants in such experiments are never aware of the presence of the threatening words, it is difficult to see how any form of response suppression could account for the results. This experiment suggests that the words are recognised at some unconscious level, that their degree of threat is appraised, and that the perceptual system changes its sensitivity in an attempt to 'block out' awareness of the threatening words. A purer experimental analogue of perceptual defence would be hard to imagine, provided that one can accept that the words used are in some way threatening to the ego.

The Swedish psychologist Ulf Kragh (1955) was interested in understanding the processes which determine how images (rather than words) are understood and interpreted. He recognised that, whilst the picture content is usually the major determinant, where this is weak (for example, when a picture is blurred, indistinct or presented for a very brief period of time), the viewer's expectations, previous experiences, etc. will also play a part – much as in the traditional rationale of projective tests. He used a tachistoscope to present a series of 20 or more exposures of a single picture, and asked his volunteers to describe and sketch what they saw at each exposure. The picture showed a central figure, known as the 'Hero', similar in age and sex to the person viewing the picture. An object (such as a toy) was nearby (the 'Attribute'), and an ugly threatening figure (the 'Secondary') loomed out of the background, as if threatening the Hero.

Kragh argued that someone viewing this series of pictures would quickly 'identify' with the central figure in the picture, so any threat directed against this person from the Secondary figure would be perceived as a threat to the viewer's ego – and defence mechanisms would be activated in an attempt to ward off this threat. Thus Kragh argued that the perceptual distortions observed from the viewer's sketch and the descriptions that were made following each presentation of the picture may give insights into the type and strength of the defence mechanisms used by that person. He drew up a detailed scheme for scoring the responses to these pictures, which seems to be based partly on Freudian theory and partly on clinical descriptions of symptoms thought to be associated with certain defence mechanisms as described by Fenichel (1946). For example, distortions that are similar to symptoms of hysteria are thought to indicate repression, and distortions that resemble obsessive-compulsive neurosis would be indicators of isolation. Unlike most projective tests, these responses can be coded reliably.

The interesting feature of the Defence Mechanism Test (DMT) is that it does seem to have external validity – it can predict behaviour in quite a wide range of situations. Cooper (1988) summarises this evidence. I argued above that individuals who use defence mechanisms to distort their perceptions and appraisals of real-life threats may be slow to recognise and respond to sudden, severe danger, e.g. warnings of fire, of being too close to the ground or of systems failure in a fighter aircraft. Papers such as those by Kragh (1962) and Neuman (Neuman, 1978, 1971) showed that the test *was* able to predict which pilots in the Royal Swedish Air Force would suffer accidents and which would have difficulty in learning to fly. As its predictive validity was so substantial, the test became part of the selection battery in the mid-1970s. Cooper *et al.* (1986) describe some further attempts to validate this test, although these were only partially successful. There is also a considerable literature on the clinical correlates of the test (e.g. Kragh, 1983).

In an attempt to overcome some of the problems associated with the use of this test (and in an attempt to move away from the psychoanalytical theory underlying its scoring system), Cooper and Kline (1989) developed an 'objectively scored' version using non-standard pictures. We used a statistical technique called Q-factor analysis to identify groups of individuals whose perceptions were distorted in similar ways, and found that this form of the test showed a substantial correlation with a measure of perceptual defence, and could accurately predict which individuals would fail RAF flying-training.

The interpretations that individuals make of ever-longer presentations of the same picture are certainly quite striking. Figure 4.1 shows the seven successive reports given by one person in response to presentations of one of the cards of the Thematic Apperception Test, a widely used projective test. This picture shows a somewhat androgynous male figure looking away from what appears to be some sort of surgical operation being performed on an old-fashioned ship – certainly one person is leaning over another brandishing a knife. There is a gun at one side and a Chianti bottle (or is it a severed arm?) in the background. Remember that each exposure was longer than the last, so one would *expect* the individual viewing this sequence to get progressively more accurate. In fact, the picture is more or less correctly identified by the fourth exposure, but was distorted on subsequent exposures so as to minimise the perceived threat, just as expected under Freudian theory. It certainly seems that something interesting can take place when people view mildly disturbing pictures under such conditions – whether or not this requires a psychoanalytical explanation is still a matter of debate. For, despite some evidence which suggests that the test can predict performance in dangerous settings as expected by Freudian theory (and the discovery that scores on the test are largely independent of the main personality factors from self-report questionnaires), hardly anyone outside Scandinavia knows about the Defence Mechanism Test. This is a shame, as it would seem to have some potential as a research tool.

Figure leaning over a table? I couldn't see whether it was a man or a woman (exposure 1)

Young man (boy) dressed in dark clothes at right of screen.
Maybe picture behind him (exposure 2)

Boy dressed in dark clothes, maybe a cap on his head, tree with thick branches behind him in the centre. The tree had no leaves on it (exposure 3)

Boy dressed in dark clothes. Behind him a middle-aged man leaning over a table looking at something on the table. He seemed to be concentrating on it. For a while I thought he might be a surgeon (exposure 4)

Boy in dark clothes. Middle-aged man looking into a car engine from the left-hand side of the car. He held a screwdriver in his right hand (exposure 5)

Boy, dressed in a dark jumper with a shirt and tie on, with dark hair, on front left of screen. Middle-aged man looking at a car engine with a screwdriver in his right hand (exposure 6)

Boy dressed in dark jumper, shirt and tie, with dark hair, on front left of screen. Middle-aged man balding (?) looking at something sunken into something, a screwdriver in his right hand pointing into the container (exposure 7)

Figure 4.1 Responses of one subject to seven successively longer exposures of a TAT card: a form of the Defence Mechanism Test.

SELF-ASSESSMENT QUESTION 4.3

What does Kragh's Defence Mechanism Test (DMT) involve people doing?

Why did Kragh expect scores on the DMT to predict whether air force pilots would crash?

Dreams and symbols

In the *Introductory Lectures on Psychoanalysis*, Freud (1917/1964) writes of the importance of symbolism, especially in dreams. Symbolism occurs when one socially acceptable object is used to represent another, 'taboo' object. Thus the use of symbols allows a 'forbidden' wish to be expressed without the defence mechanisms recognising what is happening and awakening the sleeper, or repressing or otherwise eliminating the threat from consciousness. These symbols are thought to be universal, and indeed if you are asked to guess what object is likely to be symbolised by umbrellas, spears, guns, watering cans, fountains, balloons, aircraft, snakes or reptiles, you will probably recognise at once that these are all symbols of the penis, which they resemble either by their shape or by their action. (One problem with this theory is that, if symbols are so easily recognised, why do they not stir up anxiety and activate the defence mechanisms?)

However, this apparent ease of recognition of symbols hardly constitutes conclusive evidence for the theory. More convincing is the work of Hammer (1953), who examined the symbolic content of prisoners' drawings of a house, a tree and a person – the so called 'House–Tree–Person Test'. Two groups of male subjects were tested. Members of one group of 20 subjects were tested after undergoing surgical sterilisation. The control group consisted of 20 men who were about to undergo other forms of surgery, and the prisoners' own scores on the test on a previous occasion. The men in the sterilisation group were expected to be anxious about their new state, and it was expected that such castration anxiety would be demonstrated symbolically in their drawings. Sure enough, their houses lacked chimney-pots and their trees had been chopped down – statistically significant results that appear to support Freud's theory of symbolism.

A second test of the theory comes from the field of linguistics. French, German, Irish, and Arabic and several other non-Indo-European languages assign words a masculine or feminine gender. If Freud's theory is correct, it seems probable that the femininity of the feminine symbols and the masculinity of the male symbols may have been recognised as the language developed. Thus the gender of words that have a symbolic meaning should be the same as the gender of the underlying symbol. For example, the words 'fountain' and 'aeroplane' should take the masculine gender, since they symbolise the penis.

Minturn (1965) compiled a list of symbols and asked a team of fluent linguists to translate these words into 10 languages. As a control, he also asked them to translate random samples of nouns, in order to establish the baseline proportion of masculine and feminine nouns for each language, some of which also have a 'neuter' class. The analyses determined whether words representing masculine symbols tended to be given the masculine gender more often than would be expected by chance. Similar analyses were performed for the female symbols in each language. It was found that words representing masculine symbols did generally take the masculine gender in the language of the symbol (masculine/feminine) and the gender of the word used to represent that symbol (masculine/feminine). Statistical analyses showed that the male symbols were found to take the masculine gender more often than would be expected by chance (there being no significant effect for the female symbols). Thus this study provides some slight evidence for the validity of this part of Freud's theory.

Meissner (1958) measured skin resistance, a physiological variable that is often used as an index of anxiety or emotionality. A total of 20 male volunteers were shown 50 words or phrases, some of which were symbols of death. It was thought that the meaning of the death symbols might be 'decoded' and lead to a rise in levels of anxiety, which would show itself as a fall in the resistance between the electrodes. The control words would not be expected to have such an effect. The results supported this hypothesis – it seems that symbols can indeed produce signs of anxiety.

Hall and van de Castle (1963) studied sex differences in the symbolic content of over 900 dreams. They postulated that the dreams of male subjects should often represent castration anxiety, and rarely represent penis envy, and that the dreams of female subjects should take the opposite form. They accordingly searched through the dream reports of 60 male and 60 female volunteers, and coded the intensity of themes symbolising castration or penis envy. Examples of the former would be injury to or loss of a part of the body or an object used by the dreamer, whilst penis envy would be inferred if the dreamer acquired a phallic symbol (e.g. picking up an umbrella that was found lying on the pavement) or admired a man's performance. It was found that different judges could code these themes reliably from the dreamers' reports, and that there was a highly significant difference between the dreams of the male subjects and those of the female subjects, consistent with Freud's theory. Male subjects' dreams often seemed to allude to castration anxiety but rarely to penis envy, whilst the opposite was true for the female volunteers. Thus this experiment, too, lends some credence to Freud's theory of dream symbolism.

SELF-ASSESSMENT QUESTION 4.4

Can you see anything wrong with Minturn's experiment?

Psychosexual development

If Freud's theory of psychosexual development is correct, one would expect to find that:

- the adult personality characteristics that Freud described (e.g. the 'anal character', with its blend of orderly, obstinate and stingy characteristics) would be found in adults;
- adults who show these characteristics to an extreme extent would have been either over- or under-indulged at the appropriate psychosexual stage.

The oral and anal character types have been studied in some detail, most recently (and arguably most rigorously) by Kline (Kline, 1967, 1968, 1969; Kline and Storey, 1977), who tried to develop questionnaires to measure the adult personality characteristics of the oral and anal characters. The anal character was found – the characteristics of orderliness, obstinacy and stinginess do seem to tend to occur together in adults, suggesting that they have a common cause, just as Freud suggested. Not one but two oral characters were found – the oral optimist (talkative with a cheerful outlook and a liking for sweet, milky things) and the oral pessimist (a much less pleasant character, who is jealous, sarcastic and pessimistic, with a liking for crunchy and spicy foods). Thus the three main adult personality types do seem to exist, much as Freud suggested, and Kline has developed three questionnaires, namely the Oral Optimism Questionnaire (OOQ), the Oral Pessimism Questionnaire (OPQ) and the Anal Interests Questionnaire (Ai3Q) to measure them.

This is not to say, of course, that the adult personality characteristics *arose* for the reasons that Freud predicted. Some workers have attempted to perform longitudinal or retrospective studies in order to determine whether people who are over- or under-indulged at the oral or anal stages of infancy go on to develop extreme levels of the corresponding adult personality characteristics, but without much success. However, the methodology was often weak (using unreliable scales to assess the adult personality trait, or using such tiny samples that the studies lacked statistical power), and in any case it has been found to be very difficult to obtain accurate retrospective data about how, precisely, children were weaned and potty-trained – parents simply cannot remember the detail. So, as Kline (1981) observes in his detailed discussion of these studies, whilst they do not confirm Freud's theories, this is as likely to be because of their methodological difficulties as it is to be due to the fact that the theory is incorrect.

SUMMARY

Very few people now accept that psychoanalysis is effective in curing neurotic symptoms, so one major aspect of Freud's theory appears to be flawed. However, the present chapter has focused on some aspects of Freudian theory that can, perhaps, be tested empirically. The convergence of the results obtained from tests measuring individual differences in perceptual defence and the Defence Mechanism Test is rather interesting, and lends support to the view that there is *some* type of force akin to a defence mechanism that makes unpleasantly emotionally toned pictures and words more difficult to perceive accurately than neutral or positively toned stimuli. The finding that scores on the DMT can also predict behaviour in settings where quick, accurate perception of threat is vital is also entirely consistent with Freud's model of the mind. My own suspicion is that there may be some truth in this aspect of Freud's theory.

The discovery of some evidence in support of Freud's theory of symbolism is also interesting, although the main findings need to be replicated. Moreover, the theory of adult psychosexual character types does appear to be supported by questionnaire studies, although whether these oral optimist, oral pessimist and anal character types arise for the reasons that Freud claimed is unclear.

There are plenty of good experiments that still need to be performed in this area. As Erdelyi (1974, 1985) has pointed out, many of Freud's notions can mesh quite well with modern information-processing and cognitive theories – indeed, there has been a distinct resurgence of interest in a cognitive unconscious. Priming experiments suggest that the meaning of a word *can* be extracted and understood before the word itself can be consciously recognised, which used to be one of the main arguments against perceptual-defence experiments. However, at present there seems to be no conclusive evidence that any part of Freud's theory is correct, although some of the evidence is suggestive.

SUGGESTED ADDITIONAL READING

There are relatively few books that study the scientific status of Freud's theories. Kline's (1981) *Fact and Fantasy* is perhaps the most useful. It critically discusses the methodological problems associated with the various experiments, and tries to ignore the technically flawed literature when drawing some broad conclusions about how well Freud's theories have stood up to empirical testing. Other useful texts are Erdelyi's (1985) *Psychoanalysis: Freud's Cognitive Psychology* (but only for those with a good background in cognitive psychology), and Fisher and Greenberg's (1996) *Freud Scientifically Appraised*, which covers much of the more recent work.

ANSWERS TO SELF-ASSESSMENT QUESTIONS

SAQ 4.1
This is a difficult question to answer, and any answer will necessarily be subjective. However, the important issues seem to me to deal with the structure and function of mind, so the id, ego, superego and repression (since it is supposedly the most important defence mechanism) seem fairly central to the theory – the theories of art, dreams, wit and humour seem to be fairly peripheral, and the others seem to me to lie somewhere in between.

SAQ 4.2
First, a sound understanding of the theory is the first prerequisite – sometimes experiments are performed to test hypotheses that Freud never really suggested. Second, there has to be a good way of assessing ('operationalising') the concept that is being tested. One cannot test Freud's hypothesis that 5-year-old girls develop penis envy unless one can find some way of measuring penis

envy! It would not be unfair to say that most questionnaires which have been developed to measure Freudian concepts simply fail to measure what they claim to assess, and so it is not possible simply to look through a catalogue of questionnaires and choose one that assesses the concept of interest, since it will almost certainly not prove adequate for the job. Finally, careful attention must be paid to experimental design, statistical analysis, ensuring that the number of subjects is large enough to give the experiment reasonable statistical power, ensuring that competing hypotheses are identified and eliminated, checking that control groups are well chosen, and so on.

SAQ 4.3

Subjects taking the test look at a screen. A picture is flashed on the screen, and each subject is asked to say and sketch what they saw. The process is repeated about 20 times, the picture being exposed for slightly longer on each occasion. The people taking the test are not told that they are seeing the same picture time and time again; most believe it is a series of different pictures. The test is scored by a trained psychologist, who looks for certain well-defined 'signs' in each picture (e.g. 'Hero (central figure) is a non-human animal') which are thought to reflect the action of certain types of defence mechanisms.

Individuals who use many defence mechanisms to keep unpleasant material out of consciousness may also defend against perceptions of stressful events. They may be unable to detect danger signs (e.g. an alarmingly low altimeter reading) or may misinterpret them (e.g. as a false alarm), rather than reacting rapidly and appropriately.

SAQ 4.4

The fact that most (although not all) of the male sexual symbols in Minturn's work do physically resemble the male genitals more than the female ones seems to me to reduce the strength of his explanation. When language was evolving, a pen or dagger might have been assigned to the 'male' gender simply because it does look more like the male than the female sexual organs – there is no need for any theory of symbolism to explain this. It would have been much more convincing if Minturn had considered only those symbols (e.g. feet) that do not bear such an obvious resemblance.

5

Trait theories of personality

BACKGROUND

In our everyday lives we tend to believe that people behave in ways that are consistent across all situations (so-and-so is 'nervy' or 'talkative', for example). This is the basis of trait theory, which seeks to discover the main ways in which people differ from one another. Trait theories are now widely believed to be the most useful means of studying personality – though there is less agreement about precisely which trait theory is the most appropriate. Several questionnaires have been developed to provide reliable and valid measures of the main personality traits, many of which have been found to have a biological basis, as discussed in Chapters 6 and 9.

Recommended prior reading

Chapters 1, 11, 13 and 14.

INTRODUCTION

The personality theories considered so far have attempted to understand the nature of personality and its underlying processes through detailed analyses of individuals. The pattern of free associations generated by Freud's small samples of patients led to elaborate and speculative theories about the structure of mind, child development, motivation and other aspects of personality structure and process. Kelly sought to understand each person's unique pattern of personal constructs – the unique cognitive framework that each individual uses to anticipate and model events in the world. Rogers' theory is still less analytical, viewing people as whole individuals who grow and develop over time, coming to like and accept themselves as they are.

One problem that is common to all three theories is the difficulty of measuring personality. 'Self-actualisation' remains a vague abstraction. There is no clearly valid way of assessing unconscious mental processes such as the extent of an individual's Oedipal fixation, or the strength of his or her defence mechanisms. Moreover, whilst the use of repertory grids may be particularly useful for understanding the number and nature of the constructs used by individuals, it cannot easily allow individuals to be compared. Three individuals might complete three different repertory grids, but ultimately there is no easy way of deciding how, precisely, their personalities differ.

It may, therefore, be useful to approach the problem from another direction. Instead of considering each individual's phenomenological world (as Kelly and Rogers did), it may be useful to develop techniques that will allow people's personalities to be compared, i.e. to try to discover the main ways in which people's personalities vary – to map out the main ways in which people differ from one another. Once the main dimensions of personality have been established, it should be possible to develop tests to show the position of each person along each of these dimensions – thus allowing people's personalities to be compared directly.

Trait theories of personality follow precisely this approach. They assume that there is a certain constancy about the way in which people behave – that is, behaviour is to some extent determined by certain characteristics of the individual, and not *entirely* by the situation. This seems to tie in well with personal experience – we very often describe people's behaviour in terms of adjectives ('bossy', 'timid', 'life and soul of the party', or whatever) implying that some feature of *them*, rather than the situations in which they find themselves, determines how they behave. (We shall discuss the role of situations in a little more detail below.) Describing people in terms of adjectives may sound a little reminiscent of Kelly's theory; after all, one use of the repertory grid is to find out which individuals are construed in similar ways. However, the crucial difference lies in the type of data used. According to Kelly's theory, an individual's *perception* of other people is what is important – it does not particularly matter whether these perceptions are accurate. However, trait theories attempt to map out the ways in which people really *do* differ from one another, and so depend on accurate (i.e. reliable and valid) techniques for measuring personality.

The basic aims of trait theories are therefore simple:

- to discover the main ways (dimensions) in which people differ;
- to check that scores on these dimensions do, indeed, stay reasonably constant across situations – for, if not, situations must determine behaviour, people have no personality, and we should all re-train as social psychologists.
- to discover how and why these individual differences come about – for example, whether they are passed on genetically, through crucial events in childhood (as Freud would have us believe), through the examples of our parents (as suggested by Bandura), or because of something to do with the biology of our nervous systems.

The present chapter deals with the first two issues, a discussion of personality *processes* being left until Chapters 6 and 9.

FACTOR ANALYSIS APPLIED TO PERSONALITY

You will recall from Chapter 1 that the main purpose of measuring traits is to describe how an individual will behave most of the time – hence personality descriptions such as 'John is an anxious type' may lead us to suspect that John will be more likely than most to leap into the air when startled, to worry about examinations, to be wary of bees, and so on. Using one word – 'anxious' – allows us to predict how John will probably behave in a whole range of situations. The first question is this: how should one decide which words to use to describe behaviour?

There are several problems in choosing adjectives at random and deciding that these are the main dimensions of personality. First, there are many potential 'personality trait descriptors' in the language. Allport and Odbert (1936) found over 4500 such descriptors, and so it would be impossible to assess people on all possible traits. Second, if different investigators choose different adjectives, it will be difficult to prove that these mean the same thing – for example, if one individual says that 'Elizabeth is retiring', whilst another says that she is 'shy', are they describing precisely the same personality characteristic? It is impossible to be certain just by looking at the meaning of the words, since language tends to be imprecise, with many adjectives having subtle nuances and/or multiple meanings (perhaps you initially thought that Elizabeth was coming to the end of her working life). Thus different people may use different words to describe the same feature of personality, and may perhaps use the same words to describe different aspects of behaviour. This does not bode well for reliable, valid measurement. Third, it is possible to develop scales that describe trivial aspects of behaviour, whilst leaving important aspects of behaviour unmeasured. For example, it would probably be easy to develop a scale to measure the extent to which individuals feel paranoid, even though paranoia is probably not a particularly important trait in the general population.

Fourth, it is very easy to use traits in a circular manner, whereby the presence of a trait is deduced from some behaviour, and then used to explain that behaviour. Doctors do this all the time. You might feel pain from swollen tonsils, visit your local doctor and be told that your throat hurts because you have tonsillitis. Except, of course, that your doctor has not explained anything, nor shown any understanding of what is wrong with you. He or she has just translated your symptom into Latin, and offered it to you as an explanation. Similarly, in the previous paragraph we noted that Elizabeth was quiet and retiring, and deduced from this that she is less *sociable* than other people. It is very tempting to then try to *explain* these behaviours by means of the trait of sociability – to assert that the reason why Elizabeth avoids parties is *because* she is low on the trait of sociability. To avoid falling into this trap it is vital to ensure that traits are far broader than the behaviours that are used to define them. Sociability would be a useful trait if (and only if) it has broader implications than a liking for parties, etc. If it could be shown to have a genetic basis, to be heavily influenced by some actions of one's parents, or possibly related to some aspect of brain or neuronal functioning, then we could be confident that the trait of sociability is a real characteristic of the individual. The behaviour (which we interpret as 'sociability') arises because of some real biological/social/developmental/cognitive peculiarity of that person – it is a manifestation of a broad 'source trait' that *leads* them to avoid social gatherings, not just a convenient label to summarise a person's behaviour. Without such evidence, traits are only convenient descriptions of behaviour – they cannot be used to explain it.

How, then, can we go about discovering these 'source traits' – these broad dispositions that cause people to behave in certain ways? In Chapter 14 we observe that factor analysis can sometimes show up the *causes* of behaviour. If we factor-analyse measures of the behaviour of people, some of whom have been drinking and some of whom have not, and some of whom have flu, whilst others do not, the technique of factor analysis tells us that two factors (causal influences) are at work. One factor corresponds to the alcohol-induced behaviours (slurring, staggering, etc.), whilst the other corresponds to behaviours caused by the virus (raised temperature, sneezing, etc.). In both cases, the factors represent true causal influences on behaviour – the chemical and the virus – and the technique of factor analysis is able to show both how many causal influences are at work, and which behaviours are influenced by which substance.

This situation is remarkably similar to that facing personality psychologists. Trait theory assumes that individuals differ in the extent to which they possess certain personality traits, the only problem being that we do not know in advance how many of these traits there are, or what they are like. However, we also assume that these traits influence behaviour. So, in order to determine what these personality traits are, it is simply necessary to measure the behaviour of a large number of people, to correlate these behaviours together, and to carry out a factor analysis as described in Chapter 15. The factors that emerge from this analysis should show which behaviours tend to occur together as a result of certain causal influences – influences that are termed 'personality traits'. If people's scores on these traits can be shown to be influenced by genetic, biological, social, developmental or cognitive variables, then we can be confident that a true 'source trait' has been identified, which can then be used to explain behaviour.

In the remaining sections, we shall consider various attempts to reveal the main personality traits through the use of factor analysis.

SELF-ASSESSMENT QUESTION 5.1

What are the four main problems involved in selecting trait descriptors?

THE LEXICAL HYPOTHESIS AND CATTELL'S THEORY OF PERSONALITY

In the previous section I suggested somewhat glibly that, in order to discover the main personality factors, it is merely necessary to measure huge numbers of behaviours, correlate them together, and factor-analyse the results. The problem is, of course, that deciding how to quantify human behaviour is a remarkably difficult task. Those with experience in comparative psychology will know that even logging the behaviour of rodents can be very difficult and time-consuming. To do this for humans would be a mammoth undertaking, and it would probably be necessary to monitor hundreds if not thousands of aspects of behaviour in order to capture the full richness of a person's personality. Measuring hundreds of behaviours of thousands of people in hundreds of different situations is such a gargantuan task as to be impossible. There is another problem, too, in that measures of behaviour often contain dependencies. For example, it is not easy for a person to eat, drink and talk simultaneously, so if an individual is eating, he or she will not be drinking or talking. We shall note in Chapter 15 that such dependencies can play havoc with factor analyses – they can produce entirely spurious factors.

Cattell (1946) argued that, instead of measuring behaviours, we should focus on adjectives. Specifically, he argues that every interesting aspect of personality would probably have been observed during the course of evolution, and a term describing it would have entered the language. Thus the dictionary should contain words that describe virtually every conceivable personality characteristic – generally in the form of adjectives such as 'happy', 'bad-tempered', 'anxious', 'uptight', 'phlegmatic', and so on. Suppose that a sample of these adjectives were to be extracted from a dictionary. It would probably be the case that some of these words meant the same as others – 'anxious' and 'uptight', for example. Wherever this happens, one or other of the adjectives could be dropped. This would produce a sample of words that describe *different* aspects of personality. Suppose now that these words were put into a questionnaire (so that people could rate themselves on each adjective), or that trained raters assessed people's behaviour on the basis of these adjectives. It would then be possible to collect data and correlate all of the responses to the various adjectives in order to find out whether 'happy' people also tend to be 'phlegmatic', etc. Factor analysis can be used to determine which of these ratings tend to group together. The factors that emerge should be the main personality 'source traits'. This assumption, that the analysis of correlations between properly sampled adjectives will reveal all of the main personality traits, is sometimes referred to as the 'lexical hypothesis'.

Cattell drew heavily on the work of Allport and Odbert (1936) when he was attempting to identify the main personality factors. These authors extracted from a dictionary a list of adjectives that could be used to describe people. Cattell eliminated synonyms from this list in order to avoid the problem of interdependent variables. When this was done, the original list of 4500 adjectives was reduced to 180 and then to 42–46 (Cattell, 1957). These terms were used to rate the behaviour of a group of people, whereupon the correlations between the 45 trait descriptors were computed and factor-analysed, yielding some 12 to 15 factors.

The assessment of behaviour through ratings is time-consuming. Furthermore, there may be some personality traits (such as feelings and attitudes) which, except in pathological cases, may not be obvious to someone who is rating behaviour – someone may feel frightened when walking down a lonely road at night, but step out bravely. Moreover, the very presence of the rater may alter some behaviours – our pedestrian may not feel as anxious as usual because of the presence of the rater. Thus Cattell has attempted to measure personality traits by methods other than observers' ratings – most notably through the use of questionnaires and 'objective tests'. The hope is that many of the personality factors identified in one medium will also appear in others.

EXERCISE

The crucial assumption of the lexical hypothesis is that single adjectives in the dictionary can describe all types of behaviour. Can you think of any patterns of behaviour that are not described by a single word? You might like to discuss some with your friends, to ensure that you all agree that the patterns of behaviour do actually exist. To get you started, I cannot think of any English word that describes taking pleasure in others' misfortunes (as in the German *Schadenfreude*), or which describes the sort of person who appears to be a paragon of society, heavily involved with charity work, etc., yet who behaves like an uncaring monster towards their family. If you can think up many such patterns of behaviour, this may indicate that the lexical hypothesis is unlikely to be able to cover the full range of behaviours (or, of course, it may just be that the behaviours that you notice in other people are illusory – you may *think* that you notice characteristics that do not, in fact, exist).

SELF-ASSESSMENT QUESTION 5.2

How do you think that one can tell whether a personality factor derived from a rating scale is the same as a factor that appears in ratings of behaviour?

Cattell's most famous tests for measuring personality are the Sixteen Personality Factor Questionnaires (16PF) (Cattell *et al.*, 1970a). I refer to these in the plural because there is a whole series of different forms of these self-report questionnaires that yield scores on 15 personality traits and also intelligence. The fifth edition (1993) is the most recent. Cattell has always championed the use of oblique rotations in factor analysis, and so these scales can themselves be intercorrelated and factored, producing second-order factors, of which there are at least four, including 'extraversion' (characterised by sociability, enthusiasm, risk-taking and needing the company of others) and 'anxiety' (nervousness, guilt, timidity, suspicion and compulsiveness). There is also a variant of this test designed for adolescents (the High-School Personality Questionnaire), 8- to 14-year-olds (the Children's Personality Questionnaire), 6- to 8-year-olds (the Early School Personality Questionnaire) and 4- to 6-year-olds (the Pre-School Personality Questionnaire). There is some variation in the number and nature of the factors measured by these questionnaires, which Cattell (e.g. Cattell, 1973) explains by suggesting that some traits develop later than others. He also explored personality in clinical groups, and developed the Clinical Analysis Questionnaire which measures (among other things) some seven distinct factors of depression.

It seems that Cattell's work is well founded in theory, care has been taken in sampling the variables that could describe personality, the scales have been factor-analysed, and many questionnaires have been developed. So why consider any alternative? The problem is that no one apart from Cattell and his colleagues can find anything approaching 16 factors in the 16PF. If the questionnaires do, indeed, measure 16 distinct personality traits, it should be possible to administer these to a large sample of people, correlate the items together, perform the factor analysis as described in Chapter 15, and discover that the items load 16 factors precisely as claimed by Cattell. The literature on this really is definitive – for whatever reason, the 16PF simply does not measure 16 factors. As Matthews (1989) observed, 'it may be worth abandoning the Cattell primary scales altogether'. Remember that the factor analysis essentially shows which items belong to which scales. It indicates which particular items should be added together when the test is scored. The discovery that the structure of the scales in the 16PF is not even remotely similar to the factor structure obtained when the items are factor analysed indicates that everyone who has been using the test has been scoring it in a meaningless fashion. For the factor analysis indicates that test items that actually measure little in common are being combined to form scales in the 16PF. Despite these very fundamental problems, the test is still widely used, particularly in occupational psychology. Other studies that fail to find Cattell's factors include those by Barrett and Kline (1982a) and Byravan and Ramanaiah (1995), and there are others, as can be verified from any search of the literature. Cattell's rejoinders to such work include Cattell (1986) and Cattell and Krug (1986). Cattell's attempts to measure personality by means of 'objective tests' were, if anything, even less successful. The 'Objective Analytic Test Battery' (Cattell and Schuerger, 1978) was an attempt to measure some of the main personality factors by means of objective tests. However, Kline and Cooper (1984a) showed that the factors resolutely refused to emerge as expected, and that the test appeared to measure *ability* rather better than it assessed *personality*.

Cattell, hardly surprisingly, disagrees with the studies which failed to demonstrate the expected structure in the 16PF. He argues that the tests that were used to determine the true number of factors were inappropriate (although these included his own 'scree test'). He also expressed concerns about the adequacy of rotation to simple structure, preferring his own subjective methods to those used and trusted by virtually every other psychometrician. The simplest way to rebut the criticisms would be for Cattell to produce a clear, 16-factor matrix arising from his studies with the 16PF. The 1970 handbook for the 16PF did not include such a table, and when one was eventually published it did not show the clear factors that everyone expected.

The reasons for these flaws are uncertain. Recall that the 16PF was constructed through factor analyses performed by hand – a laborious and error-prone process. It may be that errors crept in here. Block (1995) suggested another possibility. The 'personality sphere' as mapped out by Cattell included not only the lexical trait descriptors, but also descriptions of personality traits arising from other psychological theories, to ensure that nothing was left out. Hence the personality descriptions used by Cattell were not *just* an exhaustive list of all trait descriptors, since several variables were included that he believed to be of theoretical importance, even though they did not seem to appear in the word sample. It is therefore unsurprising that some of Cattell's hypotheses were borne out.

Thus, although Cattell is one of the few psychologists to appreciate the need for careful sampling of the domain of trait descriptors, the inclusion of items from previous theories presents a problem. It also seems that there are fewer personality traits than suggested by Cattell, and that tests designed to measure Cattell's personality traits are flawed. Given these problems, it is hardly worthwhile discussing the nature of Cattell's factors or considering the evidence for the validity of the 16PF. Instead, we shall consider a more modern lexical approach to personality measurement.

SELF-ASSESSMENT QUESTION 5.3

Why is it important to check that the items that form factors when a test is factor-analysed correspond to the items that are added together when the test is being scored conventionally?

THE 'BIG FIVE' PERSONALITY FACTORS

Most personality psychologists these days regard a five-factor model of personality as absolutely fundamental, and so it is educational to trace how this view of personality developed, since it seems to have a somewhat weaker basis in theory than one might expect. For, although all these studies were rooted in Cattell's 'personality sphere' concept, they broke away and ended up by analysing items that were written in order to *test* a particular preconceived model, rather than to *discover* what the main personality factors actually are.

Strangely enough, the most important paper in this area (Tupes and Christal, 1961) has only recently been published (Tupes and Christal, 1992), having previously been available only as a US Air Force technical report. It basically sought to re-analyse the results of applying Cattell's rating scales, described in the previous section. As before, the aim was to correlate and factor-analyse the correlation between the adjectives in order to reveal the fundamental dimensions of personality.

Technically, this work was by no means perfect. The samples were predominantly young and male, and being composed of officers and officer candidates were hardly representative of the general population. Personality ratings were made by untrained raters (some of whom hardly knew the people they were rating!) over a very short period of time. In addition, Block (1995) points out that the particular form of factor analysis used may well have suggested that the five factors were far more prevalent than they actually were. These deficiencies went unrecognised, and this work was to acquire an influence far beyond anything Tupes and Christal could have envisaged. A vast superstructure of theory and scale construction has been based on the premise that these studies really did demonstrate five consistent personality traits.

Norman was the first to base a theory on these findings. Following an earlier replication of the work of Tupes and Christal, Norman (1967) sought to update Cattell's work in defining the 'personality sphere' – a list of trait descriptors which, when used to assess behaviour and subsequently factor-analysed, may reveal the main dimensions of personality. He produced 1431 terms, and later sorted these into 75 clusters in accordance with the Tupes and Christal factors. Note that these traits were *subjectively assigned to a pre-existing model* rather than emerging through a process of factor analysis. Goldberg (1990) reports studies showing that five factors emerge when the 75 'Norman clusters' are used as the basis of a self-rating scale, which is perhaps less than surprising given that Norman *designed* the 75 clusters in order to yield five factors. Much is made of the fact that the Norman/Goldberg five-factor model is not restricted to the English language. Trait descriptors can be grouped according to the five-factor model in languages as diverse as German and Filipino (Angleitner *et al.*, 1990; Church *et al.*, 1996). I am not entirely convinced that this demonstrates the universality of the five-factor model, since these sortings of adjectives show how individuals *believe* behaviours group together, and not how they actually *do* intercorrelate. The first issue is a matter of linguistics, while the second is an empirical, psychological matter.

The strongest proponents of the five-factor model are Paul Costa and Robert McCrae, who began by using a technique known as cluster analysis to investigate correlations between items in Cattell's 16PF (Costa and McCrae, 1976). (Cluster analysis was developed as a 'quick and dirty' approximation to factor analysis during the 1930s, before powerful computers were available. I have never quite understood why it is still used.) They found two clear clusters of items which appeared to measure 'extraversion' (sociability, confidence, optimism, cheerfulness, etc.) and 'neuroticism' (worrying, guilt-proneness, anxiety, etc.), plus a tiny third cluster. More items were added on the basis of no particularly compelling theoretical rationale, and three clusters were then derived (Costa and McCrae, 1978), the third being known as 'openness to experience' and measuring the ways in which people deal with novel events, such as fantasy, aesthetics, feelings and actions. They then decided, quite arbitrarily, that each of these factors should be measured by six aspects of behaviour that they termed 'facets'. These represent lower-level forms of behaviour which, taken together, define the factor. For example, worrying is one facet of neuroticism – it could be assessed by items such as 'do you sometimes worry?', 'do your worries keep you awake at night?' and so on. The obvious objection to this technique is that the facets are often so narrow in content that their items are *guaranteed* to form scales. For example, someone who says 'yes' to the second item above is *bound* to say 'yes' to the first. However, Costa and McCrae ignored such problems and developed $6 \times 3 = 18$ sets of eight items, which eventually managed to form factors much as they were designed to. However, by this stage all attempts to keep to a lexical sampling model had been abandoned – the items were designed to measure a particular set of facets and factors.

Two further factors were later added to this three-factor model in order to allow Goldberg's two factors of 'agreeableness' and 'conscientiousness' to be measured, although some violence was done to Goldberg's five-factor model in the process. No one argued about the basic factors of extraversion and neuroticism, but Goldberg's third factor (previously identified as 'intellect') was altered so that it more closely resembled 'openness'. These five factors, namely openness, conscientiousness, extraversion, agreeableness and neuroticism (acronym OCEAN), constitute the currently popular five-factor model of personality, whose factors are usually measured using the NEO-PI(R) questionnaire (Costa and McCrae, 1992a). I have described its evolution in some detail, since there are several major problems with this theory that are sometimes glossed over.

First, it can be seen that everything really hinges on the work of Tupes and Christal, since this is what led Norman to categorise his traits in the way that he did, and this (via Goldberg's work) led to the five-factor model which was taken up by Costa and McCrae. Is the Tupes and Christal work really adequate? It certainly has a great many technical problems, not least the quality of the ratings performed. Cattell (1957) had painstakingly laid out a list of nine principles that were necessary for adequate ratings of personality. These included adequate sampling of items to be rated, a representative sample of individuals to be rated, careful training of raters, ensuring that ratings were performed over a long period of time, plus some technical points that need not concern us here. Few of these admirable principles were implemented in the studies by Tupes and Christal. The second problem is that most investigators seem content to identify a factor merely from examining its loadings – a notoriously dangerous principle, as argued by Zuckerman (1992), among others. To ensure that they are genuine personality traits (and not artefacts of measurement, such as a 'halo effect', social desirability, or even factors measuring mood or ability) it is desirable both to measure the traits by other means (e.g. ratings of behaviour and self-report) and to carry out experiments to validate the factors. For example, to check that 'openness to experience' does indeed measure something about the way in which people adapt to novelty, it would be interesting to measure people's behaviour when confronted with some entirely novel situation, and to determine whether this bears any resemblance to scores on this trait. If it does not, the interpretation of the trait's psychological meaning must be suspect. Finally, it is generally thought necessary to determine the psychological *processes* that cause a factor to show itself. Why do some people score higher on openness than others? Is it something to do with the way they are educated? It is linked to the nature of their interaction with their parents? Does it have a genetic component? A trait is only properly understood when its origins and mechanisms of operation are well grasped – and in my view this is not the case for all of the Big Five factors.

There are other problems reported in the literature. One might expect the NEO-PI(R) to yield five factors when its facets are subjected to a confirmatory factor analysis (described in Chapter 15), whereas some evidence suggests that it does not (Parker *et al.*, 1993). Facets that supposedly belong to quite different factors can turn out to be quite highly correlated. A related problem is that some of the five factors are themselves highly correlated. Block (1995) mentions a correlation of −0.61 between neuroticism and conscientiousness in a female sample. It really does not seem that the five factors are truly independent, as Costa and McCrae originally supposed. Thus, although 'Big Five' models are enormously popular, there are still some real doubts as to whether all of the scales of the NEO-PI(R) actually measure what they claim to.

THE WORK OF EYSENCK

Whereas Cattell's approach to exploring the main personality traits has been essentially data-driven – a 'bottom-up' process – Hans Eysenck has instead advocated a 'top-down' method of analysis in which likely personality traits are identified from the clinical and experimental literature. He has spent fully 50 years investigating the three main aspects of personality described in his 1947 book *Dimensions of Personality*, namely introversion vs. extraversion (Eysenck spells this word with an 'a'), neuroticism vs. emotional stability, and psychoticism (or tough-mindedness) vs. humaneness. The first two terms, in particular, have a long history. Eysenck (e.g. Eysenck and Eysenck, 1985) have shown that these stretch back over two thousand years to Galen and Hippocrates, were subsequently adopted in 1798 by Immanuel Kant, and surfaced again in the writings of the Swiss psychoanalyst Karl Jung during the 1920s. The basic premise of all these writers is that there are two basic dimensions of personality, rather as shown in Figure 5.1.

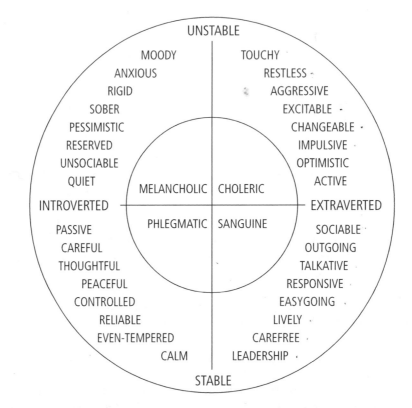

Figure 5.1 The personality dimensions of neuroticism and extraversion. Reproduced from Eysenck and Eysenck (1985) with the kind permission of Plenum Publishing.

The vertical line in Figure 5.1 represents the personality dimension of emotional instability, or 'neuroticism'. Highly neurotic individuals are moody, touchy and anxious, whereas those low on neuroticism are relaxed, even-tempered and calm. The second dimension is that of extraversion. Extraverts are hearty, sociable, talkative and optimistic individuals – the types who insist on talking to you on train journeys. Introverts are reserved, pessimistic and keep themselves to themselves. The fact that these two lines are at right angles suggests that these two dimensions of personality are independent (uncorrelated). Figure 5.1 also shows the four 'Galen types' (melancholic, choleric, phlegmatic and sanguine) relative to these axes, and around the outside are descriptions of behaviours which might be observed from various combinations of these dimensions. Thus someone who is neither particularly stable nor unstable, but very introverted, might be described as quiet or passive, a stable extravert might be described as responsive and easygoing, and so on.

This diagram does not show Eysenck's third major dimension of personality, which was only formally added to the theory in 1976. Eysenck's dimensions of extraversion and neuroticism could not differentiate between schizophrenics, or borderline schizophrenics, and normal subjects. A third dimension, psychoticism, was introduced to the model in an attempt to achieve this. Individuals scoring high on psychoticism would be emotionally cold, cruel, risk-taking, manipulative and impulsive. Those scoring low on psychoticism would be warm, socialised individuals. (If you prefer to think in terms of stereotypes, your least favourite politician is probably someone whom you regard as having high levels of psychoticism. So too are criminals.) Psychoticism is thought to be largely uncorrelated with either extraversion or neuroticism, and so Eysenck's model of personality can be represented by three, mutually orthogonal personality dimensions – extraversion, neuroticism and psychoticism.

Over the years, Eysenck has devised several techniques to measure these three dimensions of personality, using scales such as the Maudsley Medical Questionnaire (MMQ), the Eysenck Personality Inventory (EPI) and, most recently, the Revised Eysenck Personality Questionnaire (EPQ-R). Some sample items are given by Eysenck and Eysenck (1985, p. 84). Unlike some of the other questionnaires considered above, the items in Eysenck's scales do form three clear factors precisely in accordance with expectations (e.g. Barrett and Kline, 1982b). A children's version of the test is also available.

Eysenck has thus concentrated on two of the personality traits which emerge from the five-factor theorists, and as 'second-order' factors from the 16PF (Hundleby and Connor, 1968), together with a dimension of psychoticism which he finds to be appreciably negatively correlated with Costa and McCrae's 'agreeableness' and 'conscientiousness'. According to Eysenck (H. J. Eysenck, 1992), Goldberg found a correlation of -0.85 between psychoticism and these two measures (combined), indicating that agreeableness and conscientiousness may well be components of psychoticism, rather than factors in their own right. There is a continuing lively debate in the journals as to whether Eysenck's three-factor model or Costa and McCrae's five-factor model is the more appropriate. My own view is that Eysenck's model of personality is more promising than those of Costa and McCrae or of Cattell, not least because the questionnaire designed to measure these traits clearly does its job.

OTHER THEORIES

We must briefly mention some other theories, since the field is strewn with alternative descriptions of personality, none of which has proved to be as influential as those discussed above. Gray's model is the simplest to describe. Look again at Figure 5.1 and imagine spinning the horizontal and vertical axes clockwise through 45 degrees. The line now passing through the 'choleric' and 'phlegmatic' sector defines a personality dimension that Gray called 'anxiety'. The other axis, through the 'sanguine' and 'melancholic' sectors, is called 'impulsivity'. Gray (e.g. Gray, 1972) argues that this model more closely fitted the results from animal studies, in which individual differences in susceptibility to punishment were related to his construct of anxiety, and individual differences in susceptibility to reward were related to impulsivity.

Zuckerman (e.g. 1979, 1991, 1994) has focused on 'sensation-seeking' as a dimension of personality. High sensation-seekers seek out thrills and excitement to avoid boredom, and this dimension has been incorporated into Zuckerman's 'alternative five' five-factor model of personality (Zuckerman et al., 1993). Guilford's work in developing personality scales through factor analysis stretches back to the 1930s, and the Guilford–Zimmerman personality scale (Guilford et al., 1976) measures 11 main factors (plus some of lesser interest), whilst second-order factoring of these scales produces Eysenck's three main factors. Jackson et al. (1995) have postulated a six-factor model, Benet and Waller (1995) have proposed a seven-factor model . . . and there are others.

Fortunately, it is possible to explain most of these discrepancies between the models, and to draw some broad conclusions. The personality factors that emerge from a study obviously depend crucially on the number and nature of the questions that are asked, and in many cases this is determined by the theoretical background of the factorist. The other main approach, namely the lexical model as used by Cattell, might not be able to sample all aspects of behaviour, as suggested by the exercise earlier in this chapter.

As mentioned in the first section of this chapter, the discovery of a trait does not mean that it is necessarily a broad determinant of behaviour. In order to determine which traits are likely to be causal, it is necessary to establish which of them can be seen as consequences of more fundamental biological, social, cognitive or developmental variables. What is clear, however, is that almost every scale either measures extraversion and neuroticism (or something very like these) directly – as in the Zuckerman and 'Big Five' models – or else these factors emerge when the scales from these questionnaires are correlated and factored (a 'second-order' factor analysis), as in Cattell's and Guilford's models. Correlations between factors or second-order analyses can also sometimes produce factors that closely resemble Eysenck's 'psychoticism' factor (e.g. H. J. Eysenck, 1992). Thus extraversion, neuroticism and psychoticism seem to crop up regularly, no matter which particular sets of items are analysed, so it seems reasonable to regard these as being the most substantive dimensions of personality. However, before they can be used as explanations for behaviour (rather than convenient descriptions of it), it is necessary to explore their underlying processes in some detail – which is the substance of Chapter 6.

DISSENTING VOICES

Before we leave this chapter, it is necessary to consider some criticisms that have been levelled against all types of trait theory. Mischel (1968) and other social psychologists have argued that it is situations, not traits, that determine behaviour. Although we choose to *believe* that individuals behave in consistent ways (corresponding to personality traits), such beliefs are at odds with the data. However, two pieces of evidence show that this view is untenable. First, if personality were determined purely by situations, personality traits simply would not exist, and so measures of these traits (such as scores on personality questionnaires) would be unable to predict any aspects of behaviour. However, sources such as Herriott (1989) show that personality traits can predict behaviour. Second, studies such as those by Rushton *et al.* (1983) and Conley (1984) show a considerable consistency in behaviour. Indeed, Conley has shown that after correcting for the use of unreliable tests, the consistency of personality traits over time is of the order of 0.98.

SELF-ASSESSMENT QUESTION 5.4

Using the data in Table 5.1, plot a graph showing how each individual's level of anxiety varies from one situation to another. What would you expect this graph to look like if:

(a) situations, not personality, determine behaviour;

(b) personality, not situations, determines behaviour;

(c) behaviour is determined by the interaction of situation and personality?

(d) Which of these best describes what is going on in your graph?

In lectures	Coffee with friends	In a statistics practical class	Watching a horror film	Reading Dickens
8	7	18	14	6
3	2	16	4	2
7	8	17	8	7

Table 5.1 Hypothetical anxiety scores of five people in five situations

Other theories such as learning theory and social learning theory have also been proposed as alternatives to traits. For if our actions are determined by our reinforcement history and/or the behaviour of our role models, then personality traits certainly cannot be said to *cause* behaviour. One way of addressing this issue is to consider the effects of such processes on personality traits. If role-modelling and reinforcement techniques are all-important in determining how a child or adult behaves, one would expect brothers and sisters to have similar personalities, by virtue of their having been brought up according to the same family ethos. To anticipate Chapter 9, the influence of this 'shared environment' on children's personalities is minuscule, and there is enormous variation in personality within families. This makes it unlikely that such learning theories will be of value as explanations for behaviour.

A third criticism of trait psychology comes from social psychologists with an interest in the 'construction process' (e.g. Hampson, 1997). Rather than viewing personality as a characteristic of the individual, these theorists delve into the processes whereby personality attributions are made – that is, how behaviours are identified, categorised and attributed to either the person ('John is a snappy person') or the situation ('John is under stress'). Personally, I have no problem with this work, except that it is social psychology rather than anything to do with individual differences! For if we view traits as being real, internal characteristics of the individual, then it matters not one jot how others view them. This approach may be useful in fostering awareness of some measurement problems inherent in personality questionnaires, but once again the acid question is whether or not scores on personality questionnaires can predict anything. If they can, then there is more to personality than a social construction process.

SUMMARY

This chapter has covered a lot of ground, and has outlined the most promising approaches to the measurement of personality. You should now be able to define traits and discuss the problem of 'circularity' in using traits to describe behaviour, and discuss Cattell's lexical hypothesis for sampling personality traits from the language – you may have your own views on the adequacy of this method. The personality models of Cattell, Costa and McCrae and Eysenck have been discussed in some detail (as has the quality of their associated psychometric tests) and you should be familiar with some criticisms of trait theory that are sometimes levied by social psychologists and learning theorists.

SUGGESTED ADDITIONAL READING

Suggesting additional reading for this chapter is somewhat more problematic than for other chapters, because the literature is developing so rapidly in this area that anything that I mention here is soon likely to be superseded. The best solution would be to consult the papers and books cited in the text, perform a literature search, browse the journals *Personality and Individual Differences* or *Journal of Personality and Social Psychology*, or visit William Revelle's excellent World Wide Web site, 'The Personality Project', at Northwestern University. This contains a good, up-to-date list of relevant references, and is updated regularly. The papers by Costa and McCrae (1992b) and H. J. Eysenck (1992) are worth reading for two conflicting accounts of the advantages of the five-factor model over the three-factor model. There are also two papers in the *Annual Review of Psychology* that may be useful (Digman, 1990; Wiggins and Pincus, 1992).

ANSWERS TO SELF-ASSESSMENT QUESTIONS

SAQ 5.1

First, there are a great many adjectives in the language, and so it is difficult to know how to choose between them. Second, if different investigators happen to choose different samples of words, it is going to be difficult to ascertain whether their tests actually measure the same underlying psychological dimensions of personality. Third, it is difficult to ensure that *all* potential personality traits have been examined – that is, that the model is comprehensive. Finally, it is necessary to show that any concept (trait) measured by a set of adjectives is broader in scope than the adjectives that are used to measure it, before it can be used as an explanation for behaviour.

SAQ 5.2

There are two possibilities, both of which require that the same large ($n > 100$) sample of people have their behaviour assessed by raters *and* fill in the questionnaire. One can either correlate the two measures together, or factor-analyse the correlations between all of the items (both ratings and questionnaire items). Factoring is the better approach, as this will also identify any items that fail to measure the trait(s) in question.

SAQ 5.3

The factor analysis shows which items measure the same underlying trait. Suppose that a 10-item test is factored, and the analysis shows that items 1 to 5 load on one factor and items 6 to 10 load on another quite different factor. Obviously the test *should* be scored so that items 1 to 5 form one scale and items 6 to 10 form another. If, on the other hand, the test handbook recommends adding together scores on items 1, 2, 3, 7, 8 and 9, the resulting total score will be a mixture of two quite different traits, and quite meaningless. (Consider, for example, how you would interpret a person's score from a test in which five of the items measured nervousness and five items measured vocabulary – it is impossible.)

SAQ 5.4

(a) Very jagged – each person's score would vary enormously from situation to situation, and there would be no differences in the *average* score of each person (computed across situations).
(b) The graphs would be entirely flat – people would yield precisely the same score in every situation.
(c) A mixture of the two.
(d) (c).

6

Biological and social bases of personality

BACKGROUND

At the start of Chapter 5 we stressed that merely identifying the main factors of personality does not imply an *understanding* of the underlying concepts, and that trying to use such factors as explanations for behaviour is dangerously circular. We suggested that in order to use factors to *explain* behaviour it is necessary to show that the traits are much broader in scope than the specific questions posed in the questionnaires – for example, to show that a trait measured by a particular personality questionnaire is just one manifestation of some rather fundamental biological or social process that also affects other aspects of our behaviour.

Recommended prior reading

Chapter 5.

INTRODUCTION

We have seen in Chapter 5 how there is now quite good agreement between theorists about two of the main personality factors (extraversion and neuroticism) – few would now disagree that these are the two main personality traits. However, merely establishing the *structure* of personality is only the first step in any scientific study of individual differences. After all, doctors have known quite a lot about the structure of the human body (the location of the main organs) for millennia, but it is only fairly recently that medical science has begun to understand how the organs operate and interact. So it is with personality. The main dimensions having been identified, the really interesting questions involve trying to understand:

- what causes certain behaviours to vary together to form these traits; and
- what causes an individual to develop a particular personality.

One possible answer to the second question is that personality traits (or rather the *potential* to show certain patterns of behaviour in certain situations) may, to some extent, be inherited from our parents. Because exactly the same techniques are used to find the extent to which *intelligence* is typically influenced by genes, the family environment or other aspects of our environment, these two issues are considered together in Chapter 9.

What, then, are the obvious possible determinants of personality? There are two main types of theory. Social theories stress the importance of the *environment* in personality development. For these theories, the prime determinant of the child's adult personality is the environment in which children are raised. Such theories generally assume that new-born children really are fairly similar in their biological make-up and potential for personality development. They also have to suggest that the environment (including social processes) is all-important in maintaining adult personality. Biological theories, on the other hand, suggest that all children are not equal at birth, if only because of their genetic make-up. They stress the importance of genetic factors and biological mechanisms (sometimes directly related to the amount of electrical activity in certain regions of the brain) in determining behaviour – or rather for creating the *propensity* for certain types of behaviour to be manifested, given the appropriate environmental conditions in both childhood and adult life.

Unfortunately, these two schools of personality theorists rather rarely talk to one another, they hold separate conferences and they tend to publish in rather different journals, so remarkably few studies consider the influence of both biological/genetic make-up and social processes on behaviour. This is a pity, since there is no *logical* reason why social theories have to assume that all individuals have functionally identical nervous systems (that is, nervous systems that operate in precisely the same way). Likewise, although biologically/genetically inclined theorists have to add the proviso 'given suitable environmental conditions' to all of their predictions about behaviour, they generally assume that people's environments (and developmental experiences) were rather similar.

SOCIAL DETERMINANTS OF PERSONALITY

Perhaps childhood experience is all-important, as Freud, Rogers and Kelly (and also theorists such as Bandura and Skinner) maintain. Freud would argue that the child's psychosexual development (over-indulgence or frustration at a particular developmental stage) will lead to the emergence of certain adult personality traits, as might the particular pattern of defence mechanisms used, degree of Oedipal conflict, degree of identification with a parent, as well as specific childhood experiences. Thus the personality traits that we observe in questionnaires such as the Eysenck Personality Questionnaire (Revised) may simply reflect the adult consequences of different child-rearing practices. The problem is, of course, that these concepts are difficult or impossible to assess, and so it is difficult or impossible to test this theory. Attempts to assess the main adult psychosexual personality types by means of questionnaires such as the Ai3 have only limited success, and attempts to tie in adult personality types to critical events during children's psychosexual development have foundered, possibly (but not necessarily) because of the difficulties encountered in obtaining good, clear data about how individual children are weaned, potty-trained, etc. (Kline, 1981).

For Rogers, the person's view of the self (plus ideal self, etc.) – the extent of self-actualisation, self-consistency and congruence – is all-important. If a child is brought up in an environment in which it feels that it is loved *unconditionally* by its parents (when bad behaviour is followed by the message 'I don't like what you have just done', rather than 'I don't like you'), then the child will view itself as lovable and will grow up congruent and self-actualising. Thus it seems reasonable to ask whether the main personality traits are themselves affected by parental attitudes.

Much of the evidence seems to suggest that they are. For example, Coopersmith (1967) found that children's self-esteem depended on unconditional, loving acceptance of the children by their parents, control using reward rather than punishment, and clear indications of what was and was not acceptable behaviour. Thus it does seem clear that self-esteem is affected by the parents' behaviour, and since scales measuring self-esteem are found to correlate with extraversion and neuroticism (Kline, 1993), it may be that these two personality factors are also affected by such social processes.

Of course there is a flaw in these arguments. Suppose that self-esteem has a substantial genetic component. In that case it is possible that children of parents who have high self-esteem will also grow up to have high self-esteem because this trait has been transmitted genetically, and *not* because of the way in which parents with high self-esteem behave towards their children. On the other hand, if the family environment is all-important (as assumed in Coopersmith's interpretation of his data), then a social explanation is entirely appropriate. Unfortunately, this is a broad criticism of virtually *all* studies that attempt to assess the impact of parental behaviour on personality (or ability, for that matter). It is vital that such studies should consider the possibility that some other variables (e.g. genes) can influence both the parents' behaviour and the eventual behaviour or personality of the children.

Kelly's theory is less than explicit about how and why a particular individual develops a particular set of constructs, and comes to construe him or herself in a particular way. We know that children's construct systems become more complex and differentiated (Honess, 1979), but how and why children develop rather *different* construct systems does not seem to be at all well understood – although I would be surprised if this was unrelated to the variety of people and events to which the child was exposed (a stimulating environment) and the perceived consistency of the behaviour of others (so allowing useful predictions to be made).

Bandura's social cognitive theory (e.g. Bandura, 1986) is generally covered in courses such as 'learning theory', 'developmental psychology' and/or 'social psychology', and I felt that readers might rebel if they encountered it again in the present book. For those who are unfamiliar with the theory, the basics are as follows. Social cognitive theory (an earlier version of which was known as 'social learning theory') is particularly concerned with 'self-efficacy' – how well a particular individual feels that he or she can cope with a particular situation. This is rather like assuming that (in contrast to Rogers' theory) a person has a different self-concept in each situation. Feelings of self-efficacy are influenced by previous experience, observations of others in similar situations, emotions (e.g. anxiety) and argument/persuasion of others. Feelings of self-efficacy are thought to be closely related to behaviour and personality, since they determine what activities a person tends to perform, and how much effort he or she invests in them. This may be interpreted as 'personality' by others. For example, someone who believes that they are unpleasant or boring might feel low self-efficacy in social settings such as parties, especially if they have poor previous experiences of parties, have observed other people's humiliation, feel anxious or depressed, and are told that they are socially inept. Therefore they may tend to avoid parties, and are likely to appear 'introverted' when answering personality questionnaires. Two other variables are also thought to be important, namely outcome expectancies (e.g. 'if I go to a party will anyone talk to me?') and outcome value ('does it matter to me if no one talks to me?'). People also set themselves goals – meeting these self-imposed goals feels pleasurable, but failing to do so can lead to feelings of guilt and depression.

The problem with all this is, once again, Bandura's assertion that the situation (or, more accurately, the 'perceived situation') is all-important in determining behaviour. It seems to me that this can make the whole theory rather circular, since it is difficult to define the 'perceived situation' other than by noting how someone behaves in it. Thus there may be a danger of concluding that certain situations are perceived as being similar because an individual feels similar levels of self-efficacy in each of them, and then arguing that Bandura's theory is supported because similar levels of self-efficacy are reported in situations that are perceived similarly. Second, since self-efficacy can be assessed only by introspection, the theory has to assume that people are both aware of and able to explain why they behave in a certain manner in a given situation. The third problem is that, by tying perceived self-efficacy so closely to situations, this becomes a theory of situations rather than a theory of personality. We saw in the previous chapter that behaviour really *is* fairly consistent across several different situations, as the trait theorists such as Cattell and Eysenck had always claimed (e.g. Block, 1977; Olweus, 1980; Conley, 1984), and that earlier work that claimed the opposite was true was often technically flawed. Thus there would be a good case for modifying the theory to allow for cross-situational consistencies in behaviour ('traits') to explore individual differences in behaviour.

It is clear from this very brief discussion that determining the social influences on personality is a remarkably difficult research question, for the following reasons.

- It is often very difficult to collect accurate, quantitative information about the types of social interactions experienced by children.
- Some theories (e.g. that of Kelly) never really attempt to explain how personality develops. The notion that this is a social process is more of an assumption than a testable proposition.
- Just because certain forms of parental behaviour are found to be associated with certain personality characteristics in the offspring, it cannot be assumed that the parental behaviour *causes* the personality characteristic to emerge. It is possible that some genetically transmitted personality traits might generally lead to certain types of parenting behaviour, but that the genes, rather than these behaviours, will cause similar traits to emerge in the children. Which of these explanations is the correct one can only be determined by the experiments discussed in Chapter 9.
- Bandura's social-cognitive theory is geared to predicting rather precisely how people will behave in certain situations, and not how people will generally behave. It is thus more of a social psychological theory than a theory of personality, since it does not consider any stable, cross-situational, individual differences.
- Quantifying social influences is a particularly difficult process. Those that will have most effect on personality will (presumably) be those that take place over a long period of time with the parents and other members of the family – in young children, at any rate. Fortunately, the methods of genetic analysis allow us to determine the extent to which the 'family ethos' influences personality without having to assess the interactions in detail. If it is assumed that parents generally treat their children fairly equally (an assumption that research does show to be reasonably true), then the 'family ethos' should influence all of the children similarly – the parents' child-rearing methods should affect all of their children to roughly the same extent. Thus by comparing the degree of similarity of the personalities of children within a family and comparing this with the similarity of personalities *between* families (after correcting for any direct genetic effects), it is possible to assess whether the family environment has much influence on the children's personality during childhood and subsequently. If this influence is small, then it seems that children grow up despite the way in which they are treated by their parents, rather than because of it.

However, there is another way of quantifying the effect of social variables, namely by attempting to determine the extent to which *biological* variables can account for individual differences in personality, and assuming that the remainder is due to various types of social factors.

BIOLOGICAL BASES OF PERSONALITY: THEORY

The biological approach suggests that all nervous systems are not the same – there may be individual differences in the structure and function of people's nervous systems, and this can account for the emergence of personality traits. That is, any group of behaviours that vary together (and are identified as traits by factor analysis) do so because they are all influenced by some brain structure(s). The useful thing about such an approach is that it is much easier to test empirically than are social theories. With modern psychophysiological techniques – including exotica such as positron emission tomography (PET) scans and magnetic resonance imaging (MRI) – it is rather easier to check whether individual differences in personality are reliably associated with individual differences in structure and function of the nervous system than it is to attempt to analyse social interactions that may have taken place years previously.

Of course, this begs the question of how and why individual differences in nervous system structure and function themselves come about. It is not impossible that such factors may affect the development of the nervous system, in which case social factors might affect personality through the mediation of neural mechanisms. However, most proponents of the biological approach do not address this question directly.

SELF-ASSESSMENT QUESTION 6.2

What I have painted here is a fairly 'reductionist' view of personality, and one with which some readers may feel uneasy. What are the objections to looking for the roots of personality in the physiology and biochemistry of the nervous system?

Hans Eysenck (1967) put forward a general biological theory to explain the origins of extraversion and neuroticism, with Eysenck and Eysenck (1985) summarising much of the empirical work that followed the publication of this theory. Gray (1982) and Zuckerman (1991) have offered their own theories, based on personality systems that are rather different from that of Eysenck, so for brevity's sake these will not be discussed in any detail.

The most obvious starting-point for any biological theory of personality is to examine the effects on personality of brain injury and brain lesions (the latter is an innocuous-sounding term for the practice of cutting the connections between certain brain structures – often performed in the 1950s and 1960s in an attempt to treat depression, etc.), and Eysenck's biological theory owes much to this form of clinical literature.

The biological basis of neuroticism

Eysenck viewed neuroticism as a factor of 'emotionality' – highly neurotic individuals will tend to give extreme emotional responses (tears, fear) to life events that may well leave more stoic, low-neuroticism individuals emotionally unmoved. Thus if some brain structure is known to control the extent of such emotional reactions, it is possible that neuroticism may simply reflect individual differences in the sensitivity of this system to external stimuli. If temperature is used as an analogy for the degree of emotional content of a thought, perception or memory, we can view neurotic and stable individuals as having their thermostats set to different levels. For highly neurotic people, a small increase in emotional temperature is enough to trigger the thermostat and activate a full emotional response. For stable individuals, the emotional response is activated only in response to a gross increase in emotional temperature.

The limbic system is one of closely linked structures (including the hippocampus, hypothalamus, amygdala, cingulum and septum) towards the base of the brain – Eysenck sometimes refers to this system as the *visceral brain*. It has long been known to be involved in the initiation of emotional activity. It affects the *sympathetic branch* of the *autonomic nervous system*, which is often known as the 'flight or fight' mechanism, since its activation can be viewed as preparing the organism for either of these two behaviours. Activation of the sympathetic nervous system results in faster heart rate, increased respiration rate, increased blood flow to the limbs, increased sweating, and a closing down of the blood supply to the gut and other organs that are not involved in urgent physical activity. Unpleasant emotional *feelings*, such as fear, anxiety or anger, are also experienced.

The terms anxiety and neuroticism are closely linked, with anxiety being a mixture of neuroticism and low levels of extraversion (Eysenck, 1973; Eysenck and Eysenck, 1985). However, in the discussion that follows I shall use the terms 'anxiety' and 'neuroticism' interchangeably, since they correlate together with a value of about 0.7 (Eysenck and Eysenck, 1985). We know that anxiety can be assessed by questionnaires, and that activity in the autonomic nervous system can be assessed by a number of techniques. These include the psychogalvanic response (PGR), in which the skin resistance is measured on a part of the body that is well endowed with sweat-glands. The burst of sweating that follows increased activity of the autonomic nervous system leads to a decrease in electrical resistance, which can be measured. Thus it is possible to test this theory directly, as people with high levels of anxiety should produce more emotional physiological responses to moderately stressful stimuli (unpleasant pictures, perhaps) than individuals with low anxiety levels. Gray's (1982) theory of anxiety (which is based on rats rather than on people) implicates certain components of the limbic system, plus the frontal lobes of the cortex and their links to the brainstem.

The biological basis of extraversion

Eysenck's theory of extraversion involves another structure at the base of the brain, known as the 'ascending reticular activating system' (ARAS). This fearsome-sounding structure simply controls the amount of electrical activity that takes place in the cortex – it is a kind of 'dimmer switch' for the electrical activity in the cortex. It should also be mentioned here, for completeness, that there are nerve fibres linking the ARAS with the limbic system, so the two systems are not entirely neurologically independent. Perhaps as a consequence of this, most workers find a correlation of about –0.3 between the extraversion and neuroticism scales of the Eysenck Personality Questionnaire (EPQ). Eysenck proposed that:

- the ARASs of introverts and extraverts operate at different levels, as a result of which the cortices of introverts are habitually much more electrically active ('aroused') than those of extraverts; and
- a moderate degree of cortical arousal is experienced as being pleasurable, whereas very high or very low levels of cortical arousal are experienced as being unpleasurable.

Of course, factors other than the ARAS can arouse the cortex, the most obvious of which is sensory stimulation. Looking at changing images, listening to music and (especially) talking to people can all lead to increases in cortical electrical activity. Eysenck argues that, under quiet conditions (e.g. working in a library), extraverts – whose cortices are normally not very highly aroused – may experience unpleasurable feelings since their level of cortical arousal is considerably below the point which is felt as pleasurable. Therefore they do something about it – talking to others, listening to music on headphones, taking frequent coffee breaks, and generally behaving in ways that are guaranteed to infuriate introverts. For introverts are *naturally* highly aroused, and any further increase in arousal level is distinctly unpleasurable. In other words, extraverts need a constant environmental 'buzz' to arouse their cortices to pleasurable levels, whereas introverts do not, and indeed would find any such stimulation over-arousing and hence unpleasurable.

It has been found that drugs which increase or decrease the level of arousal in the cortex also affect the ease with which animals learn a conditioned response. This suggests another extension of the theory, and Eysenck claims that introverts should therefore condition more easily than extraverts because of their higher levels of cortical arousal. He regards neurotic symptoms as conditioned emotional responses, which, of course, naturally suggests that behaviour therapy is the technique of choice for *removing* such symptoms. For example, if a person who scores high on the trait of neuroticism has several unpleasant emotional experiences in a particular setting (e.g. turning over an examination paper and not knowing any of the answers), he or she should be more likely than an extravert to develop feelings of fear, depression or anxiety when entering that room, or to show avoidance behaviour.

This is Eysenck's theory of extraversion, and it is also empirically testable.

Measuring electrical activity in the ARAS is admittedly difficult (because of its position), but assessing the electrical activity of the cortex is relatively straightforward, as is assessing the ease with which classical or operant conditioning takes place. Other techniques are possible, too, as will be seen in the next section.

The biological basis of psychoticism

Psychoticism is much less well understood, and some researchers (including the five-factor theorists) (and see also Zuckerman, 1991, 1994) have suggested alternatives to the factor of psychoticism. However, Eysenck noted that levels of psychoticism were much higher in males than in females, and that criminals and schizophrenics (both of whom tend to have high P-scores) also tend to be male. Therefore Eysenck suggested (e.g. Eysenck and Eysenck, 1985) that psychoticism is linked to levels of male hormones such as androgens, and perhaps to other chemicals such as serotonin and certain antigens. Once again, this theory (although rudimentary) is clearly testable.

SELF-ASSESSMENT QUESTION 6.3

How might one test whether Eysenck's theory of psychoticism is correct?

Problems with biological theories

Eysenck therefore suggests that the three main personality dimensions may be directly linked to the biological and hormonal make-up of the body. We may display certain patterns of personality because our nervous systems work in slightly different ways, and it is these individual differences that are picked up by factor analysis and interpreted as personality traits. It is tempting to argue that certain people 'just are' extraverted because of the level of arousal which their ARAS imparts to their cortex, and that there is no need to consider any environmental explanations at all. However, even if individual differences in cortical activity were found to *explain completely* the individual differences in extraversion, this begs the question of why one person's ARAS works at a rather different level from that of another. Could *this* be influenced by life events? This is where genetic studies of personality (discussed in Chapter 9) are so useful, as they can indicate the relative importance of biological and environmental determinants of personality at any age.

Eysenck's theories are hardly subtle, and our understanding of brain structure and function has changed considerably since his book was published in 1967. The theories also fail to take into account other important phenomena, e.g. lateralisation. Zuckerman (1991) points to a huge body of evidence from brain-damaged patients showing that personality change following damage to the cortex depends on whether the left or the right hemisphere is affected. However, Eysenck's theory of extraversion does not distinguish between the left and right hemispheres. There is more concern about the concept of autonomic arousal, since empirical evidence suggests that 'arousal' in the autonomic nervous system is not nearly as simple as was previously thought. In particular, it seems that different individuals *express* signs of autonomic arousal in different ways. For example, when frightened, some people may sweat more, others may show more muscle activity (twitching or trembling), some will show a marked increase in heart rate, and others may show an increase in pupil size. However, very few individuals show *all* of these responses. Surprisingly, although almost all neurotic people *claim* to feel sweaty hands, churning stomachs, pounding hearts, and so on, when the electrodes are attached, all of these symptoms simply cannot be observed. The psychophysiological measures do not form a factor. Some of the reasons why this might be the case have been discussed by Lacey and Lacey (1970) and Pennebaker (1982).

However, the great advantage of the biological theories is that they are clearly testable – they can be shown to be incorrect. This is in stark contrast to very many (one is tempted to say 'most') of the mechanisms suggested by other theorists – terms such as self-actualisation, id processes, defence mechanisms, self-congruence, and so on, are difficult to define and assess, and belong to models that are so complex that they cannot easily be verified. The simplicity of Eysenck's model probably means that it will be unable to explain the origins of personality *perfectly*, although one should surely always prefer a simple but empirically verifiable model to a complex model which cannot be shown to be incorrect.

THE BIOLOGICAL BASIS OF PERSONALITY: EMPIRICAL RESULTS

Because of the problems that have emerged concerning the whole concept of arousal in the autonomic nervous system since the publication of Eysenck's 1967 book, in this section we shall merely examine some of the evidence for the biological basis of extraversion.

Eysenck and Eysenck (1985) consider a number of hypotheses that flow naturally from the cortical arousal theory of extraversion, together with a discussion of the main research findings, and this section owes much to their work.

If extraversion is biologically based, it seems reasonable to suggest that individual differences in the underlying brain structures may be genetically transmitted. Hence studies of the genetics of extraversion may be valuable for testing the broad idea that extraversion may have a biological basis. This does *not*, of course, test the specific arousal hypothesis discussed above. However, if extraversion could be shown to be determined entirely by the way in which children are reared, it is perhaps less likely that it would be related to individual differences in neurology than if it could be seen to have a strong genetic component. This entire issue is covered in some depth in Chapter 9, which concludes that there is evidence that individual differences in extra-version have a substantial genetic component.

Extraversion and the electroencephalogram (EEG)

By comparison with extraverts, one would expect introverts with higher levels of arousal to show:

- greater habitual levels of cortical arousal;
- stronger responses to novel stimuli.

The electroencephalogram (EEG) is a technique for analysing electrical activity in the brain by attaching metal electrodes to the surface of the scalp in carefully standardised positions and measuring the differences in voltage between each electrode and a neutral point (such as the ear lobe). The electrical signals travel around inside the head in a fairly complicated manner, but it is possible to measure the electrical activity in several of the main brain structures by this method, and fortunately the cortex is one of these areas (being just beneath the skull). The EEG is usually plotted as a graph of electrical voltage against time, and is often analysed (using a mathematical technique known as 'Fourier analysis') in order to determine whether there are regular, periodic variations in the electrical activity and, if so, their frequency.

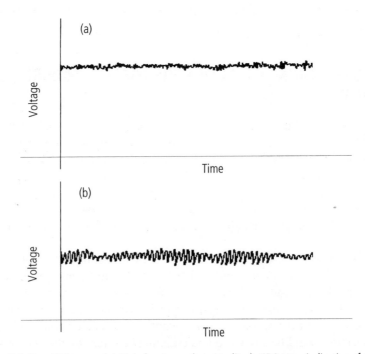

Figure 6.1 Two EEG traces. (a) High-frequency, low-amplitude EEG trace indicative of alertness. (b) Low-frequency, high-amplitude EEG traces, indicative of relaxation.

For example, Figure 6.1a shows regular low-amplitude, high-frequency electrical activity. 'Low amplitude' means that the changes in voltage from peak to trough in the graph are fairly small, of the order of 25 to 100 microvolts (millionths of a volt). 'High frequency' means that the voltage changes direction quite often. Low-amplitude brainwaves that change direction with a frequency of between 8 and 13 cycles per second are known as *alpha activity*. Alpha activity is typically found when people are wide awake and alert, so the simplest possible test of Eysenck's cortical arousal hypothesis would merely involve assessing how cortically aroused people were (as indicated by the EEG) and correlating this with their scores on the extraversion scale of the EPQ(R).

Tony Gale (1983) reviewed the literature and found that introverts were more aroused than extraverts in 22 out of 38 studies, thus providing evidence in support of Eysenck's theory. However, the effect is sometimes difficult to detect (even in exceptionally well-controlled studies using modern equipment, e.g. Matthews and Amelang, 1993). Whether it is found also seems to depend on how arousing the situation is (moderately arousing conditions are best), and it seems that the variable that influences the EEG is not full extraversion but *impulsiveness*, which is one of the components of extraversion in Eysenck's theory (O'Gorman and Lloyd, 1987). My own view of the evidence is that the data are suggestive, rather than conclusive – 10 years ago one could still argue that technical problems in the measurement of EEG traces could explain the inconsistent results, but one cannot use that excuse for ever!

The picture is somewhat clearer when changes in the EEG are monitored, following stimulation. Imagine that we attached some electrodes to a volunteer's head, made them sit in a chair, monitored their EEG, and then we played some sound. There would be a characteristic burst of neural activity shown in the EEG as the person noticed the tone, wondered what it meant, and so on – this is the 'orienting reflex'. If we were to play the same sound again a few seconds later, the physiological response would be rather smaller. If we were to keep on playing the sound at irregular intervals, eventually it would produce no response at all. The speed with which the volunteer comes to ignore the tone is known as the 'rate of habituation of the orienting reflex', and there is evidence that introverts' orienting reflexes take longer to habituate than those of extraverts (Eysenck and Eysenck, 1985), supporting Eysenck's theory. However, the strength of the stimulus (the loudness of the tone) and, surprisingly, its pitch also seem to have an effect on habituation rate, which is an unexpected finding.

PET scans and extraversion

The easy (but expensive!) way to check what is going on in the brain is to throw away the electrodes and examine how much energy each part of the brain is metabolising. Positron emission tomography (PET) scans examine this directly, and involve injecting radioactively labelled glucose into a vein, and monitoring which part(s) of the brain eventually use it. Do introverts' cortices really seem to use more glucose than those of extraverts? Unfortunately, we do not know the answer, since only one study seems to have employed the technique, and this used a small sample of anxiety-neurotics rather than normal individuals (Haier *et al.*, 1987). A similar technique (again using a radioactive tracer) that examined the amount of blood flow in various parts of the brain did reveal significant correlations of between –0.21 and –0.41 between the amount of blood flow and extraversion, in several different areas of the cortex (Mathew *et al.*, 1984). This finding supports Eysenck's theory, but needs to be replicated. More recently, Ebmeier *et al.* (1994) conducted a similar experiment, and found that extraversion was associated not with significantly decreased activity in the cortex, but with increased activity in the cingulate area – a part of the brain that has been linked to attentional processes. This opens up the basis of a new theory for extraversion, but needs to be replicated.

Classical and operant conditioning

You will recall that drugs which affect cortical arousal also affect the ease with which animals form conditioned responses. If extraversion is linked to cortical arousal, one might therefore expect ease of conditioning to be related to scores on extraversion in humans. The main problem here is that cognitive factors (e.g. conscious awareness of the reinforcement contingencies – the nature of the reinforcement schedule being used) are thought to complicate matters whenever conditionability is being assessed in humans, as can the precise detail of the conditioning task (e.g. the strength of the unconditioned stimulus).

The most commonly used paradigm for humans is classical conditioning of the eye-blink response to a tone. A tone is followed by a puff of air to the eye, which elicits the eye-blink response. After several such pairings, the tone alone will produce the eye-blink, and the number of trials before this is achieved is a measure of the person's conditionability. However, the problem is that when speed of conditioning is measured in the same individuals using a number of different experimental paradigms, the results simply do not show substantial correlations between the different paradigms. So, for humans, there is probably no such thing as general 'conditionability' (Eysenck and Eysenck, 1985). If one just examines the results from the eye-blink paradigm, several studies do find consistent negative correlations between extraversion and conditionability (Eysenck and Levey, 1972), but once again it seems to be narrow impulsivity (rather than full-blown extraversion) that is the key factor.

Sedation thresholds

One rather crude way of assessing the activity of a cortex involves determining the amount of a sedative drug required to make individuals unconscious (as assessed by the EEG, or lack of responsiveness to words). As introverts are more cortically aroused, they may require higher doses than extraverts to make them unconscious (although many other factors may also affect the required dosage). This is so – but only for moderate or high-level neurotics (Claridge *et al.*, 1981).

SELF-ASSESSMENT QUESTION 6.4

Why is it important to discover the processes that cause personality?

SUMMARY

This chapter has examined theories that view personality as either a social or a biological phenomenon, and it should be clear by this stage that neither of the views is exclusively correct. Chapter 9 will reveal that the main personality factors have a substantial genetic component, which suggests that purely social explanations of behaviour are unlikely to be adequate. However, when we delve into the psychophysiological literature, it is equally clear that relatively few experiments provide unequivocal evidence in support of Eysenck's model of extraversion. Stimulus intensity has an annoying habit of confusing results, presumably because of its effects on arousal, and impulsivity (one of the *components* of extraversion) often seems to correlate more strongly with psychophysiological indices than does extraversion itself. However, the fact that several of the studies do show significant correlations seems to suggest that there is some underlying truth in the premise that extraversion is related to the degree of arousal in the cortex. The theory may need to be refined rather than abandoned.

Perhaps this is to be expected. The biological theory of extraversion essentially assumes that the *only* determinant of whether a person is lively, sociable, optimistic and impulsive is the amount of electrical activity in their ARAS, and it really does seem fairly likely that myriad other social, cultural, motivational, cognitive and time-of-day variables that are difficult to assess will also affect people's behaviour. These uncontrolled variables will, of course, all tend to reduce the strength of the correlation between psychophysiological measures and extraversion, so the finding that some measures (such as cortical blood flow) can explain up to about one-seventh of the variability in people's levels of extraversion is, perhaps, about as good as could reasonably be expected.

There is currently much research activity in this area, with many more paradigms and empirical results than can be presented here in a single chapter. Sources such as Eysenck (1994, 1997), Zuckerman (1991) or Barrett (1997) can be recommended to those who wish to explore these matters further.

SUGGESTED ADDITIONAL READING

There is no shortage of good texts and papers on the biological basis of personality. The main problem is that some of them are very technical, whilst others go into such detail that it is difficult to keep sight of the broad picture. Eysenck (1994, 1997), Barrett (1997), Bates and Wachs (1994), Gale and Eysenck (1992) and the special issue of Volume 58 of the *Journal of Personality* (1990) are fairly approachable, and Gale (1980) makes some still relevant points about the conceptual problems of brain research. Zuckerman (1991) is excellent, although very detailed. Parts of Revelle (1995) are also useful.

ANSWERS TO SELF-ASSESSMENT QUESTIONS

SAQ 6.1
There is generally no control group (or sophisticated statistical analysis) to guard against the possibility that the child *might* have developed in much the same way had it been brought up in a completely different family environment – the child may show certain patterns of personality because of its genetic similarity to its parents. The genes may influence the parents to bring up the child in a certain way, and also influence the child's personality, and there may be no causal link between parental behaviour and personality at all. One way round this would be to perform such studies using only adopted children.

SAQ 6.2
Several objections to reductionism can be entertained. First, it may be unwise to point to brain structures as explanations for behaviour unless one knows why, precisely, these brain structures developed in the way that they did. For it is possible that life events (e.g. child-rearing practices) can influence the brain structures. In this case, a 'biological' theory of personality could be explained by social processes! There is a tendency to assume that the biology of the nervous system is fixed, immutable and thus somehow more fundamental than social theories, although the evidence for this is not always clear. Second, the theories clearly fail to take into account the importance of interactions between personality types and certain environments. It seems quite likely that certain life events will have a profound impact on those who are biologically disposed to react in a certain way. If this is so, then any attempt to explain personality by purely biological (or purely social) processes will clearly be unsatisfactory. On the other hand, it may be sensible to explore how adequately simple (e.g. purely social or purely biological) models can predict personality before beginning the much more complex task of developing models that are based on interactionism.

SAQ 6.3
There are several possible approaches. The most obvious would be to measure the levels of male hormones, etc. in a sample of 'normal' male volunteers, and to correlate the levels of such chemicals with their scores on the P-scale of the EPQ(R) (or else use a statistical technique called 'multiple regression' to determine how much of the variation in the P-scale can be predicted by

individual differences in the levels of several such chemicals). Consideration could be given to the feasibility (and ethicality) of an intervention study in which some individuals' levels of such hormones are increased, whilst a control group would receive a placebo. A one-between and one-within analysis of variance could then establish whether P-scale scores increase more in the experimental group. However, this design is probably not feasible (even if it were ethical) because it would presumably need to be carried out over a period of days or weeks. Another approach might be to compare the P-scale scores and hormonal levels of normal controls and violent criminals, in the expectation that the group with higher P-score would also have higher levels of hormone. However, this approach does not show the size of the relationship between hormones and the P-score in the general population, and for this reason the first design is probably the better.

SAQ 6.4

We have not had space to discuss this in much detail, but many of the reasons should be fairly clear. First, it allows us to answer two criticisms that are levelled at personality theory by social psychologists, namely that personality theories are 'circular' (inferring personality from behaviour, and then trying to *explain* the behaviour by invoking a personality trait), and that they are not genuine properties of the individual, but rather the results of stereotyping, attributional biases, etc. If it can be shown that the main personality traits are linked to behaviour in quite different domains (e.g. patterns of electrical activity in the cortex), then it will be clear that the personality questionnaires are measuring some rather broad property of the organism. Nor can they merely reflect attributional biases, etc. The second reason for studying processes is, of course, scientific curiosity – a desire to understand how and why certain individuals come to display characteristic patterns of personality. Finally, such work may have some important applications. For example, if a 'negative' adult personality trait such as neuroticism or psychoticism could be shown to be crucially dependent on some kind of experience during infancy, society might well want to ensure that all children receive special attention at this stage.

7

The structure and measurement of abilities

BACKGROUND

The study of individual differences in ability is one of the very oldest areas of psychology, and is certainly one of the most applicable. Tests assessing individual differences in mental ability have been of great practical value in occupational, industrial and educational psychology. The psychology of ability is one of the four main branches of individual differences (the others being personality, mood and motivation), and the present chapter outlines what is now known (and generally accepted) about the nature and structure of human abilities.

Recommended prior reading

Chapters 11, 14 and 15.

INTRODUCTION

Howard Wainer (1987) reminds us that ability testing has a long and illustrious history, stretching back four thousand years to when the Chinese used a form of ability testing to select for their civil service. He also notes a biblical reference to forensic assessment of ability (Judges 12: 4–6). This is hardly surprising, for few areas of psychology have proved of such practical usefulness as the capacity to measure human abilities. The accurate identification of which individuals will best be able to benefit from an advanced course of education, or which job applicants are likely to perform best if selected (rather than selecting randomly, or on the basis of time-consuming and potentially unreliable procedures, such as interviews), brings important financial and personal benefits. Tests of ability are also useful for identifying other forms of potential and problems, e.g. to identify outstanding musical talent, or to help in the diagnosis of dyslexia and some types of brain disease.

It is probably sensible to begin by attempting to define some terms. The word 'mental ability' is used to describe a person's performance on some task that has a substantial information-processing component (i.e. that requires thinking, sound judgement or skill) when that person is trying to perform that task as well as possible. For example, writing a sonnet, adding the numbers 143 and 228, designing a building, reading a map, structuring an essay, inventing a joke and diagnosing a fault in a computer are all examples of mental abilities if (and only if) they are assessed when individuals are really trying to do their best. Some other abilities (e.g. pruning a rose-bush, running a race) do not require vast amounts of cognitive skill for their successful completion, and so are not usually regarded as mental abilities.

Neither are tests of attainment, which (as discussed in Chapter 11) are designed to assess how well individuals have absorbed knowledge or skills *that have been specifically taught*. For example, an attainment test in geography might take a sample of facts and skills that pupils should have learned, e.g. by sampling items from the syllabus. Tests of ability, on the other hand, involve *thinking* rather than remembering, and use test items that the individual will not have encountered previously. Thus mental abilities should be measured by assessing a well-motivated person who is asked to do their best in performing some task with a substantial cognitive component, the exact nature of which is unfamiliar to them, but for which they have the necessary cognitive skills.

Mental abilities, then, are traits that reflect how well individuals can process various types of information. They reflect cognitive processes and skills, and since one of the functions of the education system is to develop some of these (e.g. numeracy, literacy), it is difficult to define what is meant by an ability without taking individuals' educational backgrounds and interests into consideration. Individual differences in the speed of solving differential equations might be regarded as an important ability for physics students or engineers, but not for many others. Thus it is not really possible to define ability independently of cultural and educational background.

For this reason, it seems to be conventional to consider only those mental abilities that everyone can be assumed to have acquired as part of a basic education, or which are not formally taught at all. Thus performance in solving cryptic crossword puzzles, evading income tax, thinking up novel uses for objects, assembling jigsaws or performing simple arithmetic would be regarded as mental abilities. Those abilities which reflect specialised knowledge or training, or which are non-cognitive in nature, would be excluded from the list. Hence being able to breathe life into a dull party, identify fungi, sprint, play the sitar, grow championship onions, recite the capitals of the US states or call a touch of Belfast Surprise Major (a *very* esoteric mental skill involving church-bells!) would not generally be regarded as mental abilities within the general population.

But how many abilities *are* there? After all, the number of 'tasks with a substantial cognitive component, the exact nature of which is unfamiliar' (our putative definition of a mental ability) is potentially enormous. In fact, it is almost infinite, meaning that it would be impossible in practice ever to understand fully a person's abilities simply by measuring all of them.

The alternative is to examine the correlations between mental abilities using factor analysis. This might show that there is some overlap between all of these tasks measuring mental abilities, and with luck this might reduce the number of distinct abilities to a manageable level. So, just as with the psychology of personality, psychometric studies of mental ability attempt to achieve two objectives:

- to establish the basic structure of abilities; and,
- once there is some consensus about the number and nature of the main abilities, to try to understand the nature of the underlying social, biological, cognitive and other processes that *cause* these individual differences to emerge.

This chapter deals with the basic structure of abilities, and Chapters 8 and 9 address some of the underlying processes.

THE STRUCTURE OF HUMAN MENTAL ABILITIES

You will already be familiar with most of the research techniques that are used in the study of mental abilities, as most authorities agree that factor analysis of the correlations between ability test items can reveal the underlying structure of abilities. Therefore precisely the same techniques that showed up personality characteristics such as extraversion and neuroticism should also be able to reveal the structure of abilities. Basically, if we measure individuals' performance on a very wide range of tasks that seem to require thought for their correct solution, correlate their scores on the items (or tests) together and factor-analyse this table of correlations, the factors that emerge should represent the main dimensions of ability.

SELF-ASSESSMENT QUESTION 7.1

Think creatively for a few minutes about how you might draw up a list of as many abilities as possible.

Which abilities should we analyse?

When studying personality, Cattell used the 'personality sphere' concept in an attempt to ensure that all possible descriptions of behaviour were included in factor analyses that were designed to reveal all of the main personality traits. No similar approach has been followed for abilities, presumably because it is recognised that the dictionary may not contain very accurate descriptions of ability. For example, I can think of no commonly used word that describes ability to solve anagrams, sing in tune, or show prodigious powers of memory. (*Phrases* are not really helpful, since they will not be turned up by a search through the dictionary.)

This can present problems, since the personality sphere at least offered a starting-point for psychologists wishing to map out the whole area of personality. Without any such guidance it is difficult to ensure that all possible abilities have been considered when trying to develop tests to cover the whole gamut of mental abilities. This can mean that certain mental ability factors will simply not be discovered. For example, if no tests of mathematical performance are given to a group of people, it is clearly impossible for any sort of mathematical ability factor to emerge when individuals' responses are intercorrelated and factor-analysed.

Cattell's Ability Dimension Action Chart (ADAC)

Cattell (1971) therefore attempted to develop a taxonomy of abilities, by means of a chart showing what types of ability could logically exist. A simplified version of this Ability Dimension Action Chart (ADAC) is shown in Table 7.1. It views abilities as consisting of three main components.

The Action domain specifies which aspect of the task is 'hard' for the individual. This might be at the *input* level – that is, the task may require

---

Action – involvement of
- input
- internal processing and storage
- output

Content – various areas such as
- verbal
- social
- mechanical
- knowledge
- sensory modality

Process – including
- complexity of relations
- complexity of processing
- amount of remembering required
- amount of knowledge required
- amount of retrieval from memory required
- flexibility/creativity vs. convergence
- speed
- fine use of muscle

Table 7.1 A short form of Cattell's Ability Dimension Action Chart (ADAC)

someone to make a fine perceptual discrimination. For example, in a test individuals may be asked to match various extremely similar colours, or attend to speech presented to one ear whilst ignoring speech presented to the other ear. The vast majority of conventional tests of ability instead rely on *internal processing and storage* – or thinking – to make the items hard. This is the second possible aspect of the Action domain. Some tasks primarily require skilled performance (e.g. singing a note in tune, tracking a moving object on a computer screen using a joystick), and so these would fall into the *output* category. The other two domains are Content (the type of material given to the individual, e.g. a mental arithmetic problem, or an anagram) and Process (which defines which mental processes the individual is supposed to perform in order to solve the problem).

The *content* of the test items can vary considerably, from verbal, mathematical and mechanical problems to social and moral issues, to pitch perception. The *processes* involved in performing the task can also take a huge number of values. Since it is highly unlikely that many tasks will involve a single process, it is necessary to categorise the *degree* to which each of them requires the use of memory, the degree of background knowledge needed, speed, the detection of relationships between objects (e.g. 'cat is to kitten as dog is to ???'), and the amount of information that needs to be processed (e.g. drawing a circle as opposed to drawing a mural). There could be a vast number of these processes, but a list could perhaps be drawn up on the basis of the main findings of cognitive psychology.

The problem is, of course, that the categorisation of tests according to this model will not generally be straightforward. How can one specify (without performing myriad experiments) how great the memory requirement of a task is relative to its speed?

SELF-ASSESSMENT QUESTION 7.2

Try to classify each of the following tasks in terms of the ADAC chart in Table 7.1.

(a) Singing the same note that is played on a piano

(b) Identifying a piece of music

(c) Learning a part in a play

(d) Solving a riddle

(e) Inventing a pun

(f) Solving this SAQ

This chart can be useful in that it reminds us that most of the abilities identified so far require an action of 'internal processing' – we know rather less about those in the input and output domains. However, the problems arise because it has no clear theoretical rationale (e.g. not drawing the list of processes from cognitive psychology), and it is almost impossible to be sure just by looking at a task which processes are involved in its solution. Thus it is probably safest to conclude that there is no single obvious, automatic technique for discovering all of the behaviours that may be influenced by ability.

The factor analysis of ability

There is an important difference in the way in which factor analysis is generally used in the study of personality and ability. Surprisingly, this is one which does not seem to have been explicitly recognised in the literature. It relates to what precisely goes into the factor analysis. You will remember that in the case of personality psychology, the responses to individual test items are usually fed straight into the factor analysis. Thus if one factor-analyses the correlations between the items in a particular personality questionnaire, the main personality factors that correspond to the scales of the questionnaire should emerge.

It is extremely rare to find a study in the area of human abilities that calculates and factor-analyses the correlations between individual test items. Almost all studies instead factor-analyse the correlations between *sub-scales* consisting of several items – for example, individuals' scores on sub-scales (each consisting of 20 or so items) measuring verbal comprehension, non-literal comprehension of proverbs, and 'odd word out' (some examples taken from Thurstone, 1938). *Most ability tests factor-analyse the correlations between groups of items, rather than between the items themselves.* How these items are grouped together in the first place can have some important consequences for the results that are obtained.

Suppose that a researcher wants to examine the structure of ability, which will include some arithmetical problems. He or she will have to decide whether it is better to include several different, separately timed and separately scored *sub-scales* measuring arithmetical ability (e.g. one for addition, one for subtraction, one for multiplication, one for division, one for geometry, one for algebra, one for long multiplication, one for long division, another for set theory, etc.) or whether to make the *assumption* that all of these skills go together and so calculate a total score from a *mixture* of these items, hoping that it will be a reliable measure of a single ability. (Most psychometricians now accept that a high level of reliability of a scale is no guarantee that its items all measure a single factor. They could instead measure two or more *correlated* factors.)

In the second case, the researcher *assumes* that these various types of problems will group together to form an ability factor, whereas the former approach allows factor analysis to *determine* whether this is so.

Thus the *factor* that is obtained when the correlations between the sub-scales are analysed is often essentially the same as the score on the *scale* that is obtained when all of the items are simply put into the same test. That is, if we factor-analyse the correlations between a number of sub-tests, calculate individuals' scores on this factor and correlate these factor scores with the sum of their scores on the sub-tests, the correlation would be very high (probably well above 0.9), showing that the factor is almost identical to the simple sum of scores.

The point to note is that by factoring *sub-scales* one might well end up with factors that are different from those that are obtained by factoring correlations between *scales*. We shall return to this distinction when we examine the work of Spearman and Thurstone.

EMPIRICAL STUDIES

Having decided (rather arbitrarily) whether to factor the correlations between scales or sub-scales, determining the basic structure of ability is rather straightforward, and is fully described in Chapters 14 and 15. All that is necessary is to:

1. administer the test(s) to a large, representative sample of the population;
2. add up individuals' scores on the various scales or sub-scales;
3. correlate these scores together;
4. factor-analyse these correlations;
5. identify the factor(s) by looking at the variables that have appreciable loadings on them;
6. validate the factor(s), e.g. by establishing their predictive and construct validity; and
7. examine the correlations between the factors – if any are appreciable, repeat steps (4) to (7) to produce 'second-order' factors, 'third-order' factors, etc., repeating the process until either the factors are essentially uncorrelated, or just one factor remains.

SPEARMAN AND THURSTONE: ONE ABILITY OR TWELVE?

Charles Spearman (1904) was one of the first to perform an empirical study of the structure of abilities – indeed, he invented the technique of factor analysis for this very purpose. He constructed some rather primitive tests which, he thought, would probably assess children's thinking ability, and administered these to a sample of Hampshire schoolchildren. He gave them tests of vocabulary, mathematical ability, ability to follow complex instructions, visualisation, matching colours and matching musical pitch.

With hindsight, it seems likely that some of the tests (vocabulary, mathematics and, perhaps, ability to follow complex instructions) would be influenced by formal education and were thus tests of attainment rather than of aptitude; however, the remaining three tests did not measure skills that were explicitly taught in school. He then added up children's scores on these six scales, correlated their scores together and factor-analysed these correlations.

Note that Spearman factored the scores between quite different scales – *not* sub-scales.

He found just one factor which he called *g* (for general ability). This result implied that, if a child performed above average on one of the tests, it was more likely than not that he or she would perform at an above-average level on all the other tests as well. It is as if there is some basic 'thinking ability' that determines performance in all areas – some children seemed to excel at everything, some performed poorly at everything, but relatively few excelled in one area and performed poorly in another.

SELF-ASSESSMENT QUESTION 7.3

Is it legitimate to say, on the basis of this analysis, that general ability *causes* someone to perform at similar levels on all tests?

Thurstone, in the USA, soon formed a different opinion, but this is largely because he analysed sub-scales rather than scales. He administered a much larger selection of tests (60 sub-scales in all) to a sample of just over 200 university students[7.1] (Thurstone, 1938). When the intercorrelations between these 60 test scores were factor-analysed (by hand), 12 distinct ability factors were extracted and rotated orthogonally. Thurstone termed these factors 'Primary Mental Abilities', and most of them made good psychological sense. For example, one factor had large loadings from all sub-scales that involved spatial visualisation, one had large loadings from all the sub-scales involving the use of language, while yet another subsumed all the sub-scales requiring numerical skills, and so on.

Thurstone's Primary Mental Abilities (PMAs) are listed in Table 7.2. Variants of the tests that Thurstone used to measure these abilities (the test of Primary Mental Abilities) are still in print, and are sometimes used to this day. Thus whilst Spearman found just one factor, namely general ability, Thurstone seems to have identified a dozen quite independent ability factors. How many ability factors *are* there?

The debate that resulted from Thurstone's work was hot and furious, and many psychologists were convinced that factor analysis was useless because it seemed to produce such inconsistent results. However, you should be able to understand precisely why the results were so different. The difference arises

---

[7.1] I ought to mention another difficulty with Thurstone's experiment that more or less guaranteed that he obtained different results from Spearman. The problem in using students is that they have most probably been *selected* on the basis of high levels of general ability. It is unlikely that many would have below-average ability. Thus the range of ability in Thurstone's sample was almost certainly much less than that in the general population. We now know that one of the effects of this will be to reduce the correlations between the sub-scales, which will reduce the likelihood of finding a single, all-pervasive factor of general ability.

Code	Factor	Brief description
S	Spatial ability	Visualising shapes, mental rotation
V	Verbal relations	Words in context: comprehension, analogies, etc.
P	Perceptual speed	Searching
N	Numerical facility	Addition, subtraction, etc., algebra
W	Word fluency	Tasks dealing with isolated words, e.g. anagrams, spelling
M	Memory	Paired-associate learning and recognition
I	Induction	Finding rules given exemplars, e.g. number series
R	Restriction	Mechanical knowledge, spatial and verbal skills
D	Deduction	Deductive reasoning: applying a rule
. . . plus three factors that could not be easily interpreted		

Table 7.2 Thurstone's primary mental abilities (Thurstone, 1938)

because Thurstone analysed correlations between sub-scales, whilst Spearman analysed correlations between scales. Indeed, some of the ability factors that were extracted from Thurstone's factor analysis (numerical ability, verbal ability and deductive reasoning/following instructions) look remarkably similar to the scales that Spearman put into his analysis. Thurstone's analysis was just performed at a lower, more detailed, level than that of Spearman.

The obvious next step is to examine the correlations between Thurstone's factors, since if they correspond to Spearman's scales, they may correlate together to give *g*.

The problem is, of course, that Thurstone forced his factors to be at right angles to each other ('orthogonal rotation') for ease of computation. Since all of the correlations between these factors are zero, it is not possible to factor-analyse these correlations between the primary abilities. There is another problem, too. Even Thurstone's work, involving 60 sub-tests, appeared to miss out some areas of ability. For example, there was nothing that measured how quickly people could come up with ideas, nothing that measured what Sternberg (1985) called 'social intelligence' (e.g. 'what's the "smart" thing to do if your potential father-in-law forbids you to marry his daughter?'), nothing that measured musical skill, judgement, co-ordination or a whole host of other abilities that may prove to be important.

Hierarchical models of ability

Later evidence shows that Thurstone's analyses were flawed in one important respect. Whereas he believed that the primary abilities were essentially uncorrelated, most subsequent research has revealed that these factors are correlated together to varying extents. It is therefore possible to factor-analyse the correlations between the primary abilities.

In addition, several investigators extended the range of sub-scales that were entered into factor analyses, and so discovered more and more primary mental abilities. Cattell's (1971) contribution is still useful here. His review of the literature identifies some 17 first-order factors that recur in several independent studies, and which seem to be acceptably broad in scope. Hakstian and Cattell (1976) later published a test designed to assess 20 primary abilities – the 'Comprehensive Ability Battery'. The 'Kit of Factor-Referenced Cognitive Tests' (Ekstrom *et al.*, 1976) is very similar, and there is good reason to believe that these two tests measure many of the most important primary mental abilities. These include abilities as diverse as originality (thinking of creative uses for objects), mechanical knowledge and reasoning, verbal ability, numerical ability, fluency of ideas (being able to produce many ideas quickly), perceptual speed (speed in assessing whether two strings of characters are the same or different), spelling, and aesthetic judgement (for works of art). Thus Cattell's analyses confirm and extend Thurstone's results.

When the correlations between these primary ability factors ('primaries') are themselves factor-analysed, a number of 'second-order' ability factors ('secondaries') emerge, rather as shown in Figure 7.1. The lines in this diagram

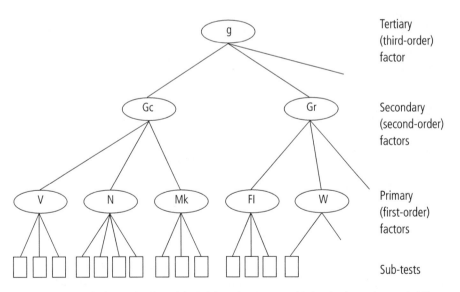

Figure 7.1 Part of a hierarchical model of ability, showing one third-order factor (general ability, *g*) which influences two second-order factors (Gc or crystallised ability and Gr or retrieval) which in turn influence primary abilities such as verbal ability (V), numerical ability (N), mechanical ability (Mk), ideational fluency (FI) and word fluency (W). At the bottom of the pyramid the squares represent various sub-tests, e.g. those measuring comprehension, knowledge of proverbs and vocabulary, ability to solve simultaneous equations, etc.

show 'significant' factor-loadings (those above 0.4, say). The raw data on which the analysis is performed are the scores on a number of sub-tests, represented by squares at the bottom of the figure. The lozenges at the next level show the factors that emerge when the correlations between these sub-tests are factor-analysed – these are the primary mental abilities. The next level up shows what happens when the correlations between the primary mental abilities are analysed. In this example, verbal ability (V), numerical ability (N) and mechanical knowledge ability (Mk) all have substantial loadings on a second-order factor called Gc, the meaning of which will be discussed shortly. Note that none of the other primary ability factors shown in the figure has a substantial loading on Gc. It might even be possible to factor-analyse any correlations between the second-order factors in order to obtain one or more third-order factors. As we move towards the top of the figure, we can see that each factor has an increasingly broad influence. For example, V (the verbal ability primary) affects performance on just three sub-scales, whilst Gc affects performance on 10 sub-scales.

Whilst there is generally good agreement about the nature of the main primary ability factors, opinions do differ somewhat about the number and nature of the second- and higher-order abilities. Vernon (1950) proposed that there were two main secondaries – one essentially corresponding to verbal/educational ability ('v:ed') and the other representing practical/mechanical abilities ('k:m'). Both of these were thought to correlate together, giving general ability (Spearman's *g*) at the third level. Vernon's v:ed factor had significant loadings from primaries such as verbal ability and numerical ability, and k:m loads primaries dealing with visualisation and spatial abilities. This theory influenced the construction of the Weschler tests of individual ability (the Weschler Adult Intelligence Scale and the Weschler Intelligence Scale for Children), which are widely used by educational psychologists and other professionals for individual assessment and guidance. These tests are still scored in order to assess verbal IQ and performance IQ (corresponding to the Vernon factors) ability, although factor analyses of the sub-tests tell quite a different story (Cooper, 1995).

Horn and Cattell (1966) and Hakstian and Cattell (1978) identified not two but six second-order factors, a finding essentially replicated by Kline and Cooper (1984b) and Undheim (1981), among others. The two most important factors in this model are known as *fluid intelligence* (Gf) and *crystallised intelligence* (Gc). Fluid intelligence is raw reasoning ability which should develop independently of schooling, and which covers areas such as memory, spatial ability and inductive reasoning, whilst crystallised intelligence requires knowledge as well, and influences primaries such as verbal comprehension and mechanical knowledge. The other four second-order factors are retrieval (Gr), which is concerned with the speed with which creative ideas are produced, visualisation (Gv), which had been identified as a primary by Thurstone, speed (Gps – a 'perceptual speed' factor that measures the speed with which individuals can compare two strings of letters or figures) and memory (Gm). Once again, these factors seem to make good sense.

SELF-ASSESSMENT QUESTION 7.4

With which of Horn's second-order factors would you expect the following measures to correlate?

(a) Locating one's whereabouts by map-reading when lost in the country.

(b) Speed of thinking what can be cooked from two eggs, an onion and a slice of bread.

(c) A child's school examination marks.

(d) Proofreading a complicated equation in a nuclear physics journal (i.e. checking whether the printed version is the same as the author's original typescript).

The main reason for the differing numbers of second-order factors probably lies in the nature of the abilities being measured, although differences in the factoring procedure may also have some effect. If a test battery contains less than two sub-tests measuring creativity or memory skills, then of course no primary or secondaries such as Gv or Gm can emerge, since the creativity or memory tasks would not show a substantial correlation with any other tasks. The other main point to remember is that fluid intelligence (Gf) bears a very striking resemblance to Spearman's g, and so it is encouraging to see that when a third-order factor analysis was performed (by factoring the correlations between the secondaries), a third-order factor affected all three secondaries (Gf, Gc and Gv) that emerged when a sample of primary abilities was factored (Gustafsson, 1981).

Where does this leave us? It seems that it is possible to conceptualise ability in several ways. First, and working our way down the hierarchy, the positive correlation between all of the primary abilities and between all of the secondaries suggests that Spearman's factor of general ability (or something very like it) is a pervasive influence on cognitive performance. Some theorists have suggested that general ability may even be linked to the speed and/or efficiency with which the nervous system operates, and some evidence for this claim will be scrutinised in Chapter 8. Thus it is perfectly legitimate to view all tasks as being affected by general ability. That said, there are also some 'clusters' of abilities which tend to rise and fall together – these are identified by the half-dozen or so main second-order ability factors. It is perhaps unsurprising to find that one of these factors (Gc) is related to school-based knowledge and skills. However, the rest seem to reflect pure thought processes. Then there are the individual primary mental abilities, over 20 of which have been discovered. These are thought to be the most basic mental skills, although as outlined earlier I have some reservations about the procedures used to identify some of them from the factor analysis of sub-tests, the factor structure of which is not always well known.

So what should one measure? Whether one should assess g (using a test such as Raven's Matrices or Cattell's Culture Fair scales), second-order abilities (using something like the Weschler scales or the General Aptitude Test Battery, or deriving scores from factoring tests of primary abilities) or simply assess primary abilities (using the Ekstrom kit or the Comprehensive Ability Battery) depends very much on the purpose of the investigation. The measurement of 20 primary abilities takes at least 3 hours, and this would be an extravagance if one just wanted to screen out low-ability applicants as part of an occupational selection process for a clerical post. Here a quick group-administered test of general ability, or perhaps perceptual speed, would be the obvious choice (depending on the nature and variety of tasks to be performed by the appointee). When assessing language ability in children in order to detect possible difficulties with language attainment, it is clearly vital to focus on just those factors that are relevant to language use. Therefore one basically selects a test at whatever level of generality seems appropriate, given some understanding of the skills and performances that one wishes to assess.

Guilford's model

It is necessary to mention Guilford's 'Structure of Intellect' model briefly, since it is still sometimes cited, despite being supported by relatively little empirical evidence. Guilford (1967) rejected factor analysis as a tool for discovering the structure of abilities, and built a model that ignored the best-known finding from half a century of research – that abilities tend to be correlated positively together. Instead, he built up a taxonomy of abilities that he felt *should* exist on theoretical grounds assuming that abilities were independent of one another. He suggested that any ability has three main qualities, the first of which he called 'content'. There were four types of content – figural, symbolic, semantic and behavioural – which defined the type of material to be presented. Tasks with a behavioural content might be based on video clips showing people's actions, those with a semantic content on words, etc.

His next quality, 'operations', defined the basic mental operations that were primarily involved in problem-solving – in other words, what made the task difficult. These were cognition, memory, divergent production, convergent production and evaluation. You may be surprised by some of these – 'cognition' would (these days) be regarded as a rather large and heterogeneous group of mental operations. Divergent production refers to the rapid and/or creative production of ideas, whilst convergent production requires someone to produce the 'best' solution to a problem. Guilford called the final quality 'products'. This defined the outcome of the problem-solving (implications, transformations, systems, relations, classes or units). Guilford thus postulated that there were 120 (4 contents × 5 operations × 6 products) distinct abilities, and devoted much energy to developing tests for these.

However, the obvious problem with this model is that it is arbitrary. Whatever the faults of factor analysis, it at least explores the structure of the data and describes what is really there. Guilford's model has no obvious theoretical or empirical rationale, and seems to have been invented 'off the top of his head'. In his scholarly review of theories of ability, Carroll (1993) uses phrases such as 'eccentric aberration' and 'fundamentally defective' when speaking of the theory (pp. 59–60) – sentiments with which it is difficult to disagree. The one good thing to come out of this work was Guilford's mention of 'divergent production' – the process of producing fast and/or imaginative ideas. These skills, which were thought to be related to 'creativity' (a matter of some concern to educators in the USA in the 1960s), had previously been overlooked by test designers. When such tests were incorporated into batteries such as the Comprehensive Ability Battery and Ekstrom Kit, they yielded a new secondary, Gv, discussed above.

STERNBERG'S TRIARCHIC THEORY OF ABILITY

The final theory to be considered here is that of Sternberg (1985). Sternberg argued that conventional ability tests were rather narrow in scope when compared to laypersons' views of what constituted 'smart' or 'intelligent' behaviour. In Sternberg's eyes there seems to be relatively little difference between being 'intelligent' and 'being successful in life in twentieth-century America'. He suggests that any definition of intelligence should take into account the following three factors.

- The context in which 'intelligent' behaviour takes place – the result of neglecting this variable is that the only behaviours seen to be relevant to 'intelligence' as measured by psychometric tests are those that are important (and can be easily measured) in a classroom testing situation. This is known as the contextual sub-theory.
- The experiential sub-theory explicitly considers the role of novelty, experience and automaticity in solving the task. (Automaticity is the smooth performance of cognitively complex operations as a result of considerable experience, e.g. driving a car or reading.)
- The componential sub-theory considers the underlying *mechanisms* (processes) of intelligent behaviour, which include 'metacomponents' (planning of actions and cognitive strategies for solving tasks) and knowledge acquisition. The more cognitive part of this sub-theory will be introduced in Chapter 8.

Sternberg's triarchic theory is an attempt to explain intelligent behaviour in terms of these three sub-theories.

A real-life example may help. My neighbour has a large and savage Rottweiler dog which lives in his garden and lunges against the hedge and barks at (and thoroughly terrifies) anyone in ours. As far as the contextual sub-theory is concerned, 'intelligent' responses to this situation might include changing the environment (moving house), modifying the environment (persuading the neighbour to take the dog into the house, or letting the dog loose in the hope that it will run away) or adapting to it (wearing ear-plugs when working, becoming friends with the dog, or turning the garden into a nature reserve so that the dog will not be disturbed).

The experiential sub-theory seeks to understand the novel demands of the situation – both the nature of the situation itself and the possible solutions. The former may include a lack of experience of fierce dogs and less-than-considerate neighbours. The latter may include a lack of experience of confrontational situations. If I had substantial previous experience in any of these areas, my responses would be more automatic (e.g. knowing precisely how to obtain the desired result when approaching the neighbours), so my overall behaviour would appear more polished and more intelligent, and would probably be more successful.

Kline (1991) raises some serious problems concerning this theory, but I am worried by a more fundamental point. By defining intelligence so broadly, it seems that Sternberg is stepping deep into the realm of personality and performance. *Style* of behaviour (which presumably includes problem-solving) was, after all, how we initially defined personality. Thus it comes as no surprise that Sternberg's focus has recently turned to understanding the relationship between (his theory of) intelligence and personality (Sternberg, 1994), which all seems rather circular. Whether I murder or release the dog, shout at or reason with my neighbour, abandon or defend my right to use the garden, plan my response to the Rottweiler problem or rush straight to a solution, these different approaches certainly sound like personality traits.

The experiential sub-theory essentially broadens the scope of 'intelligence' to cover individual differences in the whole of human performance (individual differences in performance of highly automatised skills, e.g. typing, driving, walking, etc.). At the start of this chapter we suggested that the concept of intelligence should be kept narrow in that it should consider relatively novel problems for which one has the necessary cognitive skills. That is, tasks should be designed so as to reduce the role of individual differences in familiarity or automaticity. It remains to be seen whether Sternberg's efforts to broaden the concept of intelligence eventually prove useful.

THE NOTION OF IQ

In the early years of ability testing it was necessary to devise a scale of mental ability which could be easily understood by parents and teachers, and so the concept of 'intelligence quotient' (IQ) was adopted. Confusingly, this term has two quite distinct meanings. Since most psychological testing was originally performed on schoolchildren, it was initially thought sensible to determine how a child's performance compared with the average performance of children of other ages. For example, Table 7.3 shows the average scores obtained on an early intelligence test by children of six age ranges. Suppose that a particular child is aged 74 months (this is their 'chronological age', or CA) and they score 30 on the test. Part (a) of Table 7.3 shows that a score of 30 is generally obtained by children aged 77 months, so the child's mental age is 77 months. The old definition of IQ (sometimes known as the *ratio IQ*) was:

(a) Test scores of children aged 72 to 80 months

Age (months)	72	73	74	75	76	77	78	79	80
Average score	23	24	25	27	28	30	31	33	35

(b) Test scores of adults aged 15 to 60 years

Age (years)	15	16	17	18	25	30	40	50	60
Average score	62	64	65	66	65	66	65	64	64

Table 7.3 Hypothetical scores on an ability test at various ages

$$IQ = \frac{\text{mental age}}{\text{chronological age}} \times 100$$

In this example, the child's IQ is $\frac{77}{74} \times 100 = 104$. An IQ of 100 shows that a child is performing at an average level for their age, an IQ greater than 100 shows that they are performing better than average, and an IQ less than 100 shows that they are performing below average.

There are several problems with this definition of IQ, which led to its decline. The most obvious drawback is related to the fact that performance on ability tests ceases to increase with age after the late teens. So suppose that someone aged 18 years scored 70 on the test. Since none of the higher age groups has an average score of 70, it is not possible to calculate this person's mental age, or IQ.

The ratio IQ was therefore abandoned 40 years ago. It should never be used, although alarmingly this is the only definition of IQ given in one recent dictionary of psychology. Instead, a new term called the 'deviation IQ' was introduced. By definition, deviation IQs have a mean of 100 for any particular age group, and a standard deviation that is almost always 16 (although two test constructors adopt standard deviations of 15 and 18, respectively). Deviation IQs also (by definition) follow a normal (bell-shaped) distribution, and the manuals of many ability tests contain a table showing which scores on the test correspond to which level of IQ.

Since deviation IQs follow a normal distribution, it is relatively straightforward to work out how extreme a particular IQ score is. One simply converts the IQ to a z-score by subtracting the mean IQ and dividing by the standard deviation – these figures are 100 and 16, respectively, by definition. One then consults the table of areas under the standard normal distribution which can be found in any statistics text. For example, an IQ of 131 corresponds to a z-score of $\frac{(131 - 100)}{16} = 1.94$, and the table of the standard normal integral shows that only 2.5 per cent of the population will have scores above this level. An IQ of 110 corresponds to a z-score of 0.625; 26 per cent of the population will have scores above this level.

It is only necessary (indeed, it is only statistically *legitimate*) to convert scores on ability tests into IQs for the purpose of understanding the meaning of an individual's score on a test. Most of us will simply calculate *t*-tests, correlations, etc. based on the raw scores from ability tests.

SELF-ASSESSMENT QUESTION 7.5

(a) What is the difference between ratio IQ and deviation IQ?

(b) How would you respond if a member of the government berated schoolteachers because, despite a supposedly huge increase in schools' resources, a recent study showed that 50 per cent of children still have IQs below 100 (the same figure as 10 years ago)?

THE PRACTICAL UTILITY OF ABILITY TESTING

Knowing a person's profile of abilities is incredibly useful for a number of applied reasons, since abilities:

- stay remarkably constant over time in adults (Conley, 1984); and
- correlate with a number of very useful real-life criteria.

If you were allowed to gather one piece of psychological data in order to predict how individuals would behave in *any* situation, then I would have no hesitation in recommending a test of general ability. Scores on such tests can predict an *enormous* number of behaviours, as shown by Herrnstein and Murray (1994), Kanfer *et al.* (1995), Cronbach (1994), Ghiselli (1966) and Snow and Yalow (1982) among many others, as the applied psychology journals quickly reveal. As Kanfer *et al.* note,

> companies have unarguably saved billions of dollars by using a merit-based selection process . . . tests of intellectual abilities are the single most predictive element in employee selection. Such tests are generally more valid than the use of academic and employment credentials – and certainly more valid than the use of personnel interviews – in predicting training and on-the-job success.
>
> (Kanfer *et al.*, 1995, p. 597)

It is not particularly difficult to produce predictive validities above 0.4 when using ability tests for selection purposes. Given that the reliability of the criterion (against which one is validating the test) is often woeful, this is rather an impressive result. In some cases (e.g. selecting computer programmers) the correlation between scores on ability tests and performance can be of the order of 0.6 to 0.7 (Cronbach, 1994). Whilst it is perhaps unsurprising to find that intelligence correlates substantially with school performance or annual income, the finding of appreciable links between abilities and variables as diverse as criminality, number of children and (most controversially of all) ethnicity is really rather surprising.

One concern shared by many academic psychologists is that the assessment of abilities has recently been heavily commercialised. The wheel has been well and truly reinvented, and many companies now sell rather unextraordinary ability tests for most extraordinary prices. When one buys an old, cheap and trusted test one can also search the literature to find out whether it is likely to yield valid predictions for the particular application for which it is intended. Almost by definition, the more recent or tailor-made tests generally lack such a wealth of firm evidence for their validity.

SUGGESTED ADDITIONAL READING

This chapter has concentrated on conveying a basic grasp of hierarchical models of ability, since these are of considerable theoretical and practical importance. Thus there has been little scope to explore Sternberg's work in any detail, but his 1985 book will repay careful study. Neither has there been much space to discuss which tests can best assess abilities. Buros is the obvious source, but texts such as those by Cronbach (1994), Anastasi (1961) and Kline (1991, 1993) also give some examples of test items. Journals such as *Educational and Psychological Measurement* and specialist journals on educational and occupational psychology can show how tests of mental abilities can predict performance in real-life settings, as can the books cited in the text. Kline's (1991) *Intelligence: The Psychometric View*, Cronbach, Anastasi and the early chapters of Anderson (1992) can be recommended as a general expansion of some of the issues discussed here. Herrnstein and Murray's book *The Bell Curve* (1994) contains some extremely controversial interpretations of the correlates of general ability – readers may like to evaluate critically both this work and also the many counter-views that have appeared on the Internet. Finally, Sternberg's massive (1982) handbook contains first-rate chapters on the nature, measurement and correlates of ability.

ANSWERS TO SELF-ASSESSMENT QUESTIONS

SAQ 7.1

There are no right or wrong answers to this question, the purpose of which was to encourage thought. Some possibilities are discussed in the next section. Others might include analysing what actions requiring intelligence seem to be performed by a wide range of people, e.g. by following students, plasterers, unemployed people, pensioners, drivers, doctors, etc. during their working lives, and either noting what problems they need to solve, or asking them to 'think aloud'. Alternatively, one can perform a massive literature search, as Carroll (1993) has done, in an attempt to identify and classify all the distinct abilities that have ever been reported in the literature. Another approach would be to start from cognitive psychology, and to try to assess individual differences in the types of things that cognitive psychologists assess, e.g. speed of mental rotation, mental scanning, semantic priming, etc.

SAQ 7.2

I cannot guarantee that these answers are correct – they represent just my view concerning the type of skills that might be most important in each of the tasks.

(a) Action – output; content – aural; process – fine use of muscle.
(b) Input, memory and knowledge.
(c) Internal processing, verbal and remembering.
(d) Internal processing, verbal and complexity of relations.
(e) Internal processing, verbal, complexity of relations and creativity.
(f) Internal processing, knowledge, convergence and remembering.

SAQ 7.3

It is probably not sensible to conclude causality because, although the examples at the start of the chapter on factor analysis suggested that factors can *sometimes* be causal, it is not possible to extrapolate this and argue that any factor *must* be causal. For it is quite possible that things other than 'general ability' (possibly quality of education, inability to understand English, anxiety) may cause the observed results. However, if g can be shown to reflect some basic feature of the individual (e.g. the speed with which their nerves work) that cannot easily be assessed by any other means, then it may be permissible to argue causality.

SAQ 7.4

(a) Gv, (b) Gr, (c) Gc, (d) Gps.

SAQ 7.5

(a) Ratio $IQ = \dfrac{\text{mental age}}{\text{chronological age}} \times 100$. Deviation IQ defines IQ as a normal distribution with a mean of 100 and a standard deviation of (usually) 16.

(b) Because of the definition of deviation IQ given above, 50 per cent of the children will *always* be defined as having IQs below 100, even if the underlying raw scores on the test all increase dramatically over the 10-year period.

8

Ability processes

BACKGROUND

This chapter considers some experiments designed to determine whether individual differences in ability have clear links to the physiology of the nervous system, and to the speed with which certain cognitive operations can be performed. If such links can be found, it may be appropriate to use general ability to 'explain' behaviour, since general ability may reflect individual differences in the biological processing power of the brain and nervous system – a notion that dates back to Hebb (1949).

Recommended prior reading

Chapter 7.

INTRODUCTION

Chapter 7 made some rather important points. It indicated that almost all human abilities are positively correlated together, and that it is possible to describe these correlations either by a single factor of general ability (as suggested by Spearman), by a set of 20 or more 'Primary Mental Abilities' (as suggested by Thurstone), by a few 'group factors' (as suggested by Burt and Vernon) or, most generally, by a hierarchical model which incorporates all of these features (as suggested by Cattell and Gustafsson). This really is quite interesting. It would logically be quite possible for human abilities to be independent of each other – after all, why *should* abilities as diverse as musical talent, mathematical skill, vocabulary, memory or ability to visualise shapes be interrelated? It is not as if there are any obvious processes (e.g. pieces of knowledge or skills taught through education) that are common to all of them, and which could account for their interrelationships.

However, knowing the *structure* of abilities does not mean that we *understand* what these abilities are. For this we need to develop 'process models' that describe intelligent behaviour in terms of lower-level biological, cognitive or neural processes. Only when we have a good understanding of precisely why some people show different patterns of ability, personality, and so on, can we profess to *understand* what is going on. Thirty years ago the structure of personality and ability was not particularly well understood, and the journals were full of articles attempting to establish the basic dimensions of ability. As there is now some consensus of opinion about the basic structure of abilities, almost all of the older theories being accommodated neatly by a hierarchical model, the focus of research has shifted. The main aim now is to identify the *processes* that cause individual differences in ability to appear.

Since abilities reflect the processing of information by the nervous system, the logical place to start looking for process models of individual differences is in the biology of the nervous system, and in cognitive psychology. Both of these areas can sensibly be regarded as lower-level, more fundamental *causes* of intelligent behaviour – it seems more likely that the way neurones work will affect general ability than vice versa. When one starts looking into the influence of social processes, personality, etc., the picture becomes much more complex, because it is difficult to be sure which variables are causes and which are effects. For example, suppose that it is found that children who perform poorly at mathematics hate the subject vehemently, whereas those who perform well have much more positive attitudes towards it. Perhaps we can argue that children's attitudes to a subject are an important indicator of their ability in that field – that is, that attitude influences ability. Thus any process model of ability ought to consider attitudes as important predictors.

However, this approach has several drawbacks. It is quite possible that the children's attitudes towards mathematics will *result from* their performance rather than vice versa. Achieving plenty of A-grades on mathematics tests, receiving approving comments from teachers, etc. might *cause* children to enjoy the subject. Failing tests, being laughed at by one's peers and having to take extra tuition might well engender a negative attitude towards the subject. Thus it is just as likely that attitudes *result* from ability as that attitudes *cause* ability. There is a third possibility, too – that attitude and performance may both be influenced by some other factor(s), quality of teaching being one obvious variable.

These problems are not (quite) insurmountable, given excellent experimental design and statistics, such as confirmatory factor analysis. However, it makes sense to explore the simplest routes (biology and cognition) first – it is possible that individual differences in these areas may be able to explain a very sizeable proportion of the individual differences in ability. If so, there is no need to consider the (methodologically more messy) social and attitudinal approaches. However, if biological and cognitive approaches are unable to explain individual differences in ability, then these other avenues should be explored.

NEURAL PROCESSING AND GENERAL ABILITY

In the 1980s, several theorists suggested that a person's general ability may, in part, be influenced by the way in which individual neurones in his or her nervous system process information. One theory suggests that high general ability may be a consequence of having nerve cells in the brain that conduct impulses rapidly (Reed, 1984), or which transmit information efficiently across synapses (Eysenck, 1986). Another theory suggests that general ability may be related to the *accuracy* with which information is transmitted from neurone to neurone (Hendrickson, 1972; Eysenck, 1982). The second point probably needs some explanation. Imagine that you are listening to a radio tuned to a distant station. It will be much more difficult to hear what is being said than when it is tuned to a nearby station, because the background hisses and crackles interfere with your ability to detect what is being said – they mask the signal. It may be the same with neurones. Perhaps some people's neurones switch from a very low to a very high rate of firing when stimulated by another neurone. Other people's neurones may fire quite frequently even when unstimulated, or may fire only moderately frequently when stimulated. In either case, information will not be transmitted very efficiently from one neurone to others. Some upstream neurones will 'think' that a neurone has fired when it has not, or they may fail to detect a modest increase in firing rate which corresponds to a real stimulus.

These theories lead to similar predictions. They suggest that people whose neurones conduct information quickly along the axon and/or which transmit information efficiently and accurately across the synapses are likely to be more efficient at processing information than those whose nerves transmit information slowly or have a low signal-to-noise ratio.

How can one measure speed/efficiency of neural conduction? Several techniques have been developed for this, including direct measurement, inspection time, reaction time, and evoked potential studies. These will be considered in turn.

DIRECT MEASUREMENT OF NEURAL CONDUCTION VELOCITY

In principle such direct measurement is easy. One merely has to apply two electrodes (as far apart as possible) to a single neurone. An electric current is applied to one electrode, to stimulate the neurone to fire. The second electrode is used to time how quickly the impulse travels down the axon of the nerve. If the distance between the two electrodes is measured with a ruler, it is a simple matter to calculate the nerve conduction velocity. If this experiment is performed with a large sample of people whose scores on a test of general ability are also known, then theory would predict that there should be a substantial positive correlation between general ability and nerve conduction velocity (NCV).

Vernon and Mori (1992) and Wickett and Vernon (1994) performed such experiments using nerves in the arm, and found that there was a significant correlation (of the order of 0.42–0.48) between general ability and NCV. Thus it does appear from these studies that intelligent people have nerves that simply transmit information more quickly than those of individuals of lower general ability. However, two other studies have failed to replicate this finding (Reed and Jensen, 1991; Rijsdijk *et al.*, 1995), which is worrying.

INDIRECT MEASUREMENT OF NEURAL CONDUCTION VELOCITY

Inspection time

Several techniques have been developed to measure NCV using indirect methods. Perhaps the simplest to understand is a technique known as inspection time (Vickers *et al.*, 1972). This simply measures how long a simple stimulus has to be presented in order to be perceived correctly. For example, suppose that either shape (a) or shape (b) in Figure 8.1 is flashed on to a screen for a few thousandths of a second, and a volunteer is then asked whether the longer line was on the left or the right. Shape (c) is presented immediately after (a) or (b) to act as a mask (if you are not familiar with the principles of masking you can safely ignore this detail). It is important to realise that inspection time is a measure of how long it takes to *see* a stimulus, and *not* of how quickly a person can *respond* to it – in the inspection-time task an individual can take as long as they want to make their decision.

The aim of inspection-time studies is to determine how long it takes an individual to see such stimuli. Since the retina is essentially an outgrowth of the brain, one might expect people with accurate and/or rapid neurones to be able to make this simple discrimination more rapidly than others. Thus it is possible

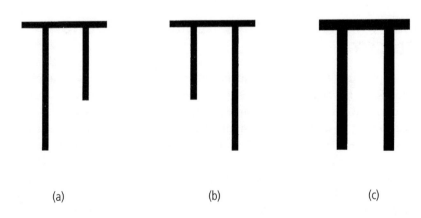

        (a)   (b)   (c)

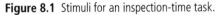

Figure 8.1 Stimuli for an inspection-time task.

that highly intelligent individuals will be able to 'see' the stimulus correctly after a shorter time than those of lower general ability – that is, there will be a negative correlation between general ability and inspection time.

The amount of time a person needs to see the figures can be estimated by repeating the experiment several times (e.g. 50–100 times) for each of several exposure periods. The percentage of correct answers can be noted, and plotted on a graph such as that shown in Figure 8.2. You can see that, at the fastest exposure time, both Person A and Person B perform at chance level. However, as the presentation time increases, it is clear that Person A can see which line is longer rather more quickly than Person B – her percentage of stimuli correctly identified rises quite rapidly. It is possible to calculate a statistic for each individual to reflect these differences – for example, the exposure time at which there is an 80 per cent chance that they will be able to solve the problem correctly. Such statistics can be correlated with measures of general ability in order to determine whether inspection time (and hence, indirectly, speed and/or efficiency of neural processing) is related to general ability.

Tens of studies show that it is. Most find that the correlations between measures of general ability and inspection time are of the order of –0.3 to –0.5. Several alternative methods of assessing inspection time have also been devised, and they yield broadly similar results. However, the interpretation of such data is a little more controversial. Without going into details, it has been suggested that the correlations between inspection time and general ability

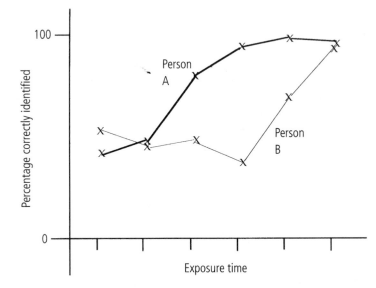

Figure 8.2 Percentage of stimuli correctly identified at several exposure durations during an inspection-time task.

may be influenced by attention span, or by the use of cognitive strategies, such as flicker detection, which will reveal whether the shorter leg of the masked stimulus was presented to the left or the right (Mackenzie and Bingham, 1985). Yet even when these are taken into account, there is still an appreciable correlation between the measures (Egan and Deary, 1992). Thus it seems that there *is* a fairly substantial link between inspection time and general ability, although this is rather less than had been claimed in the early studies. Deary and Stough (1996) offer a thoughtful recent review.

SELF-ASSESSMENT QUESTION 8.1

Why would it be serious if inspection time *was* shown to be influenced by cognitive strategies, such as flicker detection?

Reaction time

Inspection time estimates the time for which a stimulus has to be presented in order to be correctly recognised, but it is also possible to assess how long it takes an individual to *respond* to a stimulus. This, too, might be related to general ability – if highly intelligent individuals have neurones that transmit information particularly quickly or accurately, these individuals should be able to respond more rapidly to a signal than people of lower general ability. This idea was first proposed by Galton (1883), who attempted to test it and eventually concluded that no such relationship existed. However, the accurate measurement of reaction times was problematic a century ago, and Jensen and Munroe (1974) were the first to re-examine this issue in the English-language journals. They measured reaction time using the apparatus shown diagrammatically in Figure 8.3.

The apparatus consists of eight green lights (here depicted by squares) arranged in a semicircle on a metal panel. Beside each light is a button (denoted by a black circle) with an additional 'home button' centred 15 cm away from all of the other buttons. The lights and buttons are connected to a computer which controls the experiment. The task is straightforward, and participants are asked to react as quickly as possible. The index finger of the preferred hand is placed on the home button. After a (random) period of a few seconds, one of the lights is illuminated – the 'target light'. The participant lifts their finger from the home button and presses the button beside this light. Two time intervals are recorded:

- the interval between the 'target' light being illuminated and the finger leaving the home button, known as the reaction time (RT);
- the interval between the finger leaving the home button and pressing the target button, known as the movement time (MT).

This is repeated several times. Measurements are also obtained for different numbers of lights (varying from one to eight), the unused lights and buttons being masked off by metal plates.

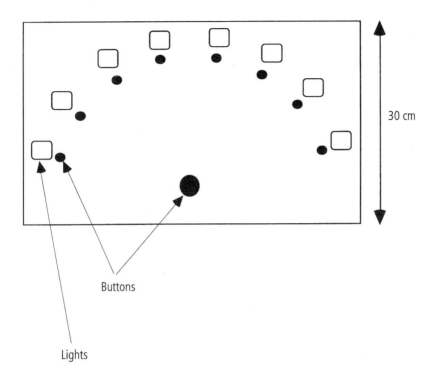

Figure 8.3 Jensen's choice reaction time apparatus.

When the mean reaction times are plotted as a function of the number of lights (do not worry about why the numbers on the x-axis are not equally spaced), a graph similar to that shown in Figure 8.4 is obtained for each individual. Straight lines may be fitted to the RT and MT graphs as shown, and the equations of these straight lines can be obtained by simple algebra. The height of these lines (the 'intercept') shows how quickly the participant reacted overall. The slope of the lines shows how much their RT (or MT) changes as the number of potential targets increases. RT typically increases as the number of potential targets increases (a phenomenon known as 'Hick's law'), whereas MT stays almost constant. We thus have four measures for each participant, corresponding to the slope and the intercept of the two lines. These measures are correlated with general ability.

It is generally found that both the slope and the intercept of the RT graph show significant negative correlations with general ability – such correlations are usually of the order of –0.3. That is, highly intelligent people respond more quickly overall, and their RT does not increase much as the number of potential target lights increases (Jensen, 1982; Barrett *et al.*, 1986). MT shows no correlation with general ability, although the *variability* in MT often does (Jensen, 1982; Barrett *et al.*, 1986).

Some objections have been raised about this interpretation of the results. Longstreth (1984) suggests that the correlations may not simply reflect a link

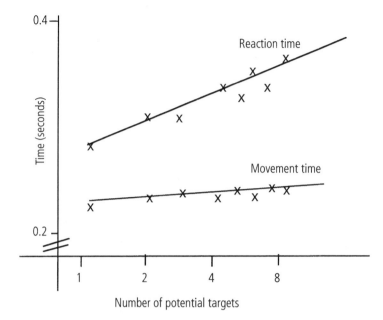

Figure 8.4 Reaction time and movement time as a function of the number of potential targets.

between RT and basic neural speed. For example, the more intelligent participants may be able to devise efficient cognitive strategies for responding quickly (Sternberg's 'metacomponents'). The correlations between RT and general ability may thus reflect the use of such strategies rather than anything more fundamental. However, experiments performed in order to test such hypotheses show that these strategies cannot explain the underlying correlation between RT and general ability (Matthews and Dorn, 1989; Neubauer, 1991). Reaction time does seem to decrease with general ability, as expected.

The problem with these experiments is that the correlation between reaction time and general ability is stronger when the task becomes more complex. For example, a reaction-time task with eight alternatives (such as that shown in Figure 8.3) produces a much higher correlation with general ability than does a two-choice or a four-choice task. Indeed, the literature suggests that simple reaction time (measured by pressing a button as quickly as possible in response to a single light or sound) shows a really rather modest correlation with general ability, of the order of –0.1 to –0.25 (Jensen, 1980). If a high level of general ability *just* reflects individual differences in the speed of processing information, then the correlations should really be higher than this.

One alternative explanation for the low correlation could be that either general ability or simple reaction time was measured with low reliability. Reaction times can have their reliability assessed in just the same way as questionnaire items, and it is unfortunate that most reaction-time studies do not estimate reliability. However, May *et al.* (1986) showed that highly reliable estimates of simple reaction time can be made from a relatively modest number of trials, and so low levels of reliability are unlikely to be the cause of the low correlations observed. It is much more probable that more complex kinds of decision-making or strategy use are at work.

SELF-ASSESSMENT QUESTION 8.2

(a) What is the difference between inspection time and reaction time?

(b) Name three measures derived from the Jensen task that have been found to correlate substantially with general ability.

Evoked potentials

A fourth way of exploring the link between neural activity and general ability relies on recording the electrical activity from brain cells. If one sticks (quite literally!) a few electrodes on the surface of the scalp and attaches these to sensitive amplifiers, it is possible to measure electrical activity in the brain – not in individual neurones, but in whole areas of the brain. Average auditory evoked potential recordings are, as their name suggests, measures of brain voltages (potentials) that are evoked by a sound. They show how the brain processes a simple sound.

In the simplest experimental design, the participant is seated in a comfortable chair, electrodes are attached to their scalp, and a pair of headphones is placed over their head. They are simply told to remain sitting, with eyes closed, and do nothing. They are informed that they will hear clicks or tones through the headphones from time to time, but that these should be ignored. A hundred or so clicks are presented over a period of about 10 minutes. What could be simpler, from a participant's point of view?

The brain's electrical activity is recorded for a couple of seconds following each click. In practice, the voltages are typically measured every thousandth of a second following the onset of the click, and at the end of the experiment each of these 1000 voltages is averaged across the 100 replications (hence it is known as the *average* auditory evoked potential). The 1000 averaged voltages may then be plotted as a graph, rather as shown in Figure 8.5, which is based on the pioneering work of Ertl and Schafer (1969). This shows time on the x-axis and voltage on the y-axis, with a time of zero corresponding to the onset of the click. You can see that these data certainly appear to show differences between low-IQ and high-IQ individuals, although you will have to take my word for the fact that there was remarkably little variation within each group of participants.

High-IQ participants appear to have longer, more spiky waveforms, and Hendrickson and Hendrickson (1980) suggested that this could usefully be detected by simply measuring the length of the graph over a particular period of time (such as 0.25 seconds). They called this the 'string measure' (since it was originally measured by putting a piece of string over graphs such as those shown in Figure 8.5, and then straightening it out and measuring its length). Using this technique, they found a correlation of 0.7 between string length and IQ in Ertl and Schafer's data. They subsequently recorded correlations of the order of 0.7 within another sample of over 200 schoolchildren (Hendrickson,

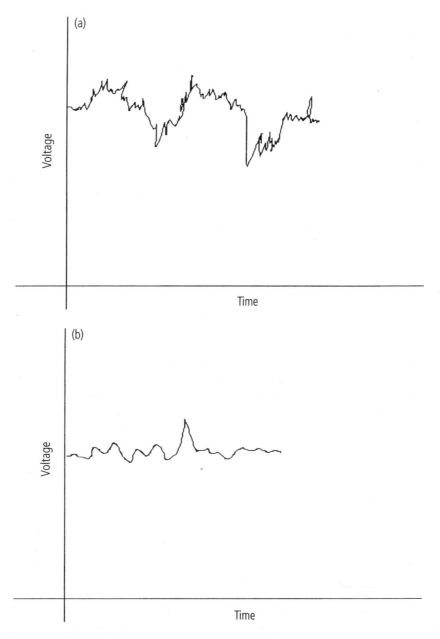

Figure 8.5 Schematic average evoked auditory potential recordings from (a) high-IQ subjects, and (b) low-IQ subjects.

1982) – a highly significant result, but one which has proved difficult to replicate.

More recent research in this area includes the work of Stough *et al.* (1990) and Gilbert *et al.* (1991), who observed an effect as expected, and Shagass *et al.* (1981) and Bates and Eysenck (1993), who did not. Most worrying of all is a technically sophisticated study by Barrett and Eysenck (1992), who could find no evidence for a positive correlation between general ability and the string measure. Indeed, if anything, the data show that the correlation should be negative. Given the scale and methodological sophistication of this study, this failure to replicate the previous findings is worrying. The measurement of evoked potentials is a highly technical business, and pushed technology to its limits in the 1960s and 1970s. There is always a nagging concern that some methodological problem may have influenced the results, particularly as Hendrickson's (1982) study involved testing at more than one site, with the sub-sample of high-ability subjects all being tested at the same location. It has also emerged that attention interacts with general ability in determining string length, even in a small sample of undergraduates (Bates *et al.*, 1995). When participants are asked to pay attention to the tones, this affects the string length of higher-ability individuals. The results of these evoked potential studies are inconsistent, which may well reflect subtle but important differences in experimental procedures and instructions. But overall there are enough strong correlations reported in the literature to suggest that there is most probably *some* underlying relationship between string length and general ability.

Many other more conventional analyses of such waveforms (e.g. measuring their amplitude and the delay between the stimulus and each peak and trough) have been performed, and Deary and Carryl (1993) have provided an excellent and thoughtful summary of this literature. Once again, the results are somewhat variable, although they generally support a link between general ability and electrical activity in the brain. However, a detailed description of these studies is beyond the scope of this chapter.

GENERAL ABILITY AND COGNITIVE TASKS

It would be amazing if the kinds of abilities studied, described here and in the previous chapter, were completely unrelated to the types of processes studied by cognitive psychologists, and so in this section and the next we shall consider some areas of overlap between the two. Carroll (1980) suggested that some of the tasks traditionally studied by cognitive psychologists, such as the S. Sternberg memory-scanning paradigm, or the Watson and Clarke sentence verification task, should be related to mental abilities. The great advantage of such tasks is that they are thought to measure single cognitive processes – the experiments were designed to measure the time taken to perform a single elementary cognitive operation (ECO). For example, the S. Sternberg memory scanning paradigm (Sternberg, 1969) presents a list of numbers or characters for several seconds, followed by a 'target character'. The participant is asked to push one button if the target character was in the preceding list, and another if it was not. The reaction time is found to be related to the length of the list. After a little statistical juggling (involving regression lines), it is possible to estimate how long it takes an individual to 'take in' the meaning of the target, and how long it takes that individual to compare the target with one of the stored representations of a character.

Two main approaches have been adopted in order to test such theories. One is fairly crude, and involves correlating the durations of various elementary cognitive operations with ability. The other involves the *modelling* of solution times to complex tasks.

The first and cruder approach simply involves estimating how long it takes each individual person in a sample to perform some of these elementary cognitive operations, using experiments such as the Sternberg memory scanning paradigm. The second stage is to check whether the people who perform these basic cognitive operations fastest also perform well on certain ability tests which may require the (repeated) use of some of these ECOs, among other things. The time taken for each subject to perform each ECO can thus be correlated with his or her scores on various psychometric ability tests. (More statistically sophisticated readers may appreciate that multiple regression techniques may be used to determine the relative importance of each ECO to each ability trait. The beta-weights may show the relative number of times each ECO is performed during the course of each ability test. However, readers unfamiliar with regression techniques can skip this detail.)

Several studies have examined the relationship between abilities and the time it takes to perform some of these ECOs. For example, Hunt (1978) suggested that verbal ability is closely related to individual differences in ability to retrieve lexical information (i.e. the meaning of letters) from long-term memory. His participants performed two experiments. In the first they were asked to decide (as quickly as possible) whether pairs of letters were the same (e.g. AA, aa, BB or bb) or physically different (e.g. AB, aA, bA, ab). In the second experiment they were asked to decide whether the two characters referred to the same letter of the alphabet (e.g. Aa, AA, aA, Bb) or not (e.g. AB, bA, ab, aB). The average time taken to make each decision (correctly) was calculated for each experiment. The average time taken to decide whether the two characters were physically identical was then subtracted from the average time taken to decide whether the two characters referred to the same letter of the alphabet. This was thought to be related to the amount of time taken to access the 'meaning' of each character in long-term memory. It was consistently found that the correlation between this statistic and verbal ability was of the order of −0.3 – statistically significant, but once again not large enough to support the claim that verbal ability is *just* speed of lexical access. So perhaps we need to perform some more complex experiments in order to try to *model* the processes that are used when solving a more complex task.

SELF-ASSESSMENT QUESTION 8.3

Is it possible that some cognitive strategies could affect performance on either of these experiments?

Plenty of other attempts have been made to explore the links between cognition and mental ability in other areas, too – see, for example, Mulhern (1997) and Stankov *et al.* (1995) for useful reviews.

The second approach involves a careful analysis of the steps involved in performing some really quite complex cognitive tasks. Bob Sternberg (1977) (no relation of S. Sternberg) performed some remarkably elegant experiments in this area. He argued that if the sequence of cognitive operations required to perform a fairly complex task was known, and if it was possible to estimate (through experiments such as those described above) how long it takes each individual to perform each of these basic cognitive operations, it might be possible to predict quite accurately how long it would take an individual to solve the problem. In other words, one first identifies all of the ECOs that are thought to be involved in a particular task, and draws up a flowchart to show how these are organised. The next step is to assess how long it takes *each individual* to perform each of these mental operations, using carefully designed experiments. Having done this, it should be possible to 'plug in' the amount of time that it takes an individual to perform each ECO in order to predict how long it should take a person to solve a particular problem.

Moreover, since most mental tasks may involve the same basic ECOs, albeit strung together according to different flowcharts, it might be possible to measure how long it takes a person to perform each ECO, and on the basis of this to predict how long they will take to solve other mental tasks. Essentially, ECO durations would replace ability traits as the unit of analysis.

Much of Sternberg's work focused on non-verbal analogy problems – for example, analogy items based on the 'people-piece' cartoon characters. These characters differed from each other in the following four basic ways:

- gender – male/female;
- height – tall/short;
- girth – fat/thin;
- colour – shaded/unshaded.

A typical analogy task using these characters would be like that shown in Figure 8.6. You have probably already encountered verbal analogies – for example, 'cat is to kitten as dog is to bitch' (*sic*). Participants would have to decide whether each of these items was true or false. Sternberg moved away from such verbal analogies because he felt that the use of language may complicate the process of solving these problems. Instead, he argued that 'people-piece' characters can be used in the same way. In Figure 8.6 the only thing that differs between the first pair of characters is their sex. Their shading, height and girth are the same. Applying the same rule to the second pair, the

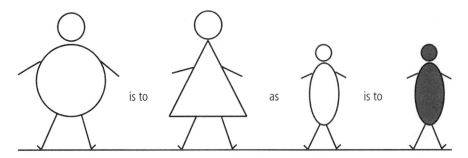

Figure 8.6 Example of a schematic analogy task, reading 'Tall fat unshaded man is to tall fat unshaded woman as short thin unshaded man is to short, thin, shaded man' – an incorrect analogy. If correct, the fourth character would show a short, thin unshaded woman.

fourth character *should* clearly be a short, thin, unshaded female. However, is not, so the analogy is false.

Sternberg argued that six main cognitive processes underpinned performance on these tasks, namely encoding (the recognition of each feature of the cartoon characters), inference (noting which features changed between the first pair of characters, thus inferring the rule to be applied to the second pair of characters), mapping the relationship between the first and third characters, applying the rule to the third character, comparing the fourth character to what it should be, and responding appropriately. He drew up several plausible flowchart models for solving these problems on the basis of these elementary cognitive operations. Through the use of some ingenious experiments involving pre-cueing (sometimes showing some of the characters before the others, thereby allowing some of the ECOs to be performed prior to the measurement of the reaction times), he was able to assess the duration of each of these components independently for each person (Sternberg, 1977).

The problem is that, even with a relatively simple task such as this, the number of plausible models for solving the analogies becomes quite large. For example, it is possible to suggest that some cognitive operations may be performed in parallel, rather than sequentially. Cognitive strategies for solving the problems can also complicate the picture enormously. For example, if three of the characters are shaded but one is not, or if one figure is a different height from the other three, then the analogy *must* be incorrect. Some (but not all) of the individuals performing this task seem to check for such possibilities before analysing the problem in detail. One attempt to replicate this work (May *et al.*, 1987) found that the model really did not fit the data very well. Nor did the estimated durations of Sternberg's six basic cognitive processes correlate very strongly with other cognitive measures.

SUMMARY

In this chapter we have looked at some biological and cognitive processes that are associated with mental abilities. The picture is still somewhat tantalising in that there are a number of variables (e.g. inspection time, RT slope, lexical access time) that show statistically significant correlations with mental abilities, although the correlations are not large enough to suggest that these variables can completely *explain* the abilities. Furthermore, more complex modelling of cognitive processes (as with Sternberg's model) soon runs into problems, since the number of potential flowcharts becomes very large, as individuals may use different cognitive strategies when solving the tasks.

So far, we have assumed that intelligence and abilities are real characteristics of individuals, perhaps related to the way in which neurones operate, or to the way in which individuals process information. That is, we have assumed that abilities exist, and that they influence behaviour. Not everyone shares this view. For example, Howe (1988) argues that these abilities are a convenient way of *describing* how people behave, but are essentially 'constructions' of the observer, rather than any real property of the individual. According to this view, it would be quite wrong to use general ability as an explanation – for example, to say that a child performs well at school because he or she is intelligent would imply that general ability is some basic property of the individual, rather than just a convenient way of describing their behaviour.

The experiments described in the present chapter all attempt to relate performance on ability tests to some more basic biological or cognitive processes. They are important because they can show whether it is legitimate to regard abilities as the behavioural manifestations of more fundamental properties of the brain and cognitive systems. If this is so, it may be legitimate to argue that abilities can truly *explain* behaviour.

Howe's argument collapses if experiments show that abilities are closely linked to some fundamental properties of individuals' nervous systems or speed of cognition, or if there is evidence for a substantial genetic influence on general ability (evidence for which will be scrutinised in a later chapter). In a rejoinder to Howe's paper, Sternberg (1988) suggests that many of Howe's points are based on a somewhat selective reading of the literature, and that several important empirical studies undermine his conclusion. You will find it very useful to consult these papers by Howe and Sternberg and draw your own conclusions.

Many of the studies described in the present chapter are really rather crude. Psychometrically, most have focused on general ability rather than a broader range of ability factors. Experimentally, none of the studies of brain electrical activity has considered that general ability may be related to the localisation of brain activity. Some evidence suggests that processing is more highly localised in high-ability individuals.

Several studies have been performed using undergraduates, who will all (presumably!) have above-average general ability. Using a sample with a small range of individual differences in mental ability will underestimate the true, underlying correlations between general ability and other variables. It also seems probable that some other variables (such as attention and personality) have not been adequately controlled for, and the task (which generally involves listening to clicks) is really rather non-demanding. My feeling is that these studies probably do indicate some overlap between general ability, cognitive processes and the way in which the nervous system operates, despite the existence of so many contradictory results. However, there is still plenty of scope for the environment to influence general ability.

SUGGESTED ADDITIONAL READING

The theoretical rationale for looking behind pencil-and-paper tests of g is to determine whether or not psychometric tests that assess general ability also reflect some rather basic biological or cognitive properties of the nervous system, e.g. the speed with which it can process information. If so, some theorists would argue, it is reasonable to use the term 'general ability' to explain why some individuals perform better than others on a very wide range of mental tasks. Two papers by Mike Howe (1988) and Bob Sternberg (Sternberg, 1988) bear directly on this issue, and make interesting reading.

More detailed accounts of the link between general ability, inspection time and reaction time are given in Ian Deary's reviews (Deary and Carryl, 1993; Deary and Stough, 1996), and a more general survey of the whole field is offered by Art Jensen (1997). However, with the exception of some of the EEG studies (which can become a little technical), few of the papers cited in this chapter should prove difficult to follow.

ANSWERS TO SELF-ASSESSMENT QUESTIONS

SAQ 8.1

The whole rationale for correlating inspection time with g is that inspection time is thought to measure a rather simple and basic physiological process, namely the speed and/or accuracy with which information can be transmitted from neurone to neurone. If it is found that performance on the inspection-time task is influenced by 'higher-order' mental processes (such as strategy use or concentration), then it is clear that inspection time cannot be a pure measure of this physiological phenomenon, and so will be less useful for testing the theory that intelligence is essentially a measure of how fast and/or accurately nervous systems can transmit information.

SAQ 8.2

(a) In an inspection-time task the experimenter controls the duration of the stimuli, and ascertains the exposure duration at which each individual has a certain probability (e.g. 75 per cent or 90 per cent) of correctly identifying the stimulus. The participant can take as long as they like to make their response. A reaction-time task, on the other hand, requires participants to respond as quickly as possible to a stimulus. In the inspection-time task, perceiving the stimulus is the important part of the experiment, whereas in the reaction-time task it is responding quickly that is crucial.

(b) The following three measures have been found to correlate substantially with general ability.

- The slope of the line obtained when response time is plotted as shown in Figure 8.4 shows a negative correlation with g.
- The intercept (height) of the line obtained when response time is plotted as shown in Figure 8.4 shows a negative correlation with g.
- The variability in the movement time (e.g. the standard deviation of individuals' movement times for a particular experimental condition) shows a negative correlation with g.

SAQ 8.3

It does seem possible that cognitive strategies might influence performance on both the Hunt and the S. Sternberg tasks. Most obviously, the standard instruction to 'respond as quickly as possible whilst trying not to make *any* errors' may well be interpreted rather differently by various individuals, some of whom will respond slowly in order to avoid making any errors, whilst others may be content to sacrifice accuracy for speed. There are other possibilities, too. For example, when scanning a list of 'target letters' in the Sternberg task, does one continue to scan to the end of the list after detecting the target, or does one stop immediately? Is it possible to scan several elements of the list in parallel, rather than serially? The evidence shows that the responses to this task are influenced by such variables. Likewise, Hunt's task can involve strategies, e.g. scanning for a straight line sticking up, which necessarily indicates a 'b' rather than an 'A', an 'a' or a 'B'.

9

Environmental and genetic determinants of personality and ability

BACKGROUND

Empirical studies of the extent to which personality and ability can be inherited provide valuable evidence as to the relative importance of biological and social factors in development. They can also show whether individual differences are 'real' characteristics of organisms (as trait/biological theorists would argue), or whether personality is best viewed as a 'social construction' – an inference drawn by others that need have no basis in fact.

Recommended prior reading

Chapter 5, 6, 7 and 8.

INTRODUCTION

The question of whether personality and ability are socially determined, or whether they are substantially influenced by our genes, is generally seen as being one of the most important issues in psychology. It is certainly one of the best researched, with studies of varying quality dating back to the early years of this century. So why is it so important to understand whether personality and intelligence are influenced by genes? The answer is quite simple. You will have gathered by now that there are two schools of individual difference theorists. The first, rooted in social psychology and sociology, claims that the *environment* is of paramount importance in determining how individuals behave. An extreme form of this view stresses that personality is not 'something inside' the individual at all. Instead, personality is inferred by other people, who may choose to 'see' constancies in behaviour that really do not exist. For these theorists, the only interesting issue in personality study is to examine the social process by which personality traits and abilities are attributed to others. On what *grounds* may I decide that John is mean? What evidence would it take to make me change my mind? You can see now that Howe (1988) took essentially this point with regard to intelligence.

Other researchers claim that personality and intelligence appear to have some clear links with the biology of the nervous system. That is, they believe that personality and intelligence are behavioural consequences of biological structures that really are 'inside' the individual. If this is so, it seems reasonable to ask whether these behaviours may be influenced by individuals' genetic make-up. If it can be shown that a trait is substantially influenced by genetics, this means that the characteristic is, in reality, 'inside' the individual, and that sociological and social psychological processes will be unable to explain individual differences completely.

No biologically based theorist goes so far as to say that the environment is unimportant in determining behaviour – after all, it is the only thing that we can alter. However, in view of the fact that environmental influences can be shown to be only about 25 per cent as powerful as genetic factors in determining the levels of some traits for some age groups, then it should be obvious that drastic environmental manipulations (e.g. special schooling programmes, improved housing, courses of psychotherapy) are unlikely to be completely effective in changing individuals' positions on these traits. Yet other characteristics (those with little or no genetic component) may benefit greatly from environmental interventions.

Many people seem to believe that if personality is influenced by genetics, then all members of the same family will be highly similar. This is not the case, of course. Since intelligence is thought to be influenced by many genes, each of which is derived randomly from one parent or the other, even if a trait does have a genetic basis there is likely to be substantial diversity within families. Some children may 'strike it lucky' and develop high levels of intelligence, sociability, etc., even though neither parent is outstanding with regard to these characteristics.

Before we start to examine the facts, it may be useful to look at the political implications of both an extreme environmental and an extreme hereditarian position. This may sound odd in a psychology text. However, the whole issue of heredity vs. environment has become heavily politicised, and generates strong emotions.

THE POLITICS OF INDIVIDUAL DIFFERENCES

Suppose that personality and abilities are completely shaped by the environment – the settings in which adults live and children develop, their interactions with other people, schools, parental attitudes to education, and so on. This is the view often taken by the political left, since it suggests that improved social conditions can allow everyone to develop to their full potential. Without such interventions, the outlook for a child being brought up in a poor environment is grim indeed – the accident of birth will mean that he or she is unlikely to develop a high IQ, for example. Since IQ is generally found to correlate with income, it means that the whole dreary cycle of poverty, low opportunity and low achievement is likely to continue from one generation to the next. On the other hand, children of the upper-middle classes, who enjoy a good education and have plenty of books, computers and encouragement will all (presumably) turn into geniuses, since there is nothing in their environment or their biological make-up to stop them from doing so. Similar arguments can be put forward for personality traits. A child who suffers a traumatic childhood will inevitably become depressed, anxious and neurotic. About the only good thing about this vision is that improvements to the disadvantaged underclass would be expected to lead to a dramatic improvement in their personality and ability.

Would the situation be any better if our traits were entirely genetically determined? Social background would not now affect IQ, since high ability would show itself no matter what happened to individuals as they grew up. A child born and reared under the most appalling social conditions might still turn out to be an Einstein. The expensive educations enjoyed by the middle classes would give them no advantage in terms of IQ and personality, and so in a meritocracy (a system in which people rise to positions of power and influence on the basis of individual merit) one would expect the power to devolve to high-ability people from both backgrounds – who will then sometimes marry each other. The children of such marriages are also likely to be of above-average ability (as we assume that ability is genetically determined) – the same is true for low-IQ individuals. So this too results in a split society, only this time based on ability rather than on the accident of being born into wealth.

Since schooling will predominantly affect a child's *knowledge* (and not their genetically determined *ability*), it probably will not matter too much if schools and universities are underfunded and crowded. What if there are clear racial or other group differences in IQ or personality traits? If members of each community tend to select partners from within that community (as seems likely in practice), these differences are unlikely to decrease over time – members of some ethnic groups will always end up being appointed to the top jobs. Worse is to follow. Since we suppose that IQ is determined purely by genetic factors, it is not difficult to increase the average IQ in the country. Indeed, this may be thought desirable since it may lead to greater economic competitiveness. For it to be achieved, it is merely necessary to ensure that high-IQ individuals produce more children (preferably with other high-IQ individuals) than do low-IQ individuals – a principle known as 'eugenics', which has been advocated by some early psychologists, as well as by dictators such as Hitler.

The latter view has, of course, been associated with the political right. Even if we ignore the implications of race differences and eugenics, both scenarios sound profoundly depressing to me. However, I mention these political fantasies (and no doubt reveal my ignorance of sociological principles!) in order to encourage you to understand some of the moral issues that can emerge from the simple question of whether individual differences arise because of nature or because of nurture – that is, because of genetic or environmental influences.

The unfortunate problem is that some psychologists and other social scientists seem to decide what the answer to the nature/nurture question *should* be, rather than looking at the evidence dispassionately. Many even argue that it is unethical to *examine* these issues, even if the methods used to do so are capable of yielding accurate results – an attitude that seems to smack of scientific Luddism.

In the sections that follow I have tried to survey the literature as objectively as possible, but you will quite probably hear rather different interpretations given by others, particularly sociologists and social psychologists, who are understandably keen to emphasise the importance of the *environment* in determining behaviour. Because of the importance of this issue, it is vital that you read the primary sources and critically evaluate the merits of any interpretation of the data – including, of course, my own.

METHODS FOR STUDYING THE NATURE/NURTURE ISSUE

You will probably remember that, during the process of conception, there is a 50-50 chance that each of the genes in the fertilised egg will be derived from the father or the mother – something rather like a vast game of musical chairs takes place, with two genes (one from the father, and one from the mother) trying to sit on one site at each position on the chromosome. This means that we would expect *about* 50 per cent of an individual's genetic material to come from their father, and the rest to come from their mother. A large number of the parents' genes will be identical (since it is the genes, after all, that determine whether the DNA produces a human hair, a frog's leg or an oak leaf), but some of the parents' genes will be different, i.e. the parents will show some *genetic variability*. This chapter considers whether individual differences in these genes do, in any way, relate to individual differences in personality or ability. This discipline is known as *behaviour genetics*.

The consequences of parents' genetic variability are rather well known so far as physical characteristics are concerned. Eye colour, hair colour, blood group, inability to taste the chemical phenylthiocarbamide and colour blindness are among the physical characteristics that can be inherited, and it can be shown that just a few genes determine each of these outcomes. That is, if the genetic make-up of the parents is known, it is possible to predict rather accurately the probability of (say) a particular hair colour.

Personality traits and abilities are rather different from these characteristics, in that they are *continuous* traits rather than taking just a few possible values. Thus geneticists suspect that most traits are influenced by a large number of genes, each of which makes a small influence in enhancing (or reducing) a person's level of a trait. Animal breeders have long known that it is possible to breed selectively individuals with certain physical characteristics. Cows that produce copious amounts of high-fat milk are repeatedly mated with bulls whose mother and sisters also produce large amounts of good-quality milk in the hope that, in some cases, the resulting calf will receive one set of 'high-milk-yielding' genes from each parent, and so will produce even more prodigious amounts of excellent-quality milk than either parent.

Animal breeders can also breed for psychological characteristics ('traits'), and so it is unsurprising that psychologists have also considered whether genetic factors underpin human abilities and personality. My neighbour's Rottweiler tries to attack me whenever I move towards her territory, whereas a golden retriever comes bounding up wagging her tail whenever I go through *her* garden gate. More formally, Tryon (1940) managed to breed selectively two strains of rat, some of which quickly learned how to run through a maze in search of food (described as 'maze bright') and others which were slow in learning to do this (referred to as 'maze dull'). The methods of *behaviour genetics* can be used to estimate the extent to which individuals' scores on psychological traits are influenced by their genes.

It follows that *if* a trait (such as general intelligence, extraversion, etc.) is influenced by our genetic make-up, we would expect individuals who have a similar genetic make-up to show similar scores on the trait. If genes have no influence on our intelligence (that is, if it is our environments alone that determine intelligence), we would not expect people who are genetically similar to have similar scores on the psychometric test unless they have also been brought up in similar environments.

This all sounds very straightforward, but there is of course one huge problem. People tend to be brought up within families. This means that genetically similar individuals (parents and their offspring) are often found to be living in the same place, sharing the benefits (or hardships) of a particular income level, and perhaps bringing to bear the same attitudes to education and learning that their parents gave to *them*. So although members of a family are genetically similar, it is *not* possible simply to conclude that any similarity between their scores on some psychological test implies that this trait has a genetic component. It is just as likely that social factors (income, attitudes, etc.) could cause their scores to be similar.

'Assortive mating' creates difficulties, too. This is the tendency of 'like to attract like' – couples may come together because they see in each other characteristics (environmentally or genetically determined) that they both share. High intelligence is a good example. It is fairly unusual for partners to show a massive discrepancy in their IQ. So can *this* explain any similarity in their offspring's intelligence? How can we tell the extent to which environmental or genetic factors influence personality or intelligence? The answer is to look at genetic similarity within families (as well as between families), although this method is rather beyond the scope of the present chapter.

Several different experimental designs have been used to examine the extent to which personality and ability traits are influenced by genetics and the environment.

Twin studies

Identical twins have identical genes; non-identical twins on average share only half the genes that vary in humans. Suppose that a trait is measured in many pairs of identical twins, and in pairs of non-identical twins, each pair of twins being brought up together in a normal family. If pairs of identical twins are found to have scores that are more similar than the scores of pairs of non-identical twins, this suggests that the trait has a genetic component – that is, that their greater genetic similarity *causes* them to have scores that are more similar than are those of pairs of non-identical twins. If pairs of identical twins are no more alike than pairs of non-identical twins, this suggests that the trait has no genetic component.

Very occasionally identical twins are separated at birth and reared in quite different environments. Studying *their* personality and abilities later in life can also yield valuable information about the genetics of personality and ability, since any similarity in trait scores can (arguably) be ascribed only to their identical genetic make-up.

SELF-ASSESSMENT QUESTION 9.1

What would you conclude if identical twins' scores on IQ tests were found to be no more similar than the scores of non-identical twins (who share only half their genes, on average)?

Family studies

Each parent shares about half their genes with each of their children, and this implies that the children will also, on average, share half their genes with each other. Figure 9.1 shows some other linkages. If a trait is influenced by genetic factors, one would expect children who are very similar genetically to show similar scores on the trait, and children who are less genetically similar to differ more. If the individual's environment determines the level of the trait, all children reared in the same environment (regardless of their genetic background) should show similar levels of the trait. Family units in which a grandchild of an older daughter may be brought up alongside uncles and aunts of a similar age may be useful here.

Adoption studies

These are valuable since they allow one to see the extent to which the environment can influence scores on a trait. An adopted child shares no variable genes with the other children in his or her adoptive family. If a study shows that adopted children generally have similar levels of a trait to other members of their adoptive family, this suggests that the trait is strongly influenced by the family environment, rather than by genetics.

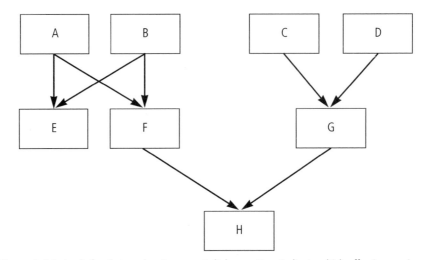

Figure 9.1 A simple family tree showing genetic linkages. Lines indicate which offspring receive about half of their genetic material from which other individuals. A, B, C and D are unrelated individuals. E and F are the children of A and B, whilst G is the child of C and D. H is the child of F and G. Siblings will share about half of their genes with each other, and with their parents, so E and F, E and A, F and A, E and B, G and C and G and D will each share about half of their genes. H will share about a quarter of her genes with her grandparents (A, B, C and D) and aunt or uncle

One has to be careful about the age of individuals in genetic studies. As Pedersen and Lichtenstein (1997) have observed, the relative importance of genetic and environmental effects is quite likely to vary with age for several reasons. First, some genes are known to influence behaviour only at specific times – the genes that control the production of certain hormones (and thus bring about puberty) are one example. Thus, even if a certain group of genes can potentially influence an individual's personality and intelligence, they need not all be active at all ages. Hence the extent to which our intelligence or personality is influenced by our genes is likely to vary over our lifespan simply because not all genes are influential all the time. Second, it might be that genetic influences on personality or ability are important only early in life. It seems quite possible that, as one gets older, the accumulation of experience and the variety of life events may become far more influential than our genetic make-up in determining how we think or behave, so perhaps genetic influences on personality and ability decline with age. Third, one can argue entirely the opposite case. It might be that the environment will tend to *magnify* any early genetically influenced individual differences in personality or behaviour. For example, a child who is identified as being of higher-than-average intelligence might be encouraged to take plenty of examinations, stretch his or her abilities to the limit by taking demanding university courses, and so on. These are fascinating empirical issues which cannot, unfortunately, be explored in any depth here.

The studies have been performed, and they indicate that our genetic background certainly continues to affect our personality and general intelligence into middle age and beyond (Pederson *et al.*, 1988; Loehlin, 1992; Pedersen and Lichtenstein, 1997). In the case of general intelligence, it seems that the influence of genetic factors is actually far more pronounced during middle age than during childhood or adolescence (McGue *et al.*, 1993). Thus it is emphatically *not* the case that our genetic background influences our behaviour only in childhood or adolescence. Rather, it seems to set us up for life.

THE METHODS OF QUANTITATIVE GENETICS

Let us consider what influences the personality or ability of children in a family. In the previous section I referred rather vaguely to 'environmental effects' as a blanket term for everything that is not genetic. However, geneticists distinguish between two types of environment. The first is the *shared environment* (sometimes also known as the *common environment* and hence denoted by 'C'), which basically represents the living conditions and the ethos experienced by all members of a family. It covers every influence that may make members of the same family show similar traits, including parental income, quality of housing, parental attitudes to education and discipline, nutrition, and any other environmental events that would be expected to influence the development of all members of the family in much the same direction.

Not every influence on a child will be shared by other children in the family. Friendships outside the family (e.g. with classmates) that are not shared with other family members, a good (or bad) relationship with a particular teacher, the effects of illnesses, disability or bullying, and every other experience that is not shared by other family members together form the individual's *unique environment* (generally referred to as 'E'). The shared environment is composed of influences that will make family members similar to one another, whereas the unique environment describes environmental influences that tend to make family members different from one another. In addition to these environmental influences, it is possible that genetic similarities between family members will also influence their levels of certain traits. We represent the influence of these genetic factors by 'A'.

We assume that individuals' scores on a particular test can be completely explained by these three sources of variance (shared environment, unique environment and genetic similarity), each of which can be expressed as a number between 0 and 1. Thus we may write:

$$\text{total variation} = 1 = A + C + E$$

The basic aim of these genetic analyses is to establish the values for A, C and E in the above equation – that is, to establish the relative importance of genetics, the shared environment and the unique environment in determining a particular behaviour.

It should be intuitively obvious that the only factor that could cause a 'family' of unrelated children (e.g. adopted or fostered children) to show similar scores on a test would be the common environment. The only factor that could cause identical twins reared in the same family to show different scores on a test would be the influence of the unique environment (as their genetic make-up and the shared environment are identical). The only factor that could cause identical twins who are separated after birth and reared in different environments to have similar levels of a trait would be their genetic similarity (since their common and shared environments are very different). So it is only necessary to administer a test to these children, and to calculate the correlation between the test scores of members of these groups, in order to be able to draw some rather powerful conclusions about the heritability of whatever trait is measured by the test. It is also possible to perform a few fancy calculations based on the relative similarity of the test scores of identical (monozygotic) and non-identical (dizygotic) pairs of twins.

SELF-ASSESSMENT QUESTION 9.2

Since dizygotic twins share half their genes and the common environment, we may write r_{dz} = 0.5A + C, whilst for monozygotic twins r_{mz} = A + C. Try to use a little elementary algebra to simplify these two equations for A and for C.

Suppose that many pairs of dizygotic twins were given the same ability test, and the scores of these twin-pairs were correlated together, giving $r = 0.4$. Suppose the experiment was repeated with monozygotic (identical) twins, giving $r = 0.6$. What would you conclude about the relative importance of the genetic make-up, shared environment and the unshared environment?

There are two main problems with the study outlined in SAQ 9.2. First, it must assume that the monozygotic twins are not more similar than non-identical twins for environmental (rather than genetic) reasons, e.g. being dressed similarly. The second problem is that measurement error (e.g. that brought about by using an unreliable test or thinking that twins are identical when they are not) can also be confused with variation due to the non-shared environment. Suppose that the correlations were found to be exactly zero for monozygotic and dizygotic twins because the test was completely riddled with measurement error. You should verify for yourself (using the equations given in the answer to SAQ 9.2) that the genetic effects and the shared environment would seem to have no influence on the trait, but that all of the variation would appear to arise from the unique environment. In a typical experiment (in which there is *some* measurement error) we may therefore expect the effect of the unique environment to be rather overestimated. Statisticians have developed ways of 'tweaking' the formulae to allow for this, but this is rather too detailed an issue for us to consider here.

You should be able to appreciate that it is possible to draw up systems of equations for other family members of known genetic similarity (e.g. cousins reared in the same environment) and so to estimate the relative importance of A, C and E by several different methods.

THE GENETICS OF ABILITY

Few issues in psychology have received as much attention as the origins of intelligence, perhaps reflecting the importance that we attach to this concept. Bouchard and McGue (1981) reviewed over 140 studies of the relative importance of genetic factors, shared environment and the unique environment for determining general intelligence. Their conclusion (and one that is entirely consistent with the later evidence) is that approximately 50 per cent of the variation in adult and child intelligence is attributable to our genes. This finding used to be highly controversial, with environmentalists such as Kamin (1974) bitterly disputing the evidence. However, most social scientists now accept that genetic factors can influence general intelligence (Snyderman and Rothman, 1987). The effects can be discerned very early in life, although the measurement of cognitive ability in young children is a notoriously difficult and unreliable process, and some studies must be discounted because they used inadequate tests.

Plomin (1988) has summarised a vast amount of data from twin, family and adoption studies. These reveal the following findings.

- Pairs of identical twins reared apart have IQs that correlate giving $r = 0.74$ (suggesting that genetic factors account for about 75 per cent of the variance in the IQ of any one child).
- Identical twins reared together have IQs that correlate 0.87, whilst fraternal (non-identical) twins reared together have IQs that correlate 0.53. Substituting these values into the formulae derived in the answer to SAQ 9.2, this suggests that IQ has a heritability of $2(0.87 - 0.53) = 0.68$, the shared environment accounts for $2 \times 0.53 - 0.87 = 0.19$ of the variation in IQ, and the unique environment explains the remaining 13 per cent of the variability.
- Pairs of unrelated children living together and adoptive parents and adoptive children show correlations in IQ of 0.23 and 0.20, suggesting that the shared environment explains about 20–25 per cent of the variation in IQ.

The really interesting findings concern the relative influence of the shared environment on IQ as children get older. Theorists such as Skinner seemed to believe that the childhood environment and childhood experiences should play an important part in children's eventual cognitive development. So, too, do parents who pay to send their children to expensive schools in order to develop their potential to the full. However, does the shared environment of childhood really influence adult IQ?

The answer seems to be a firm *no*. Studies of pairs of unrelated children brought up in the same family show that the correlations between their IQs fall to zero by adulthood – the shared environment has *no* influence on children's eventual cognitive ability. (Note that this applies to *all* children, not just those who are adopted. The purpose of considering adopted children is to eliminate genetic influences.) Family influences have no impact whatsoever on adult intelligence, which is certainly a good thing for those children reared under difficult circumstances.

A great many studies have examined the general intelligence of identical and non-identical twins who are brought up in a normal family environment. These studies are based on rather large samples – the Louisville Twin Study alone considers some 500 pairs of twins. Wilson (1983) reports the correlations between the cognitive functioning of pairs of twins during early life. Between the ages of 3 and 18 months, identical twins and non-identical twins show rather similar correlations (of the order of 0.55 to 0.7). However, at 18 months of age the correlation is 0.82 for identical twins but 0.65 for fraternal twins, the values at 24, 30 and 36 months being broadly similar. This suggests (as you should verify using the formulae derived in your answer to SAQ 9.2) that genetic factors seem to account for about a quarter to a third of the variation in the cognitive abilities of even these young infants. Later analyses suggest that the heritability increases from about 0.4 at 1 year of age to 0.57 at 4 years and 0.7 at 7 years (Cherny *et al.*, 1996).

What happens as children get older? It used to be supposed that their environments (learning experiences, schooling, etc.) become more varied and so the effects of genetic make-up on ability would decrease. In fact, quite the opposite is found. Thompson (1993, p. 112) cites evidence from the Western Reserve Twin Project (based on 148 pairs of identical twins and 135 pairs of fraternal twins aged 6–12 years) which suggests that general cognitive ability has a heritability of 0.5 at this age level (that is, genetic factors account for 50 per cent of the variation in the children's scores on the test), and that the shared environment accounts for an additional 42 per cent of the variance, with the unique environment having relatively little effect. In other words, the genes and the 'family ethos' are of almost equal importance as influences on the child's intelligence at this age.

After this age, the influence of the shared environment almost disappears. When the same experiment is repeated with adolescents, the genetic influence is much the same, but the shared environment has a negligible effect on the mental abilities of young teenagers (LaBuda *et al.*, 1987). This is a surprising finding. It seems that, at this age, it simply does not matter what family background, facilities, encouragement or difficulties the children enjoy – their intellectual ability appears to be influenced in equal measure by their genetic background and their non-shared environments. The influence of the family seems to have virtually no effect on the child's intellectual ability after the very early teenage years.

This raises some interesting issues concerning the effectiveness of educational interventions, suggesting (as it does) that any environmental intervention (e.g. 'hothousing' children by providing an enhanced non-shared environment) is unlikely to have the potential to change any child into a genius, since genetic factors will also influence the child's ultimate intellectual performance. The 'Head-Start' programmes in the USA were 1- or 2-year interventions designed to provide a stimulating pre-school experience for children from socially deprived backgrounds. At first the results seemed impressive, and the children's IQs increased by half a standard deviation. However, when the children were retested 7 to 10 years later, those who had taken part in the Head-Start programmes had IQs that were identical to those of control groups. Other studies, based on more intensive stimulation starting at a younger age, show an increase in IQ of approximately one-third of a standard deviation (Royce *et al.*, 1983; Ramey, 1992) after a similar time period. These findings suggest that the effects of an enriched environment at some critical stage of development are not as massive as had been expected. The results are consistent with the evidence that general intelligence has a substantial genetic component.

This is not necessarily a bad thing, of course. It means that even the most ghastly learning environment will not be able to 'pull down' all children's IQs. It also seems that factors outside the family are much more potent influences on the adolescent's IQ than any family influences, although family influences can be important for younger children. The most consistent finding to emerge from these hundreds of studies is that some children do appear to have a definite advantage in life when it comes to IQ, and that these genetic influences do not decline with age. About 50 per cent of the variability in IQ can be explained by a knowledge of individuals' genetic backgrounds, and this applies to adults at least as much as it does to children.

This is not to say that educational interventions should not be attempted. After all:

- the interventions are designed to improve educational performance rather than IQ, and since the studies never really sought to boost IQ, it may be unreasonable to conclude that because they cannot do so, no intervention is likely to prove effective in increasing intelligence;
- they may be able to motivate children to work hard, and motivational/attitudinal influences may have a profound influence on educational performance (although not necessarily on IQ);
- genetic factors account for only about 50 to 70 per cent of the variability, implying that environmental improvements can have a marked influence on IQ.

However, the evidence does show very clearly that theories which seek to 'explain' intelligence purely in terms of social processes will, at best, be able to explain 50 per cent of the variation in IQ. Although many of us would wish that it were not so, the literature indicates that an individual's genetic make-up is as important as *all* of their environmental influences in determining their ultimate level of intelligence. Children are simply not born with equal intellectual potential.

THE GENETICS OF PERSONALITY

The issue of the genetics of personality is much less controversial than the genetic basis of ability, simply because society does not really care too much whether an individual has an extreme personality type. Individuals who are three standard deviations above the mean on extraversion are, on the whole, treated in much the same way as individuals who are three standard deviations *below* the mean. They are not (some would add 'thankfully') encouraged to develop their extraversion to its maximum extent. Rates of pay will not be influenced by levels of extraversion. Thus the social consequences of having a particular type of personality are much less marked than those of ability.

Several studies have examined the extent to which the main personality traits are determined by genetic make-up, using the methodologies described above – for once again we make the assumption that an individual's position along a particular personality trait is influenced by the additive effects of a large number of genes. For example, John Loehlin (1992) used twin and adoption data to determine the extent to which each of the 'Big Five' personality factors of Costa and McCrea (Costa and McCrae, 1992a) is influenced by genetic make-up. The heritability values for these scales range from about 0.3 to 0.5 (the best-agreed factors of extraversion and neuroticism having the highest levels of heritability). Zuckerman (1991) provides useful summaries of the older literature, again showing that:

- the heritabilities are substantial;
- the influence of genetic effects does not disappear by adulthood;
- the shared (family) environment really plays a rather minor part in determining personality at any age, the non-shared environment being a much more potent influence on all personality traits.

For example, Table 9.1 shows the correlations between the personality-test scores of identical twins and fraternal twins for three broad types of personality factors (these are grouped, since not all investigators used the same scales), namely extraversion/sociability, neuroticism/emotionality, and psychoticism/impulsivity/unsocialised sensation-seeking. The figures in each column vary somewhat, since the studies used different tests (that varied in reliability and validity). You will see that some of these studies are based on *enormous* samples of identical and fraternal twins, and that there is a considerable degree of consistency in the results. If genetic make-up had no influence on personality, one would expect pairs of identical twins to have personality traits that were about as similar as pairs of fraternal twins – that is, the correlations in the 'I' columns in Table 9.1 should be about the same size as the correlations in the 'F' columns for the same trait. You do not need any fancy statistical analyses to see that this simply is not so. Pairs of identical twins have really quite similar levels of extraversion (r-values of between 0.46 and 0.61), whereas pairs of non-identical twins tend to be considerably less alike in their degree of extraversion (r-values ranging from 0.06 to 0.42). Similar trends can be seen for the other two main personality traits. This

Study	Age	Number of pairs		Personality trait					
				E-Sy		N-Emo		P-Imp	
		I	F	I	F	I	F	I	F
Loehlin and Nichols (1976)	18	490	317	0.61	0.25	0.54	0.22	0.54	0.32
Tellegen et al. (1988)	21	217	114	0.54	0.06	0.54	0.41	0.58	0.25
Rose (1988)	14–34	228	182	0.60	0.42	0.41	0.22	0.70	0.41
Floderus-Myrhed et al.	17–49	2279	3670	0.47	0.20	0.46	0.21	—	—
(1980)	17–49	2720	4143	0.54	0.21	0.54	0.25	—	—
Rose et al. (1988)	24–49	1027	2304	0.46	0.15	0.33	0.12	—	—
Rose et al. (1988)	24–49	1293	2520	0.49	0.14	0.43	0.18	—	—
Eaves and Young (1981)	31	303	172	0.55	0.19	0.47	0.07	0.47	0.28
Pedersen et al. (1988)	59	151	204	0.54	0.06	0.41	0.24	—	—

Table 9.1 Correlations between test scores of pairs of identical twins (I) and fraternal twins (F) (reared together) on personality scales assessing the three major dimensions of personality, namely extraversion (E-Sy), neuroticism (N-Emo) and psychoticism/impulsivity (P-Imp). Adapted from Table 3.2 of Zuckerman (1991)

strongly suggests that these three main personality traits have a substantial genetic component. When the correlations from the Floderus-Myrhed studies (chosen because they involve the largest samples of twins) are entered into the formula shown in the answer to SAQ 9.2, the estimated heritability of extraversion can be seen to be of the order of 0.54 to 0.66. Similarly, the influence of the shared environment is essentially zero.

Like the finding that the shared environment is of little importance in determining adult intelligence, the last-mentioned result is, I feel, one of the most remarkable discoveries in the whole of psychology. Given all that has been written about the importance of the family in childhood, it is truly amazing to discover that personality seems to be almost entirely uninfluenced by the type of family in which one is brought up. It matters not a jot whether a child is brought up in a gentle, kind, loving family or a violent, abusive one – any influences on the child's later personality must be understood in terms of the genes that are inherited from their parents, and *not* in terms of their childhood experiences *per se*. The correlation between genetically dissimilar children who are brought up (adopted) in the same family is typically almost zero (Zuckerman mentions an *r*-value of 0.07).

As Brody and Crowley (1995) have observed, 'if shared environmental influences are close to zero, most of the variables that have typically been studied by developmental psychologists have little or no influence on personality' and 'it is usually a mistake to study environmental influences on personality and intelligence without a consideration of possible genetic effects'. Given that virtually *all* of the studies point to the same conclusion, it is difficult to argue with this analysis. It certainly appears that all of the ingenious environmentally based developmental theories of Rogers, Freud, Skinner, Bandura, etc. are simply incorrect (at least in that the family environment spectacularly fails to influence the two major personality traits, namely extraversion and neuroticism). This kind of result is not at all popular with social psychologists or sociologists, and I personally would wish that the evidence pointed towards a social explanation of personality and ability, but it simply does not do so.

The evidence suggests that personality is determined by a mixture of genetic factors and the non-shared environments of children – the influence of particular teachers on a child, the 'special' relationship between a child and other members of his or her family, or the influence of friends from outside the family. However, it is necessary to qualify this assertion somewhat. *Some* personality traits (or behaviours) *have* been found to be substantially influenced by the common environment. For example, Stevenson's (1997) twin study examined the extent to which pro-social behaviour (empathy, helping behaviour and altruism), antisocial behaviour (aggression or destructive behaviour) and sociability were genetically determined. Antisocial behaviour was found to have a comparatively small genetic component (0.24, as opposed to 0.54 and 0.67, respectively) and was the only behaviour for which the influence of the shared environment was substantial (0.54, as opposed to 0.2 and 0, respectively). Thus it is clear that some behaviours, at least, can be moulded by the family – it just so happens that the main personality traits are not shaped in this way.

The study by Pedersen *et al.* involved 59-year-old males, whilst participants in the studies by Loehlin and Nichols (1976) and Tellegen *et al.* (1988) were aged 18 and 21 years, respectively. The influence of genetic factors on personality does not seem to decline with age. If it did, Pedersen's identical twins and fraternal twins would show similar correlations. If anything, the data suggest that genetic influences become relatively *more* important as one gets older.

SUMMARY

We now know a great deal about the relative importance of environmental and genetic influences on personality or intelligence. The problem is that social psychologists, sociologists and the like are unhappy with the idea that one's genetic make-up can moderate (and arguably dominate) the effects of the environment, whilst eugenicists are reluctant to acknowledge the very potent influence of the unshared environment. There are certainly many facts that the simple models described above cannot explain, e.g. the 'Flynn effect'. It has been noted that IQ scores are rising steadily, year by year, throughout much of the world (Flynn, 1987). Eugenicists stress the importance of genetic influences on IQ, and point to evidence that low-IQ individuals tend to produce more children than high-IQ individuals. Thus they would predict that global IQ should be *falling*! Given that the annual increase in IQ cannot be attributed to genetic factors, what aspects of the children's shared or unshared environments can be causing it to rise? The answer is that no one really knows, although improvements in nutrition have been suggested (Lynn, 1993). Vitamin supplements have been found to have a dramatic effect on children's IQ even in the UK (Benton and Roberts, 1988). However, the increase in IQ remains unexplained.

Plomin *et al.* (1985) suggested that the child's unique environment may itself be influenced by genetic factors, which at first glance seems a bizarre proposition. However, suppose that intelligence/personality *is* substantially influenced by genetic factors. It seems quite likely that the intelligent child will actively seek out intellectually stimulating environments – playing chess, asking parents for educational games, joining several clubs at school, reading educational magazines, and perhaps making friends who are also of above-average ability. Thus the child's environment may be determined, at least in part, by his or her genetic make-up (i.e. intelligence). The lifestyle of the extravert (their unshared environment) may also be created so as to allow the free expression of extraverted behaviour, whilst that of the neurotic may be designed to be as safe, predictable and unthreatening as possible. Thus the types of unshared environments experienced by individuals may, at least in part, be influenced by their genetic make-up. This is an interesting idea that is beginning to be explored.

Much exciting research involves examining the effects of individual genes on behaviour, and on scores on tests of personality and ability. One of the most promising findings here is that a gene has been identified which seems to be closely related to levels of anxiety (Lesch *et al.*, 1996). It is remarkably fortunate that a gene which has such a strong link to a psychological construct has been discovered since, as argued earlier, we would expect traits such as anxiety, intelligence and extraversion to be influenced by many genes, each of which exerts a relatively small influence.

Given the exciting nature of the findings discussed in this chapter, it is necessary to remind ourselves of one basic point before moving on to the next chapter. You will recall that there is some opposition to the very notion of traits. Intelligence is seen not as a real property of people, but as a convenient social abstraction (Howe, 1988), whilst personality traits have received the same treatment at the hands of some social psychologists (Hampson, 1997). The finding that intelligence and personality traits all have a very substantial genetic component seems to suggest that neither of these views can be entirely correct, and that the individual differences that we measure by means of psychological tests are, to a considerable extent, the behavioural consequences of individual differences in certain biological structures.

SUGGESTED ADDITIONAL READING

There are several excellent texts and journal papers that introduce basic genetic concepts (such as those described here) before going on to describe more complex issues, such as multivariate models. These include (in no particular order) Bouchard (1993), Stevenson (1997), Bouchard (1995), Pedersen and Lichtenstein (1997), Plomin and Daniels (1987), Plomin (1988), Plomin and Rende (1991), Brody and Crowley (1995) and Eaves *et al.* (1989), and there are plenty of others. Kamin (1974) gives a very early, strongly environmentalist view. However, it might also be worth reading some reviews of that book before taking his arguments to heart.

ANSWERS TO SELF-ASSESSMENT QUESTIONS

SAQ 9.1
You would conclude either that the trait has a genetic component, or that it is influenced by the environment and the identical twins are treated more similarly than non-identical twins. I have not considered the latter possibility in much detail in the text, since studies suggest that the types of ways in which identical twins are treated more similarly than fraternal twins (e.g. being dressed similarly) are unlikely to have much effect on their personality or intelligence.

SAQ 9.2
Subtracting the two equations gives

$$r_{mz} - r_{dz} = 0.5A + 0$$

Multiplying both sides by 2 gives $A = 2(r_{mz} - r_{dz})$

Multiplying both sides of the first equation by 2 and subtracting the second equation gives:

$$2r_{dz} - r_{mz} = 0 + C$$

So substituting in the values for the correlations:

$$A = 2(0.6 - 0.4) = 0.4$$

$$C = 2 \times 0.4 - 0.6 = 0.2$$

Hence

$$E = 1 - A - C = 1 - 0.4 - 0.2 = 0.4$$

showing that, in this hypothetical case, genetic influences and the unique environment are of equal importance, and each is about twice as important as the shared environment in determining scores on that trait.

These important results were included as a self-assessment question since it might be easier (and safer) to derive the formulae from first principles during an examination, rather than trying to memorise them.

10

Mood states and motivational states

BACKGROUND

Most of this book has been concerned with traits, i.e. those stable features of behaviour that are classified as ability and personality. However, in this chapter we shall take a brief look at the psychology of mood and motivation, which are generally regarded as *states* that vary over time, and are sensitive to life events.

Recommended prior reading

Chapter 5.

INTRODUCTION

So far we have only considered stable personality characteristics, and have made the assumption that traits – the main building blocks of personality and ability – are more or less constant features of the individual. The wealth of evidence that links personality and ability traits to the biology of the nervous system (e.g. work on inspection time and reaction time, the discovery that personality and ability have a very substantial genetic component, and research into the psychophysiology of personality) indicates that this approach is broadly correct. We seem to have identified the main dimensions of personality, and shown that they are characteristics of individuals, rather than social processes or situations.

No one has ever suggested that the trait model is all that is needed, as it fails to address two rather obvious types of individual differences, namely moods[10.1] and motivation. This chapter will look at some basic theories of mood and

---

[10.1] Whether or not moods are the same as emotions is a fairly contentious issue. See, for example, Morris (1985) and Cooper (1997).

motivation. The often thorny issues concerning the ways in which these can be assessed are described in Chapter 19.

The main characteristics of both emotions and motivation are as follows:

- they change over time; and
- they will often change in response to situations.

For example, many of us have experienced feelings of euphoria (or despair!) after taking part in a race or hearing the results of an examination, feelings of terror after a near miss on the roads, or surges of love following someone's kind act – these are all examples of moods.

Motivation is what propels us into action. You will remember the importance that Freud attached to sex, but other factors too can motivate us. Fear of failure may drive us to study hard before an examination. Hunger-pangs may lead us into the kitchen when we are working late into the night. However, once we have satisfied our lust/completed the examination/nibbled the biscuits, our interest in sex/psychology/food is likely to decline for a while. Thus these motivating variables, too, are states rather than traits.

Considerably less is known about the psychology of moods and motivation than is known about personality and ability traits, and I believe that there is a very good reason for this. Measures of traits are immensely useful in many branches of applied psychology, e.g. for identifying those job applicants who have the greatest ability in a particular area, for deciding which individuals are likely to be stable enough to cope with the stresses of living for long periods in a submarine or spacecraft, or to help to determine whether a child appears to be dyslexic. Knowing a person's position on the main personality and ability traits can allow one to predict how that individual will generally behave. However, as we argued earlier, states are both situation-specific and transient.

Worse still, a huge number of cognitive variables may affect states. The emotions that you experience when a stranger pours a drink over you will vary enormously depending on whether or not you believe it was an accident. We can also evaluate whether or not we are experiencing negative moods ('stress') and explore our options for reducing such feelings (e.g. dropping out of university, improving our time-management skills, blaming lecturers' unrealistic expectations rather than ourselves, or heading for the bar). Different individuals may adopt different cognitive 'coping strategies' when faced with stressful life events, and these will influence their resulting moods (e.g. Folkman and Lazarus, 1980). Thus states are influenced by both external events and internal processes (such as coping strategies).

Because states vary over time and from one situation to another, and may be heavily dependent on self-monitoring of mood and the use of coping strategies, a single measure of mood state is really not much use for predicting how a person will react next week or next month, or in another situation. Thus measures of mood are of limited use in areas of applied psychology such as personnel selection and guidance.

Much the same applies to tests measuring motivation. At first sight, this claim seems rather odd. In the case of personnel selection, for example, one might have thought that it would be useful to assess applicants' motives for applying for a post. However, even if we assume that motives can be assessed accurately, the motives that impel one to join an organisation (e.g. a desperate need to pay off one's debts, a need for feelings of self-worth as a result of being employed) may be rather different from the motives that keep an individual in the post (good social atmosphere, intrinsic enjoyment of 'trouble-shooting'), which is why it makes rather little sense to take a 'snapshot' of motives on one occasion.

Of course, states may be much more important to us *as individuals* than are traits. For example, bouts of anxiety or depression may make us feel intensely miserable – the motivation to drink or gamble may prove irresistible, and a need to 'put down' or humiliate the other partner may spell the end of many a relationship. However, with the exception of educational and clinical psychology, psychologists tend not to be too keen to explore these interesting questions.

It is also necessary to consider which *aspect* of states we should assess. When measuring traits there is only one sensible thing to assess, namely the person's level of the trait, which is assumed to be a stable feature of that individual. However, many more options are available when measuring mood or motivational states. For example, one could choose to measure:

- a person's level of the state(s) at one particular instant, e.g. their level of anxiety prior to an examination;
- the extent to which an individual's state score changes between two situations, e.g. their level of anxiety before an examination minus their level of anxiety when sitting relaxing on a beach;
- a person's *average* level of the state(s), e.g. the average strength of a person's sex drive over a period of weeks or months;
- the variability of a person's state(s) from hour to hour, day to day or week to week. Some individuals' levels of anxiety may vary widely from hour to hour or from day to day, possibly (although not necessarily) as a result of a rich variety of life events, whilst other people may have levels of anxiety that are remarkably consistent over time;
- periodic fluctuations in states, e.g. the extent to which a person's level of state(s) can be predicted by some regular daily, weekly, monthly or annual cycles, such as circadian rhythms, or the yearly cycles of seasonal affective disorder;
- the speed with which a person's score on a state changes following some intervention, e.g. the speed with which levels of anxiety return to their habitual level after a person is exposed to a standard anxiety-inducing stimulus, such as an unexpected loud noise.

Whilst with traits it was only necessary to try to understand which variables affected the *level* of the trait (e.g. the biological basis of intelligence), it is clear that any comprehensive study of moods and motivational states will need to consider all of the above-mentioned variables, at least. This makes it difficult to construct and test any comprehensive theories of mood and motivation, and ensures that the field is far too broad to be covered in any depth in this chapter! For those who are interested in such issues, I have summarised some of the empirical results in Cooper (1997).

SELF-ASSESSMENT QUESTION 10.1

Which aspects of mood can usefully be studied experimentally?

DIMENSIONS OF MOOD AND MOTIVATION

Mood

Much of the research on mood has taken place because of interest in its clinical consequences, e.g. the development of tests to assess patients' levels of anxiety and depression. Thus many inventories have been designed to measure depression, anxiety, hopelessness, 'negative affect' and the like, with rather few attempting to assess the more pleasant moods, such as elation, sociability or *joie de vivre*. There are two problems with this approach. First, it means that different investigators may have devised scales that measure the same construct, but may have labelled these constructs differently. One person's 'anxiety' scale may measure precisely the same thing as another theorist's scale of 'state neuroticism', 'tense arousal' or 'negative affect', and this can create enormous confusion until the scale items are jointly factored to reveal the extent of their overlap. The second problem is that this *ad hoc* approach to the construction of mood scales may leave certain important aspects of mood unmeasured. Apart from the work of Storm and Storm (1987) (which did not use factor analysis) and a little early work by Cattell (mentioned in Cattell, 1973), there has been little attempt to ensure that mood scales – even supposedly comprehensive ones – actually measure the full range of possible moods. Different mood theorists tend to use different samples of items and so discover different numbers of factors.

Re-analysis of the correlations between mood scales (Watson and Tellegen, 1985) and hierarchical factor analyses of mood items drawn from the major mood scales (such as McConville and Cooper, 1992b) reveals five primary mood factors: depression, hostility, fatigue, anxiety and extraversion (also known as 'positive affect'). Since the first four of these are very substantially intercorrelated, it is possible to group these four scales together and call them 'negative affect'. Thus one can conclude that there are either five main dimensions (the five primary factors) or two main dimensions ('positive affect' and 'negative affect') of mood.

It is a great pity that the terms 'positive affect' and 'negative affect' were used to describe the two main dimensions of mood, since there is much confusion in the literature about what these scales mean – you will often find misunderstandings about this in journal articles and in books. The key point is that positive and negative affect are *not* opposite ends of the same dimension of mood. Instead, they represent two very different aspects of mood. Negative affect is recognisable as the proverbial 'bad mood' (feelings of depression, anxiety, anger, etc.), but the opposite of negative affect is *not* positive affect. Instead, positive affect refers to feelings of energy, enthusiasm and high activity level. A person who scores high on positive affect would report feeling active, excited and enthusiastic; someone who scores low on positive affect would report feeling drowsy or sluggish. Individuals scoring high on negative affect would describe themselves as distressed, jittery or anxious, whereas those scoring low on negative affect would describe themselves as calm and content. However, it is quite possible that some important aspects of mood have not been found, simply because no one has asked the relevant questions when compiling mood questionnaires. It would be very useful if someone could follow Cattell's personality sphere approach for mood items, and fully explore the nature of mood.

There are some problems with all of this work, which is why it has been discussed only briefly. The obvious drawback is that an inappropriate method of factor analysis has been used. As will be argued in Chapter 19, it is really necessary to carry out longitudinal studies (based on P or chain-P technique) in order to identify the test items that tend to move up and down together, thus forming a state. Such research simply has not been attempted for most of these questionnaires. Furthermore, it is not entirely obvious where the items came from, how synonyms were eliminated, and how the tedium of completing the questionnaires may have affected the nature of the factors that emerged.

SELF-ASSESSMENT QUESTION 10.2

List some adjectives that might describe:

(a) high positive affect;

(b) high negative affect;

(c) low positive affect;

(d) low negative affect.

Motivation

Even less is known about the main dimensions of motivation. Freud suggested that sex and aggression were the fundamental forms of motivation, although the complex transformations of these basic drives (e.g. the orally fixated individual who achieves sexual satisfaction by eating milk puddings) make this aspect of Freudian theory, like so many others, almost impossible to test. Cattell has identified around 20 main dimensions of motivation, and has developed a test (the Motivation Analysis Test) to measure them. However, as is shown in Chapter 19, it seems most unlikely that this test works properly.

Apter *et al.* have coined the terms 'telic' and 'paratelic' states to distinguish between essentially goal-oriented activities (e.g. reading a statistics book, making a sandwich, walking to work) and those that involve focusing on feelings about the self (e.g. feeling bored, noticing feelings of hunger, enjoyment of walking for pleasure). They suggest that there are four main goals, which could be interpreted as four main forces of motivation. These are physiological needs (e.g. avoiding danger, reducing pain, overcoming strong hunger), social goals (e.g. activities that lead to feelings of status, power or affiliation/'belonging'), goals that are related to self-esteem (e.g. obtaining a degree in psychology, being seen to have a stable relationship) and those goals that involve family and friends (e.g. looking after a sick relative). This suggests that some activities are intrinsically satisfying (and so may perhaps be regarded as basic drives) and are performed for this reason. Listening to music is one obvious example. Other activities are performed as a means to some other end (e.g. someone enduring an awful job because the pay allows them to indulge their hobbies). Apter and his colleagues (Apter, 1975) have studied how, why and when people 'flip' between these two types of motivation, and the emotional and other consequences of doing so.

However, this theory lacks any firm basis in fact. It sprang from introspections, it is not entirely clear that the four categories described above are independent, and it is not entirely obvious how it can all be empirically tested. It also assumes that we know – or can know (if we introspect) – our true reasons for performing some action, which seems a little restrictive. There are, in any case, more sophisticated theories (such as Cattell's, which is discussed in Chapter 19, since it is closely linked to some important measurement issues), so Apter's work will not be discussed in greater detail.

Overview

Having read this far, you can see that the psychology of mood is not particularly well understood. About five main dimensions of mood have been discovered, and these generally seem feasible (corresponding quite neatly to certain clinical syndromes). However, I argue that several important aspects of mood may have yet to be discovered. The situation is far worse when we turn to the psychology of motivation. Here there is an almost total lack of knowledge of the main motivational states, and it certainly seems that we cannot assess any of them using questionnaires, for Cattell's Motivation Analysis Test simply does not work, and others seem to measure personality traits rather than mood states. Thus there is plenty of potential for further research here.

EVENTS THAT INFLUENCE MOOD LEVEL

Environmental effects

In this section we shall ignore motivational states, partly in order keep the chapter to a reasonable length, and partly because much less is known about the factors that influence human motivational states than about those which influence moods.

It is surprisingly easy to alter levels of mood experimentally, using the 'Velten technique' (Velten, 1968; Martin, 1990) and its derivatives. In the original version of this technique, subjects read a standard series of statements and were asked to try to experience the mood implied by them. The first statements are fairly innocuous (e.g. 'I'm feeling a little "down" today'), but they soon plumb the depths of despair (e.g. 'I feel so wretched that I just want to die'), and after working their way through the series of cards individuals really do seem to feel the depression. This is reflected in their scores on questionnaires, and also in other 'objective tests' of depression (such as longer decision times). Thus this does seem to be a genuine effect, rather than some kind of 'demand characteristic' (in which the participant sees the purpose of the experiment and resolves to give the experimenter the sort of results that they want). The two main problems with the technique are that:

- for reasons that are not at all well understood, it simply does not appear to work well for men (Morris, 1985), and so most studies using the technique are performed on female samples; and
- little attempt has been made to use the Velten technique to induce moods other than anxiety/depression.

Following Velten's work, other interventions (such as viewing video-clips and listening to extracts of music) have also been used.

Aficionados of music, literature, drama and film will probably find the above account rather unsurprising. *Of course* reading emotionally charged literature will affect our moods – that is probably why we enjoy it. However, the technique does provide a convenient way of changing moods in the laboratory, and can be used in experiments to investigate many of the variables discussed in the previous section (e.g. by assessing the time-course of mood change), the only problem being that few of the experiments have actually been attempted.

Life events, both positive and negative, also affect mood. What *is* surprising is the very substantial impact of minor 'hassles' (such as rainy weather, missing a train or losing an umbrella) on mood (e.g. Gruen *et al.*, 1988). Likewise, apparently trivial *positive* events (such as finding some small change left in a public telephone) can induce pleasant moods (Isen and Levin, 1972).

Physiological effects

Life soon becomes complicated when we turn to the physiological causes of mood, as a bewildering variety of chemicals can influence moods – yet it is not nearly so clear whether levels of mood are normally associated with elevated (or lowered) levels of certain neurotransmitters, such as the catecholamines. As Schnurr (1989) observes, the evidence now seems to suggest that moods such as depression are not simple functions of the levels of these chemicals, and not all depressed individuals show similar (low) levels of these chemicals.

Cognition and anxiety

One state that has been well researched is anxiety, one of the primary mood factors mentioned at the start of this chapter. Several questionnaires have been designed to measure this state, most of them containing rather unsubtle items such as 'how anxious do you feel right now?'. Of these, Spielberger's 'State–Trait Anxiety Inventory' (STAI) (Spielberger *et al.,* 1970) is a well-known, reliable and valid measure of both the state of anxiety and its corresponding trait (habitual level of anxiety). Scores on the trait version of the STAI correlate substantially with scores on Eysenck's 'neuroticism' scale, suggesting that anxiety is an important component of neuroticism (M. W. Eysenck, 1992).

There is general acceptance that feelings of anxiety are associated with many psychiatric conditions (including phobias, panic disorder, obsessive-compulsive disorder, post-traumatic stress disorder) as well as 'generalised anxiety disorder' (DSM-IV criteria) itself, whilst anyone who has experience of taking examinations, public speaking, acting, or asking someone for a date will have felt its milder forms.

Jeffrey Gray's work on anxiety, mentioned in Chapter 6, was initially targeted at examining how anxiety-reducing drugs (such as alcohol and benzodiazepines) operate. In fact there is clear evidence that various anti-anxiety drugs work by affecting a part of the brain known as the 'septo-hippocampal system', part of the limbic system discussed in Chapter 6. Gray could tell this by noting that anxiety-reducing drugs and surgical interference with this area of the brain (in rats) produced almost identical changes in behaviour (Gray, 1982, 1985). He also suggested that anxiety is experienced when we encounter novelty, i.e. when the world does not behave as we expect. An unexpected noise downstairs late at night or an unnoticed car heading towards us as we cross the road will lead to feelings of anxiety (a view which has some interesting but unexplored links with Kelly's personality theory).

However, as Michael Eysenck (1992) observes, *pleasant* unexpected events (e.g. winning the lottery) are unlikely to make us anxious, which suggests that the theory is incomplete. In particular, because the theory is based on an animal model, it cannot include cognitive processes (e.g. an appraisal of how one can best *deal* with feelings of anxiety) that are essentially human. Nor is the sensitivity-to-novelty aspect of the theory well supported by physiological data.

Since a physiologically based theory seems to have some limitations, can a cognitive theory fare any better? Perhaps anxiety arises in conjunction with certain types of cognitive activity. For example, suppose that a person remembers only the unpleasant, threatening stories from the daily newspapers.

It seems reasonable to suggest that he or she will soon develop a view that the world is a dangerous, hostile place, and will appear anxious. An individual who remembers both the good and the bad news stories should be less likely to become anxious. Aaron Beck's theory (e.g. Beck and Emery, 1985) makes essentially this point. The main problem with the theory is that it does not seem to be particularly well supported by the empirical data. Experiments designed to detect 'retrieval biases' (the tendency to remember threatening rather than non-threatening information) do not find that these biases are more pronounced in highly anxious individuals (e.g. Mogg *et al.*, 1987). Moreover, whilst Bower's theory of state-dependent memory (e.g. Bower, 1981) has excited much interest among cognitive psychologists, it says rather little about individual differences in mood and cognition, and so will not be considered here.

Michael Eysenck's hypervigilance theory is well supported by empirical results. He suggests (Eysenck, 1992) that anxiety is related to the amount of attention that is paid to potentially threatening stimuli in the environment. For example, in one experiment (Eysenck and Byrne, 1992) participants were seated in front of a computer screen, given a button to hold in their left hand and another to hold in their right hand, and asked to press the left-hand button if the word 'left' appeared on the screen, and the right-hand button if the word 'right' appeared on the screen. Their reaction time was then recorded. However, the word 'left' or 'right' was not presented on its own on the screen – two other words or groups of letters were presented too, and the participants were asked to ignore these. Sometimes the other words were two 'nonsense words', composed of random letters, sometimes they were two pleasant words (e.g. 'happy', 'relaxed'), sometimes two neutral words (e.g. 'table', 'shopping'), and sometimes two socially threatening words (e.g. 'failure', embarrassed') or two physically threatening words (e.g. 'murder', 'cancer').

If highly anxious people spent more time processing the environment for signs of threat, then they might be expected to slow down when they found the words 'left' or 'right' – that is, once they saw threatening words on the screen they would process them more deeply than would non-anxious individuals. This is (broadly) what Eysenck and Byrne found. An unpublished experiment of my own gave the same kind of result. It involved taking low-state-anxious subjects and using music to induce either high state anxiety or low state anxiety before they took part in the experiment. Once again, high-state anxious individuals slowed down when faced with threatening words, whereas low-state-anxious people did not, which again supports Eysenck's theory. The only real question is whether hypervigilance is a cause of high anxiety, a consequence of high anxiety, or whether some other variable(s) lead to both feelings of high anxiety and hypervigilant behaviour.

Cognitive coping strategies are also thought to alter mood, the basic model assuming that individuals may realise that they are feeling stressed or anxious, and decide to do something about it. Lazarus (1991) suggests specific links between the way in which individuals appraise their relationship with their environment and the emotion (mood) that is felt. Zeidner (1995) makes the point that, since general ability may influence the process of appraisal of threat (and the number of coping options considered), it should also have an indirect influence on the moods experienced in stressful situations. The nature of coping strategies is both extensive and well researched, although it is not entirely clear whether tests measuring 'coping mechanisms' are distinct from those that measure personality traits. However, the stress and coping literature is really rather too complex to explore here in any detail. The crucial point is that it seems rather likely that our experience of negative emotions will be related to our perceptions of their origins, our options for dealing with them, and the success of the coping strategies adopted in any particular situation.

The cyclical nature of mood

The time-course of moods has also been extensively studied, although one immediately encounters a formidable methodological problem. It is extremely difficult to separate the effects of time from the effects of life events. For example, suppose it was found that individuals showed a dip in certain moods each evening. Would this indicate that these moods were under the control of some 'biological clock' that causes the levels of mood to rise and fall with a particular frequency (e.g. every 24 hours)? The answer is, of course, that it would not. Moods may dip at a particular time of day because of fatigue, the physiological after-effects of a large dinner, or a whole host of other factors that just happen to occur at the same time each day because we tend to live fairly regular lifestyles (getting up and eating at approximately the same times each day).

Some studies have circumvented this problem by monitoring the mood of individuals who are kept in a laboratory in which there are no windows and the length of the 'day' is artificially changed (generally increased) from its 24-hour norm. If the daily frequency of moods changes, this will indicate that the moods are a by-product of life events. If the moods remain locked to their 24-hour cycle, this would suggest that they are under the direct control of a biological clock, possibly mediated by chemicals such as cortisol. One such study found that individuals' levels of happiness were influenced both by their life events and by the 24-hour cycle (Boivin *et al.*, in press), suggesting that this mood is, to some extent, under physiological control.

Several studies also suggest that a 7-day cycle influences mood levels (e.g. Larsen and Kasimatis, 1990). However, it is not altogether clear whether the 7-day cycle is biological in origin, or whether it reflects social habits that happen to be tied to a 7-day week (perhaps socialising at weekends and feeling gloomy when returning to work on Monday).

SELF-ASSESSMENT QUESTION 10.3

What influences mood level?

FACTORS THAT AFFECT THE VARIABILITY OF MOOD

Mood variability is a particularly interesting issue, since there are remarkably large individual differences in the extent to which people's moods change over time. For example, Chris McConville (1992) asked people to complete a mood scale each day for about 30 days. Figure 10.1 shows the daily mood scores of two participants in this study. It can be seen that one participant shows considerable variability from day to day, whilst the other person's moods vary relatively little.

It is a well-established finding that *all* of a person's moods vary to a similar and characteristic extent (Wessman and Ricks, 1966). This implies that we can regard mood variability as a kind of trait, and postulate some type of 'regulating mechanism' that controls the extent to which individuals' moods swing either side of their habitual level. However, the mechanisms that underlie mood variability are not at all well understood. When mood variability is correlated with the main personality studies, there is an almost complete lack of agreement between studies. Some have found that extraversion affects mood variability, whilst others have not, and some have found that neuroticism has a powerful effect, whilst others have not. Moreover, some have found that psychoticism has an effect, whilst others have not (McConville and Cooper, 1992a). We simply do not know why individual differences in mood variability are found, or whether any underlying regulatory mechanism has a physiological basis.

However, mood variability does seem to show a very substantial correlation with levels of depressed mood among normal people (Larsen and Kasimatis,

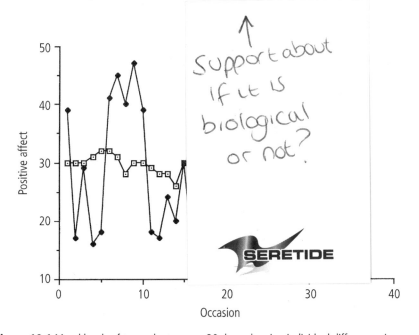

Figure 10.1 Mood levels of two volunteers on 30 days, showing individual differences in variability of mood (from McConville, 1992).

1990; McConville and Cooper, 1996). Depressed individuals seem to have remarkably variable moods, in strange contrast to the *Diagnostic and Statistical Manual* (DSM) definitions, which would appear to suggest that flattening of affect (i.e. low variability) is associated with depression. Similar results have been reported for clinically depressed patients (Hall *et al.*, 1991) so this does seem to be a fairly reliable finding. It implies that the level of one mood (depression) is related to the variability of other moods (positive affect and negative affect), although it is not at all clear whether feelings of depression cause mood swings, mood swings cause depression, or some other variable(s) influence both mood variability and depression.

AVERAGE MOOD AND PERSONALITY

Cattell (Cattell, 1973; Cattell and Kline, 1977) has made the eminently sensible suggestion that individuals' average levels of moods should be closely related to their personality. After all, some items in personality questionnaires refer to feelings (e.g. 'I am generally an anxious sort of a person'), as well as to behaviours, so it would be amazing if items such as these did not correlate with a person's average level of anxious mood (assessed by administering a questionnaire designed to measure state anxiety on several occasions and averaging the results). In fact this is what the literature shows.

If an individual is given a scale that measures some state (e.g. anxiety, positive affect or negative affect) on several occasions, their data may be plotted rather as shown in Figure 10.2. Here the shaded area shows an

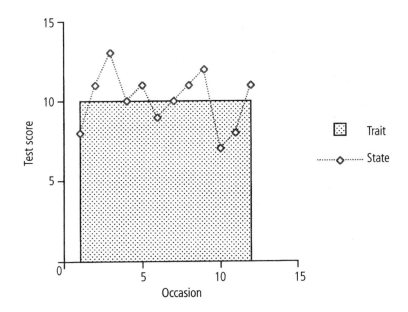

Figure 10.2 Results of adminstering a mood scale to one individual on 12 occasions.
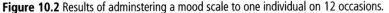

individual's average (habitual) score on that state, which should correspond to the trait. Hence the logical implication of this approach is that *each personality state may have a corresponding mood state*. Sure enough, the two main mood states (positive affect and negative affect) do measure the same thing as Cattell's 'state extraversion' and 'state anxiety' scales from the Eight State Questionnaire (Cooper and McConville, 1989), although the nearest that we have to state measures of psychoticism would seem to be impulsivity. There is no obvious mood state corresponding to openness, conscientiousness or agreeableness, and it would be interesting to rectify this using the techniques described in Chapter 19.

We should finally note that this approach to mood measurement reveals very clearly that taking and interpreting a single measurement of mood is of little use. For example, the same score on a mood scale could be produced by either a generally low-anxious individual on a particularly stressful occasion, or a generally highly anxious individual on a particularly relaxed occasion – two very different types of person. However, most studies that do use once-measured mood seem to be unaware of the fact that they may be confusing mood with personality.

SUMMARY

This chapter has examined some interesting aspects of mood and motivation, and has raised far more problems than it has solved. For example, as there is arguably no truly effective questionnaire for assessing motivation (since several that claim to do so actually measure personality), it is almost impossible to comment on the structure, nature and correlates of motivation. Hence the chapter has concentrated on states in general, and moods in particular.

I have argued that, as well as examining the *level* of states, several other interesting measures can be considered. These include the extent to which mood states swing either side of their habitual level (variability), the extent of any regular (periodic) fluctuations over time, their average level, the speed with which they change, and the extent to which they change following some intervention.

From this brief survey of the factors that influence mood level and mood variability, it seems that both thoughts and life events can have a significant influence on mood levels, a finding that should come as no great surprise. However, there do appear to be substantial (and ill-understood) individual differences in susceptibility to the Velten technique which make its use problematical. There is evidence to suggest that the levels of some moods vary according to a regular cycle, although separating the effects of a regular (daily or weekly) biological rhythm from regular life events is a tricky and time-consuming task. Finally, I have introduced some theories of anxiety, and suggested that Eysenck's cognitive theory may be one of the better ways of understanding levels of both this mood state and the corresponding trait.

I have argued that mood variability is another interesting phenomenon whose origins are not at all well understood, and whose relationship to levels of depression merits investigation. Finally, I have pointed out that average mood would appear to be equivalent to a trait, which may indicate that each trait should have a corresponding mood state, as suggested by Cattell.

SUGGESTED ADDITIONAL READING

Apart from Apter's work, it is difficult to recommend any texts on the psychology of motivation, as Cattell's book (Cattell and Child, 1975) is not easy to read, and the measurement issues (discussed in Chapter 19) need to be firmly grasped. Paul Barrett (1997) argues that 'somewhere along the line psychometricians seem to have forgotten about motivation', a point with which I wholeheartedly agree.

However, mood is a great deal easier. M. W. Eysenck (1992) provides a lucid description of his theory about the cognitive correlates of anxiety (plus a review of several other relevant theories), Zajonc's (1980, 1984) papers speculate about some links between mood and cognition, which will be of interest to the cognitively inclined, whilst Morris (1985), Cattell and Kline (1977), Watson and Tellegen (1985) and Watson *et al.* (1988) introduce the psychology of moods and the broad factors of positive affect and negative affect. McConville and Cooper (1992a) and Hepburn and Eysenck (1989) are typical of the mood variability studies.

ANSWERS TO SELF-ASSESSMENT QUESTIONS

SAQ 10.1
Aspects of mood or motivation that merit study include:

- level at one moment/situation;
- difference in mood/motivation between two situations;
- average mood/motivation;
- variability over time;
- periodicity (the extent to which mood/motivation follows a regular biological cycle);
- rate of change of mood/motivation in some standard setting.

SAQ 10.2
(a) lively, active, energetic, 'peppy' – anything implying energy and enthusiasm.
(b) anxious, uptight, distressed, fearful, jittery – a tense, unpleasant mood.
(c) sleepy, tired, lethargic, sluggish – the opposite of (a)
(d) relaxed, calm, at rest, placid – the opposite of (b)

SAQ 10.3
Relatively trivial life events (physiological variables probably do *not* have a direct effect), interventions such as the Velten technique, time of day, the appraisal/coping process in the case of stressful situations, possibly hypervigilance (although it is not obvious whether this causes anxiety or vice versa).

Section B: Assessment of Individual Differences

11

Measuring individual differences

BACKGROUND

This chapter provides an introduction to psychometrics, the branch of psychology that deals with the measurement of individual differences. It introduces the concepts of trait and state, and shows how knowledge of an individual's traits and states may be used to predict behaviour. Various types of psychological tests are then outlined, and the interpretation of individual scores through the use of norms is discussed. Finally, some guidance is given as to how to select a test and use it ethically.

Recommended prior reading

Chapter 1.

INTRODUCTION

One of the most important distinctions between the discipline of psychology and other disciplines that also claim to give insight into 'the human condition' is that of measurement. Students of literature are happy to make suggestions about the personality, motives and moods of figures such as Hamlet, Hannibal or Hagar, and although these contributions may be highly scholarly, they are not truly scientific in that they cannot ever be shown to be wrong. This is where psychology differs radically from other methods of understanding how humans function. Whilst great literature, religious doctrines, therapists' explanations, old wives' tales, psychoanalytical interpretations of the causes of neurosis, armchair speculation and 'common sense' *may* provide some accurate and useful insights, it is perfectly possible that some or all of these are simply wrong.

We certainly cannot tell what is true just by our emotional reactions. A favourite trick of academics is to ask students to complete personality questionnaires which are then taken away for computerised scoring. The next week, the students are given a talk about the ethics of testing, are handed sealed envelopes each holding a computer-generated analysis of their personality and asked to rate how accurate they find it. In my experience, most students are amazed by how insightful and accurate the results are, and astounded by the depth of these insights. Asking members of the class to compare their descriptions is probably the kindest way of showing that everyone in the class has received precisely the same personality assessment! The point is that one simply cannot trust one's emotional judgements to sort out fact from fiction. The fact that the results obtained from some personality test 'feel right' to an individual is not an adequate criterion. This of course is unsurprising – given that we are all human beings, it will be possible to make some broad descriptions about how human beings *in general* behave, which is a far cry from the scientific assessment of individual differences. Instead, we need to develop more rigorous techniques.

Psychometrics is the branch of psychology concerned with the measurement of individual differences, and you will have noted that half of this book is devoted to psychometric principles. This is because the accurate assessment of individual differences, using proper psychological tests or other techniques, is absolutely vital for a proper, scientific study of the discipline. It is important for three reasons.

First, it is generally possible to test theories only if individual differences can be measured accurately. For example, in the nineteenth century, Galton surmised that intelligent people might be able to react faster to some simple task (e.g. pressing a button when a light comes on) than less intelligent people. – a theory that has some value in so far as it suggests that intelligence may be linked to the speed with which our nervous systems can process information. To test this hypothesis it is necessary to measure some individuals' reaction times, *and also their intelligence* – the analysis might involve correlating these two scores together. Without an effective measure of intelligence the hypothesis is untestable.

In other words, we have assumed that individuals' scores on some psychological test are proportional to their level of ability. We are using scores on the intelligence test as if they were a measure of the abstract concept, intelligence. This is sometimes known as making an *operational definition*. For of course the kinds of terms used in theories of individual differences ('self-concept', 'cortical arousal', 'spatial ability', 'sex drive') are all lofty and abstract, whereas what is required is some method of actually *measuring* these things in real people (e.g. a questionnaire, a reading on a meter attached to carefully positioned electrodes, performance when solving a set of problems, the difference between mean reaction times measured under two different experimental conditions, or behavioural ratings.

Making an operational definition essentially means assuming that some observable measure can be used as if it was the abstract concept. To return to the reaction-time example, if we chose a different intelligence test from the catalogue and repeated the experiment, we would (hopefully!) obtain very similar results, but these results would probably not be quite identical, since it is unlikely that either of our tests would be *perfect* measures of ability. The extent to which a test measures what it is supposed to is known as validity (we shall return to this in Chapter 13). Thus we need psychological tests in order to check whether theories are correct. Without tests, theories are mere speculations, of little scientific value.

The second reason for studying psychometrics is that almost all modern models of personality, ability, mood and motivation are based on a psychometric technique called 'factor analysis'. Without understanding the basic principles of this it is impossible to grasp how these theories have developed, their strengths and weaknesses, and whether a particular theory is based on a sound methodology.

The third reason for studying psychometrics is because psychological tests are so widely used in applied psychology. Occupational psychologists and personnel managers use tests to assess the potential of job applicants. Educational psychologists may use tests to detect learning difficulties, difficulties in using language, etc. Medical psychologists may use a questionnaire to identify individuals whose 'Type A' personality puts them at risk of a heart attack. It is vitally important that test users understand how these instruments are constructed, how they should be administered, scored and interpreted, and the importance of assessing measurement error, bias, and other important and potentially litigious issues.

Furthermore, the types of test used are likely to become increasingly complex. Printed tests will almost certainly be replaced by computer programs which present different people with quite different sets of test items. Some participants will sit very easy tests, and some will sit very difficult tests. Yet although people have taken tests that differ greatly in difficulty, the programs can estimate the relative ability of all those taking part. Once again, test users will need to grasp the basics of these methods in order to be able to interpret the results of such measures.

SELF-ASSESSMENT QUESTION 11.1

(a) What is an operational definition?

(b) Try to think what you might use as operational definitions of French-speaking ability and meanness.

Thus it seems likely that many readers of this book will eventually use psychological tests in some shape or form, either as dependent variables for testing psychological theories or in applied psychology, whereas everyone will need an appreciation of some basic principles of psychological measurement in order to grasp modern theories of ability and personality. Given the prevalence and importance of psychological tests in academic and applied psychology, it is somewhat embarrassing to have to admit that many are simply not worth the paper that they are printed on. Some patently useless tests are both widely used and slickly marketed, and so one aim of this book is to teach you enough about the basics of psychological measurement to allow you to decide whether a particular test is likely to be of any use for a given purpose – in other words, whether scores on a particular test will provide a suitable operational definition for the concept that you have chosen to assess.

TRAITS AND STATES

Most psychological tests measure 'traits' of one kind or another. Traits are simply useful descriptions of how individuals generally behave. For example, 'sociability' is generally regarded as a trait, since few people are the life and soul of the party one day and a virtual recluse the next. Since individuals tend to have a characteristic level of sociability we term it a trait. There are plenty of others.

SELF-ASSESSMENT QUESTION 11.2

Try to decide which of the following are probably traits

(a) musical ability;

(b) hunger;

(c) liberality of attitudes;

(d) anger;

(e) good manners.

It is conventional to group traits into three classes, namely attainments, ability traits and personality traits. Measures of attainment are of little interest to psychologists. They measure how well an individual performs *in a certain area, following a course of instruction*. School examinations are an example of attainment tests. If children attend lessons and read and memorise the textbook, they should be able to achieve a perfect mark in a knowledge-based attainment test. Levels of attainment are specific to a particular area. If a pupil has a first-rate knowledge of British social history in the nineteenth century, it is not possible to say whether or not they know anything about modern economic theory, seventeenth-century history, or anything else. It all depends what they have been taught. The distinction becomes a little more blurred at university level, where students are required to search out references, think about their implications, and make a coherent argument when writing an essay – in this situation, abilities, personality traits and motivational factors will also play a part. Here an essay mark will, in part, measure attainment, but will also be influenced by motivation, the students' ability to express themselves, and so on.

Ability traits are concerned with a person's level of cognitive performance in some area, e.g. how well he or she can read maps, solve mental arithmetic problems, solve crossword clues, visualise shapes, understand a passage of prose, or come up with creative ideas. These refer to thinking skills (rather than knowledge) either in areas that are not explicitly taught (e.g. visualisation of rotated shapes) or in areas in which everyone can be presumed to have had the same training (e.g. being taught to read and comprehend prose). Abilities are related to future potential, i.e. thinking skill in a particular area, rather than to achievement.

Personality traits, on the other hand, reflect a person's *style* of behaviour. Words such as 'slapdash', 'punctual', 'shy' or 'anxious' all describe how (rather than how well) a person usually behaves. These are broad generalisations, since how we behave is obviously also influenced by situations – even the most bubbly extrovert is unlikely to tell *risqué* jokes during a funeral service. Nevertheless, like abilities, these traits may be useful in helping us to predict how individuals will probably behave most of the time.

Cattell (e.g. Cattell, 1957) also argues that it is necessary to consider two types of 'states'. Unlike traits, states are short-lived, lasting for minutes or hours rather than months or years. Moods (or emotions, as the distinction is not clear) refer to transient feelings such as fright following a near miss when driving, or joy or despair on learning one's examination results. He also identifies 'motivational states' – forces that direct our behaviour. For example, the basic biological drives (food, sex, aggression, company, etc.) can direct our behaviour, but only for a short time. After we have eaten, our desire for food declines. So these, too, are states, not traits.

MEASURING TRAITS

How might we measure individual differences in practice? We shall consider the measurement of states in Chapter 19, and so this section will focus on personality and ability traits. The key point about *all* psychological tests is that the individuals taking them should have precisely the same experience, no matter who administers the test, or in which country it is given. Great care has to be taken to ensure that the testing situation is standardised. Time limits must be strictly followed, the test instructions must be given precisely in accordance with directions, and no variation should be made to the format of the question booklet or answer sheet lest these should affect performance. The way in which the test is scored (and interpreted) also has to be precisely explained and followed rigidly.

Ability tests and personality questionnaires

Some tests are designed to be administered to just one person at a time – for instance, those involving equipment, or in which there is a need to build up a good testing rapport. However, most tests are designed for administration to groups of people, either in a classroom or in a computer laboratory.

Ability tests are simply samples of problems, each of which is thought to rely on a particular mental ability. For example, a test designed to assess mathematical ability might consist of some puzzles involving addition, subtraction, multiplication, fractions, geometry, simultaneous and quadratic equations, algebra, calculus, etc. However, it is not possible merely to put together a set of items and call it a test. For example, there is absolutely no guarantee that all of these items do, in fact, measure the same underlying ability – it is possible that the ability to perform addition, subtraction, multiplication and division is quite unrelated to the other, 'higher-level' mathematical skills. This can be checked using the techniques discussed in Chapter 14. Ability tests involve free responses (e.g. 'which number comes next: 1, 8, 27, . . .?') or multiple choice questions ('the next number is (a) 32, (b) 36, (c) 48, (d) 64'), although other options are available. These may include asking a child to insert the most appropriate missing word (from a list) into a space in a sentence, or to make up a test item in order to show that they have understood a concept. As Gulliksen (1986) has observed, psychologists and educators are not particularly creative in the ways in which they devise test items, and he offers some valuable alternative formats.

Perhaps the most obvious way of measuring personality is through self-report questionnaires. However, it is important to bear in mind two points about such tests. First, it is not possible simply to devise a few questions, decide how the responses should be scored, and then administer the test. The reasons for this will be covered in some detail in Chapters 13, 17 and 18, but the basic point is that there is no guarantee that the questions that you ask will measure the trait that you expect. Instead, it is necessary to perform some statistical analyses and to check that the scale appears to measure what it is intended to before using the test.

The second important point is that, just because someone ticks a box in a questionnaire in a certain way, this does not imply that we can accept their response at face value. Some reasons for this will be discussed in Chapter 17. To borrow an example from Cattell (1973), suppose someone strongly agreed with an item in a questionnaire that said 'I am the smartest man in town' (although not the most modest, one assumes).

One can treat this piece of information in two ways. The first would be to assume that what the person said is accurate, and credit them with high intelligence, and Cattell terms this 'Q'-data'. A response is treated as Q'-data if the psychologist chooses to believe that the person has made a true, accurate observation about him- or herself. This is common practice in social psychology, but is regarded as rather naive by many of those who work in the field of individual differences, and is one of the main reasons why there is some friction between these two groups.

The second approach pays no heed to the apparent meaning of the answer, but only to its pattern of relation to other things. Responses to questionnaires are regarded as 'box-ticking behaviours' for statistical analysis, rather than as true, insightful descriptions of how the individual behaves. Cattell calls this 'Q-data', and argues that lack of self-insight, deliberate attempts to distort responses, and other variables considered in Chapter 18 make Q'-data of little value for a scientific model of personality.

This is an important point that is often misunderstood both by psychologists and by individuals who are exposed to psychological tests. *Most psychologists do not believe that people are making true statements about themselves when they answer items in personality tests.* They do not *need* to do so when the responses are analysed statistically. For example, suppose that a firm wants to use some kind of test to identify those applicants who will develop into highly successful salesmen. They may find (by asking existing sales staff to complete a questionnaire) that successful sales staff all strongly agree that 'they are the smartest man in town', whilst no one else holds this belief. This is an empirical fact, and need not be tied to any theory. Thus it would be reasonable just to *use* this question as part of the selection procedure. No one is interested in whether the applicants are *really* the smartest individuals (logically they could not *all* be!), so the response is treated as Q-data rather than as Q'-data. Techniques for developing tests along similar lines are discussed in Chapters 14, 15, 16 and 18.

The main problem with questionnaires is that responses are quite easy to fake. For example, most individuals will try to paint a favourable impression when completing a personality scale as part of an employment selection process. It is possible to detect such behaviour. Eysenck favours the use of a 'lie scale' – a list of common but socially undesirable peccadilloes embedded in the personality questionnaire, e.g. 'did you ever cheat at a test in school?'. Someone who admits to few of these is either a saint, out of touch with how they really behave, or distorting their responses. However, is a personnel manager justified in rejecting a candidate just because they appear to be a paragon of virtue? It might be difficult to defend such an action at an industrial tribunal.

Ratings of behaviour

The second main form of evidence stems from ratings of behaviour. Raters can be carefully trained how to classify behaviours according to a particular check-list. If they then follow individuals around for a long period (months, rather than days) in a wide variety of situations, these ratings of how people behave in their everyday life may give useful insights into their personality or abilities. Cattell terms this 'L-data' (for 'life-record'). Ratings of behaviour are often used to assess personality during interviews and other selection exercises, and there are probably some important characteristics (e.g. leadership quality, social skills) that are difficult to assess by other means. However, because behaviour is observed only for a short time, and in one or two situations, it is unreasonable to expect such assessments to be highly accurate – and indeed they are not (see, for example, Cronbach, 1994).

Objective tests

The third form of evidence stems from analyses of the behaviour of individuals (generally in laboratory situations) who are either unaware of which aspect of their behaviour is being measured, or are physically unable to alter their response. These tests should therefore overcome the principal objection to questionnaires, which is that responses can easily be faked. For example, Cattell and Warburton (1967) suggest that highly anxious people are likely to fidget more than others. In order to measure fidgeting (and hence anxiety), they fitted a special chair with microswitches and left it in a waiting-room outside the laboratory. Volunteers arriving for testing sessions sat in the chair without realising that their behaviour was being measured – a procedure that raises some interesting ethical problems.

In another even more bizarre example, equipment was used to measure volunteers' skin resistance under three conditions – whilst sitting relaxed in a chair, whilst reading the words 'frightful horror' on a card, and following the firing of a starting pistol just behind the volunteer's head. (Ethical standards were obviously not fully appreciated in the 1960s.) Here the unfortunate volunteer would be unable to control the reaction of their autonomic nervous system, which would result in a dramatic fall in their skin resistance. Cattell termed the data from such experiments 'T-data' (since they arose from objective Tests) and argues that they should form an excellent basis for measuring personality, since they are entirely objective. In particular, since individuals do not know which aspect of their behaviour is being measured, or are unable to manipulate their responses, such tests are difficult to fake. However, it is very difficult to devise and develop suitable objective tests, and few have so far been found to be of any practical use, as will be shown later.

Objective tests can also be used to assess ability – here they are often known as 'performance tests'. For example, children could be timed to see how quickly they can complete jigsaws, arrange some wooden blocks to form a certain pattern, or arrange a series of cartoon pictures into the most logical order. Job applicants can be presented with a sample of the types of problems that they would be expected to deal with if they were appointed, and simply told to get on with solving them – the so-called 'in-basket' approach. Their performance on these tasks can later be assessed (although this is not usually a straightforward procedure). Alternatively, some specific skills can be measured, e.g. tests of manual dexterity assess the amount of time it takes applicants to use tweezers and screwdrivers to assemble objects using small nuts and bolts.

Projective tests of personality

'Projective tests' provide a fourth source of evidence about personality. In these tests, individuals are presented with some ambiguous, unclear or completely meaningless stimuli and are assumed to reveal their personalities, experiences, wants, needs, hopes, fears, etc., when describing these. The Rorschach inkblots are probably the most famous projective test. In this test, participants are shown a series of inkblots, rather similar to that shown in Figure 11.1, and are

Figure 11.1 An example of an inkblot, similar to those used in Rorschach's test.

asked to describe in their own words what they 'see' in them. (Be warned that replying 'an inkblot' is classed as distinctly pathological!) Their responses are scored according to any one of about three main scoring systems, and are supposed to reveal hidden depths of personality. Unfortunately, despite (or perhaps because of) the Byzantine complexity of the scoring schemes, such tests simply do not work, and are now rarely used. However 'multiple-choice' projective tests (in which respondents choose responses from a list, rather than describing the pictures in their own words) may be of some value (e.g. Holmstrom *et al.*, 1990).

SELF-ASSESSMENT QUESTION 11.3

What is or are

(a) Q-data?

(b) L-data?

(c) Q'-data?

(d) T-data?

(e) Projective tests?

SCORING TESTS

Every test, whether it measures personality or ability, must have some clearly defined technique for converting an individual's responses into some kind of score. Details of how to administer, score and interpret the test will almost always be given in the test manual. This is generally a substantial booklet that contains other information which may be useful in assessing the merit of the test, although some tests rely on journal articles to provide this information. In the vast majority of cases (projective tests being the only real exception) the score will be a number, since the test seeks to *quantify* the ability or personality trait. Multiple-choice ability tests are perhaps the easiest to score. In the vast majority of cases one point will be awarded for each correct answer. Sometimes, in an attempt to prevent guessing, one point will be deducted for each incorrect answer. Items that have not been attempted almost invariably score zero. Multiple-choice tests are generally scored either by computer (most test publishers provide a postal scoring system – at a price) or by using templates. These are usually acetate sheets that are positioned over the top of the answer sheet, and which clearly indicate the correct answer for each item. The beauty of this system is that it is almost 100 per cent accurate, and requires no subjective judgements. Cattell (never one to resist a neologism) calls such scoring schemes highly 'conspective' (literally 'looking together'), meaning that different markers will arrive at the same conclusion, as opposed to essays, for example.

Scoring free responses from ability tests can be problematic. Much depends upon the quality of the test manual and the skill of the person administering the test. For example, suppose that in a comprehension test a child is asked to define the meaning of the word 'kitten' and they reply that it is 'a type of cat' – an answer that is neither completely correct nor totally wrong. Good test manuals will provide detailed instructions, with examples, to show how such answers should be scored. Where actions are timed (e.g. the amount of time to solve a jigsaw is recorded), the test manual will show how many points to award for a particular solution time.

Most personality scales do not have answers that are either right or wrong. A typical item measuring sociability might be as follows:

I enjoy big, wild parties

(a) strongly agree (b) agree (c) neutral (d) disagree (e) strongly disagree

where one of the choices (a) to (e) is marked. Since there are five possible answers that form a scale of degree of liking for parties, a response of (a) would generally be given 5 points, (b) 4 points and so on. If another item in the scale was phrased in the reverse direction, such as

I like nothing better than a quiet night at home

(a) would receive 1 point and (e) would receive 5 points. Most personality scales urge participants to answer all of the questions, and so there should be no missing items, unlike ability tests, in which time-limits often mean that most individuals will fail to complete all of the items.

The scoring of most projective tests is very complex, which is why they are now rarely used. Those who wish to use these tests professionally have to serve an apprenticeship under the guidance of an experienced user of the test in order to appreciate fully the intricacies of the scoring system. Even so, the level of conspection of most projective tests is lamentably low: two different people are likely to come to vastly different conclusions when interpreting the same set of responses, a point that has been made with some force by Eysenck (1959). However, there seems to be no good reason why responses to projective tests cannot be coded objectively, using some form of content analysis – that is, specifying a large list of characteristics (e.g. 'mentions any non-human animal'), each to be coded as present or absent.

EXERCISE

Suppose that Jane completes a 20-item test of musical ability, and gives correct responses to 15 items. What can be concluded about her musical ability?

The answer is simple – nothing. You may possibly have thought that, since there were 20 items in the test and Jane answered more than half of them correctly, this would indicate that her score was above average, but of course it does not, for in almost all cases (the important exception being discussed in Chapter 16), a person's score on a test depends upon the level of difficulty of the test items. The items may have been so trivially easy that 99 out of 100 children might have obtained scores *above* 15 on this test, in which case Jane would be markedly *less* musical than other children of her age. To interpret the meaning of an individual's test score it is necessary to use *norms*.

Tables of test norms simply show the scores of a large, carefully selected sample of individuals. For example, the test might be given to 2035 8- to 9-year-old children, ensuring that the sample contains equal numbers of males and females, that they are sampled from different regions of the country (in case some regions are more musical than others), and that the proportion of children from ethnic minorities is consistent with that in the general population. A frequency distribution of these scores can be drawn up in a similar way to that shown in Table 11.1. The first column shows each possible test score, the second column shows the number of children in the sample who obtained each score, the third column shows the number of children who obtained each score *or less*, and the fourth column shows this figure as a percentage – a figure known as the percentile.

Many test manuals show the percentile scores, so it is a simple matter to interpret an individual's test score – it is merely necessary to look across and

Score	Number of children with this score	Number of children with this score or lower	Percentile
0	3	3	$\frac{3}{2035} \times 100 = 0.15$
1	2	3+2=5	0.25
2	6	3+2+6=11	0.54
3	8	19	0.93
4	8	27	1.33
5	13	40	1.97
6	17	57	2.80
7	23	80	3.93
8	25	105	5.16
9	33	138	6.78
10	57	195	9.58
11	87	282	13.86
12	133	415	20.39
13	201	616	30.27
14	293	909	44.67
15	357	1266	62.21
16	270	1536	75.48
17	198	1734	85.21
18	126	1860	91.40
19	100	1960	96.31
20	75	2035	100.00

Table 11.1 Norms for a test of musical ability, based on a (hypothetical) random sample of 2035 children aged 8–9 years

discover that 62 per cent of the children scored 15 or less on the test. Sometimes, however, percentiles are not shown. If these scores follow a normal (bell-shaped) distribution whose mean and standard deviation are known, it is still quite a straightforward matter to estimate the percentage of the population having a score as low as any particular test score. For example, the mean ($\bar{x}$) of the scores shown in Table 11.1 is 14.47, and the standard deviation (s) is 4.978. Suppose that we want to estimate what percentage of the population has a score of 15 or below. To do this, simply calculate:

$$z = \frac{15 - \bar{x}}{s} = \frac{(15 - 14.47)}{4.978} = 0.106$$

A table of the standard normal distribution (found in almost any statistics book) will then show the proportion of individuals having a score lower than this value, which is 54 per cent. This figure is similar (but not quite identical) to the one that we read directly from Table 11.1. The discrepancy arises because we assumed that the scores follow a normal distribution, whereas in fact they do not quite do so. However, this approach can be useful if you know the mean and standard deviation, but do not have access to the full table of norms.

Most test manuals contain several different tables of norms, e.g. those collected in different countries, separate norms for each sex, and (almost invariably in the case of ability tests) at different ages. All that is necessary is to choose the table that is the most appropriate for your needs, ensuring that it is based on a large sample (a minimum of several hundred) and that care has been taken to sample individuals properly.

SELF-ASSESSMENT QUESTION 11.4

Why are different norms used for different ages in ability tests?

Finally, I ought to mention that tables of norms are only necessary for the interpretation of one individual's score on a test. Researchers will often just want to correlate scores on a test with individuals' scores on other variables (e.g. correlating intelligence with head size), or to compare the test scores of two groups (e.g. using a t-test to determine whether males and females are equally musical). Then it is not only unnecessary to convert the norms to percentiles, but also bad practice, for you will find that the original distribution of scores is much more bell-shaped than that of the corresponding percentiles, and this is an assumption of most statistical techniques.

USING TEST SCORES TO PREDICT BEHAVIOUR

The psychometric model, as defined by Cattell, proposes that if we could measure all of an individual's abilities, personality traits, motivational states and mood states, we should be able to predict their behaviour. More specifically, he suggests that the likelihood of any particular behaviour in a particular situation can be predicted by what he calls a 'specification equation'. This shows how the probability of someone acting in a particular way depends on each of the following:

- how strongly each of the traits or states predicts the behaviour of interest. This can be estimated from another sample of individuals using a statistical technique called multiple regression, and these values will appear as numbers in the equation, known as 'weights'. A positive weight indicates that a high score on that trait/state increases the probability of the behaviour occurring. A near-zero weight implies that the trait or state is irrelevant when predicting the behaviour. A negative weight means that the higher a person's score on a trait or state, the less likely he or she is to show the behaviour;
- the individual's score on each of the traits and states. This might be

measured by psychological tests, or by other techniques discussed above. Since the tests will probably have different means and different standard deviations, it is necessary to re-scale the scores so that they have a mean of zero and a standard deviation of 1.0 (standardised scores, or z-scores) by subtracting the mean and dividing by the standard deviation.

So if the weights and an individual's scores on all of the traits and states are known, it should be possible to determine which of several courses of action a person is most likely to follow by plugging these numbers into the 'specification equations' for each course of action in order to determine which gives the highest value. For example, suppose that you buy a videotape of a favourite film and discover that the picture quality is poor. There might be three common responses to this situation:

- returning to the shop and asking for a replacement;
- moaning to one's friends but doing nothing;
- throwing the tape in the bin.

The equation for the first action might be as follows:

$$0.7 \times \text{drive for assertion} + 0.6 \times \text{angry mood} - 0.3 \times \text{neuroticism}$$

and for the second:

$$- 0.6 \times \text{drive for assertion} - 0.4 \times \text{angry mood} + 0.4 \times \text{neuroticism}$$

By inserting an individual's scores on tests of these variables into the equations, it should be possible to work out which action is the most likely. Thus knowledge of a person's traits and states may lead directly to predictions about how that individual is likely to behave.

The technique is particularly useful in applied psychology. For example, it can be used to predict how well each job applicant is likely to perform if appointed.

OBTAINING AND USING TESTS

Psychological tests cannot be bought over the counter by anyone. There are two reasons for this. First, imagine what would happen if a photocopy of a commercial intelligence test reached sixth-form common-rooms. Groups of students would no doubt while away some time by trying to solve the items, and (given that it is a group effort with unlimited time) might well succeed in solving most items in the test. Suppose some individuals were then given the same test as part of a screening test for employment. Those who had had previous experience of the test might well be able to remember at least some of the correct answers, and so would score higher than they 'should' do, reducing the effectiveness of the test in selecting the best applicants.

Second, it would be disastrous if tests were given out to people who had no training in test administration, scoring or interpretation. They might use a test that was inappropriate for a particular application (as discussed in Chapter

13), or which was manifestly useless for measuring *anything*. Even if they did choose an appropriate test, they might not be able to score it, they might give the individuals who had been tested incorrect feedback, and they might fail to keep the test results confidential. In other words, test users may not adhere to proper ethical standards. For these reasons, test publishers will supply tests only to properly trained users, and may require users to attend a training course before supplying them with a particular test.

It is thus vitally important that all test users adhere to ethical principles when conducting research or using tests for guidance, diagnosis, selection or other purposes. The professional associations of most countries (e.g. the British Psychological Society and the American Psychological Association) have laid down guidelines for the use of psychological tests. These provide broad principles covering the selection of appropriate tests, guidance for their administration, their scoring and the interpretation of results, and some principles to be followed when giving feedback about test performance. One typical set of standards is shown in Appendix B, and this should be studied carefully.

There are four main ways of finding out which tests are available to measure a particular aspect of personality or ability. First, one can search test publishers' catalogues – these are glossy brochures that invariably describe tests in glowing terms. Second, one can consult a book, such as Sweetland and Keyser (1991), which lists brief details of tests, including the age groups for which they are suited, as well as details of publishers and prices. The problem is that neither of these sources is very evaluative – they will not help you to distinguish between the Rolls-Royce and the Lada of tests. This is why it is far preferable to consult the *Mental Measurements Yearbooks*. These weighty volumes were introduced by Oscar Buros in 1938 to provide a 'consumer's guide' to commercially published psychological tests. They contain indices listing tests by type, by name and by author, but the real value of these volumes lies in the critical reviews of tests, which have been written by psychometric specialists. These will often state, quite bluntly, that a particular test is so severely flawed that it should be avoided, or only be considered for research purposes. In my view it is absolutely vital to read such reviews before deciding to use any test for any purpose.

The three sources of information discussed so far cover only commercially published tests. Unfortunately, several tests (particularly those beloved by social psychologists) are printed as appendices to journal articles rather than being commercially published. This means that they are more difficult to track down (requiring a search of the literature), and it can be even harder to find the necessary psychometric information, tables of norms, and so on. The safest method is to perform a citation search (using the *Social Science Citation Index* or its computerised equivalent) to find out who cites the paper that contains the test. However, when using such tests you lack the guidance of the contributors to the *Mental Measurements Yearbooks*, and it is vital that you consider dispassionately whether a test is really going to suit your needs. Issues of reliability, validity and bias (discussed in Chapters 13 and 17) are of particular importance, and you should also be wary about using a test developed in a different cultural setting.

SUMMARY

After having read this chapter, you should be able to describe what is meant by traits and states, describe the main types of mental tests, discuss how individual test scores may be interpreted through the use of norms, outline the ethical principles associated with test use, and show an understanding of how traits and states may be used to predict behaviour through the use of a specification equation.

SUGGESTED ADDITIONAL READING

If you have not already done so, you should consult Appendix B of this book (or its equivalent) in order to learn about standards of testing procedure. You may find it interesting to browse through the *Mental Measurement Yearbooks* and search out some reviews, e.g. reviews of the Rorschach test, Sixteen-Personality-Factor test, Lüscher Colour Test, Adjective Checklist and/or the Weschler Adult Intelligence Scale. You may also find it interesting to glance at any standard psychometrics or occupational psychology textbook (e.g. Cronbach, 1994) to see what some typical test items look like, or to practise scoring and interpreting tests (as well as satisfying your natural curiosity) by testing your own personality or ability with Eysenck (1962) or Eysenck and Wilson (1976).

ANSWERS TO SELF-ASSESSMENT QUESTIONS

SAQ 11.1

(a) Any score from a psychological test or other device that is used as if it measured some theoretical concept.

(b) A person's score on a test of appropriate difficulty consisting of whatever items are thought to make up the concept of 'French-speaking ability', e.g. items measuring knowledge of colloquialisms and vocabulary, and ratings of quality of accent and fluency. The measurement of meanness is a much more difficult proposition. Direct self-report questions will probably not work – who would admit to this quality? Asking if any regular payments to a charity are made from bank accounts may be more useful. Ratings by friends may be a possibility, as may 'objective tests' (e.g. asking for a loan, or observing behaviour in the vicinity of a beggar). However, most of these measures could indicate 'poverty' instead of 'meanness'.

SAQ 11.2

(a), (c), (e)

SAQ 11.3

(a) Responses to questionnaire items that are analysed in ways that do not assume the truth of what the respondent is saying.

(b) Ratings of behaviour.

(c) Responses to questionnaires that are analysed as if the respondents are making some true comment about themselves. For example, if a person strongly agrees that they are happy, the psychologist would conclude that they are indeed happy.

(d) Data from objective tests of personality – tests whose purpose is hidden from the test participant, or in which the test participant physically cannot alter his or her response.

(e) Personality tests in which an individual is asked to describe or interpret an ambiguous stimulus (e.g. a picture, an inkblot or a sound). The rationale for such tests is that the way in which the stimuli are interpreted will provide some insight into the individual's personality, needs and experience. Scoring the responses to such tests is notoriously difficult, as Eysenck has shown.

SAQ 11.4

Because abilities tend to increase with age. In order to determine whether a particular child is performing markedly better or worse than 'the average child', it is important to compare him or her with other children of the same age. Almost all abilities increase with age as a result of physiological maturation and education. Suppose that a test had a table of norms that covered a fairly broad range of ages (e.g. children aged 6–10 years). It would not be possible to use these to interpret a child's score, since an 'average' (or median) score could indicate a 6-year-old who was performing much better than most 6-year-olds, an 8-year-old of average ability, or a 10-year-old whose performance was below average. The best ability tests give norms at 3-month intervals (e.g. one table for children aged 74–76 months, another table for children aged 77–79 months, etc.).

12

Personality through introspection: testing the theories of Kelly and Rogers

BACKGROUND

Whilst Chapter 2 introduced the theories of Rogers and Kelly, it gave no hint as to how the self-concept or personal constructs could be assessed. The present chapter outlines some popular techniques for assessing these concepts, and also raises some associated methodological problems.

Recommended prior reading

Chapters 1, 2 and 11.

INTRODUCTION

Whilst Chapter 2 gave a basic overview of the personality theories of Rogers and Kelly, it gave few clues as to how their theories could be tested – or indeed how an individual's self-concept or their system of personal constructs could be discovered. If it is not possible to measure these concepts accurately, then the theories are essentially untestable – it is impossible to tell whether they are correct or incorrect. We can happily theorise about the relationship between the way we construe the world and emotions (as discussed in Chapter 2), but if it is not possible to *measure* the way in which a person's construct system operates, it is impossible ever to know whether these theories fit the facts.

In Rogers' theory, incongruence occurs when a person's behaviour is manifestly different from that suggested by their self-image. It is supposedly associated with feelings of anxiety and tension. However, if there is no accurate way of measuring a person's self-image, then there is no possible way of testing whether or not this assertion is actually correct, or whether it needs to be modified in the light of empirical evidence.

THE CLINICAL METHOD AND Q-SORT

According to Rogers, an individual can best come to understand their personality in the context of a close clinical relationship with a therapist who is congruent (i.e. self-aware), empathic (i.e. able to view the world from the other person's perspective) and has unconditional positive regard for the client (i.e. the client feels that the therapist likes and values them as a person, and that this is not conditional on what they say or do). The therapist will listen attentively, ask when unsure about some precise detail, and often give reflective feedback so that the client is aware that the therapist understands the personal meaning of what has been said or implied. From this the therapist builds up a picture of the client's feelings, concerns and nature, and can help the client to consider their options for action, their feelings, any discrepancies between their self and their ideal self, and other clinically relevant issues.

There are plenty of examples of therapists' reflective comments in Rogers' writing. The following extract is from Rogers (1967), and follows a somewhat tortuous account of how a previously murderous client feels that there is something about her that is totally without hate:

> Therapist: I'd like to see if I can capture a little of what that means to you. It is as if you've gotten very deeply acquainted with yourself on kind of a brick-by-brick experiencing basis, and in that sense have become more *self*-ish, and the notion of really, – in the discovering of what is the core of you as separate from all the other aspects, you come across the realization, which is a very deep and pretty thrilling realization, that the core of the self is not only without hate, but is really something more resembling a saint, something really very pure is the word I would use. And that you can try to depreciate that. You can say, maybe it's a sublimation, maybe it's an abnormal manifestation, screwball and so on. But inside of yourself you know that it isn't. This contains the feelings which could contain rich sexual expression, but it sounds bigger than, and really deeper than that. And yet fully able to include all that could be a part of sex-expression.
>
> Client: It's probably something like that.
>
> (Rogers, 1967, p. 96)

It can be seen that measuring attitudes to the self by such means can be a long, difficult process requiring great sensitivity and insight – and there is always the nagging doubt that the therapist may 'lead' the client down routes that will support his or her own theoretical stance through choosing to emphasise some aspects of the dialogue rather than others. However, there are other techniques for measuring attitudes towards the self, ideal self, etc.

The Q-sort is a measure designed by Stephenson (1953) to determine how an individual views his or her self. The client is given a pile of 100 or so cards, on each of which is a self-descriptive statement (drawn from clinical interviews) such as 'I usually like people', 'I don't trust my emotions', 'I am afraid of what other people may think of me', and so on. The client is asked to sort these into several piles (about five) ranging from statements that are most characteristic of them to those that are least characteristic of them. The number of cards to be placed in each pile is usually specified, so that the number of cards in each group follows a normal distribution.

The whereabouts of each card is recorded, and the exercise is repeated under other conditions, e.g. after several sessions of therapy, or after asking the client to sort the cards according to his or her 'ideal self' rather than actual self. It is a simple matter to track changes in the way in which the cards are sorted, and thus to build up a picture of how the self-concept is evolving, or the precise ways in which the self is seen to be rather different from the ideal self, and these can be usefully explored during the therapeutic interview.

There seems to be no reason why a sensitive clinician should not make up his or her own cards, and this might be useful for exploring particular issues that may have been raised or hinted at, but not fully explored. There also seems to be no reason why the items in any standard personality questionnaire could not be transferred on to cards and administered in this way, but the tendency is to use a standard set of items (the California Q-set) to cover most of the standard feelings about the self. Block (1961) gives full details on the use of the Q-sort technique in various settings. This measure provides a quick method of allowing individuals to express their feelings about themselves in a quantifiable manner.

Several questionnaires have also been developed to measure self-concept. They are quite widely used in clinical and social psychology, and Kline (1993) discusses them in some detail. They are certainly popular, with just one test, the 'Self-Esteem Scale' (Rosenberg, 1965), being cited well over 1000 times in the literature. The items in this 10-item scale are very similar to each other, and basically they just ask 'do you like yourself?' in 10 different ways. The test also shows *very* high correlations with other tests measuring anxiety and depression (−0.64 and −0.54, respectively), and as Kline points out, the evidence that either this scale or alternative measures that he discusses actually measure self-esteem itself is rather flimsy.

The Twenty Statements Test (Kuhn and McPartland, 1954) has also been proposed as a way of exploring the self. As its name suggests, individuals being tested are just asked to describe themselves using 20 short statements. There are several ways of scoring this test, e.g. the number of items that are job-related, the number of physical descriptions, and so on. The order in which the statements are produced is also thought to be significant. Once again, whilst it might be clinically quite interesting to note whether some individuals pay a disproportionate amount of attention to one particular aspect of their self (e.g. their looks), this is not a particularly sophisticated technique for exploring the self.

SELF-ASSESSMENT QUESTION 12.1

How might you test whether the Q-sort gives accurate results?

THE REPERTORY GRID TECHNIQUE

Although Kelly developed the repertory grid (discussed below) as a way of formalising individuals' systems of personal constructs, he also believed in the use of good listening skills. 'If you want to know what is wrong with someone,' he once wrote, 'ask them: they *may* tell you'. Moreover, he believed that the technique of self-characterisation could be useful for understanding individuals. He suggested that if one wanted to learn what a particular person was like, he or she should be invited to write a short self-description *as if it were written by a close friend*. His books contain several examples of these. They (and the repertory grid techniques, described below) were used therapeutically in what is known as 'fixed role therapy'.

In fixed role therapy the therapist noted how the individual tended to view him- or herself and others (their constructs), and asked that person to 'play-act' being a very *different* person. For example, if a person construed him- or herself as being 'quiet', 'unemotional' and 'anxious', the therapist might ask them to try *acting* as if they felt the opposite (normally for a period of some weeks) so that they could explore what it felt like to construe themselves differently. This contrasts enormously with Rogers' approach. For Rogers, the basic aim of therapy was to let individuals discover themselves and explore their feelings about themselves as they really are. Kelly's approach involves actively encouraging the individual to try being someone else for a few weeks (at least) in an attempt to develop their construct system.

However, the most popular method for determining how individuals construe their private worlds is the repertory grid technique. You will recall from Chapter 2 that, according to Kelly, each person tends to classify objects and people ('elements') by means of 'personal constructs'. These can be verbalised as two terms that have opposite meaning to that individual, e.g. good/bad, miserable/happy or lively/boring, although sometimes one pole is not obvious to the individual. If we can find a way to determine the nature of these dimensions ('constructs') that the person uses to impose some structure on the world, four interesting questions immediately arise.

- What constructs does an individual use? In other words, what aspects of other people seem to matter most to this individual? What characteristics does he or she find useful in attempting to predict how others will behave?

Are there any obvious features which simply do not seem to be considered? Are there any very idiosyncratic constructs?

- How does the individual construe certain key 'elements' in his or her life? In particular, how does the person construe him- or herself, as well as their family and their friends? The technique offers yet another method for exploring feelings about the person's self. Moreover, there is no reason why the person who is completing the grid should not be asked to use 'myself as I would like to be' as one of the elements, thus allowing self/ideal-self discrepancies to be directly observed.

- What are the relationships between the constructs? It is quite possible that the constructs will be correlated. For example, we could find that a patient views 'lively' (rather than 'dull') people as 'untrustworthy' (rather than 'honest') – which may open up all kinds of fruitful avenues for clinical enquiry.

- What are the relationships between the elements? Which individuals tend to be viewed in much the same way? For example, do men choose for their wives people whom they construe in much the same way as they do their mothers? Might it be of clinical interest to discover that a woman construes her husband in much the same way as she construes sex criminals?

The repertory grid technique can help to address all of these issues. The basic idea is very simple. Each participant is asked to write down the name of one real person who occupies a particular role in their life – *real individuals* are generally used rather than vague stereotypes. Thus a participant would be asked to think of one particular brother, rather than a mixture of all of their brothers. The names of these individuals are known as 'elements'. About a dozen of these *role titles* are generally used. They might typically include the participant, their mother, father, partner, a particular brother, a particular sister, someone whom the participant dislikes, someone they feel sorry for, their boss at work, a close friend of the same sex, a well-liked teacher, etc., and are usually chosen so as to cover the main relationships in the participant's life, with disliked as well as liked individuals featuring on the list.

The elements may be specially chosen for clinical applications. For example, a therapist who wanted to understand a person's self-concept might include 'myself as I would like to be', 'myself as I am now', 'myself as my family see me', 'myself 5 years ago'. A therapist who wanted to understand a client's addiction might include 'myself before drinking', 'myself after drinking', 'myself as I believe I will be after drinking', and someone trying to sort out marital problems might include 'myself as I appear to my partner' as well as 'my partner'. The scope to tailor the repertory grid to the circumstances of any individual is one of the great strengths of the technique. However, for now we shall merely consider the types of elements that might be appropriate for 'normal' individuals.

The participant taking the grid shown in Figure 12.1 has filled in the names of five appropriate individuals under their 'role titles' in the first row of the grid.

	Father Peter	Mother Fiona	Self David	Boss Mark	Friend Fred	
Mean						Generous
Happy						Miserable
Lively						Quiet
etc.						etc.

Figure 12.1 Example of a repertory grid.

The participant is then given just three of these names, which have been chosen more or less at random, and is asked to think of one important *psychological* way in which any one of these individuals differs from the other two. For example, they might see Peter and Mark as being 'mean' – this is the 'emergent pole' of the first construct. They would then be asked to describe the opposite of 'mean'. It could be 'generous', 'helpful', or many other possibilities, and it does not have to be a *logical* opposite in the sense of a dictionary definition. However, let us suppose that our participant decides that the opposite of 'mean' is 'generous' – this is the 'contrast pole' of the construct. The words describing the emergent and contrast poles of the construct are entered into the first row of the repertory grid, as shown in Figure 12.1. The process is then repeated using another three elements, until sufficient constructs have been generated or until the participant is unable to produce any new constructs. Few people can produce more than a dozen or so different constructs. If someone gets 'stuck' and finds it difficult to think of a new construct, it is useful to encourage them to group the elements differently. Rather than looking for a construct which differentiates one's boss from oneself and one's brother, one could reflect on how one differs from one's brother and one's boss, or how one's brother differs from one's boss and oneself.

Two points need to be borne in mind when encouraging someone to reveal their constructs. First, they should be encouraged to produce constructs that are psychological characteristics and not (for example) physical features (e.g. tall vs. short, male vs. female) or anything to do with an individual's background or habits (e.g. poor vs. wealthy, city-dweller vs. countryman, drinker vs. teetotaller). The second important principle is that each construct should be different from those given previously. Gentle questioning is necessary to ensure that the participant feels that this is the case.

	Father Peter	Mother Fiona	Self David	Boss Mark	Friend Fred	
Mean	1	4	5	1	2	Generous
Happy	4	5	1	5	3	Miserable
Lively	5	4	2	5	3	Quiet
Hedonistic	5	4	3	5	4	Moral
Friendly	4	1	1	3	1	Aloof
etc.						etc.

Figure 12.2 Completed repertory grid.

Once the participant's constructs have been discovered, it is necessary to find out how they view ('construe') each of the elements. There are several ways of doing this. The simplest is to ask the participant to rate each element on a five-point scale. A rating of 1 indicates that the phrase in the left-hand column (the 'emergent pole') of the construct describes the element very accurately – for the first construct in Figure 12.1 this is 'mean'. A rating of 5 indicates that the phrase in the right-hand column (the 'contrast pole' of the construct) describes the element very accurately – 'generous' in this case. A rating of 2 would show that the element was fairly mean, a rating of 4 that they were fairly generous, and a rating of 3 that they were neither particularly mean nor particularly generous. Each person or 'element' is rated in this way, and one then moves on to the next construct. The repertory grid eventually looks something like that shown in Figure 12.2.

SELF-ASSESSMENT QUESTION 12.2

What is meant by (a) a construct, (b) a role title, (c) an element and (d) a triad?

THE ANALYSIS OF REPERTORY GRIDS

Whole books have been written about how to analyse these grids, and the possibilities are virtually endless. Simply looking at the grids can help one to obtain a general impression of how an individual construes him- or herself, and some clinical work relies on this approach. However, most analyses explore two main areas – patterns of similarities between the constructs, and similarities between the elements.

Similarities between the constructs are interesting because they reveal the 'stereotypes' which were discussed earlier. You can see this for yourself from the grid shown in Figure 12.2. If an element has a rating of 1 or 2 on the 'happy vs. miserable' construct, then they also tend to have a rating of 1 or 2 on the 'lively vs. quiet' construct. The same is true for ratings of 4 and 5. This shows that the individual perceives happy people as being lively, and miserable individuals as being quiet, which is really rather an interesting finding.

The obvious way to analyse these relationships is to correlate the rows of the matrix together, but there is a problem with this technique. Consider for now the two constructs 'hedonistic/moral' and 'friendly/aloof'. It is clear that the ratings given to the elements on these two constructs are not very similar. However, if you examine the correlations between these two rows (a useful exercise if you have a computer available) you will find that they are quite large. This is because correlation coefficients ignore differences in the mean scores (and standard deviations) of each variable. You should beware of this when interpreting correlations between constructs. It is not sensible to conclude that, because these constructs show a high correlation, the participant views hedonistic people as friendly and moral people as aloof. You can see from the grid that this is patently untrue. This individual does not view *anyone* as being particularly hedonistic. Use the word 'relatively' to remind you of this – the participant sees those who are *relatively* more friendly as *relatively* more hedonistic.

There is no reason at all why you should not invent your own statistics for comparing the *absolute* similarity of the ratings given to two constructs. You could, for example, add up the differences between two rows, ignoring any minus signs, e.g. the similarity between friendly/aloof and hedonistic/moral constructs would then be $5 - 4 = 1 + 3 + 2 + 2 + 3$, or 11. For happy/miserable and lively/quiet constructs this statistic is 3. Alternatively, you could take the square root of the average squared difference between the pairs of ratings:

$$\sqrt{\frac{(5-4)^2 + (4-1)^2 + (3-1)^2 + (5-3)^2 + (4-1)^2}{5}} = 2.3$$

for the friendly/aloof and hedonistic/moral constructs, whilst for happy/miserable and lively/quiet constructs this statistic is 0.8. The only drawback of using this approach is that it is not possible to tell whether a particular value of one of your home-made statistics is significant. However, when one is dealing with individuals in a clinical setting this will probably not matter too much, since the therapist will probably be interested in discovering which pair(s) of constructs are most similar (i.e. the rank-order of the measures of similarity), rather than anything sophisticated involving significance tests, and the home-made statistic is quite capable of showing this.

The second way of analysing grids is to look for similarities between its *columns*. This shows whether the participant sees two *elements* as being similar. For example, look at the columns representing the participant's father and their boss (Mark) in Figure 12.2. You can see that this participant tends to place these two individuals in similar positions on each of the constructs. When one has a rating of 1 or 2 the other is likely to have a similar rating. This shows that the participant regards these two individuals as having much the same type of personality. Here I feel that it is really *essential* to use a statistic such as those described in the last paragraph in preference to a correlation coefficient.

Some psychologists perform much more complex analyses on the data from repertory grids. One popular technique, called 'factor analysis', will be discussed in Chapters 14 and 15. My own view is that most such analyses should be avoided at all costs, since the data rarely if ever meet the statistical requirements for these analyses. Quite apart from the fact that the analysis is performed upon correlations (an approach which, as we have seen, is of dubious value when correlating elements together), the small amount of data produced by the repertory grids means that each of the correlations has a large amount of error associated with it – so that a small change to one of the numbers in a grid can have quite a dramatic effect on the size of the correlations. This in turn can have a drastic influence on the results from the factor analysis. It is really much safer to keep the analyses simple. Although several packages are available for analysing repertory grids, I would counsel against their use.

EXPLORING REPERTORY GRID TECHNIQUES

You may find it interesting either to complete a repertory grid yourself, or to assist a close friend in doing so. (In the latter case, do make certain that you treat the results from this exercise confidentially, and that you offer sensitive feedback – see Chapter 2.) The first step is to draw up a list of 'elements' for the person who will complete the grid. Give a list of 'role titles' such as self, mother, father, partner, a same-sex friend, someone who is disliked, an opposite-sex friend, an influential teacher, someone who is pitied, least-favourite politician, a brother, a sister, self in 10 years' time. You should choose about a dozen characters who seem appropriate for the person concerned.

Next you should decide how many constructs to elicit – again, about a dozen is probably a reasonable number. Assuming that you are going to elicit 12 constructs, you should prepare a list of 12 different 'triads' of elements, e.g. 'mother/self/least-favourite politician', 'same-sex friend/opposite-sex friend/ brother'. It should not matter too much whom you use, but it would be sensible to check that you use each element at least twice.

The third step is to draw the grid on a sheet of paper, using Figure 12.1 as a model. Your grid should have 14 columns (for the 12 elements plus the two poles of each construct) and 12 rows. Having constructed the grid, you are ready to start testing.

First of all, you should explain the purpose of the experiment and ensure that the participant is happy for you to know what they think of all the important people in their life. If you detect any kind of reluctance you should simply complete the grid yourself. You should then ask the participant to write in the name of one individual who fills each of these 12 roles that you have written in the first row of the grid: these will be the 12 *elements*. Each person's name should appear only once, and if some role titles seem inappropriate (e.g. 'brother' for an only child), the participant should be encouraged to think of the name of a person whom, for example, they *think of* as a brother.

The next step is to present first triads of elements from your list and ask the participant to think of the most obvious way in which any *one* of the three individuals differs from the other two. Their response, in the form of a word or short phrase, should be written down in the first column. You should then ask the participant to name the opposite of this characteristic, and enter that word or phrase in the final column. This is then repeated for the remaining 11 triads. You should check that each construct is a *psychological* characteristic, and that it appears different from those that have gone before. If two constructs look similar, you should ask the participant whether (for example) 'content/up-tight' means the same to them as 'relaxed/anxious'. If it does, you should invite them to try to think of another construct. If they experience difficulty in doing so, suggest that they think about using the triad in a different way. For example, instead of thinking about how they differ from their father and their mother, they could consider how their mother differs from them and their father, for example. It may happen that the participant is eventually unable to produce any new constructs, and in this case you should either move on to the next triad or simply carry on to the next stage.

The final stage involves placing people on each of the constructs. Several techniques for doing this are discussed in the literature. Some experimenters ask participants to rank-order the elements on each of the constructs (a difficult and time-consuming task), whilst others may ask participants to assign half of the elements to the emergent pole of the construct (these being marked by crosses in the grid), the remainder being assigned to the contrast pole of the construct. However, the simplest technique is simply to use a five-point scale, where a rating of 1 implies that the emergent pole describes the element very well, a rating of 5 suggests that the contrast pole is an excellent description of their character, etc.

In order to analyse the grid, you should transfer these ratings to either a spreadsheet or your favourite statistics package and perform the analyses described in the previous section. You will probably want to correlate all possible pairs of constructs together (a 12×12 grid like this will yield 66 correlations, which is why it is best to use a computer for such analyses). You may want to perform significance tests to determine which of these are significantly different from zero, and you should explore these findings with the person who completed the grid. For example, if you found an extremely high correlation between 'happy/depressed' and 'adventurous/timid' constructs, you would conclude that the person probably views adventurous people as being happy and timid people as being depressed. People are very often unaware of the way in which their constructs are related, and the discussion of such interrelationships can prove quite insightful.

You may then like to compute some statistic to show how similarly each pair of elements is construed, possibly using the 'total absolute difference' or 'root-mean-square difference' statistics discussed above. This will show which pairs of individuals are viewed most similarly, and again this can yield interesting results of which the participant is unaware. We run a repertory grid practical at the university where I teach, and each year I am amazed by how many of the female students' boyfriends are construed in much the same way as their fathers!

The test–retest reliability of the repertory grid has been quite widely studied (e.g. Feixas *et al.*, 1992), and it is generally concluded that students produce rather similar grids if they are retested on another occasion, but that the grids of schizophrenics can vary quite markedly from one time to another.

Repertory grids have a very wide range of uses, since they can be designed for specific applications as diverse as understanding how individuals categorise works of art and eliciting experts' knowledge which can then be used as the knowledge-base for 'expert-system' computer programs.

SELF-ASSESSMENT QUESTION 12.3

How might you use repertory grid techniques to discover how individuals categorise complex stimuli, such as works of art?

There have also been some elaborations of Kelly's theory. Hinckle's work (1965, unpublished results) on the 'implication grid' attempts to explore some of the relationships between the constructs in more detail. In particular, this technique aims to discover a hierarchical (pyramid-like) structure of constructs rather like that shown in Figure 12.3. Here some constructs are thought to be *subordinate* to others, or affected by the way in which other constructs are used. In Figure 12.3, the way in which an element is evaluated on the good/bad construct will influence the way in which they are evaluated on the honest/dishonest and open/secretive constructs, *but not vice versa*. Moreover, 'open/secretive' will in turn influence 'friendly/unfriendly' and 'kindly/hard'. Thus if a person is construed in a certain way using one of the higher-order constructs, this will influence the way in which they are construed on some other constructs in the system. Unfortunately, there is no space to consider the details of this procedure, but they are provided in several books (e.g. Bannister and Mair, 1968; Bannister and Fransella, 1971) and journal articles (e.g. Caputi *et al.*, 1990).

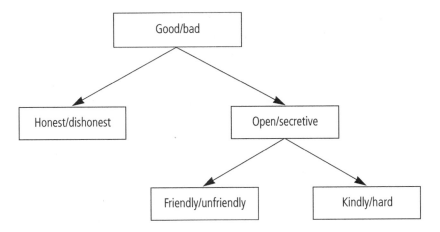

Figure 12.3 Hypothetical hierarchical arrangement of constructs.

CRITIQUE OF REPERTORY GRIDS

Although it offers plausible explanations about the way in which we perceive ourselves and others, Kelly's model of personality is almost purely descriptive. It says relatively little about the processes which govern our choice and use of constructs. What, specifically, makes a person decide to try out a particular construct in the first place? What are the criteria used to determine whether the construct system requires revision, and what determines how this is done (e.g. the introduction of new constructs or the re-evaluation of certain elements)? Why do people develop such different construct systems?

Second, theories should by definition be testable. How could one determine whether Kelly's view of 'man-the-scientist' is correct? The theory may 'feel right' to individuals, but does this necessarily mean that it is an accurate description of their behaviour? I mention in Chapter 11 that if students are given a personality test and each of them is later handed an individually addressed 'personality profile' allegedly laying bare the innermost secrets of their personality, most individuals express amazement as to how accurate and insightful the test results are – even when all of the students in the group are presented with exactly the same feedback, which bears absolutely no relationship to the way in which they answered the personality test. People are generally happy to believe nice things about themselves, a phenomenon known as the 'Barnum effect' (after the showman). This means that subjective reactions to grid interpretations are really a rather unreliable way of establishing whether they are accurate. You may like to ask yourself what firm evidence there is that people do actually walk about mentally rating other individuals on constructs, and you may perhaps question whether constructs may not be laboratory phenomena that bear little or no relationship to real life. Can the theory be disproved?

Third, it is rather difficult to make specific predictions on the basis of the theory. Constructs are extremely useful for describing how people view their worlds, but not for predicting behaviour in specific circumstances. If a person uses constructs such as 'idiot/OK guy', 'tough/weak' and 'determined to get own way/compliant' (rating themselves as being an 'OK guy' who is tough and determined to get their own way), then it seems reasonable to suspect that they may be somewhat aggressive – but under what circumstances? And in what way are they aggressive? Engaging in heated political debate as a professional politician, partner-beating, or viewing violent videos? The theory cannot tell us.

Fourth, the repertory grid basically consists of a series of self-reports. The theory therefore has to assume that individuals are conscious of their true feelings towards themselves and others, a view with which some theorists (e.g. Freud and his followers) would disagree.

Finally, it should be clear from your own experience of administering and interpreting another person's repertory grid that phenomenology is both the greatest strength and the greatest weakness of Kelly's theory. Whilst the clinician may find it very useful to try to understand how an individual views his or her phenomenological world, problems can arise when we try to interpret precisely what someone means by their constructs.

Suppose that one person uses 'nervous/confident' as one of their constructs, someone else uses 'uptight/cool', and a third person uses 'anxious/sane'. Do any of these constructs mean the same thing? There is simply no way of telling. This makes it virtually impossible to compare repertory grids produced by different people. You might think that simply forcing individuals to use the same construct (that is, *supplying* a standard set of constructs to be used when completing the grid) would solve this problem. In my view it does not. Your definition of 'anxious' and/or 'sane' might be quite different from mine, so we might use the 'anxious/sane' construct in quite different ways. Thus Kelly's theory, like that of Rogers, is strictly a psychology for understanding individuals. It does not easily allow for the comparison of different people.

SUGGESTED ADDITIONAL READING

The various editions of Bannister and Fransella's book *Inquiring Man* (e.g. 1971), *Experimenting with Personal Construct Theory* (Fransella and Thomas, 1988) and Fransella and Bannister's (1977) manual for the technique are good starting-points, and Neimeyer (1985) traces the development of the technique. There is also a considerable literature on the application of grid methodology, although these articles tend to appear in specialised journals that are not widely available. There are also some excellent personal-construct psychology sites on the World Wide Web. The obvious source of information on Q-sort methodology is Block's (1961) book, and also his account of a large longitudinal study in which Q-sort methodology was used to tame an unruly mass of qualitative data (Block, 1971).

ANSWERS TO SELF-ASSESSMENT QUESTIONS

SAQ 12.1

There is no simple way of testing this. After all, the individual is the only person who can really comment on some of his or her deepest, most personal feelings. However, it might be possible to attempt some experiments. One approach could involve giving the Q-sort twice, after a gap of a week or two, and checking that the person produces roughly the same arrangement of cards. If there *is* a marked discrepancy (and the client cannot think of any reason why their self-image may have altered), then it may be unwise to proceed with the technique. Alternatively, the cards (and particularly those towards the extremes of the distribution, which best and least describe the individual) could be put into a questionnaire, and other people (e.g. partner, parents, close friends) could be asked to rate the client on each quality. This would show whether the client's self-image was consistent with other people's impressions of them.

SAQ 12.2

(a) A construct is a psychological dimension which an individual finds useful when classifying a certain set of elements (usually people).

(b) A role title is the name of a type of person with whom the individual is likely to be well acquainted (e.g. a brother). A wide range of role titles is used to ensure that the individual considers a wide range of people when completing the grid.

(c) An element is a particular individual who fills one of the role titles (e.g. John, who is 'a brother').

(d) A triad is a group of three elements used to elicit constructs by asking the individual to name one psychological way in which any one of the elements in the triad is very different to the other two.

SAQ 12.3

Either provide or elicit a list of elements, e.g. paintings, smells, faces or pieces of music. Present three of these and ask the individual to describe how one differs from the other two – then continue and analyse as before. The ratings given to the constructs can perhaps be correlated with features of the stimuli (e.g. the year in which they were painted or written) in order to help to identify the constructs.

13

The reliability and validity of psychological tests

BACKGROUND

Chapter 11 made the point that individuals' scores on psychological tests are often used as operational definitions of abstract psychological concepts. It is thus vitally important to be able to check that the scores on any psychological test have little random measurement error associated with them (high reliability) and do, in fact, measure what they *purport* to measure (high validity).

Recommended prior reading

Chapters 1 and 11.

INTRODUCTION

This chapter covers some basic principles about measurement – both in the physical world and when assessing individual differences. In particular, we shall examine the concepts of systematic and random errors of measurement, and see how these principles lead naturally to an important aspect of psychometrics known as *reliability theory*. Finally, we shall consider how we can determine whether a test really measures what it claims to – that is, whether it is *valid*.

One fundamental and entirely uncontroversial characteristic of psychological tests is that each scale should assess one (and only one) psychological characteristic. For example, suppose that the four-item test shown in Table 13.1 was given to an individual. Its items are scored by giving a score of zero points for a 'no' response, a score of one point for an 'uncertain' response, and a score of two points for a 'yes' response. Suppose that one individual obtained a total score of 4 on this scale. What conclusion might you draw about his or her personality?

Item 1 I often feel anxious	Yes/Uncertain/No
Item 2 A good, loud party is the best way to celebrate	Yes/Uncertain/No
Item 3 I have been to see my doctor because of 'nerves'	Yes/Uncertain/No
Item 4 I hate being on my own	Yes/Uncertain/No

Table 13.1 Hypothetical four-item personality questionnaire

The answer is, quite simply, that one cannot hope to draw *any* conclusion from a person's scores on this scale, since its items seem to measure two distinct concepts. Items 1 and 3 appear to assess anxiety, whilst items 2 and 4 appear to measure sociability. Thus a total score of 4 on this test could arise if an individual was:

- anxious and unsociable (scoring 2, 0, 2, 0);
- non-anxious and sociable (scoring 0, 2, 0, 2);
- moderately anxious and moderately sociable (scoring 1, 1, 1, 1);

... etc.

It should be intuitively obvious that when tests are scored in this way, it is possible to interpret their meaning only if all of the items in a scale measure the same underlying psychological characteristic. If all four items measured anxiety, the higher a person's score on the test, the more anxious they would be. However, such an interpretation is not possible when the items measure two or more quite different characteristics, as in the above example. Thus it is vital to ensure that all of the items in a particular scale measure one (and only one) trait. There are two basic ways of achieving this. In the present chapter, we shall consider reliability theory – a theory that initially *assumes* that all items measure the same characteristic, and tests whether this is likely to be the case. In Chapters 14 and 15 we shall examine a technique that allows us to *explore* how many characteristics are measured by a particular set of items.

PSYCHOLOGICAL AND PHYSICAL MEASUREMENT

Measurement of everyday objects can be achieved with remarkable precision. Although there is always some 'error of measurement' associated with measures of size, mass or volume, this is generally quite a small percentage of the quantity being measured. The digital scales in my kitchen weigh flour to an accuracy of 2 g, so when weighing 225 g of flour, the measurement error is of the order of plus or minus 1 per cent. A surveyor's tape-measure may have markings every centimetre, so the error involved in measuring the position of either end of this tape may be approximately plus or minus 0.5 cm. Thus the total error in measuring the size of a 300-cm wall in my study will be of the order of plus or minus $\frac{2 \times 0.5 \text{ cm}}{300 \text{ cm}}$, or 0.3 per cent. Even more accurate techniques are available to measure such distances with a greater degree of precision when required.

The error associated with making each measurement can be regarded as 'random', in that it will vary randomly from one occasion to another. If the wall were to be measured 100 times, its length would sometimes seem to be as much as 301 cm or as little as 299 cm, but when the 100 measurements were averaged, they should give a better estimate of the true length of the wall than would be obtained from only one measurement, since these random errors of measurement will tend to average each other out.

Other methods of measuring the length of my study include the use of a digital tape-measure. This measures how long it takes for a pulse of sound, transmitted from a small box held against one wall, to travel to the other end of the room and be reflected back. Finally, we could measure the circumference of a small wooden roller and count the number of rotations it makes as it is passed over the wall. Multiplying the circumference of the roller by the number of rotations should give the length of the room.

As well as ensuring that measurement errors are as small as possible, measuring instruments are designed to ensure that the readings obtained are influenced by only one physical variable, namely the one that it is supposed to measure. For example, the readings obtained on the digital scales should not be affected by the time of day when the measurement is made, the temperature of the room, the colour or nature of the object being measured – or anything else except its mass. This is directly equivalent to the principle demonstrated using the four-item test – measuring instruments should measure only *one characteristic* of an object.

In practice, this is not quite so simple as it sounds. Assume for now that the measuring tape, the digital tape-measure and the roller are completely free from measurement error – the 'random errors' mentioned above. Does this imply that the length of my study can be measured with complete accuracy? Unfortunately it does not, since none of these tools measures *only* length. The surveyor's tape-measure will expand and contract slightly as the temperature and the humidity change, and so it will give a slightly different reading on a cold, humid day to that on a hot, dry one. The accuracy of the digital tape-measure will be slightly affected by air pressure, so it would give a slightly different reading if my study were transported to the top of Everest. If the wallpaper is heavily embossed, the roller would measure the overall length of the peaks and troughs in the paper in addition to the length of the room.

Thus, even though we may *assume* that these devices all measure length (and length alone), the measurements shown on any of these devices will actually be influenced by several different variables. We call these sources of 'systematic error'. Unlike the random errors discussed above, sources of systematic errors will not tend to cancel out when repeated measurements are made under the same physical conditions. If we measure the length of the room

100 times with a tape-measure on a cold wet day, the reading will *always* be slightly overestimated, since the tape-measure will have shrunk.

This is shown diagrammatically in Figure 13.1, together with the influence of random error (error in reading the tape). Here the sources of error are denoted by ellipses, and arrows indicate that each of these influences the reading that is obtained (designated by the rectangle). Since there is also some random error associated with reading the tape-measure, this too is included in the diagram. The numbers against each arrow indicate the relative importance of each of these factors in determining the reading on the tape-measure. Thus it can be seen that the reading on the tape-measure is influenced far more by the length of the room than by anything else, with humidity, measurement error and temperature being the next three most important variables.

Given that these three ways of measuring the length of my wall (i.e. a tape-measure, roller or digital tape-measure) are all influenced by different physical variables, how should one estimate the 'real' length on the basis of three slightly different readings? The obvious solution is to average the three readings. Hopefully it will be intuitively obvious that the average of three measures is likely to be closer to the 'true' value than any one measure alone.

We can summarise this in a few basic principles as follows.

- 'Good' measurement instruments are those that are little influenced by random error.
- 'Good' measurement instruments are also uninfluenced by sources of systematic error.

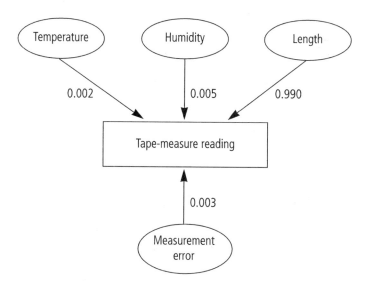

Figure 13.1 Variables affecting readings on a measuring tape. The figures against each arrow show the relative importance of each of these in determining the reading.

- Taking multiple measurements under any set of physical conditions and averaging the results reduces the impact of random errors.
- Averaging measurements from different instruments will tend to reduce the effects of systematic error.

MEASUREMENT IN PSYCHOLOGY

In psychology, the response that an individual makes to a test item is analogous to the measure of length obtained by one of the methods described above – with one important practical difference, particularly in the case of personality measures.

EXERCISE

Suppose that you asked a student the question 'do you enjoy drunken parties?' in a personality questionnaire, and they then responded by marking a five-point scale ranging from 'strongly agree' to 'strongly disagree'. Try to make a list of half a dozen factors that might influence which response they mark.

Apart from those variables that are likely to show little variation within the group (such as being able to understand all of the words in the sentence) my list includes the following:

- their level of extraversion (a personality trait);
- the number of parties they have recently attended (their liver may need a rest);
- their age;
- their religious beliefs/ethnic background;
- social desirability – some students may find it difficult to admit that they would much rather be working in the university library than partying, and so would tend to overstate their true liking for parties;
- the context in which the question is asked – a potential employer and a psychology student might well obtain different answers to this question;
- the student's impression of what is being assessed – for example, one person may read the question, assume that it is being used to assess whether they have a drinking problem, and answer it accordingly, whereas someone else may believe that it measures their level of extraversion, and so answer it accordingly;
- the way in which a person uses the five-point scale – some individuals use scores of 1 and 5 quite freely, whilst others never use the extremes of the scale;
- a tendency to agree – it has been found that people tend to agree with statements;
- the student's mood;
- random error – if you asked the student the same question a couple of minutes later you might obtain a slightly different result.

Your list probably contains other important variables, too. A whole host of these 'nuisance factors' determines how an individual will respond to a single item in a personality test, and we shall consider some of these in Chapter 17. Much the same applies to ability tests. Performance here might be affected by anxiety, luck in guessing the correct answer, misunderstanding of what is expected, social pressures (deliberately under-performing so as not to stand out from the group), perceived importance of obtaining a high mark, and so on, as well as ability. We could make a similar case for ratings of behaviour (when aspects of the rater's personality and sensitivity would also affect the ratings made). Thus every piece of data collected when assessing individual differences is likely to be influenced by a vast number of factors, as shown in Figure 13.2.

It would be possible to conduct experiments in order to determine the extent to which each of these variables influences an individual's response to this particular question. If the question is designed to measure the trait of extraversion, it will be a 'good' item if the effects of all the other variables are small, in much the same way as a 'good' measure of length is influenced by distance and not temperature, air pressure or anything else. In the previous example, involving measurement of the length of the wall, the actual length of the wall is by far the most important influence on the reading obtained on the tape-measure. Unfortunately, in psychology, this is not the case. It is almost impossible to find a personality test item for which the personality trait accounts more than 20 to 30 per cent of the variation in individuals' responses to the items. Most of the variation is due to other factors.

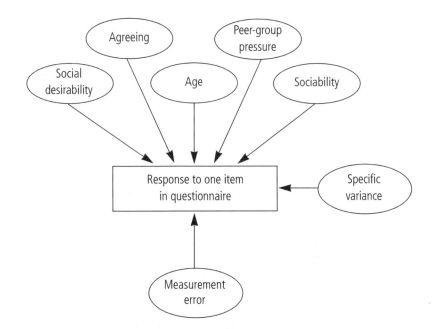

Figure 13.2 Some variables that may influence a person's response to one item on a personality inventory.

This is rather embarrassing. It seems that it is difficult or impossible to devise items that are pure measures of a trait, since individuals' responses to a single test item are going to be influenced by a whole host of traits, states, attitudes, moods and luck. So how can we ever hope to assess personality or ability with any degree of accuracy?

Fortunately, there is a way. It is possible to list some other items measuring extraversion, each of which is affected by a *different* set of 'nuisance factors'. Chapter 5 shows that Eysenck views extraverts as being sociable, optimistic, talkative and impulsive, etc., so it would be possible to phrase questions to measure these variables, too. An item such as 'do you keep quiet on social occasions?' would be influenced by a number of nuisance factors, only a few of which would be the same as for the first item. Thus if a questionnaire were constructed from a number of items, each affected by a different set of nuisance factors, the influence of the nuisance factors would tend to cancel out, whilst the influence of the trait would accumulate. Thus in order to produce a more accurate measure of a personality trait, it is simply necessary to:

- write several items, each measuring a different aspect of that trait, and thus affected by a different set of 'nuisance factors';
- score these items; and
- add the scores together.

The total (or average) score on the questionnaire will inevitably be a better estimate of an individual's trait score than the response to any one item, since the 'nuisance factors' will have cancelled each other out. This is exactly the same principle as was suggested in the previous section. There I argued that, in order to obtain the 'best' estimate of the length of the room from three measurements that are all slightly different (because each is affected by a different set of nuisance factors), we should simply take the average of these values. When we do this, 80 per cent, 90 per cent or even more of the variation in the total score on a test is caused by the personality trait, which is far better than the 20 to 30 per cent that can be achieved by even the best individual item. This simple principle forms the basis of 'reliability theory', which will be discussed in the next section.

Before we leave this section, it is necessary to explain what is meant by the term 'specific variance', which crept unannounced into Figure 13.2. The rest of the arrows in this figure suggest that an individual's response to this item can be *entirely understood* in terms of five basic processes (plus some measurement error, which we can ignore). However, this need not be so. It is quite possible that someone who is not extraverted, who does not enjoy drinking and whose response is not much influenced by any of the other 'nuisance factors' may nevertheless just happen to enjoy drunken parties. That is, someone might happen to strongly agree with this question, even though it would be impossible to predict that they would do so from a knowledge of all their attitudes, personality traits, and the rest of the nuisance factors. It is necessary to take this into account, and the term called 'specific variance' does so.

THE RELIABILITY OF MENTAL TESTS

In the previous section I showed that, whilst an individual test item is a poor measure of a trait, a much better estimate of the value of a trait can be obtained if we add up the scores on a number of items, each of which measures some different aspect of the trait. Suppose that about 20 or so items are listed to measure a certain trait, and are then administered to about 200 people. Here we *assume* that all of the items measure the trait – we shall discuss how to test this assumption and eliminate items that are poor measures of the trait in Chapter 18. Specialised computer programs (such as the SPSS 'reliability' procedure) can be used to calculate a statistic from these data which various authors have referred to as the 'reliability' of a test, 'alpha', 'coefficient alpha', 'KR-20', 'Cronbach's alpha' or 'internal consistency'. The details of how the statistic is calculated need not concern us here, but can be found in most psychometrics texts. As you might expect from reading the previous section, coefficient alpha is influenced by two factors:

- the average size of the correlation between the test items. Since we assumed in the previous section that different test items are affected by different 'nuisance factors', the only reason why individuals' responses to any pair of items *should* be correlated is because both of these items measure the same underlying trait. Thus if all of the items in a test measure the same trait, the correlations between them will be large and positive (after scoring);
- the number of items in the scale. Again, I pointed out that the whole purpose of building a scale from several test items is to try to ensure that the nuisance factors cancel out. It should hopefully be obvious that the more items there are in a scale, the more likely it is that these nuisance factors will all cancel out. The Spearman–Brown formula (given in any standard psychometrics text) is useful here. It allows one to predict how the reliability of the scale will increase or decrease if the number of items in the scale is changed.

	Item 1	Item 2	Item 3	Item 4	Item 5
Item 1	1.0				
Item 2	−0.02	1.0			
Item 3	0.10	0.28	1.0		
Item 4	0.15	0.31	0.24	1.0	
Item 5	0.12	0.25	0.27	0.36	1.0

Table 13.2 Correlations between five hypothetical test items

What you *should* remember is that the reliability of a test is simply a statistic that can be calculated from any set of data (so long as there are more than about 200 people in the sample). Remember, too, that its maximum possible value is 1.0 (its minimum value can, under some circumstances, be less than zero). It is amazingly important. For long tests, the square root of coefficient alpha is a very close approximation to the correlation between individuals' scores on a particular mental test and their 'true score' on a trait (Nunnally, 1978). Thus a coefficient alpha of 0.7 implies a correlation of $\sqrt{0.7}$ or 0.84 between scores on the test and individuals' true scores, whereas an alpha value of 0.9 implies that the correlation is as high as 0.95. Since the whole purpose of using psychological tests is to try to achieve as close an approximation as possible to a person's true score on a trait, it follows from this that tests should have a high value of alpha.

A widely applied rule of thumb states that a test should not be used if it has an alpha value below 0.7, and that it should not be used for important decisions about an *individual* (e.g. for assessment of the need for remedial education) unless its alpha value is above 0.9.

SELF-ASSESSMENT QUESTION 13.1

Five test items measuring extraversion were given to a large sample of people. The correlations between the test items were calculated, and are shown in Table 13.2.

(a) What does the correlation between any pair of items show?

(b) Which item seems to be the least effective measure of extraversion?

(c) Suppose that you calculated alpha from the correlations shown in Table 13.2 and found that it was lower than 0.7. What might you do?

This seems straightforward enough, but we have not yet said anything about the *content* of the test items. The problem is that it is very easy to boost the average correlation between test items by essentially asking the same question more than once, only slightly rephrasing it each time. This will ensure that all of the 'nuisance factors' that affected the first item will also affect the second one. Since both questions refer to the same behaviour, they will also share much of their *specific* variance. Thus one would expect the correlation between the two items to be close to 1.0. Two such items might be 'I enjoy parties' and 'I enjoy social gatherings'. Since these two items essentially ask exactly the same question, it is difficult to imagine that many people could possibly strongly agree with one and strongly disagree with the other. The responses to the two items are *bound* to have a huge positive correlation. Given that the correlations between test items are usually small (at best of the order of 0.2 to 0.3), a correlation of 0.9 inserted into this table from two virtually identical items will greatly increase the average correlation. In the example shown in Table 13.2, changing the correlation between Item 1 and

Item 2 from −0.02 to 0.9 increases the mean correlation from 0.206 to 0.298. The effect of this will be to boost alpha massively. However, it should be clear that we have broken two of the main assumptions – that each item will be influenced by a different set of 'nuisance factors', and that each will have its own 'unique variance' which is not shared with any other item.

It is thus vitally important to ensure that the items in any scale are broadly sampled. In some cases this is easy. For example, in the case of a vocabulary test it is merely necessary to sample items from a dictionary (perhaps excluding those that occur below a certain level of frequency, or which are rude, technical or archaic). When this is done, the only thing that will affect the correlation between the responses to a pair of items is the extent to which they each measure the underlying trait (spelling ability) – a principle sometimes known as 'local independence'. There is no magic formula for achieving this automatically when constructing tests. It is up to the person writing the items to ensure that the only possible reason why the responses to any pair of items should be correlated together is because of the underlying personality or ability trait which they are both assumed to measure. Unfortunately, some approaches to test construction, e.g. that advocated by Costa and McCrae (1992a), virtually guarantee that many artificially high correlations will be generated, and so will lead to an over-estimate of alpha. Cooper (in press) suggests how the magnitude of this problem may be estimated in existing scales.

It is also important to ensure that the sample of individuals whose test scores are used to compute alpha is similar to the group on whom the test will be used. It is pointless to find an alpha value of 0.9 with university students and then conclude that the test will be suitable for use with the members of the general population, for university students are not a random sample of the population, as they are generally young, academically talented, middle-class, literate and numerate. Again, there is no numerical way to determine whether a test that has a high alpha value in one sample will also work in another group – it is a matter of using common sense. I would certainly be wary about assuming that a personality test which was developed using American college students will work for the general population of the UK (or vice versa), but not everyone shares these misgivings. It is safest to calculate alpha whenever one uses a test, although this does presuppose that a large sample of people will be tested (Nunnally recommends a minimum of 200).

When used properly, alpha is very useful. Any test can be regarded as a sample of items from some larger *domain* of items that could, potentially, have been asked. For example, a spelling test is a sample of words from the dictionary. A test measuring anxiety is a sample of all the (many!) items that could conceivably have been listed to measure the many aspects of anxiety. A test of mathematical ability is a sample of the near-infinite number of mathematical items that could possibly have been written.

I have used the phrase 'true score' before, but have not defined its meaning. An individual's *true score* on a trait is the score that they would have obtained if they had been given every possible item in the domain. If you measured someone's ability to spell every word in the dictionary, you would know their exact spelling ability – there would be no measurement error associated with it whatsoever. However, in a test we take a small sample of items from the domain, and assemble them together. If (and only if) the items in the test form a representative sample of items in the domain, the square root of coefficient alpha closely estimate the correlation between a person's score on the test and their true score (the score that they would have obtained if they had been given all of the items in the domain to complete).

The higher the value of alpha, the less error there is in the measurement of a trait, and it is possible to derive a statistic called the 'standard error of measurement' (SEM) from a knowledge of the reliability of the test and the standard deviation of the test scores. This shows how much measurement error is likely to be associated with each measurement. One could find that if a person's score on a test is 35 one can be 99 per cent confident that their true score lies somewhere between 30 and 38.[13.1] The formula for the standard error is

$$SEM = SD \times \sqrt{1 - alpha}$$

where SD is the standard deviation of the test scores. Thus a test with a standard deviation of 10 and a reliability of 0.7 would have a standard error of 5.4. If its reliability was 0.9, the SEM would fall to 3.1. Thus a knowledge of a test's reliability allows one to draw some interesting conclusions about the amount of error that is likely to be associated with any measurement – provided, of course, that the test items can genuinely be regarded as forming a representative sample of items from the domain.

SELF-ASSESSMENT QUESTION 13.2

(a) What are KR-20 and Cronbach's alpha?

(b) Why is it unwise to paraphrase the same item a number of times when designing a questionnaire?

(c) What does the standard error of measurement tell you?

(d) Suppose that we have two tests that claim to measure anxiety. Test 1 has a reliability of 0.81, and Test 2 has a reliability of 0.56. What will be the correlation between each of these tests and the true score? What is the largest correlation that you are likely to obtain if you correlate individuals' scores on Test 1 with their scores on Test 2?

[13.1] Should you ever want to do this in practice, it is highly advisable to consult Nunnally (1978, p. 241) beforehand. The procedures given in most test manuals (even widely used ones such as the WISC-III) and in many psychometric textbooks are incorrect.

OTHER APPROACHES TO THE MEASUREMENT OF RELIABILITY

Prior to the advent of computers, it was tedious to calculate alpha by hand, so an approximation was used. Instead of adding together all of the items in a test to derive a total score, two scores were calculated – one based on the odd-numbered test items and the other on the even-numbered items. These two scores were then correlated together, and after applying the Spearman–Brown formula (since the set of the odd or even items is only half as long as the full test), this yielded the *split-half reliability*. There seems to be no good reason to use this today.

Test–retest reliability, sometimes known as temporal stability, is a completely different entity. As its name suggests, it checks whether trait scores stay more or less constant over time. Most tests are designed to measure traits such as extraversion, numerical ability or neuroticism, and the definition of a trait stresses that it is a relatively enduring disposition. This implies that individuals should have similar scores when they are tested on two occasions (say several weeks apart), provided that:

- nothing significant has happened to them in the interval between the two tests (e.g. no emotional crises, developmental changes, or significant educational experiences that might affect the trait); and
- the test is a good measure of the trait.

If a test shows that a child is a genius one month and of average intelligence the next, either the concept of intelligence is a state rather than a trait, or the test is flawed.

Assessment of test–retest reliability typically involves testing the same group of people on two occasions, which are generally spaced at least a month apart (in order to minimise the likelihood of people remembering their previous answers), yet not *too* far apart (in case developmental changes, learning or other life events affect individuals' positions on the trait). Test–retest reliability is simply the correlation between these two sets of scores. If it is high (implying that individuals have similar levels of the trait on both occasions) it can be argued that the trait is stable, and that the test is likely to be a good measure of the trait.

The problem is, of course, that the test–retest reliability is based on the total score – it says nothing about how people perform on individual items. Whereas alpha shows whether a set of items measures some single, underlying trait, a set of items that had nothing in common could still have perfect test–retest reliability. For example, if you asked someone to add their house number, their shoe size and their year of birth on two separate occasions, this statistic would show impressive test–retest reliability, although the three items have nothing in common.

Parallel-forms reliability will now be mentioned for the sake of completeness. Test constructors sometimes create more than one test from a set of items. In order to create two parallel forms of a test, items are administered to a large sample of people, and pairs of items with similar content and difficulty are identified. For example, both may involve the solution of seven-letter anagrams, the answer being a word with a similar frequency of occurrence in the language, and only about 25 per cent of the sample will be able to solve each one. One item will then be assigned to Form A of the test, and the other to Form B. These two tests are marketed separately and (in theory) it should not matter which one is used for a particular application, since care is generally taken to ensure that the two versions produce similar distributions of scores (thus allowing the same tables of norms to be used for each form of the test). If both tests measure the same trait, one would expect a high positive correlation between individuals' scores on the two forms of the test. This correlation is known as the parallel-forms reliability. However, as relatively few tests *have* parallel forms, it is rarely used.

Generalisability theory (Cronbach *et al.*, 1972) is another approach to reliability theory. A good account may be found in Cronbach (1994). This theory essentially requires investigators to be very precise about what inference is to be drawn from a set of test scores. It attempts to identify all of the sources of error that may arise in an assessment, rather as shown for individual test items in the previous section. It seeks to assess each of these independently, and to correct each individual's score for the influence of these 'nuisance factors'. Suppose that some children completed a spelling test on two occasions – the same data could be analysed in many ways, e.g. to estimate the temporal stability of the spelling test, to determine how consistently children perform in spelling, or to chart whether the spelling performance of the class has increased. The problem is that determining (and measuring) all of these variables is a very involved and ponderous procedure, and since the variables will probably shift in importance from one sample to another (pensioners may try less hard to cheat on ability tests than students, for example), it has not so far been of great practical use.

TEST VALIDITY

We have seen that reliability theory can show whether or not a set of test items seem to measure some underlying trait. What it cannot do is shed any light on the *nature* of that trait, for just because an investigator *thinks* that a set of items should measure a particular trait, there is no guarantee that they actually do so. In the early 1960s a considerable literature built up concerning the 'Repression-Sensitisation Scale' (R-S Scale). This scale was designed to measure the extent to which individuals used 'perceptual defence' – that is, tended to be less consciously aware of emotionally threatening phrases than neutral phrases when these were presented for very brief periods of time. The items formed a reasonably reliable scale, so everyone just assumed that this scale measured what it claimed to do – it generated a lot of research. Then Joy (1963, cited by Kline, 1981) found that scores on this test showed a correlation of –0.91 with a well-established test of social desirability. The maximum correlation between two tests is limited by the size of their reliabilities, so a correlation of –0.91 actually implied that *all* of the variance in the R-S Scale could be accounted for by social desirability. It was not measuring anything new at all.

This tale conveys an important message. Even if a set of items appears to form a scale, it is not possible to tell what that scale measures just by looking at the items. Instead, it is necessary to determine this empirically by a process known as test validation.

A test is said to be valid if it does what it claims to do, either in terms of theory or in practical application. For example, a test that is marketed as a measure of anxiety for use in the general UK population should measure anxiety, and not social desirability, reading skill, sociability or any other unrelated traits. A test that is used to select the job applicants who are most likely to perform best in a particular occupation really *should* be able to identify the individual(s) who will perform best. However, whilst the reliability of a test can be expressed as a certain number (for a particular sample of individuals), the validity of a test also depends on the purpose of testing. For example, a test that is valid for selecting computer programmers from the UK student population may not be useful for selecting sales executives. A test that is a valid measure of depression when used by a medical practitioner will probably not be valid for screening job applicants, since most individuals will realise the purpose of the test and distort their responses.

It follows that reliability is necessary for a test to be valid, since low reliability implies that the test is not measuring *any* single trait. However, high reliability itself does not guarantee validity, since as shown above this depends entirely on how, why and with whom the test is used.

There are four main ways of establishing whether a test is valid.

Face validity

Face validity merely checks that the test *looks* as if it measures what it is supposed to. The R-S Scale débâcle described earlier shows that scrutinising the content of items is no guarantee that the test will measure what it is intended to. Despite this, some widely used tests (particularly in social psychology) are constructed by writing a few items, ensuring that alpha is high (which is generally the case because the items are paraphrases of each other) and then piously assuming that the scale measures the concept that it was designed to assess. It is *vital* to ensure that a test has better credentials than this before using it.

Content validity

Very occasionally it is possible to construct a test which *must* be valid, by definition. For example, suppose that one wanted to construct a spelling test. Since, by definition, the dictionary contains the whole domain of items, any procedure that produces a representative sample of words from this dictionary has to be a valid test of spelling ability. This is what is meant by content validity. To give another example, occupational psychologists sometimes use 'workbasket' approaches in selecting staff, where applicants are presented with a sample of the activities that are typically performed as part of the job, and their performance on these tasks is in some way evaluated. These exercises are not psychological tests in the strict sense, but the process can be seen to have some content validity. The problem is that it is rarely possible to define the domain of potential test items this accurately. How would one determine the items that could possibly be included in a test of numerical ability, for example? Thus the technique is not often used.

Construct validity

One useful way of checking whether a test measures what it claims to assess is to perform thoughtful experiments. Suppose that a test is designed to measure anxiety in UK university students. How might its validity be checked through experiment?

The first approach (sometimes called 'convergent validation') is to check that the test scores relate to other things as expected. For example, if there are other widely used tests of anxiety on the market, a group of students could be given both tests, and the two sets of scores correlated together. A large positive correlation would suggest that the new scale is valid. Alternatively, the test could be administered to a group of students who claim to have a phobia about spiders, before and after showing them a tarantula. If their scores increase, then the test might indeed measure anxiety. The basic aim of these convergent validations is to determine whether the test scores vary as would be expected on theoretical grounds. Unfortunately, a failure to find the expected relationships might be due to some problem either with the test or with the other measures. For example, the *other* test of anxiety may not be valid, or some of the individuals who say that they are phobic about spiders may not be. However, if scores on a test do appear to vary in accordance with theory, it seems reasonable to conclude that the test is valid.

Studies of 'divergent validity' check that the test does not seem to measure any traits with which it should, in theory, be unrelated. For example, the literature claims that anxiety is unrelated to intelligence, socio-economic status, social desirability, and so on. Thus if a test that purportedly measured anxiety actually showed a massive correlation with any of these variables, doubt would be raised as to whether it really measured anxiety at all.

Predictive validity

Psychological tests are very often used to predict behaviour, and their success in doing so is known as their predictive validity. For example, a test might be given to adolescents in an attempt to predict which of them would suffer from schizophrenia later in life, or a psychological test might be used to select the most promising candidate for a post as a salesperson – the test would have predictive validity if it could be shown that the people with the highest scores on the test made the most sales. This process sounds remarkably straight-forward, but in practice tends not to be.

The first problem is the nature of the criterion against which the test is to be evaluated. For although noting a diagnosis of schizophrenia or the volume of sales achieved is quite straightforward, many occupations lack a single criterion. A university lecturer's job is a case in point. Mine involves teaching, administration and research, the supervision of postgraduate students, providing informal help with statistics and programming, supporting and encouraging undergraduates, and so on – the list is a long one, and it is not obvious how most of these activities can be evaluated, or their relative importance determined. In other cases (e.g. where employees are rated by their line-manager) different assessors may apply quite different standards.

A second problem is known as 'restriction of range'. Selection systems generally operate through several stages, e.g. initial psychometric testing to reduce the number of applicants to manageable proportions, followed by interviews and more detailed psychological assessments of individuals who get through the first stage. Applicants who are eventually appointed will all have similar (high) scores on the screening tests (otherwise they would have been rejected before the interview stage), so the range of scores in the group of individuals who are selected will be much smaller than that in the general population. This will create problems for any attempt to validate the screening test, since this restricted range of abilities will tend to reduce the correlation between the test and any criterion. There are ways around this (see Dobson, 1988, who offers one of the better solutions), but these two examples show how difficult it can be to establish the predictive validity of a test.

SELF-ASSESSMENT QUESTION 13.3

(a) Must a reliable test be valid?

(b) Must a valid test be reliable?

(c) What is meant by the construct, content and predictive validity of a test?

(d) What are 'convergent validity' and 'divergent validity'?

SUMMARY

The reliability of a test is important because it shows how closely the test score approximates to a person's true score on the trait being measured. Hence it shows whether it is reasonable to treat the score on a particular test as if it measured the underlying trait. Unfortunately, it is easy to overestimate the reliability coefficient alpha by including items in a test that are virtual paraphrases of one another – an obvious problem that is not well recognised in the literature. To avoid this, test designers need to check all pairs of test items to ensure that the assumption of local independence seems reasonable.

It is vitally important to establish the content validity, construct validity and/or predictive validity of a test before using it for any purpose whatsoever. A test with low reliability cannot be a valid measure of a trait. However, high reliability does not guarantee high validity.

SUGGESTED ADDITIONAL READING

All psychometrics textbooks and many statistics books give accounts of reliability theory. Among the best are Cronbach (1994 and other editions), Anastasi (1961 and other editions) and Guilford and Fruchter (1978). The book that psychometricians usually recommend is Nunnally (1978), and this derives many of the formulae mentioned above – for example, showing how reliability is related to the true score (equation 6.1) and how close the estimate of reliability (calculated from one sample of individuals) is to its true value (Nunnally, 1978, p. 208; beware the misprint in equation 6.13 on p. 207).

ANSWERS TO SELF-ASSESSMENT QUESTIONS

SAQ 13.1
(a) Assuming that each pair of items is influenced by a different set of nuisance factors, the correlation will show the extent to which the pair of items assesses the trait being measured – extraversion in this case.
(b) Since Item 1 shows low correlations with all of the other items, it would appear to be a poor measure of extraversion.
(c) The obvious thing would be to write more test items, give the old and new items out to a new sample of individuals (at least 200 of them) and re-compute the correlations and alpha. Since coefficient alpha depends in part on the number of items in the test, increasing the number of items will increase alpha. There is also another possibility. We saw in the answer to (b) that Item 1 really is not very good – it shows low correlations with all of the other test items. Removing this item from the test will both increase the average correlation between the remaining items (from 0.206 based on 10 correlations to 0.285 based on 6 correlations) and reduce the length of the test. The first factor will tend to increase alpha, and the second will tend to decrease it. Thus it is possible – although not certain – that removing Item 1 may also increase alpha. We shall return to this in Chapter 18.

SAQ 13.2
(a) Alternative names for the internal consistency or reliability of a test, which I have termed alpha throughout this book.
(b) Doing so is bound to produce a very high reliability, as the items share specific variance as well as measuring the same trait.

(c) The SEM shows how accurate an assessment of an individual's score is likely to be. For example, if one test suggested that a person's IQ was 100 with an SEM of 3, we would be more confident that the child's IQ really *was* 100 than if the test had an SEM of 5.

(d) $\sqrt{0.81} = 0.9$ and $\sqrt{0.56} = 0.75$. Suppose that Test 2 was completely reliable. The correlation between Test 1 and Test 2 would then be the same as the correlation between Test 1 and the true score, i.e. 0.9. However, as Test 2 is *not* perfectly reliable, the correlation will be lower. It can be shown that the largest correlation that one can expect between two tests is the product of the square roots of their reliabilities. In this case one would not expect the tests to correlate together by more than $\sqrt{0.81} \times \sqrt{0.56} = 0.9 \times 0.75 = 0.68$. This is how I was earlier able to claim that *all* of the variability in the R-S Scale could be explained by social desirability, although the correlation between the two scales was only –0.91, not –1.0.

SAQ 13.3

(a) Most certainly not. High reliability tells you that the test measures some trait or state, not what this trait or state is.

(b) Yes. Although beware if the reliability of a short scale appears to be too high (e.g. 10-item scales with a reliability of 0.9). This may suggest that the same item has been paraphrased several times.

(c) See text.

(d) In construct validation, convergent validity is a measure of whether a test correlates with the characteristics with which it *should* correlate if it is valid – for example, whether an IQ test correlates with teachers' ratings of children's academic performance. Divergent validity checks that a test shows insubstantial correlations with characteristics to which it should theoretically be unrelated. For example, scores on the IQ test could be correlated with tests measuring social desirability, various aspects of personality, etc., the expectation being that these correlations will be close to zero.

14

Factor analysis

BACKGROUND

Factor analysis is a statistical tool that lies at the very heart of individual differences research. Its many uses include constructing tests, discovering the basic dimensions of personality and ability, and showing how many distinct psychological dimensions (e.g. traits) are measured by a set of tests, or test items. This chapter introduces the broad concepts of factor analysis. Details of how to perform and interpret factor analyses are covered in Chapter 15.

Recommended prior reading

Chapters 1, 11 and 13.

INTRODUCTION

We should start by mentioning that the term 'factor analysis' can refer to two rather different statistical techniques. *Exploratory factor analysis* is the older (and simpler) technique, and forms the main basis of this chapter and the first section of Chapter 15. *Confirmatory factor analysis* and its extensions (sometimes known as 'path analysis', 'latent variable analysis' or 'Lisrel models') are useful in many areas other than individual differences, and are particularly popular in social psychology. A brief outline of *this* technique is given at the end of Chapter 15. Authors do not always make it clear whether exploratory or confirmatory factor analysis has been used. If you see the term 'factor analysis' in a journal, you should assume that it refers to an exploratory factor analysis.

Chapter 13 showed why it is important that the items in a scale all measure one (and only one) psychological variable, and introduced coefficient alpha as a measure of the reliability of a scale. This technique *assumed* that all of the items in a test formed one scale, and the reliability coefficient essentially tests whether this assumption is reasonable.

An alternative approach might involve examining a sample of test items and *discovering* how many distinct scales they contain, and which items belong to which scale(s). Suppose that a psychologist administered some vocabulary items, some comprehension items and some anagram problems to a group of volunteers. It would be most useful to know whether the vocabulary items formed one scale, the comprehension items a second scale, and the anagram-solving items a third scale, or whether (for example) the vocabulary and comprehension items formed one scale whilst the anagram problems formed another. However, let us first consider a simpler example. Suppose that, in the interests of science, you were to collect the following pieces of data from a random sample of (say) 200 fellow-students in the bar of your university or college.

- V1, body weight (kg);
- V2, degree of slurring of speech (rated on a scale from 1 to 5);
- V3, length of leg (cm);
- V4, volubility of talking (rated on a scale from 1 to 5);
- V5, length of arm (cm);
- V6, degree of staggering when attempting to walk in a straight line (rated on a scale from 1 to 5).

It seems likely that V1, V3 and V5 will all vary together, since large people will tend to have long arms and legs, and be heavy. These three items all measure some fundamental property of the individuals in your sample, namely their size. Similarly, it is likely that V2, V4 and V6 will all vary together – the amount of alcohol consumed is likely to be related to slurring of speech and talkativeness, and to difficulty in walking in a straight line. Thus although we have collected six pieces of data, these questions measure only two 'constructs', namely size and drunkenness. In factor analysis, the word 'factor' is usually used instead of the word 'construct', and we shall follow this convention from now on.

Exploratory factor analysis essentially does two things.

- It shows how many distinct psychological constructs (factors) are measured by a set of variables. In the above example there are two factors (size and drunkenness).
- It shows which variables measure which constructs. In the above example, it would show that V1, V3 and V5 measure one factor, and that V2, V4 and V6 measure another, quite different factor.

Some forms of factor analysis can in addition allow the factors to be correlated together, and can calculate each person's score on each factor ('factor scores').

Scores on entire tests (rather than test items) can also be factor-analysed – indeed, this is how the technique is normally used. Factor analysis can then show whether tests which purportedly measure the same construct (e.g. six tests that claim to measure anxiety) actually produce one factor, or whether several factors are required (indicating that the tests actually measure several different things). Factor-analysing the scores from complete tests can be extremely useful for discovering what, precisely, is measured by a group of tests, as the imprecision of language means that the same construct may be given several different names by different researchers. One person's 'anxiety' may be the same as another's 'neuroticism' or a third person's 'negative affect'. The number of terms used in individual differences psychology is potentially enormous, and without factor analysis there is no reliable way of telling whether or not several scales actually measure the same basic psychological phenomenon. For example, if a publisher's catalogue shows that there are psychological measures of 'neuroticism', 'anxiety', 'hysteria', 'ego strength', 'nervousness', 'low self-actualisation' and 'fearfulness', it seems reasonable to question whether these are indeed six quite distinct concepts, or whether the same characteristic has been given different names by researchers of different theoretical persuasions. Factor analysis can answer precisely this question, and so is extremely useful for simplifying the structure of personality and abilities.

The technique is not restricted to test items or test scores. It would be possible to factor-analyse reaction times from various types of cognitive test in order to determine which (if any) of these were related. Alternatively, suppose that one took a group of schoolchildren who had no specific training or practice in sport, and assessed their performance in 30 sports by any mixture of coaches' ratings, timings, mean length of throw, percentage of maiden overs obtained, goals scored, or whatever performance measure is most appropriate for each sport. The only proviso is that each child must compete in each sport. Factor analysis would reveal many useful findings, such as whether individuals who were good at one ball game tended to be good at all of them, whether short-distance and long-distance track events formed two distinct groupings (and which events belonged to which group), and so on. Thus instead of having to talk in terms of performance in 30 distinct areas, it would be possible to summarise this information by talking in terms of half a dozen basic sporting abilities (or however many abilities the factor analysis revealed).

EXPLORATORY FACTOR ANALYSIS BY INSPECTION

The top section of Table 14.1 shows a six-item questionnaire. Six students were asked to answer each question, using a five-point rating scale as shown in the table, and their responses are shown towards the bottom of the table. These indicate the extent to which each individual agrees with each statement.

EXERCISE

Look at the students' responses in the bottom section of Table 14.1. Try to decide on the basis of these figures whether there is any overlap between any of the six items – and if so, which. Spend about 5 minutes on this exercise.

	Q1	Q2	Q3	Q4	Q5	Q6
Q1	I enjoy socialising	1	2	3	4	5
Q2	I often act on impulse	1	2	3	4	5
Q3	I am a cheerful sort of person	1	2	3	4	5
Q4	I often feel depressed	1	2	3	4	5
Q5	It is difficult for me to get to sleep at night	1	2	3	4	5
Q6	Large crowds make me feel anxious	1	2	3	4	5

For each question please circle ONE NUMBER which describes your reaction to each statement.

Circle '5'   if you strongly agree that a statement describes you
Circle '4'   if it describes you fairly well
Circle '3'   if you are neutral or unsure about whether the statement describes you
Circle '2'   if you feel that the statement does not really describe you
Circle '1'   if you feel strongly that the statement does not describe you

	Q1	Q2	Q3	Q4	Q5	Q6
Stephen	5	5	4	1	1	2
Ann	1	2	1	1	1	2
Paul	3	4	3	4	5	4
Janette	4	4	3	1	2	1
Michael	3	3	4	1	2	2
Christine	3	3	3	5	4	5

Table 14.1 Six-item personality questionnaire and responses of five students

The first thing you may have done is to look at the mean response to each item. You can see from this that individuals tend to disagree with question 4, which has a mean rating of 2.16, whereas most individuals tend to agree with question 2, which has a mean rating of 3.5. You might also have thought of examining the variance of scores in order to see whether some questions elicit a greater range of responses than others. However, interesting though these may be, they do not really help us to understand the relationships *between* the variables. It would be useful to know whether the six questions measure six quite distinct concepts, or whether they overlap at all – and tables of means cannot show this.

In Chapter 11 it was explained that questionnaires are generally scored by adding up individuals' scores on all of the constituent items. It is tempting to do the same to the data in Table 14.1, and calculate that Stephen has a score of 18 on the questionnaire, etc. If you have attempted this, you should read through Chapter 11 again before continuing. Remember that it is sensible to add together individuals' scores only if the items all measure the same psychological concept – and we have no idea whether the six items in this questionnaire measure one, two, three, four, five or six quite distinct concepts.

The whole point of the present analysis is to answer this question, so this is not an appropriate strategy either.

Eagle-eyed readers may have noticed some trends in these data. You may have observed that individuals' responses to questions 1, 2 and 3 tend to be similar. Stephen tends to agree with all three of them, Ann tends to disagree with them, whilst the others feel more or less neutral about them. These are rough approximations, of course, but you can see that no one who rates him- or herself as '1' or '2' on one of these three questions gives him- or herself a '4' or '5' on one of the others. This may suggest that enjoying socialising, acting on impulse and having a cheerful disposition tend to go together, and so these three items might be expected to form a scale. Much the same applies to items 4 to 6. Again, people such as Stephen or Ann who give themselves a low rating on one of these three questions also give themselves a low rating on the other two questions, whilst Christine gives herself high ratings on all three questions.

Thus there seem to be two clusters of questions in this questionnaire. The first group consists of questions 1, 2 and 3 and the second group consists of questions 4, 5 and 6. However, spotting these relationships is very difficult. Had the order of the columns in Table 14.1 been rearranged, these relationships would have been difficult or impossible to identify by eye.

Fortunately, however, a statistic called the *correlation coefficient* makes it possible to determine whether individuals who have low scores on one variable tend to have low (or high) scores on other variables. A brief summary of correlational methods is given in Appendix A, which should be consulted now, if necessary.

Table 14.2 shows the correlations calculated from the data in Table 14.1. (The detailed calculation of these correlations is not shown, as statistics books such as Howell (1992) explain this in great detail.) These correlations confirm our suspicions about the relationships between the students' responses to questions 1 to 3 and questions 4 to 6. Questions 1 to 3 correlate strongly together (0.933, 0.824 and 0.696, respectively) but hardly at all with questions 4 to 6 (−0.096, etc.). Similarly, questions 4 to 6 correlate highly together

	Q1	Q2	Q3	Q4	Q5	Q6
Q1	1.000					
Q2	**0.933**	1.000				
Q3	**0.824**	**0.696**	1.000			
Q4	−0.096	−0.052	0.000	1.000		
Q5	−0.005	0.058	0.111	**0.896**	1.000	
Q6	−0.167	−0.127	0.000	**0.965**	**0.808**	1.000

Table 14.2 Correlations between the six items of Table 14.1

(0.896, 0.965 and 0.808, respectively), but hardly at all with questions 1 to 3. Thus it is possible to see from the table of correlations that questions 1 to 3 form one natural group and questions 4 to 6 form another – that is, the questionnaire actually measures two constructs or 'factors', one consisting of the first three questions and the other consisting of the final three questions.

Whilst it is easy to see this from the correlations in Table 14.2, it should be remembered that the correlations shown there are hardly typical. Specifically, the reasons for this are as follows.

- The data were constructed so that the correlations between the variables were either very large or very small. In real life, correlations between variables would rarely be larger than 0.5, with many in the range 0.2–0.3. This makes it difficult to identify patterns by eye.
- The questions were ordered so that the large correlations fell next to each other in Table 14.2. If the questions had been presented in a different order, it would not be so easy to identify clusters of large correlations.
- Only six questions were used, so there are only 15 correlations to consider. With 40 questions there would be $\frac{40 \times 39}{2}$ or 780 correlations to consider, making it much more difficult to identify groups of intercorrelated items.

There are several other problems associated with performing factor analysis 'by eye', not least of which is that different people might well reach different conclusions about the number and nature of the factors – the whole process is rather unscientific.

Fortunately, however, well-known mathematical methods can be used to identify factors from groups of variables which tend to correlate together, and even the very largest factor analyses can now be performed on a desktop computer. Several statistics packages can be used to perform factor analysis, including SPSS, BMDP, SYSTAT, Statview and SAS. To understand how computers can perform this task, it is helpful to visualise the problem in a slightly different way and adopt a geometrical approach.

A GEOMETRICAL APPROACH TO FACTOR ANALYSIS

Child (1990) has shown that it is possible to represent correlation matrices geometrically. Variables are represented by straight lines which are of equal length, and which all start at the same point. These lines are positioned such that the correlation between the variables is represented by the cosine of the angle between them. The cosine of an angle is a trigonometric function which can either be looked up in tables or computed directly by all but the simplest pocket calculators – you do not need to know what cosines mean, but just where to find them. Table 14.3 shows a few cosines to give you a general idea of the concept. Remember that when the angle between two lines is small, the cosine is large and positive. When two lines are at right angles, the correlation (cosine) is zero. When the two lines are pointing in opposite directions, the correlation (cosine) is negative.

Angle (in degrees)	Cosine of angle
0	1.000
15	0.966
30	0.867
45	0.707
60	0.500
75	0.259
90	0.000
120	−0.500
150	−0.867
180	−1.000
210	−0.867
240	−0.500
270	0.000
300	0.500
330	0.867

Table 14.3 Table of cosines for graphical representation of correlations between variables

It is but a small step to represent entire correlation matrices geometrically. A line is drawn anywhere on the page representing one of the variables – it does not matter which one. The other variables are represented by other lines of equal length, all of which fan out from one end of the first line. The angles between the variables are, by convention, measured in a clockwise direction. Variables which have large positive correlations between them will fall close to each other, as Table 14.3 shows that large correlations (or cosines) result in small angles between the lines. Highly correlated variables literally point in the same direction, variables with large negative correlations between them point in opposite directions, and variables which are uncorrelated point in completely different directions. Figure 14.1 shows a simple example. The correlation between V1 and V2 should be 0, and this is represented by a pair of lines of equal length joined at one end but at right angles (90°) to each other, as indicated in Table 14.3. The correlation between V1 and V3 is 0.5, and that between V2 and V3 is 0.867, so V3 is positioned as shown.

SELF-ASSESSMENT QUESTION 14.1

Figure 14.2 shows the geometric representation of the correlations between five variables. Use Table 14.3 to try to answer the following questions:

(a) Which two variables have the highest positive correlation?

(b) Which variable has a correlation of zero with V3?

(c) Which variable has a large negative correlation with V3?

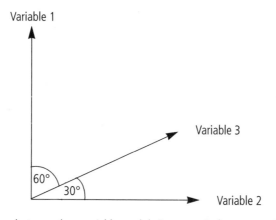

Figure 14.1 Correlations between three variables and their geometrical representation.

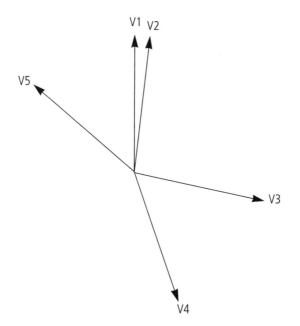

Figure 14.2 Geometrical representation of correlations between five variables.

EXERCISE

Without turning the page, try to sketch out roughly how the correlations between the six test items shown in Table 14.2 would look if they were represented geometrically.

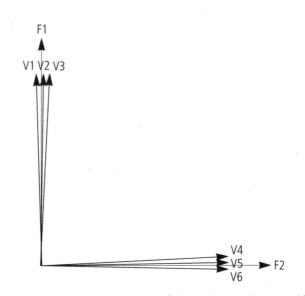

Figure 14.3 Approximate geometrical representation of the correlations shown in Table 14.2.

It may have occurred to you that it is not always possible to represent correlations in two dimensions (i.e. on a flat sheet of paper). For example, if any of the correlations in Figure 14.1 had been altered to a different value, one of the lines would have to project outward from the page to some degree. This is no problem for the underlying mathematics of factor analysis, but it does mean that it is not possible to use this geometric technique to perform real-life factor analyses.

Figure 14.3 is a fairly good approximation of the data shown in Table 14.2. Ignoring lines F1 and F2, you can see that the correlations between variables 1, 2 and 3 shown in this figure are all very large and positive (that is, the angles between these lines are small). Similarly, the correlations between variables 4 to 6 are also large and positive. As variables 1 to 3 have near-zero correlations with variables 4 to 6, variables 1, 2 and 3 are at 90° to variables 4, 5 and 6. Computer programs for factor analysis essentially try to 'explain' the correlations between the variables in terms of a smaller number of factors. It is good practice to talk about 'common factors' rather than just 'factors' – they mean the same thing, but it helps to be precise. In this example, it is clear that there are two clusters of correlations, so the information in Table 14.2 can be approximated by two 'common factors', each of which passes through a group of large correlations. The common factors are indicated by long lines labelled F1 and F2 in Figure 14.3.

It should be clear that, from measuring the angle between each common factor and each variable, it is also possible to calculate the *correlations* between each variable and each common factor. Variables 1, 2 and 3 will all have very large correlations with factor 1 (in fact variable 2 will have a correlation of nearly 1.0 with factor 1, as factor 1 lies virtually on top of it).

Variables 1, 2 and 3 will have correlations of about zero with factor 2, as they are virtually at right angles to it. Similarly, factor 2 is highly correlated with variables 4 to 6, and is virtually uncorrelated with variables 1 to 3 (because of the 90° angle between these variables and this factor). Do not worry for now where these factors come from, or how they are positioned relative to the variables, as this will be covered in subsequent sections.

In the above example, the two clusters of variables (and hence the common factors) are at right angles to each other – what is known technically as an 'orthogonal solution', a term that you should note. However, this need not always be the case. Consider the correlations shown diagrammatically in Figure 14.4. Here it is clear that there are two distinct clusters of variables, but it is equally clear that there is no way in which two orthogonal (i.e. uncorrelated) common factors, represented here by lines F1 and F2, can be placed through the centre of each cluster. It would clearly make sense to allow the factors to become correlated, and to place one common factor through the middle of each cluster of variables. Factor analyses where the factors are themselves correlated (i.e. not at right angles) are known as 'oblique solutions'. The correlations between factors form what is called a 'factor pattern correlation matrix'. Try to remember this term – it will be helpful when you come to interpret printed output from factor analyses. When an orthogonal solution is performed, all of the correlations between the various factors are zero. (A correlation of zero implies an angle of 90° between each pair of factors, which is another way of saying that the factors are independent.)

It is possible to show all the correlations between every item and every common factor in a table, called the 'factor matrix' or sometimes the 'factor structure matrix'. The correlations between items and common factors are usually known as 'factor loadings'. By convention, the common factors are shown as the columns of this table, and the variables as the rows. The values

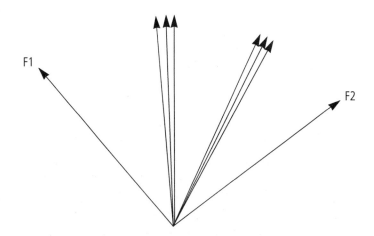

Figure 14.4 Correlations between six variables showing two factors at right angles.

in Table 14.4 were obtained by looking at the angles between each common factor and each variable in Figure 14.3, and translating these (roughly) into correlations using Table 14.3.

Variable	Factor 1	Factor 2
V1	0.90	0.10
V2	0.98	0.00
V3	0.90	−0.10
V4	0.10	0.85
V5	0.00	0.98
V6	−0.10	0.85

Table 14.4 Approximate factor structure matrix from Figure 14.3

SELF-ASSESSMENT QUESTION 14.2

Without looking back, try to define the following terms:

(a) oblique solution;

(b) factor loading;

(c) factor structure matrix;

(d) orthogonal solution;

(e) factor pattern correlation matrix.

The factor matrix is extremely important, as it shows three things.

First, it shows which variables make up each common factor. This can be seen by choosing an arbitrary cut-off point, and noting which variables have loadings that are more extreme than this value (positive or negative). By convention, the cut-off value is 0.4 or 0.3, which implies an angle of 60° to 75° between the variable and the common factor. The easiest way to see which variables 'belong' to a factor is thus to underline those that have loadings higher than 0.4 (or less than −0.4). Thus in Table 14.4 one would deduce that factor 1 is a mixture of V1, V2 and V3 (but not V4, V5 or V6, as their loadings are less than 0.4). Likewise, factor 2 is a mixture of V4, V5 and V6. Thus the factor matrix can be used to give a tentative label to the common factor. For example, suppose that 100 ability items were factored, and it was found that the variables which had substantial loadings (> 0.4) on the first common factor were concerned with spelling, vocabulary, knowledge of proverbs and verbal comprehension, whilst none of the other items (mathematical problems, puzzles requiring objects to be visualised, memory tests, etc.) showed large loadings on the factor. Because all of the high-loading items involve the use of language, it seems reasonable to call the common factor 'verbal ability', 'language ability', or something similar. Be warned, however, that there is no guarantee that labels given like this are necessarily correct. It is necessary to validate the factor exactly as described in Chapter 13 in order to ensure that this label seems to be accurate. However, if the items which define a common factor form a reliable scale that predicts teachers' ratings of language ability, correlates well with other well-trusted tests of verbal ability and does not correlate at all strongly with other measures of personality or ability, it seems likely that the factor was correctly identified.

You will remember that the square of the correlation coefficient (i.e. the correlation coefficient multiplied by itself) shows how much 'variance' is shared by two variables – or in simpler language, how much they overlap. Two variables with a correlation of 0.8 overlap to the extent of 0.8^2 or 0.64. (Consult Appendix A if this is unfamiliar ground.) As factor loadings are merely correlations between common factors and items, this implies that the square of each factor loading shows the amount of overlap between each variable and each common factor. This simple finding forms the basis of two other main uses of the factor matrix.

The factor matrix can reveal the amount of overlap between each variable and all of the common factors. If the common factors are at right angles (an 'orthogonal' solution), it is simple to calculate how much of the variance of each variable is measured by the factors, by merely summing the squared factor loadings across factors. (When the common factors are not at right angles, life becomes rather more complicated.) It can be seen from Table 14.4 that $0.90^2 + 0.10^2$ (= 0.82) of the variance of Test 1 is 'explained' by the two factors. This amount is called the *communality* of that variable.

A variable with a large communality has a large degree of overlap with one or more common factors. A low communality implies that all of the correlations between that variable and the common factors are small – that is, none of the common factors overlap much with that variable. This might mean that the variable measures something which is conceptually quite different from the other variables in the analysis. For example, one personality item in among 100 ability test items would have a communality close to zero. It might also mean that a particular item is heavily influenced by measurement error or extreme difficulty, e.g. an item which is so easy that everyone obtained the correct answer, or which was ambiguously phrased so that no one could understand the question. Whatever the reason, a low communality implies that an item does not overlap with the common factors, either because it measures a different concept, because of excessive measurement error, or because there are few individual differences in the way in which people respond to the item.

Finally, the factor matrix shows *the relative importance of the common factors*. It is possible to calculate how much of the variance each common factor accounts for. A common factor that accounts for 40 per cent of the overlap between the variables in the original correlation matrix is clearly more important than another which explains only 20 per cent of the variance. Once again it is necessary to assume that the common factors are orthogonal (at right angles to each other). The first step is to calculate what is known as an *eigenvalue* for each factor. This can be computed by squaring the factor loadings and summing down the columns. Using the data shown in Table 14.4, it can be seen that the eigenvalue of factor 1 is $0.90^2 + 0.98^2 + 0.90^2 + 0.10^2 + 0.0^2 + (-0.10)^2$ or 2.60. If the eigenvalue is divided by the number of variables (six in this instance), it shows what proportion of variance is explained by each common factor. Here factor 1 explains 0.43 or 43 per cent of the information in the original correlation matrix.

SELF-ASSESSMENT QUESTION 14.3

Try to define the terms *eigenvalue* and *communality*. Then look back at Table 14.4 and:

(a) calculate the communalities of variables 2, 3, 4, 5 and 6;

(b) calculate the eigenvalue of factor 2;

(c) work out what proportion of the variance is accounted for by factor 2;

(d) work out, by addition, the proportion of variance accounted for by factors 1 and 2 combined.

Before we leave the factor matrix, it is worth clarifying one point which can cause confusion. Suppose that one of the factors in the analysis has a number of loadings which are large and *negative* (e.g. –0.6, –0.8), some that are close to zero (e.g. –0.1, +0.2), but no large positive loadings. Suppose that the items with large negative loadings are from items such as 'are you a nervous sort of person?' and 'do you worry a lot?', where agreement is coded as '1' and disagreement with the statements as '0'. The large negative correlations imply that the factor measures the *opposite* of nerviness and tendency to worry, so it may be tentatively identified as 'emotional stability' or something similar. Whilst it is perfectly acceptable to interpret factors in this way, it may sometimes be more convenient to reverse *all* of the signs of *all* of the variables' loadings on that factor. Thus the loadings mentioned above would change from –0.6, –0.8, –0.1 and +0.2 to +0.6, +0.8, +0.1 and –0.2. It is purely a matter of convenience whether one does this, as SAQ 14.4 will reveal. However, if you do alter the signs of all factor loadings you should also:

- change the sign of the correlation between the 'reversed' factor and all of the other factors in the factor pattern correlation matrix; and
- change the sign of all of the 'factor scores' (discussed below) calculated from the factor in question.

SELF-ASSESSMENT QUESTION 14.4

(a) Use Table 14.3 to represent graphically the sets of correlations between one factor (F1) and two variables (V1 and V2) shown in Table 14.5.

(b) Next, change the sign of the correlation between the variables and F1 and re-plot the diagram.

(c) From this, try to explain how reversing the sign of all of a factor's loadings alters the position of a factor.

When you completed part (d) of SAQ 14.3 you will have noticed something rather odd. The two common factors combined only account for 83.4 per cent of the variance in the original correlation matrix. Similarly, all of the communalities are less than 1.0. What happened to the 'lost' 17 per cent of the variance?

Factor analysis is essentially a technique for summarising information – for making broad generalisations from detailed sets of data. Here we have taken the correlations between six variables, observed that they fall into two distinct clusters, and so decided that it is more parsimonious to talk in terms of two factors rather than the original six variables. In other words, the number of constructs needed to describe the data has fallen from six (the number of variables) to two (the number of common factors). Like any approximation, this one is useful but not perfect. Some of the information in the original correlation matrix has been sacrificed in making this broad generalisation. Indeed, the only circumstance under which no information would have been lost would have been if V1, V2 and V3 had shown an intercorrelation of 1.0 (likewise for V4, V5 and V6), and if all the correlations between these two groups of variables had been precisely zero. Then (and only then!) we would have lost no information as a result of referring to two factors rather than six variables.

This, then, is the first part of the explanation of the 'missing variance'. It may be regarded as a necessary consequence of reducing the number of constructs from six to two. Suppose, however, that instead of extracting just two factors from the correlations between the six variables, one extracted six factors (all at right angles to each other and hence impossible to visualise).

	F1	V1	V2
F1	1.000		
V1	−0.867	1.000	
V2	−0.867	0.500	1.000

Table 14.5 Correlations between two variables and one factor

Since there are as many factors as there are variables, there should be no loss of information. One might expect that the six factors should be able to explain *all* of the information in the original correlation matrix.

PRINCIPAL-COMPONENTS ANALYSIS AND FACTOR ANALYSIS

Whether or not this is the case depends on how the factor analysis is performed. There are two basic approaches to factor analysis. The simplest, called 'principal-components analysis', assumes that six factors can indeed fully explain the information in the correlation matrix. Thus each variable will have a communality of precisely 1.0, and the factors will between them account for 100 per cent of the variation between the variables.

More formally, the principal-components model states that, for any variable,

total variance = common factor variance + measurement error

and that when as many factors are extracted as there are variables, these common factors can explain all of the information in the correlation matrix.

The assumption that anything that is not measured by common factors must just be measurement error is rather a strong one. Each test item may have some morsel of 'unique variance' that is unique to that item, but which cannot be shared with other items. Suppose that a pupil gives the correct answer to the question 'what is the capital of Venezuela?' in a geography test. This could indicate either that they generally have a good standard of geographical knowledge, or that they just happen to possess the one specific piece of knowledge required to answer this item correctly, and may know no other geographical facts whatsoever.

Another way of looking at this is to say that no two items are completely equivalent. One person may know the capital of Venezuela, but not that of Ecuador; another person with the same overall level of geographical knowledge may just happen to know the name of the capital of Ecuador, but not that of Venezuela. Thus it is not possible to regard these two items as being precisely equivalent. Whether someone gets an item correct depends on both the common factor(s) being measured by the test (geographical knowledge, etc.) *and* something quite unique to the individual item. The principal-components model assumes that all of the variation in subjects' responses to items is explicable by 'common factors' (such as geographical knowledge) alone. It cannot consider the possibility that each item also measures a certain amount of specific knowledge or skill which is unique to itself. The 'specific variance', by definition, cannot be predicted from any of the common factors. Thus even if one extracts as many common factors as there are variables, the communalities of the variables will not be 1.0, but will generally be smaller, the 'missing variance' being explained by 'specific variance'. The *factor-analysis* model thus assumes that for any item:

$$\text{total variance} = \text{common factor variance} + \text{specific factor variance} + \text{measurement error}$$

It follows that factor analysis is a more complicated process than component analysis. Whereas component analysis merely has to determine the number of factors to be extracted and how each variable should correlate with each factor, factor analysis also has to estimate (somehow) what the communality of each variable would be if as many factors as variables were extracted. In other words, it must also work out how much of an item's variance is 'common-factor' variance, and how much is unique to that particular variable and cannot be shared with any other item. The good news is that, in practice, it does not seem to matter too much whether one performs a component analysis or a factor analysis, as both techniques generally lead to similar results. In fact, the authorities on factor analysis can be divided into three groups. Some believe that factor (rather than component) analysis should never be used (e.g. Leyland Wilkinson, who according to Stamm (1994, personal communication) fought to keep factor-analysis options out of his SYSTAT statistics package. Commercial pressures eventually won). Some maintain that a form of factor analysis is the *only* justifiable technique (e.g. Carroll, 1993), and finally, some pragmatists argue that, as both techniques generally produce highly similar solutions, it does not really matter which of them one uses (e.g. Tabatchnick and Fidell, 1989; Kline, 1994).

One slightly worrying problem is that the loadings obtained from component analyses are always larger than those which result from factor analyses, as the former assume that each variable has a communality of 1.0, whereas the latter computes a value for the communality which is generally less than 1.0. Thus the results obtained from a component analysis always look more impressive (i.e. have larger loadings) than the results of a factor analysis. This has clear implications for many rules of thumb, such as regarding factor loadings above 0.4 (or less than –0.4) as being 'salient', and disregarding those between –0.39 and +0.39, but unfortunately these have not been addressed in the literature. It is also vitally important that authors of papers should state clearly whether they have followed the factor-analysis or component-analysis model. Few do this, and some authors mention 'factor analysis' in the text even though they have performed principal-components analysis.

USES OF FACTOR ANALYSIS

Factor analysis has three main uses in psychology. First, it may be used to construct tests. For example, 50 items might be written to measure some ability, personality trait or attitude (such as conservatism). The items would then be administered to a representative sample of several hundred individuals, and scored (in the case of ability tests) so that a correct answer is coded as 1 and an incorrect answer as 0. Responses that are made using rating scales (as with most personality and attitude questionnaires) are simply entered in their raw form – one point if box (a) is endorsed, two if (b) is chosen, etc. The responses to these 50 items are then correlated together and factor-analysed. The items that have high loadings on each factor measure the same underlying psychological construct, and so form a scale. Thus it is possible to determine how to score the questionnaire in future simply by looking at the factor matrix: if items 1, 2, 10 and 12 are the only items that have substantial loadings on one factor, then one scale of the test should be the sum of these four items, and no others. It is likely that some items will fail to load substantially on any of the factors (i.e. show low communalities). This could happen for a number of reasons: in the case of ability tests the items could be so easy (or hard) that there is little or no variation in people's scores. Personality items may refer to uncommon actions or feelings where there is again little variation – e.g. 'there are occasions in my life when I have felt afraid', an item with which *everyone* is likely to agree. Or items may fail because they are severely influenced by measurement error, or because they measure something different from any of the others that were administered. Test constructors do not usually worry about why, precisely, items fail to work as expected. Items that fail to load a factor are simply discarded without further ado. Thus factor analysis can show at a stroke:

- how many distinct scales run through the test;
- which items belong to which scales (so indicating how the test should be scored);
- which items in a test should be discarded.

Each of the scales then needs to be validated, e.g. by calculating scores for each person on each factor, and examining the construct validity and/or predictive validity of these scales. For example, scores on the factors may be correlated with scores on other questionnaires, used to predict educational success, etc.

The second main use of factor is in data reduction, or 'conceptual spring-cleaning'. Huge numbers of tests have been developed to measure personality from different theoretical perspectives and it is not at all obvious whether these overlap. Suppose that half a dozen scales have been marketed to measure subtly different aspects of personality: one might claim to measure 'negative reactivity', one 'ego strength', another 'intuitive thinking', and so on. Do they *really* measure six quite distinct dimensions of personality? Might they perhaps all measure the same thing? Or is the truth that the tests measure two, three, four or five distinct aspects of personality? To find out it is simply necessary to administer the test items to a large sample, then factor the correlations between the items, and the factor analysis will show precisely what the underlying structure truly is. For example, two factors may be found. The first factor may have large loadings from all the items in tests 1, 5 and 6. All the substantial loadings on the second factor may come from items in tests 2, 3 and 4. Hence it is clear that tests 1, 5 and 6 measure precisely the same thing, as do tests 2, 3 and 4. Any high-flown theoretical distinctions about subtle differences between the scales can be shown to have no basis in fact, and any rational psychologists seeing the results of such an analysis should be forced to think in terms of two (rather than six) theoretical constructs – a considerable simplification.

The third main use of factor analysis is for checking the psychometric properties of questionnaires, particularly when they are to be used in new cultures or populations. For example, suppose that the manual of an Australian personality test suggests that it should be scored by adding together the scores on all the odd-numbered items to form one scale, whilst all the even-numbered items form another. When the test is given to a sample of people in the UK and the correlations between the items are calculated and factor-analysed, two factors should be found, with all the odd-numbered items having substantial loadings on one factor and all the even-numbered items loading substantially on the other. If this structure is *not* found it shows that there are problems with the questionnaire, which should not be scored or used in its conventional form.

It is thus easy to see why factor analysis is so important in individual differences and psychometrics. The same statistical technique can be used to construct tests, resolve theoretical disputes about the number and nature of factors measured by tests and questionnaires, and check whether tests work as they should, or whether it is legitimate to use a particular test within a different population or a different culture. You may even have wondered whether the size of the eigenvalue obtained when factoring a test that has just one factor running through it has any link to the test's reliability . . .

SUMMARY

This chapter has provided a basic introduction to the principles of factor analysis. It has left many questions unanswered, including the following ones.

- How does one decide how many factors should be extracted?
- How can computer programs actually perform factor analysis?
- What types of data can usefully be factor-analysed?
- How should the results obtained from factor-analytical studies be interpreted and reported?

These and other issues will be explored in Chapter 15.

SUGGESTED ADDITIONAL READING

Eysenck's ancient paper on the logical basis of factor analysis (Eysenck, 1953) is well worth reading, whilst Child (1990) and Kline (1994) offer two 'student-friendly' basic introductions to factor analysis.

ANSWERS TO SELF-ASSESSMENT QUESTIONS

SAQ 14.1

(a) The smallest angle between any pair of variables in Figure 14.2 is that between V1 and V2. Hence these variables are the most highly correlated.

(b) The angle between V3 and V2 is approximately 270° (moving clockwise). Table 14.3 shows that this corresponds to a correlation of 0.

(c) The angle between V5 and V3 is approximately 210°, which corresponds to a correlation of –0.87.

SAQ 14.2

(a) An oblique solution is a table of factor loadings in which the factors are not at right angles, but are themselves correlated together.

(b) A factor loading is the correlation between a variable and a factor.

(c) The factor structure matrix is a table showing the correlations between all variables and all factors.

(d) An orthogonal solution is a table of factor loadings in which the factors are all uncorrelated (i.e. at right angles to each other).

(e) A factor pattern correlation matrix is a table which shows the correlations between all of the factors in a factor analysis. For an orthogonal factor analysis, all of the correlations between factors will be 0 (as they are independent). For oblique solutions, the correlations will be values other than zero.

SAQ 14.3

The eigenvalue associated with a factor is the sum of the squared loadings on that factor, calculated across all of the variables. The communality of a variable is the sum of the squared loadings on that variable, calculated across all of the factors.

(a) The communality of variable 2 is $0.98^2 + 0^2 = 0.9604$. The communalities of variables 3, 4, 5 and 6 are likewise 0.82, 0.7325, 0.9604 and 0.7325, respectively.

(b) The eigenvalue of factor 2 is $0.10^2 + 0.0^2 + (-0.10^2) + 0.85^2 + 0.98^2 + 0.85^2$, or 2.4254.

(c) As there are six variables, factor 2 accounts for $\dfrac{2.4254}{6}$ or 0.4042 of the variance between them.

(d) The worked example in the text shows that factor 1 accounts for 0.423 of the variance. As the factors are orthogonal, factors 1 and 2 combined account for $0.43 + 0.4042 = 0.834$ of the variance between the variables.

SAQ 14.4
(a)

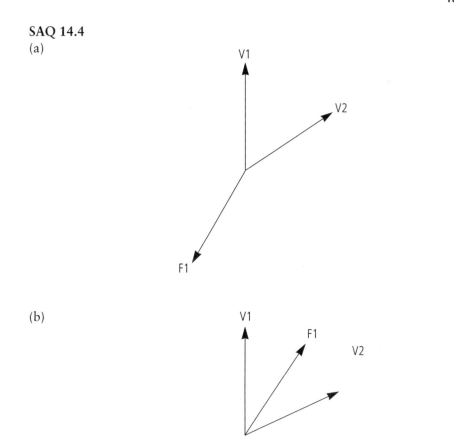

(b)

(c) Reversing all of the loadings between the variables and a given factor in effect causes the factor to have a correlation of −1.0 with its previous position. Table 14.3 shows that this corresponds to its pointing in the opposite direction (180°) to its previous position. Large negative correlations between a variable and a factor imply that the factor points away from the variables which have the largest correlation with it. Reversing the signs of all of the correlations reverses the direction of the factor so that it passes through the cluster of variables.

15

Performing and interpreting factor analyses

BACKGROUND

Whilst Chapter 14 gave an overview of the basic principles of factor analysis, it deliberately omitted some of the detail which is needed either to perform factor analyses or to evaluate the technical adequacy of published studies. Many journal articles which employ factor analysis are so technically flawed as to be meaningless, so it is vital that one should be able to identify (and discount) such studies when reviewing the literature.

Recomended prior reading

Chapter 14.

INTRODUCTION

Although it is quite possible to perform exploratory factor analyses by hand, and older texts such as Cattell (1952) provide detailed instructions for doing so, such exercises are best suited to the enthusiast or masochist who has several weeks to spare. The calculations involved are lengthy and repetitious, so are best performed by computer. Most of the main statistical packages contain good exploratory factor-analysis routines which will typically run analyses in minutes rather than hours, the time taken to perform an analysis being roughly proportional to the cube of the number of variables. Confirmatory factor analyses (which will be described towards the end of this chapter) require specialised packages, and analyses can sometimes take hours to run.

EXPLORATORY FACTOR ANALYSIS

No matter whether the analysis is being performed using an abacus or an IBM, there are eight basic stages involved in performing an exploratory factor analysis, each of which is discussed below.

Stage 1. Ensure that the data are suitable for factor analysis.

Stage 2. Decide on the model – factor analysis or component analysis.

Stage 3. Decide how many factors are needed to represent your data.

Stage 4. If using factor (rather than component) analysis, estimate the communality of each variable.

Stage 5. Produce factors giving the desired communalities (factor extraction).

Stage 6. Rotate these factors so that they pass through the clusters of variables, checking to ensure that 'simple structure' has been reached.

Stage 7. Optionally compute factor scores.

Stage 8. Optionally perform hierarchical analyses, if appropriate.

One of the problems with factor analysis is its power. The computer programs used will almost always produce an answer of some kind, and by trying to analyse the data using many different techniques, taking out different numbers of factors and concentrating on different subsets of variables, it is possible to pull something semi-plausible from the most ghastly study. One occasionally encounters journal articles in which the technique has clearly been used in a desperate attempt to salvage something from a poorly designed experiment. Indeed, there are some areas of the discipline, such as personal construct psychology, in which such practices are the norm. Thus it is vital that those who use the technique or read the literature should have an understanding of the design and execution of factor-analytical studies. No-where is the computer scientists' maxim of 'garbage in, garbage out' more appropriate than in factor analysis, so the present chapter begins with a look at the types of data which may usefully be factor-analysed.

Suitability of data for factor analysis

Not all data can be factor-analysed. Factor analysis may be appropriate if the following criteria are fulfilled.

1. All of the variables in the analysis are continuous – that is, measured on at least a three-point interval scale (such as 'yes/?/no', coded as 2/1/0). One cannot normally factor-analyse *categorical* data which form a nominal scale, such as colour of hair (black/brown/red), country of residence, voting preference or occupation. It is sometimes possible to choose codes for categorical data which will convert them into some kind of interval scale which can legitimately be factored. For example, support for a communist party may be coded as '1', for a social democratic party as '2', for a conservative/ republican party as '3', and

for a right-wing party as '4'. These numbers form a scale of 'right-wingness', which could legitimately be factored.

2. All of the variables are (approximately) normally distributed, with outliers properly identified and dealt with; see, for example, Tabatchnick and Fidell (1989, chapter 4). Skewed data can be transformed if necessary; see, for example, Tabatchnick and Fidell (1989) or Howell (1992).

3. The relationships between all pairs of variables are approximately linear, or at any rate not obviously U-shaped or J-shaped.

4. The variables are independent. The easiest way to check this is to go through all of the formulae and ensure that each measured variable affects no more than one score that is being factor-analysed. If individuals produce scores on four test items, it would be permissible to create and factor new variables such as

$$\left\{(\text{score 1} + \text{score 2}) \text{ and } \frac{\text{score 3}}{\text{score 4}}\right\}$$

or $\{(\text{score 1} + \text{score 2} - \text{score 3}) \text{ and } 1 - \text{score 4}\}$,

but not $\{(\text{score 1} + \text{score 2} + \text{score 3}) \text{ and } (\text{score 1} + \text{score 4})\}$

or $\{(\text{score 1}) \text{ and } (\text{score 1} + \text{score 2} + \text{score 3} + \text{score 4})\}$

as in the latter two cases, one of the observed test scores ('score 1') affects two of the variables being factored. Common instances in which this principle is broken include the following:

(a) factor analysis of a set of variables, some of which are computed from other variables in the analysis. For example, factor analysis of scores on six test items together with individuals' *total* score on these six test items;

(b) items of the following form:

'Question 1: What is 2×3?'

'Question 2: What is the square of the answer to Question 1?'

For if Question 1 was answered incorrectly, Question 2 must be answered incorrectly as well.

It can sometimes be more difficult to detect such interdependencies. For example, an experimenter might record several measures of voltage from various parts of the brain, together with muscle activity from two sites, and intend to factor-analyse the mean level of these responses along with some questionnaire items. As readers with experience in psychophysiology will know, it is unlikely that all of these measures will be independent. Muscle movements (such as eyeblinks and heartbeats) can show up in *all* such physiological recordings unless considerable care is taken. This can result in all of the various electrical signals being interdependent, and thus unsuitable for factor analysis.

(c) It is not possible to factor-analyse all of the scores from any test where it is impossible for a person to obtain an extremely high (or extremely low) score on *all* of its scales (known as 'ipsatised tests'), as all of the scales of such tests are bound to be negatively correlated. Advocates of these tests claim that it is possible simply to drop one of the scales before factoring. However, the interpretation of the results will be affected by the (arbitrary) choice of which scale to omit.

5. The correlation matrix shows several correlations above 0.3. If all of the correlations are tiny, then one should seriously question whether any factors are there to be extracted. If the correlations are small because of the use of tests with low reliability, it may be appropriate to correct for the effects of unreliability as shown by Guilford and Fruchter (1978) among others. Likewise, if poor experimental design led to data being collected from a group of restricted range (e.g. ability scores being obtained from a sample of university students rather than from a sample of the general population), it might be appropriate to correct the correlations for this using the formula of Dobson (1988) before factor-analysing. However, such pieces of psycho-metric wizardry should be used with caution, and are really no substitute for sound and thoughtful experimental design.

   The Bartlett (1954) test of sphericity tests the hypothesis that all of the off-diagonal correlations are zero, and it is routinely computed by packages such as SPSS. However, the test is very sensitive to sample size, and minuscule correlations between variables from a large sample will lead the test to indicate that factor analysis is appropriate. It is much safer just to look at the correlation matrix.

6. Missing data are distributed randomly throughout the data matrix. It would not be wise to factor-analyse data where a proportion of the sample omitted to take complete blocks of items. For example, some subjects may have taken tests A, B and C. Others may have taken tests A and C only, and others may have taken only tests B and C. Because of this, it would not be legitimate to factor-analyse these data, although several statistical packages will do so without a murmur.

7. Any missing values have either been estimated (Tabatchnick and Fidell, 1989), or the computer program has been told ignore them. It is very easy to code missing data as '99' (or whatever) when typing them in, and then to forget to instruct one's statistical package that values of 99 represent missing data. This will obviously invalidate the whole analysis.

8. The sample size is large. Experts vary in their recommendations, but factor analysis should not be attempted if the number of subjects is less than 100, as the standard errors of the correlations would otherwise be unacceptably large. This would mean that the correlation matrix from the sample of testees would not much resemble the 'true' correlation matrix. In other words, analyses based on small samples are unlikely to be replicable, nor are they good approximations of what the relationships between the variables really are. It used to be thought that it is also necessary to relate sample size to the number of variables being analysed. For example, Nunnally (1978) advocates that there should be at least 10 times as many cases as variables. More recent studies, such as those by Barrett and Kline

(1981) and Guadagnoli and Velicer (1988), show that, so long as there are more subjects than variables, the ratio of subjects to variables is not as important as absolute sample size and the size of the factor loadings. Thus if the factors are well defined (e.g. with loadings of 0.7, rather than 0.4), one needs a smaller sample to find them. If the data being analysed are known to be highly reliable (e.g. test scores, rather than responses to individual items), it should be possible to relax these guidelines somewhat. However, attempts to factor-analyse small sets of data (such as repertory grids) are doomed to failure, as the large standard errors of the correlations ensure that the factor solution will be both arbitrary and unreplicable.

A problem arises with dichotomous data – that is, scores which can assume one of only two values. These are often encountered during analysis of responses to test items (1 = 'yes', 0 = 'no', or 1 = 'correct answer', 0 = 'incorrect answer'). When dichotomous items are correlated together, the correlation can only approach 1.0 if both of the test items have similar difficulty levels. Thus a small correlation can suggest that either:

- there is no relationship between items of similar difficulty; or
- the two items have widely differing difficulties.

Thus factor analysis of the usual Pearson product-moment correlations between dichotomous items tends to produce factors of 'item difficulty', as only items of similar difficulty levels can possibly correlate together and form a factor. Other items that measure the same construct but which have very different difficulties will, because of this, show low loadings on the resulting factor. However, it is remarkably difficult to circumvent this problem using the standard statistical packages, which offer no alternative to the use of Pearson correlations. Other types of correlation coefficients which avoid these problems are available, and Chambers (1982) gives a useful, if somewhat technical, précis of the literature. The legitimacy of factoring these coefficients is still a matter for debate (Vegelius, 1976), although plenty of people routinely do so. In short, life is made very much easier if one can simply avoid using dichotomous data altogether.

SELF-ASSESSMENT QUESTION 15.1

A colleague is studying the mathematical skills of a sample of 100 11-year-old children as part of her project work. She has collected data on 120 test items, each of which she has scored as being answered correctly or incorrectly. She has also coded the county of residence for each person, and is keen to factor-analyse all of these responses in order to (re-)discover the basic dimensions of mathematical ability and to investigate whether some mathematical abilities are higher in some counties than in others. What advice would you offer her?

Factor analysis vs. component analysis

One school of thought maintains that factor (rather than component) analysis should never be used because of the difficulty in estimating communalities – the estimation of factor scores also turns out to be surprisingly tricky. The second school of thought maintains that, as the factor model is a priori much more likely to fit the data, any attempt to estimate communalities is better than none. The principal-components model, they would argue, is simply inappropriate when applied to test items and other data which one would expect to contain unique variance. Authors such as Carroll (1993) maintain that it is nonsensical to use a principal-components model, as this is known to be inappropriate for the types of data that are usually analysed, although many of us argue that, in practice, it matters little which technique is used, as it is rare for different methods of analysis to give very different results. Interested readers should see Velicer and Jackson (1990) for a more detailed discussion of this topic.

Tests for the number of factors

Several tests have been developed to help analysts to choose the 'correct' number of factors. These tests require careful consideration – one cannot rely on computer packages to make this important decision, as most of them (e.g. SPSS) use a technique which is known to be flawed, and fail to incorporate some of the more useful tests. Determining the number of factors to be extracted is probably the most important decision that one has to make when conducting a factor analysis. A faulty decision here can produce a nonsensical solution from even the clearest set of data. There is no harm in trying several analyses based on differing numbers of factors, and in using several different tests to guide the choice of factors.

The first guides are theory and past experience. One may sometimes want to use factor analysis to ensure that a test is performing as expected when used within a different culture, patient group, or whatever. Confirmatory factor analysis can be used for this purpose (see below), but if exploratory factor analysis is preferred, the previous results can be used to guide one in deciding how many factors to extract. If a (technically adequate) factor analysis of a test in the USA revealed seven factors, any attempt to factor-analyse the tests in another culture should at least consider the seven-factor solution.

Theory and past practice are all very well, but most factor analyses are truly exploratory in nature. The researcher will often have no good theoretical rationale for deciding how many factors should be extracted, and previous studies will sometimes be so technically flawed as to be useless. There are a number of other techniques which can be used in such circumstances, all of which seek to determine the number of factors which should be extracted from a correlation matrix. The problem is that few of them have been implemented in the computer packages likely to be encountered by non-expert users, and so they are simply not available. Second, the various techniques do not always yield consistent results. One test may point to six factors, another to eight, and previous research to nine! In circumstances such as this it is safest to consider a number of solutions, and check them for psychological plausibility. Users should also consider whether:

- increasing the number of factors increases the 'simplicity' of the solution (such as decreasing the proportion loadings in the range of −0.4 to 0.4). If increasing the number of factors does little or nothing to increase the simplicity of the solution, it is arguably of little value;
- any large correlations between factors emerge when performing oblique rotations. These can indicate that too many factors have been extracted, and that two factors are trying to pass through the same cluster of variables. Correlations between factors larger than around 0.5 could be regarded as suspect;
- any well-known factors have split into two or more parts. For example, if a myriad of previous studies show that a set of items form just one factor (e.g. extraversion), yet they seem to form two factors in your analysis, it is likely that too many factors have been extracted.

One of the oldest and simplest tests for the number of factors is that described by Kaiser (1960) and Guttman (1954), and known as the 'Kaiser–Guttman criterion'. It has the advantage of being very straightforward. One simply performs a principal-components analysis on the data, extracting as many factors as there are variables, but without performing an operation known as 'rotation' (to be discussed below). The eigenvalues are calculated as usual by summing the squared loadings on each component. One then simply counts how many eigenvalues are greater than 1.0 – this is the number of factors to be used.

There are many problems with this technique, the most obvious being its sensitivity to the number of variables in the analysis. As each eigenvalue is simply the sum of the squared factor loadings, if the number of variables is large, so too will be the eigenvalue. A test for the number of factors should really give the same result whether or not there are four or 40 variables representing each factor, and the Kaiser–Guttman test manifestly will not do so. Furthermore, Hakstian and Mueller (1973) observed that the technique was never intended to be used as a test for the number of factors. Because it is extremely easy to implement automatically, most statistical packages will perform a Kaiser–Guttman test by default. It should *always* be overridden.

The scree test, devised by Cattell (1966), is also conceptually simple. Like the Kaiser–Guttman criterion, it is based on the eigenvalues of an initial unrotated principal-components solution. However, it draws on the *relative* values of the eigenvalues, and so should not be sensitive to variations in the number of variables being analysed. Successive principal components explain less and less variance, and so the eigenvalues decrease. The scree test is based on visual inspection of a graph showing the successive eigenvalues, such as that illustrated in Figure 15.1. This graph should be plotted as accurately as possible, using graph paper or a graph-plotting package. The accuracy of plots produced by some statistical packages is inadequate for this purpose.

The basic idea is simple. It is clear that the points on the right-hand side of

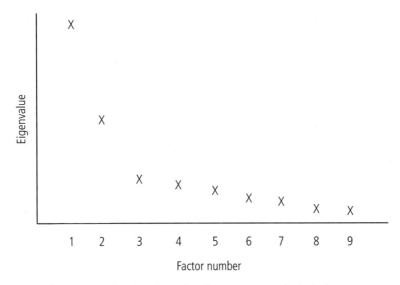

Figure 15.1 The scree test showing eigenvalues from an unrotated principal-components analysis of nine variables. The graph indicates that two factors should be extracted.

Figure 15.1 form a straight line, known as a 'scree slope'. It is possible to put a ruler through these points, and to determine how many eigenvalues lie well above this line. This is the number of factors which should then be extracted. Thus Figure 15.1 depicts a two-factor solution. Further examples of scree tests are given in Cattell (1966), in chapter 5 of Cattell (1978) and by Cattell and Vogelman (1977). Several popular texts on factor analysis describe the scree test incorrectly, by asserting that the number of factors corresponds to the number of eigenvalues above the scree line *plus one*. They would thus advocate extracting three factors from the above solution. It is not obvious where this confusion arose, as Cattell's papers and 1978 book are quite clear on the matter: 'the last real factor is that before the scree begins' (Cattell and Vogelman, 1977).

A problem with the scree test is that it does rely on subjective judgement and may sometimes have several possible interpretations, particularly when the sample size or the 'salient' factor loadings are small (Gorsuch, 1983). Sometimes more than one clearly identifiable straight scree slope is found. In such cases, one simply looks for the eigenvalues which lie above the leftmost scree slope.

The MAP test (Velicer, 1976) is a good technique for determining the number of factors to be extracted. It is numerically too complex to be performed by hand, but it is not implemented in the main commercial packages for performing factor analysis, despite being one of the more consistently accurate techniques (Zwick and Velicer, 1986). There are several other methods available but these, too, remain unimplemented in the major packages. In the absence of the MAP test, computer simulation studies have shown that the scree test is probably the most accurate guide for making the all-important decision as to the number of factors to be extracted from a correlation matrix.

SELF-ASSESSMENT QUESTION 15.2

In the graph shown below, how many factors would the scree test and the Kaiser–Guttman criterion indicate?

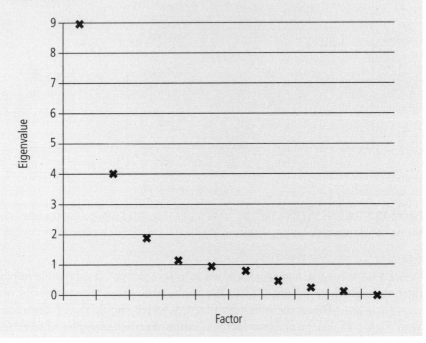

Estimation of communalities

The communality of a variable is the proportion of its variance which can be shared with the other variables being factor-analysed. In the case of component analysis, it is assumed that this is potentially 100 per cent – that is, that the correlations between variables are entirely attributable to common factor variance and measurement error. In the case of factor models, it is further assumed that each variable has some amount of reliably measured variance which is 'unique' to that variable – and so cannot be shared with any of the other variables in the analysis. This is the variable's 'unique variance', so in factor-analysis models the variables' communalities are in general less than 1.0, because of the 'unique variance' associated with each variable.

The estimation of communalities is a process which worries factor analysts, as there is no easy way of checking that one's estimates are correct. Sometimes the procedures used lead to ridiculous estimates of communalities, such as those that are larger than 1.0 ('Heywood cases'). Indeed, the problems associated with this can drive many analysts to use the simpler component model.

Different techniques for factor extraction differ in the way which the communalities are estimated. The simplest is principal-factor analysis, in which communalities are first of all estimated through a series of multiple regressions, using all of the other variables as 'predictors'. Since the communality is defined as the proportion of a variable's variance that can be shared with the other variables in the analysis, it has been claimed that this gives the 'lower bound' for the communality – the smallest value that the communality could possibly have, although a paper by Kaiser (1990) challenges this view. Many packages (such as SPSS) then modify these values several times through a process known as 'iteration', until they become stable. Unfortunately, however, the theoretical rationale for repeated iteration is dubious, and there is no guarantee that it will produce sensible estimates of the true values of the communalities. It is also possible to specify the communalities directly, and some packages allow users to choose other values, such as the largest correlation between each variable and any other. Maximum likelihood estimation arguably tackles the communality problem in the most sensible way. That said, it rarely seems to matter much in practice which technique one uses.

Factor extraction

There are a number of techniques available for extracting factors, all with different theoretical backgrounds. Most statistical packages offer users a choice between principal-factor analysis, image analysis (also known as 'Kaiser's second little jiffy'), maximum-likelihood analysis, unweighted least-squares ('MINRES') and generalised least-squares. Most of these techniques have their own individual methods of estimating communalities. In practice, given the same number of factors and communality estimates, all methods will usually produce results that are nearly identical.

However, we must now admit that the previous chapter over-simplified the way in which factors are moved through the clusters of variables. In practice, this is a two-stage process. First, the factors are placed in some arbitrary position relative to the variables, and then another procedure (called *factor rotation*) is used to move the factors through the clusters of variables.

All of the above-mentioned techniques for factor extraction therefore place the factors in essentially arbitrary locations relative to the variables. Typically, the factors are positioned so that each successive factor is placed:

- at right angles to previous factors; and
- in a position where it 'explains' a substantial proportion of the variance of the items (i.e. where its eigenvalue is large).

Figure 15.2 shows the correlations between four variables V1 to V4. It can be seen that V1 and V2 are highly correlated, as are V3 and V4. Inspection of the figure shows that a two-factor solution would be sensible, with one factor passing between V1 and V2, and another between V3 and V4. However, the initial extraction does not place the factors in this sensible position. Instead, the first factor passes between the two clusters of variables, rather than through the middle of either of them. All of the variables will have moderate

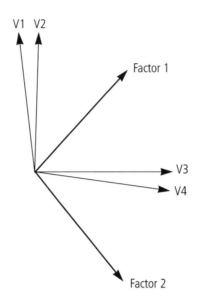

Figure 15.2 Typical positions of two factors relative to four variables following factor extraction.

positive loadings on this factor. The second factor is at right angles to the first, and has a positive correlation with V3 and V4 and a negative correlation with V1 and V2. In neither case does a factor pass through the middle of a pair of highly correlated variables.

Factor rotation

Factor rotation changes the position of the factors relative to the variables so that the solution obtained is easy to interpret. As was mentioned in Chapter 14, factors are identified by observing which variables have large and/or zero loadings on them. The solutions which defy interpretation are those in which a large number of variables have 'mediocre' loadings on a factor – loadings of the order of 0.3. These are too small to be regarded as 'salient' and used to identify the factor, yet too large to be safely ignored. Factor rotation moves the factors relative to the variables so that each factor has a few substantial loadings, and a few near-zero loadings. This is another way of saying that the factors are rotated until they pass through the clusters of variables, between V1 and V2, and between V3 and V4 in Figure 15.2, for example.

Thurstone (1947) was probably the first to realise that the initial position of the factor axes was arbitrary, and that such solutions were difficult to interpret and harder to replicate. He coined the term 'simple structure' to describe the case in which each factor has some large loadings and some small loadings, and likewise each variable has substantial loadings on only a few factors. His 'rules of thumb' are neatly summarised in Child (1990, p. 48).

Table 15.1 demonstrates how much easier it is to interpret rotated rather than unrotated factor solutions. The unrotated solution is difficult to interpret,

	Unrotated		Rotated (VARIMAX)		h^2
	Factor 1	Factor 2	Factor 1	Factor 2	
Comprehension	0.4	0.3	0.50	0.00	0.25
Spelling	0.4	0.5	0.64	0.00	0.41
Addition	0.4	−0.4	0.13	0.55	0.32
Subtraction	0.5	−0.3	0.06	0.58	0.34
Eigenvalue	0.59	0.73	0.68	0.64	1.32

Table 15.1 Unrotated and rotated factor solutions

as all of the variables have modest loadings on the first factor, whilst the second factor seems to differentiate the 'mathematical' from the 'language' abilities. After rotation, the solution could not be clearer. The first factor looks as if it measures language ability (because of its substantial loadings from the comprehension and spelling tests), whilst the second factor corresponds to numerical ability. The eigenvalues and communalities of the variables are also shown. This indicates that, during rotation, the communality of each variable stays the same, but the eigenvalues do not.

One crucial decision has to be made when rotating factors. Should they be kept at right angles (an 'orthogonal rotation'), or should they allowed to become correlated (an 'oblique rotation')? Figure 15.3 shows clearly that an oblique rotation is sometimes necessary to allow the factors to be positioned sensibly relative to the variables. However, the computation and interpretation of orthogonal solutions is considerably more straightforward, which accounts for their popularity.

Kaiser's (1958) VARIMAX computer program is the overwhelmingly popular choice for orthogonal rotations, and many computer packages will perform it by default. For those who are interested in such procedures, it is conceptually quite straightforward. Table 15.2 shows the *squares* of each of the loadings of Table 15.1 (squaring is performed to remove the minus signs, if any). The bottom row of Table 15.2 shows the variance (the square of the standard deviation) of these four squared loadings. You will see that, because some of the loadings in the 'rotated' matrix were large whereas others were small, the variance of the squared rotated loadings is much greater than the variance of the loadings in the unrotated solution (0.041 and 0.034, as opposed to 0.002 and 0.006). Thus if the factors are positioned so that the variance of the (squared) loadings is as large as possible, this should ensure that 'simple structure' is reached. And this (with a minor modification which need not concern us here) is how the VARIMAX program operates. It finds a rotation which MAXimises the VARIance of the (squared) factor loadings.

	Unrotated		Rotated (VARIMAX)	
	Factor 1	**Factor 2**	**Factor 1**	**Factor 2**
Comprehension	0.160	0.090	0.250	0.000
Spelling	0.160	0.250	0.410	0.000
Addition	0.160	0.160	0.017	0.302
Subtraction	0.250	0.090	0.003	0.336
Variance of squared loadings	0.002	0.006	0.038	0.034

Table 15.2 Squared loadings from Table 15.1 to demonstrate the principle of VARIMAX rotation

Oblique rotation is more complicated. The first problem is in detecting whether a rotation has reached simple structure. You will recall that the 'factor structure matrix' shows the correlations between all of the variables and all of the factors. In Figure 15.3 it is clear that, although each factor passes neatly through a cluster of variables, because the factors are correlated it is no longer the case that each variable has a large loading (correlation) with just one factor. Because the factors are correlated, the correlations between V1, V2 and V3 and factor 2 are not near-zero. Likewise, although V4, V5 and V6 will have a massive loading on factor 2, they will also have an appreciable correlation with factor 1. This means that the factor structure matrix can no longer be used to decide whether 'simple structure' has been reached.

Another matrix, called the 'factor pattern matrix', can be calculated for this purpose. It does not show *correlations* between the variables and the factors – indeed, the numbers it contains can be larger than 1.0. Instead, it shows which variables 'belong' with each factor by essentially correcting the structure matrix for the correlations between the factors. Thus it can be used to

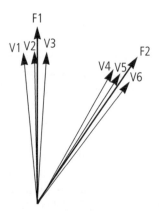

Figure 15.3 Six variables and two correlated factors.

determine whether simple structure has been reached. For the data shown in Figure 15.3, the factor pattern matrix would resemble the VARIMAX-rotated entry of Table 15.1. (In the case of orthogonal rotations such as VARIMAX, the correlation between the factors is always zero, and so there are no correlations between factors to correct for. Thus the numbers in the pattern matrix are the same as the numbers in the structure matrix.)

Alarmingly, opinions are divided as to whether the factor structure matrix or the factor pattern matrix should be interpreted in order to identify the factors, or to report the results of factor analyses. For example, Kline (1994, p. 63) states that 'it is important . . . that the structure and not the pattern is interpreted', yet Cattell (1978, chapter 8) and Tabatchnick and Fidell (1989, p. 640) hold precisely the opposite view. Brogden (1969) suggests that if the factor analysis uses well-understood tests but the interpretation of the factors is unknown, then the pattern matrix should be consulted. Conversely, if the nature of the factors is known, then the structure matrix should be consulted. Brogden's justification for this position seems to be sound.

Readers may wonder how one would ever be able to identify a factor, but not the variables which load on it. However, this is possible. For example, a selection of behavioural or physiological measures may be correlated and factored. Factor scores might be computed for each person, and these may be correlated with other tests. If a set of factor scores shows a correlation of 0.7 with the subjects' scores on a reputable test of anxiety, it is fairly safe to infer that the factor measures anxiety. Alternatively, a few well-trusted tests may be included in the analysis to act as 'marker variables'. If these have massive loadings on any of the rotated factors, this clearly identifies the nature of those factors.

Several programs have been written to perform oblique rotations, and Clarkson and Jennrich (1988) and Harman (1976) discuss the relationships between the various methods. Techniques such as Direct Oblimin (Jennrich and Sampson, 1966) are among the more useful. Almost all such programs need 'fine tuning' in order to reach simple structure (Harman, 1976), usually by means of a parameter which controls how oblique the factors are allowed to become. This is set by default to a value which the program author rather hoped would be adequate for most of the time. Using this value blindly is a dangerous, if common, practice. Harman (1976) suggests performing several rotations, each with a different value of this parameter, and interpreting that which comes closest to simple structure. I have found this to be sound advice.

SELF-ASSESSMENT QUESTION 15.3

What is simple structure, and why is 'rotation to simple structure' almost always performed during the course of a factor analysis?

Factors and factor scores

Suppose that one factor-analyses a set of test items which measure some mental ability, e.g. the speed with which people can visualise what various geometric shapes would look like after being rotated or flipped over. Having performed a factor or component analysis on these data, one might find that a single factor explains a good proportion of the variance, with many of the test items having substantial loadings on this factor. It is possible to validate this factor in exactly the same way as one would validate a test (as discussed in Chapter 13). For example, one can determine whether the factor correlates highly with other psychological tests measuring spatial ability, measures of performance, etc. However, in order to do this it is necessary to work out each person's score on the factor – their 'factor score'.

One obvious way of calculating a factor score is to identify the items which have substantial loadings on the factor, and to simply add up each person's scores on these items, ignoring those with tiny loadings on the factor. For example, suppose that response times to only four items were factor-analysed, and that these had loadings of 0.62, 0.45, 0.18 and 0.90 on a factor (after rotation). This suggests that items 1, 2 and 4 measure much the same construct, whereas item 3 measures something rather different. Therefore it would be possible to go through the data file and average each person's response times to items 1, 2 and 4 only. Thus each person would obtain a 'factor score' which is a measure of the speed with which they can solve the three items with substantial loadings on the factor. Another way of looking at this is to say that each person's scores are 'weighted' using the following numbers – 1, 1, 0 and 1. A weight of '1' is given if the factor loading is thought to be substantial (above 0.4, for example), and a weight of zero corresponds to a small, insignificant factor loading. Thus a person's factor score can be calculated as

$$1 \times RT_1 + 1 \times RT_2 + 0 \times RT_3 + 1 \times RT_4, \text{ or } RT_1 + RT_2 + RT_4$$

where RT_1 to RT_4 are the response times to items 1 to 4, respectively. The 'weights' (the 0s and 1s) are called 'factor score coefficients'. If each person's factor scores are calculated, they can be correlated with other variables in order to establish the validity of this measure of spatial ability.

Whilst this technique for calculating factor scores is sometimes seen in the literature, it does have its drawbacks. For example, although items 1, 2 and 4 all have loadings above 0.4, item 4 has a loading which is very substantially higher than that of item 2. That is, item 4 is a very much better measure of the factor than is item 2. Should the weights – the 'factor score coefficients' – reflect this? Rather than being 0s and 1s, should they be linked somehow to the size of the factor loadings? This approach clearly does make sense, and factor analysis routines will almost invariably offer users the option of calculating these factor score coefficients – one for each variable and each factor. Having obtained these, it is a simple matter to multiply each person's score on each variable by the appropriate factor score coefficient(s), and thus to calculate each person's 'factor score' on each factor. Most computer packages will even do this calculation for you.

For completeness, I ought to mention that factor score coefficients are not applied to the 'raw' scores for each item, but to the 'standardised' scores. Consider item 1. If a person has a response time of 0.9 second to this item, whereas the mean response time of the rest of the sample to this item is 1.0 second, with a standard deviation of 0.2 second, the response time of 0.9 second would convert to a standardised value of $\dfrac{0.9 - 1.0}{0.2}$ or -0.5. It is this value, rather than the original value of 0.9 second, which is used in the computation of factor scores.

The actual mechanics of the calculation of the factor score coefficients need not concern us here. Good discussions are given by Harman (1976, chapter 16), Comrey and Lee (1992, section 10.3) and Harris (1967) for those who are interested. Whereas it is a straightforward matter to compute factor scores when principal-components analysis is used, the problem becomes much more complex in the case of any form of factor analysis. Here there are several different techniques available for calculating factor scores, each with its own advantages and disadvantages. Bartlett's method is one of the better ones (as argued by McDonald and Burr, 1967), and is available as an option on many factor-analysis packages.

SELF-ASSESSMENT QUESTION 15.4

Suppose that a personnel manager factor-analyses applicants' scores on a number of selection tests. How might she use this analysis to decide which tests no longer predict how well employees will perform?

Hierarchical factor analyses

When one performs an oblique factor rotation, the factors which are obtained are generally correlated. The 'factor pattern correlation matrix' describes the angles between the factors. This matrix of correlations between factors can *itself* be factor-analysed – that is, the correlations between the factors can be examined, and any clusters of factors identified. This is what is meant by a 'second-order' or 'second-level' factor analysis (factoring the correlations between the variables being the 'first-order analysis'), and researchers such as Cattell have made considerable use of the technique. An example may illustrate the usefulness of the method.

Chris McConville and I recently wondered what the basic dimensions of mood might be (McConville and Cooper, 1992b). We accordingly factor-analysed the correlations between over 100 mood items, and extracted and obliquely rotated five first-order factors, corresponding to the basic dimensions of mood discussed in Chapter 10. We then factor-analysed the correlations between these first-order factors, and discovered that four of these five first-order factors correlated together to form a second-order mood factor called 'negative affect'. The fifth mood factor had a negligible loading on this factor. Thus there was a hierarchy of mood factors as shown in Figure 15.4.

If there are plenty of second-order factors, and these show a reasonable degree of correlation, it would be quite legitimate to factor the correlations between the second-order factors to perform a third-order factor analysis. The process can continue either until the correlations between the factors are essentially zero, or until just one factor is obtained.

A problem inherent in these hierarchical analyses is that it can be remarkably difficult to identify or conceptualise second- and higher-order factors. Whereas first-order factors can be tentatively identified by inspecting the items with substantial loadings, the second-order factor matrix shows how the first-order factors load on the second-order factor(s). Because of this, it can be quite difficult to identify the second-order factors. For example, what would one make of a factor which seemed to measure the primary abilities of spelling, visualisation and mechanical ability? It would be much easier to see what was going on if a dozen or so variables could be shown to have large loadings on a second-order factor, rather than trying to interpret the second-order factor in terms of just a couple of large loadings from first-order factors.

Several techniques have been devised to overcome this problem. They all relate second- and higher-order factors directly to the observed variables (Schmid and Leiman, 1957). In the example given above, the second-order factors would be defined not in terms of the primary factors (spelling, visualisation, mechanical ability, etc.), but in terms of the actual variables. McConville and Cooper (1992b) give an example of this technique in practice. None of the standard factor-analysis packages include the Schmid–Leiman

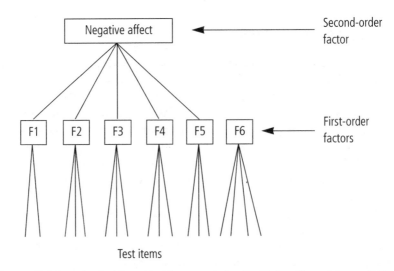

Figure 15.4 Example of a hierarchical factor analysis, after McConville and Cooper (1992b).

technique, but packages such as EQS and LISREL (described below) can perform similar analyses.

A second problem with these analyses concerns measurement error. Sometimes several quite different positionings of the first-order factors are almost equally satisfactory so far as the criterion of meeting simple structure is concerned. However, the more or less arbitrary choice of one such solution will have a powerful effect on the correlations between the factors, and hence the number and nature of the second-order factors. Factor analyses should be performed with above-average care if hierarchical solutions are to be produced.

CONFIRMATORY FACTOR ANALYSIS

A complete treatment of this topic is beyond the scope of this text. The purpose of this section is merely to mention that the technique exists, and to give an example of its usage. Whereas exploratory factor analysis seeks to determine the number and nature of the factors which underlie a set of data through rotation to simple structure, confirmatory factor analysis (as its name suggests) tests hypotheses, or rather it allows the user to choose between several competing hypotheses about the structure of the data. For example, suppose you were interested in using a questionnaire to measure attitudes to eating. On reviewing the literature you might find that one piece of previous research claims that 10 of the 20 items form one factor, the remaining 10 items form another factor, and that these factors have a correlation of 0.4. Another piece of research with the same test might indicate that all 20 items of the test form a single factor. It is vitally important to know which of these claims is correct. The first will lead to two scores being calculated for each person, whilst the second will produce only one score. Confirmatory factor analysis can be used to determine which of these competing models is most appropriate for the data.

It is possible to specify either factor-analytical or principal-components models for confirmatory factor analysis. However, almost all studies are based on factor models, where the communality of each variable is estimated. Indeed, it is possible to perform hierarchical factor analyses, and to test a huge range of models using the technique. Good descriptions of confirmatory factor analysis and its parent technique, structural equation modelling, are given by Long (1983), Loehlin (1987) and in chapters 12 and 13 of Comrey and Lee (1992), among others. Kline (1994) and Child (1990) offer simpler introductions to the subject.

A number of computer programs have been written to perform confirmatory factor analysis. The best known is LISREL, written by Karl Jöreskog, the statistician who devised the technique. EQS (Bentler, 1989) is another program which is arguably simpler to use than LISREL. As confirmatory factor analysis is one of the simplest forms of structural equation modelling, any such program should be able to perform these analyses.

Confirmatory factor analysis views the basic data (test scores, responses to test items, physiological measures, etc.) as being brought about or caused by one or more factors (often known as 'latent variables'). Thus a set of equations can be drawn up, each showing which factor(s) are thought to influence which variable(s).

For example, suppose we postulate two factors – general intelligence ('g') and test anxiety ('TA'). Also suppose that the scores on a test, Test 1, are influenced by both of these factors – but more by general intelligence than by test anxiety. We can represent this by a simple equation, such as:

$$\text{Test } 1 = 0.8 \times g + 0.1 \times \text{TA} + \text{unique variance}$$

The numbers 0.8 and 0.1 show the size of the relationship between the variables and each factor – the factor loadings. Each of these numbers can be either:

- specified directly, as a number (as in the above example);
- estimated by the computer program; or
- set equal to other values which are then all estimated. For example, one could specify that all of the tests are affected by test anxiety to an equal but unknown extent. (This option can be problematical in practice.)

In confirmatory factor analysis, one normally draws up an equation for each variable, showing which factor (or factors) are thought to influence scores on this variable – although not normally the *size* of the loadings. Any factor loadings which are not specified are assumed to be zero. It is also necessary to specify that the variance of each factor is 1.0. The computer program then estimates the best possible values for each of the loadings, and also computes statistics showing how closely the postulated structure fits the actual data. It is common practice to try out several different models, and to choose the one which gives the best fit – that is, which is best supported by the data.

Loehlin (1987) gives a good discussion of how to interpret the various indices of goodness of fit. Whilst these measures of goodness of fit are useful for choosing between competing models, they are not particularly effective for working out the absolute goodness of fit of a particular model. That is, the technique cannot easily determine whether or not a pattern of factors and factor loadings is found in the data, but can be useful in deciding which of three competing models is the most appropriate.

It is common practice to represent the relationships between the variables, common factors and unique factors by means of a diagram called the 'path diagram'. An example should make this clear.

Ignoring the numbers, Figure 15.5 shows two factors, F1 and F2, each of which is thought to influence some observed variables (V1 to V6). You will notice that V4 is influenced by both of the factors, and the other variables are influenced by just one of them. Also shown are the unique variances of each variable (U1 to U6). Each of the lines linking a factor to an observed variable has an arrow at one end, indicating that the factor is presumed to cause a particular observed score (rather than vice versa). The curved line between F1 and F2 represents a correlation – factor 1 and factor 2 may be correlated. Thus this diagram corresponds to an oblique factor solution.

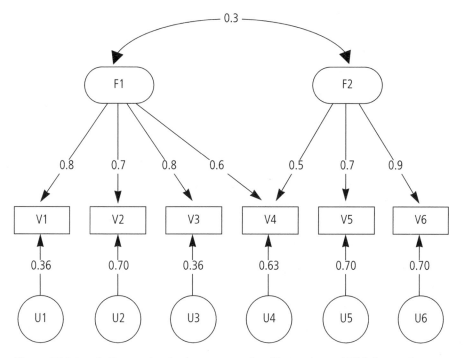

Figure 15.5 A path diagram showing how two correlated factors (F1 and F2) influence the values of six observed variables (V1 to V6). The variables' unique variances (U1 to U6) are also shown.

The numbers on each of the lines represent the factor loadings (in the factor pattern matrix) or, in the case of the curved line, the correlation between these factors. Some of these values might have been specified by the user at the start of the analysis. More usually, however, all of the numbers will have been estimated by the program. Thus the path diagram in Figure 15.5 corresponds to the factor pattern matrix shown in Table 15.3.

Several other plausible path diagrams can be drawn up on the basis of theory or previous research, and each can be tested in order to determine how closely it fits the data. In this way, the researcher can choose between various competing theoretical models. However, there are some risks involved in the use of these techniques. It is all too easy to embark on a 'fishing trip', modifying a model over and over again in order to improve its goodness of fit, regardless of its psychological plausibility. Indeed, EQS and LISREL encourage this practice by suggesting which parts of the model need modification. However, the computer program knows nothing about psychology or the theory of factor analysis, and will frequently suggest something nonsensical, such as allowing the unique variances of different variables to become correlated. Such a model may fit the data from a particular sample wonderfully well, yet make little psychological sense (and be unlikely to replicate in other samples). However, whenever there is a need to choose between competing theoretical models, confirmatory factor analysis can prove to be a very useful tool.

Variable	Factor 1	Factor 2	h^2
V1	0.8	0.0	0.64
V2	0.7	0.0	0.49
V3	0.8	0.0	0.64
V4	0.6	0.5	0.61
V5	0.0	0.7	0.49
V6	0.0	0.7	0.49

Table 15.3 Factor pattern matrix equivalent to the path diagram in Figure 15.5

The account given above has been deliberately simplified, and readers who intend to use the technique should in particular ensure that they understand from other sources:

- that analyses are usually performed on covariances, rather than correlations; and
- what is meant by the 'identification' of a model.

SUMMARY

Factor analysis is a tremendously useful technique for clarifying the relationships between a number of interval-scaled or ratio-scaled variables. It can be applied to any such data – from physical and physiological measures to questionnaire items. This chapter has described how to perform a technically sound factor analysis, and has highlighted some common errors which occasionally creep into published papers. Finally, it has introduced confirmatory factor analysis as a useful technique for choosing between various competing factor-analytical models.

SUGGESTED ADDITIONAL READING

This has been largely indicated in the text. The books by Child and Kline are the simplest, but those by Gorsuch and Comrey are also fairly accessible to non-mathematicians.

ANSWERS TO SELF-ASSESSMENT QUESTIONS

SAQ 15.1
There are problems with this proposal, the most obvious one being that 'county of residence' is not an interval-scaled variable. When the numerical

codes were being allocated, it was entirely arbitrary whether a '1' referred to Cornwall or Cumbria, so the codes do not represent a scale of any kind. Therefore they must be excluded from the factor analysis. (To check for differences in mathematical ability between counties you could suggest that your colleague calculates factor scores on each of the factors and then performs an analysis of variance using 'county' as the between-subjects factor.)

The other problem is that there are more variables being analysed than there are people in the sample. Thus although the number of subjects is greater than the 'magic' number of 100, these data are not suitable for factor analysis. You could suggest that your colleague collects some more data so as to increase the sample size to at least 150. You could usefully warn her about the problems inherent in factoring dichotomous data such as these – where the only possible answers are 0 or 1 – and if the items are found to differ drastically in their difficulty values (the proportion of individuals answering each item correctly) you could consider consulting the literature for alternatives to the Pearson correlation which are suitable for factor analysis.

Finally, you could usefully check with your colleague that the children were given plenty of time to attempt all of the test items, and ask whether the items that were not attempted have been coded as being answered incorrectly, or given a special code and treated as missing data. If items that were not attempted are given the same code as 'incorrect answer' (e.g. '0'), it is clear that problems can arise if not all of the children managed to finish the test in the time allocated. The items towards the end would appear to be more difficult than they really are, simply because only a few children managed to reach them. In circumstances such as these it might be better just to analyse the first 50 items (or whatever), in which case there is no need for your colleague to collect any more data, as the sample of 100 would be adequate for this number of items.

SAQ 15.2
Three and four. You should probably extract three factors, given that the scree test has been found to perform better than the Kaiser–Guttman technique.

SAQ 15.3
Simple structure is a measure of the extent to which each factor passes through a cluster of variables. Let us suppose that the factors are being kept at right angles – an orthogonal rotation. If the rotation has reached simple structure, each factor will have few sizeable correlations (above 0.4 or below −0.4) with some variables, and correlations close to zero (e.g. ±0.1) with the rest. There should be very few medium-sized correlations, in the range of ±0.1–0.4. Similarly, when the rows of the factor matrix are examined, each variable should have a large loading on only one or two factors. The position is much the same for oblique rotations (where the factors are not kept at right angles), except that the 'factor pattern matrix' which is used to assess the simplicity of the solution does not contain correlations between the variables and the factors, although it is interpreted in the same way.

Since the initial position of the factors relative to the variables is essentially arbitrary, different researchers would report quite different results if rotation to simple structure were not carried out. It is thus important for ensuring that factors can be consistently identified across several different studies.

SAQ 15.4

The factor analysis will show the nature and the extent of the overlap between the test scores, and will probably produce several factors measuring personality and/or ability. Scores can be calculated for each applicant on each of these factors ('factor scores'), and each of these factor scores can be validated in precisely the same way that tests are validated, as described in Chapter 13. For example, the applicants could be followed up and their factor scores correlated with measures of productivity or with supervisors' ratings of performance. Alternatively, ANOVA may be used to determine any differences in factor scores between various groups of employees, e.g. those who are later promoted, or those who leave.

If some of the factor scores do seem to be useful in the selection process, the tests which have high loadings on the factors in question could usefully be retained. Those which do not load on any of the useful factors could probably be dropped from the assessment battery.

16

Item response theory

BACKGROUND

This chapter introduces a completely different approach to assessing ability from test scores – one that does not require the use of norms and does not even require that respondents should take the same tests. As its name suggests, the technique considers how people respond to individual items in a test, rather than their total scores. It leads naturally to 'tailored testing', namely the administration of test items by computer such that the difficulty of the items presented is appropriate to each individual's ability level, and is one of the most exciting recent developments in psychometrics.

Recommended prior reading

Chapters 11 and 12.

INTRODUCTION

Thus far we have always assumed that a person's total score on a psychological test provides the best measure of their ability or their endowment with a particular personality trait. We are so familiar with adding up the number of items answered correctly (or totalling scores on Likert scales) and comparing these scores with norms in order to interpret their meaning for an individual that it is difficult to see what is wrong with this method of scoring tests, or how it could be improved.

One problem with using the total score as a measure of ability is that someone who answers four easy items correctly but fails all of the difficult items ends up with the same score as someone who (through boredom?) answers one easy item and three of the difficult items correctly, which seems wrong. For the total score completely ignores the (easily available) information about the difficulty of the test items. An individual will obtain a high score given an easy test, and a low score if they are given a difficult test, even though they show the same ability in each – necessitating the use of norms.

There are certainly plenty of alternatives to computing a person's total score as a measure of their ability. If the difficulty levels ('p-values', i.e. proportion of individuals passing) of items are known, one could therefore use the p-value of the most difficult item that was answered correctly (or the easiest item that was answered incorrectly) as a measure of ability. Alternatively, one could calculate the average difficulty of the items that were answered correctly. There is a whole host of possibilities, most of which have remained unexplored in the literature.

SELF-ASSESSMENT QUESTION 16.1

The purpose of this exercise is to encourage you to think about how statistics other than the total score can reflect someone's level of ability, including one based on the difficulty of the hardest item passed, and another based on the easiest item that was failed. The following table shows the responses of two individuals to nine test items that were administered to a larger sample of people. The p-values show the proportion of people who answered each item correctly.

(a) Work out the total score and the other three ability measures for Person 2.

Item	1	2	3	4	5	6	7	8	9
p-value	0.9	0.1	0.4	0.5	0.7	0.4	0.3	0.8	0.3
Person 1	1	0	1	0	1	0	0	1	0
Person 2	1	0	0	0	0	0	0	1	0

	Total score	1 – Min. p correct	1 – Max. p incorrect	1 – Mean p correct
Person 1	4	$1 - 0.4 = 0.6$	$1 - 0.5 = 0.5$	$1 - \dfrac{2.8}{4} = 0.30$
Person 2	?	?	?	?

(b) Why is it probably *not* sensible to assess ability on the basis of the 'hardest item passed' or 'easiest item failed' criteria?

The problem is that a very large number of indices could be calculated from the data shown in SAQ 16.1. How does one decide to use one rather than another? One approach may be to use an explicit mathematical model to describe what may be going on when individuals respond to test items. For simplicity we shall assume for now that we are dealing with a free-response test (so guessing is not a problem), each item of which can be scored as true or false.

THE ITEM CHARACTERISTIC CURVE

Three assumptions that can probably safely be made are that:

1. the chance of someone getting an item correct depends on both their ability and the difficulty of the test item;

2. the chance of someone getting a particular item correct is not influenced by the correctness of their responses to any other items, other than as a function of that person's ability (this is known as the assumption of 'local independence');
3. all of the items in a scale measure just one construct.

The assumption of local independence basically means that each item should be an entirely novel problem, and there should be no carry-over from one item to the next – either positive (where a correct answer to one question either is necessary or provides a clue as to how to answer another) or negative (where it may be necessary to break the 'set' used in previous questions to arrive at the correct answer). Thus the assumption of local independence would not hold for items such as item 1: 'What is 4 + 5', and item 2: 'What is the square root of the answer to item 1', since if item 1 is answered incorrectly, then item 2 must be, too.

For the sake of simplicity, let us just consider a single test item. Assumption (1) above tells us that the chance of someone getting this item correct depends on their ability and the difficulty of this test item. So what is the best way to model this relationship mathematically? You might initially think that a straight line linking ability and performance would provide the simplest relationship. After all, psychometricians usually assume linear relationships between variables when computing correlations, and so on. Thus perhaps we could describe the relationship between ability and item performance by a straight line? One such graph is shown in Figure 16.1 (ignore the letters A, B and C for now).

Figure 16.1 implies that we can estimate the chances of someone passing this item using the equation of a straight line, that is,

$$\text{probability of passing} = a + b \times \text{ability}$$

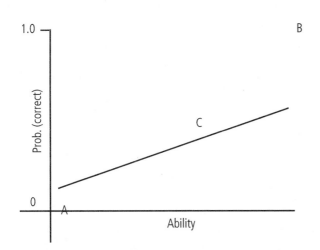

Figure 16.1 A possible linear relationship between ability and item performance.

where a and b are constants (numbers) that could be estimated, e.g. through regression. Unfortunately, there seems to be quite a lot wrong with this graph. For a start, we know that the probability of getting an item correct can only range between 1.0 and 0. Unless the line is horizontal (which itself indicates that the chances of passing an item are completely unrelated to ability!), the straight line is bound to imply that students with very low or very high ability will have a below-zero or better-than-perfect chance of passing the item, and this is clearly absurd. There is a second problem here, too. The position of a line on Figure 16.1 is determined by two parameters, namely its slope and its height, so both of these have to be estimated when evaluating the relationship between ability and performance on an item. Perhaps there is a better way of describing this relationship, one which does not allow the probability to be greater than zero or less than one, and which relies on just one parameter.

For the sake of simplicity we shall assume that we are dealing with a 'free-response test' in which respondents are asked to produce an answer (e.g. 'What is the capital of Ecuador?', rather than choose between several alternatives (e.g. 'The capital of Ecuador is (a) Quito (b) Bogotá (c) Montevideo). Given this, it seems reasonable to make the following assumptions.

- The probability of someone with extremely low ability correctly answering a test item of moderate difficulty should be fairly close to zero, so the curve should pass through point A on Figure 16.1.
- The probability of someone with extremely high ability correctly answering an item of moderate difficulty should be fairly close to 1.0, so the curve should pass through point B on Figure 16.1.
- The point where a respondent has a 50 per cent chance of answering an item correctly can be identified (as point C on Figure 16.1). This point corresponds to the difficulty level of the item.
- There will be a range of abilities on either side of this point where the probability of answering the item correctly moves smoothly between zero and 1.0.
- For now, we shall assume that this spread of abilities is the same for each item.

Given these fairly common-sense constraints, I suggest that the shape of the curve linking ability to item performance could look somewhat like that shown in Figure 16.2. This shows the probability of individuals of various ability levels answering this item correctly. The difficulty level of this item is 1.0 – this is the point on the x-axis where an individual has a 50 per cent chance of answering the item correctly. Graphs such as these are known as *item characteristic curves* (ICCs) – an important term.

You will have noticed that the ability scale has negative as well as positive values. Do not worry about this.

You can see that the chances of a person with ability levels below −1.5 answering this item correctly are rather small, and that at ability levels above 3.5 the vast majority of people will answer the item correctly. Different test items will generally have different difficulty levels, and these can conveniently be represented on the same graph, as shown in Figure 16.3, which shows three items of difficulty levels 0, 2 and 3.

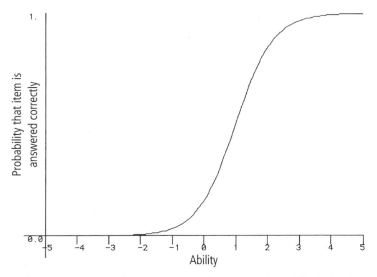

Figure 16.2 An item characteristic curve for an item whose difficulty level is 1.0.

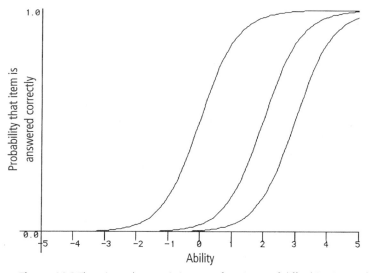

Figure 16.3 Three item characteristic curves from items of difficulties 0, 2 and 3.

SELF-ASSESSMENT QUESTION 16.2

Suppose that someone with an ability of 1.0 had answered the three questions whose item characteristic curves (ICCs) are shown in Figure 16.3. Roughly what are the chances that they would get each item correct? What would be the chances of someone with an ability of 0 answering each of these three items correctly? The curve for an item of difficulty 1.0 is not shown, but can you nevertheless say what the probability is that a person whose ability is 1.0 would answer such an item correctly?

In the examples discussed above, we assume that the items vary only in terms of their difficulty. Thus the ICCs run parallel to each other, with the more difficult items to the right of the ability scale. Since item difficulty is the only parameter that makes one ICC different from another, the ICCs shown in Figure 16.3 are examples of what is known as a 'one-parameter model'.

The graphs shown in Figures 16.2 and 16.3 can be described by a fairly simple mathematical equation, known as the 'logistic function'. There are two main reasons for working with the logistic function. First, (unlike the linear model) the shape of the curve looks sensible according to the criteria outlined above, and it guarantees that the probability of a person answering an item correctly can never stray outside the range of 0 to 1.0. Second, it is easy to work with mathematically in that it does not require any integrations or similar 'messy' techniques to be performed. It starts off at zero, moves smoothly upwards at a point determined by the item's difficulty, and then flattens out as it approaches a probability of 1.0.

Suppose that we have one item (item i) and we wish to work out the probability that a person with a particular level of ability (ϑ) will get this item correct. The equation for the one-parameter logistic function is:

$$P_i(\text{correct} \mid \vartheta) = \frac{e^{1.7(\vartheta - b_i)}}{1 + e^{1.7(\vartheta - b_i)}} \qquad \text{(Equation 16.1)}$$

which is actually not quite so fearsome as it first appears. The left-hand side of the equation reads 'the probability that a person will get item "i" correct given that they have a level of ability that is ϑ'. On the right-hand side of the equation, 'e' is simply a number whose approximate value is 2.718, ϑ is the person's ability, and b_i is the difficulty level of item 'i'. In SAQ 16.1 you were asked to estimate the probability that someone whose ability was 1.0 would pass an item whose difficulty was 2.0, by looking at the graphs in Figure 16.3. Now we can calculate this directly from the logistic function.

$$P(\text{correct} \mid 1) = \frac{e^{1.7(\vartheta - 2)}}{1 + e^{1.7(\vartheta - 2)}} = \frac{e^{1.7(1 - 2)}}{1 + e^{1.7(1 - 2)}} = \frac{e^{(-1.7)}}{1 + e^{(-1.7)}}$$

$$= \frac{0.183}{1.183} = 0.15$$

which agrees with Figure 16.3. The only step that may have caused you any problems here is the evaluation of $e^{-1.7}$. Many calculators will work this out for you, or alternatively mathematical tables of e^x may be consulted.

The important point to grasp is that the one-parameter logistic function allows us to calculate the probability of any person passing any item, given a knowledge of that person's ability and the item's difficulty. The difficulty of an item is defined as being that point along the ability scale that is half-way along the sloping part of the ICC. Since in this case the curve starts at a value of 0 and flattens out at a value of 1.0, the difficulty level of an item is that point where the probability of passing the item is $\dfrac{1.0 - 0}{2} = 0.5$.

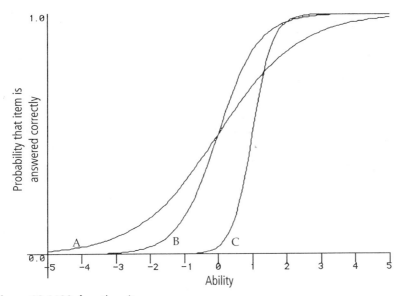

Figure 16.4 ICCs from three items.

So far we have assumed that every item has an equal 'spread' on either side of its difficulty value. This is actually quite a restrictive assumption. It seems quite probable that items' ICCs may have different slopes (or levels of 'discrimination'), as shown in Figure 16.4. A small value of discrimination indicates that individuals with a broad range of abilities have a reasonable chance of answering the item correctly. A high value of discrimination indicates that the ICC is much more upright. (The mathematically minded might like to view the discrimination parameter as being the slope of the ICC at its point of inflection.)

SELF-ASSESSMENT QUESTION 16.3

Two of the items in Figure 16.4 have a difficulty level of 0. Of these, one has a discrimination of 0.5 and the other has a discrimination of 1.0. The other item has a difficulty of 1.0 and a discrimination of 2.0. Can you identify which is which?

It is very easy to modify the formula for the one-parameter logistic formula to take account of this second discrimination parameter, which is usually written as a_i. The modified formula is:

$$P_i(\text{correct} \mid \vartheta) = \frac{e^{1.7\,a_i(\vartheta - b_i)}}{1 + e^{1.7\,a_i(\vartheta - b_i)}} \qquad \text{(Equation 16.2)}$$

and so the probability of a person with an ability (ϑ) of 3.0 answering an item that has a difficulty (b_i) of 2.0 and a discrimination (a_i) of 0.5 correctly is:

$$P_i(\text{correct} \mid \vartheta) = \frac{e^{1.7 \times 0.5(3-2)}}{1 + e^{(1.7 \times 0.5(3-2))}} = \frac{e^{0.85}}{1 + e^{0.85}} = \frac{2.34}{3.34} = 0.70$$

It should come as no surprise to learn that this function is known as the 'two-parameter logistic function', the two parameters defining each item being discrimination (a_i) and difficulty (b_i).

A final variant of the logistic model is very useful in cases where subjects are given a multiple-choice test. Suppose that a sample of individuals was asked to choose the correct answer from four alternatives. Here it is clear that someone of very low ability would have an approximately 25 per cent chance of guessing the correct answer (assuming that the four alternatives were equally attractive), and so the ICC should level out not at a probability of zero, but at a level rather above this. The problem is that we cannot assume that this value will be exactly 0.25, for in practice the various (incorrect) alternatives will not be exactly equally attractive to those taking the test. Thus rather than using the fixed value of $\frac{1}{n}$ (where n is the number of alternatives offered), it may be better to estimate for each item the best value for the point where the curve levels off. The 'three-parameter logistic model' allows us to make such allowances for guessing. Its form is:

$$P_i(\text{correct} \mid \vartheta) = c_i + (1 - c_i)\frac{e^{1.7\,a_i(\vartheta - b_i)}}{1 + e^{1.7\,a_i(\vartheta - b_i)}} \qquad \text{(Equation 16.3)}$$

where a_i represents the item's discrimination and b_i represents its difficulty as before, and where c_i represents the probability that a respondent of very low ability answers the item correctly. Figure 16.5 shows three ICCs, one with $a_i = 1.0$, $b_i = 0.5$ and $c_i = 0.2$, another with $a_i = 0.5$, $b_i = 1.0$ and $c_i = 0.25$ and a third

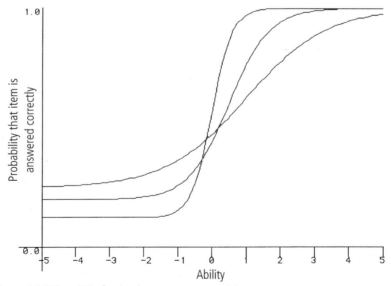

Figure 16.5 Three ICCs for the three-parameter model.

with $a_i = 2.0$, $b_i = 0$ and $c_i = 0.125$. You will see how each of them levels out at the left-hand side to a value of c_i, which of course allows for the probability of 'lucky' guessing. You should be careful when establishing the difficulty level of items under the three-parameter model, since the ICC does not now start off at a probability value of zero. If the curve starts at a value of 0.3 and flattens out at a value of 1.0, the difficulty level of an item is that point where the probability of passing the item is $0.3 + \dfrac{1.0 - 0.3}{2} = 0.65$.

You may have noticed that each of the formulae given above is a slight elaboration of the previous one. Thus if we set c_i equal to zero in Equation 16.3, we end up with Equation 16.2. If we also set the item discrimination parameter a_i to 1.0, then we end up with Equation 16.1.

This section has introduced three mathematical models which could reasonably be expected to describe the relationship between a person's ability and his or her likely performance when confronted with a single test item. The two-parameter model is perhaps the most appropriate for free-response data, whilst the three-parameter model may be useful in cases where a multiple-choice test has been given. We have shown how it is quite straightforward to work out the likelihood of a person answering any item correctly provided that one knows the item parameters and the person's ability. The basic aim of item response theory is to perform this trick backwards. Having obtained individuals' responses to the test items, item response theory attempts to estimate the most likely values for:

- the one, two or three parameters associated with each item; and
- each person's ability.

ESTIMATING ABILITIES AND ITEM PARAMETERS

As mentioned above, the basic aim of item response theory is to estimate the difficulty level of each item in the test, and (at the same time) to estimate the ability of each person who takes the test. Thus if a test consists of 20 items and the responses of 100 children are analysed, we will need to estimate 20 measures of item difficulty and 100 measures of ability for the one-parameter model, plus 20 item discriminations if we opt for the two-parameter model, plus a further 20 guessing indices if we opt for a three-parameter model. How should we go about doing this?

One possibility is simply to look at the data. Table 16.1 shows the responses made by eight people to five test items. A 'correct' response is shown as a 1, and an incorrect response is coded as zero.

EXERCISE

Spend 5 minutes or so looking at the data in Table 16.1. Try to identify the easiest and most difficult items, and the most and least able people.

	Item 1	Item 2	Item 3	Item 4	Item 5
James	1	0	1	1	0
Sharon	1	1	1	1	0
Brian	1	1	1	0	1
Linda	0	1	0	0	0
Michael	0	1	1	0	0
Susan	0	0	1	0	0
William	1	0	0	0	0
Fiona	1	1	1	0	0

Table 16.1 Scores of eight people on five test items

It seems probable that, when we ignore the difficulty levels of the individual items, Sharon and Brian (with four items answered correctly) have higher scores on the trait in question than the others, with William, Linda and Susan having the lowest scores (one item answered correctly). Now consider the columns. Which items seem to be the most difficult? Only one person (Brian) answers item 5 correctly, and only two people (James and Sharon) answer item 4 correctly, so it seems reasonable to assume that these are difficult items, whilst item 3 (which only two people fail to answer correctly) is easy.

Now consider the abilities of the people taking the test. Both Sharon and Brian have total scores of 3, and so according to 'classical' test theory they would be considered to have equal ability. However, you can see from Table 16.1 that such an assumption is rather simplistic, since we argued earlier that item 5 is likely to be rather more difficult than item 4. Brian thus managed to answer a difficult item correctly, but failed an easier item. Sharon answered the easier item correctly, but failed the more difficult one. So it seems reasonable to believe that Brian should have a higher score on the trait than Sharon.

EXERCISE

Consider the scores obtained by James and Fiona. Which do you think is the more able, and why?

The crucial point to bear in mind here is that when we estimate the difficulty level of the items, we try to take the ability of the respondents into account, and vice versa. In a clumsy and informal kind of way we are trying to estimate what a person's ability score would be independent of (that is, after taking into consideration) the difficulty level of the test items that happened to be administered. Likewise, we try to estimate the difficulty of each item having taken into account differences in the ability of the respondents.

This is a vitally important point to remember – item response theory sets out to measure ability independently of the difficulty of the particular items that were administered. It also seeks to estimate item difficulty/discrimination/guessing in a manner that is quite independent of the sample of individuals who happened to take the test. This is in stark contrast to classical test theory, in which a person's score is regarded as their measure of ability, and this is totally confounded with the difficulty of the test items. The same score could be obtained by a highly able student confronted with difficult test items, or a low-ability student presented with easy test items.

I argued earlier that the item characteristic curve (ICC) shows the probability of individuals with various levels of ability passing a particular test item. Perhaps a computer program can be written that would first make a rough 'guesstimate' of the abilities of the various people (perhaps on the basis of the number of items answered correctly) and then, given these abilities, would estimate the difficulty levels of each of the items. The same process could subsequently be repeated backwards, with the students' abilities being estimated from the item difficulty statistics. This process could be repeated time and time again, yielding better estimates of the ability and item parameters at each stage, until the estimates of the students' ability and the items' difficulties could not be improved further. In other words, such a program could attempt to find the most appropriate values for all of the item parameters and abilities. Swaminathan and Gifford (1983) have shown that when the number of items and individuals is fairly large, the estimates of the parameters that are obtained in this way are quite close to their true values for the one- and two-parameter models, whilst the three-parameter model is rather more problematical.

Put like this, it sounds a simple enough procedure, although the statistical and numerical estimation of all these parameters can be a process of toe-curling complexity. You should not worry about the details too much. Several computer programs have been written to perform such analyses. LOGIST (Wingersky *et al.*, 1982), RASCAL, RSP, XCalibre and ASCAL (Assessment Systems Corporation, 1989) are programs that attempt to estimate these person-parameters and item-parameters simultaneously by a variety of methods. The important point to grasp is that these programs can simultaneously estimate both individuals' abilities and the various item parameters. They also provide statistics which show how closely a particular model fits the data – for example, they allow one to determine whether the two-parameter logistic model is adequate, or whether it is also necessary to calculate the guessing parameters for each item.

In order to demonstrate that the programs work in much the same way as our common-sense analysis, Table 16.2 shows the ability and item difficulty estimates that were obtained by analysing the data shown in Table 16.1 using a two-parameter logistic model. The ICCs corresponding to the data in Table 16.2 are shown in Figure 16.5. Do not take these results too seriously – it is normally thought necessary to base such analyses on samples of several hundred people and tests that consist of more than five items. However, it does

	Ability	Item	Difficulty	Discrimination
James	0.424	1	−0.534	1.440
Sharon	0.915	2	−0.531	1.004
Brian	1.026	3	−0.956	1.609
Linda	−0.943	4	0.970	1.317
Michael	−0.376	5	1.474	1.565
Susan	−0.733			
William	−0.791			
Fiona	0.264			

Table 16.2 Item difficulties and ability estimates for the data in Table 16.1, based on the two-parameter logistic model

show that the programs appear to produce results that are broadly in line with our previous expectations – you should check for yourself that the results in Table 16.2 are consistent with our earlier 'eyeballing' of the data.

This section ends with a caution. Like many other statistical techniques, programs that estimate item parameters and abilities almost always produce answers, and there is a great tendency for users simply to report these without being too concerned about whether the chosen model (e.g. the one-, two- or three-parameter logistic model) actually fits the observed data. If it does not, then everything that we have said about the invariance (independence) of ability from the item parameters simply fails to apply, and the test items will be useless. Hambleton *et al.* (1991, chapter 4) provide a good introduction to this most vital issue.

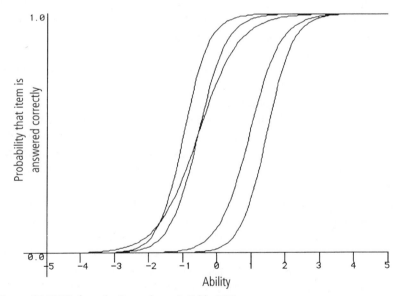

Figure 16.6 ICCs from the items shown in Table 16.2.

BENEFITS OF ITEM RESPONSE THEORY

The wonderful thing about item response theory is that the estimates of individuals' ability are divorced from the characteristics (difficulty, discrimination and guessability') of the particular sample of items that was administered. *We would expect to obtain precisely the same estimates of ability whatever sample of items individuals were presented with.* This is a far cry from conventional testing, in which test scores can be interpreted only by reference to expensively gathered norms, and item difficulties and so on also depend on the characteristics of the sample to whom the test was administered.

For example, suppose that a vocabulary test item was administered to a random sample of the population. We might find that 50 per cent of the sample answer the item correctly. Now suppose that we add a large number of university graduates to the sample – highly able people, most of whom will tend to answer the item correctly. We might now find that, because the sample includes a disproportionately large number of highly verbal people, 80 per cent of the second sample will answer the item correctly. Thus traditional item difficulty indices ('p-values') tend to alter according to the composition of the sample. You should take it on trust that the same thing does not happen with item response theory. Provided that there is a good spread of abilities in the sample, the estimates of item difficulty will not depend at all on the number of people at each ability level. This is what it means to estimate item difficulty independently of ability. Precisely the same thing holds for the other item indices – discrimination (a_i) and guessing (c_i). It makes the whole process of test construction much easier, for one does not have to go to the expense of tracking down random samples of the population from which to estimate the item parameters. Any convenient group of people will do, so long as it contains a reasonable spread of abilities. However, the number of people at each ability level will not affect the estimates of the item parameters.

How about the process of estimating individuals' abilities from test items? Much the same kind of thing applies. Using item response theory we can administer any convenient sample of test items in order to obtain an estimate of respondents' abilities, just so long as the item characteristic curves are not all bunched up at one position – that is, so long as several of the items discriminate at each ability level. If this is the case (as it usually will be, provided that the items vary considerably in difficulty and have low to moderate discrimination parameters) it is possible to estimate respondents' ability without worrying at all about the number of items at each difficulty level.

When one is assessing ability by means of a conventional test, in which the number of items answered correctly forms the estimate of the respondents' abilities, it is clear that the number of easy and difficult items in the test will affect the estimates of ability. Respondents sitting a test in which the majority of the items are easy will obtain higher total scores than those sitting a test where the majority of the items are difficult. This is not a problem with ability measures derived from item response theory. Since these ability measures are divorced, statistically, from the difficulty of the test items, the number of questions at each difficulty level does not really matter.

That said, some items are more useful than others for gleaning information about an individual person's ability. Consider Figure 16.7. Suppose that someone failed items C and D, and passed items A and B. It seems reasonable to suspect that their ability lies somewhere in the range between 0 and 1, but it will be difficult to work out precisely where, for at this range of abilities the probability of a person answering any of the items correctly is, in each case, either very close to 1.0 or very close to 0. There would be a considerable amount of measurement error associated with any estimate of ability in this region.

It can be shown that test items whose difficulty levels lie close to the person's ability, which have steep slopes (i.e. high discrimination power), and for which the guessing parameter is low, provide the most information about a respondent's precise ability. Lord and Novick (1968) have shown that it is possible to calculate the 'item information function', a statistic which shows the range of abilities for which each item provides useful information. Should you ever want to calculate one, the formula is

$$I_i(\vartheta) = \frac{2.89a_i^2\,(1-c_i)}{(c_i + e^{1.7\,a_i(\vartheta - b_i)})\,(1 + e^{1.7\,a_i(\vartheta - b_i)})^2}$$

where the left-hand side of the equation reads 'the information provided by item i (having item discrimination, difficulty and guessing parameters a_i, b_i and c_i) at an ability level ϑ'. Thus if we have estimated the item's three parameters, we can now establish whether it is likely to tell us anything useful about a certain level of ability. Moreover, it is an easy matter to work out the ability

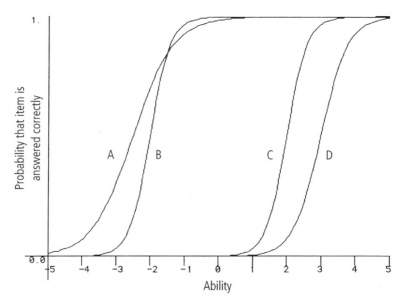

Figure 16.7 Four ICCs that yield little information about abilities in the region between 0 and 1.

level at which a particular item yields most information about ability. Thus, were we to compute the item information functions for the four items shown in Figure 16.7, this would reveal that none of them could give much information in the region between 0 and 1. Therefore the item information function provides a convenient way of computing what is obvious from Figure 16.7 – that to make precise estimates of ability requires highly discriminating items with difficulty levels close to the true ability level of the person being tested. Establishing a person's ability level involves determining which items (of known difficulty, etc.) they can usually answer correctly, and which ones they reliably fail to answer correctly. Their ability lies somewhere in between the difficulty of these two sets of items. Hence it follows that items which are either very difficult or very easy tell us little about a person's precise ability, but items that tax the person to their limit allow us to pinpoint precisely where their ability lies.

ADAPTIVE TESTING

Conventional ability tests normally operate over a fairly narrow range of abilities, in order to avoid making respondents feel dispirited when confronted with large numbers of very difficult items, or bored when presented with many very easy items. This sometimes places the users of conventional tests in the paradoxical position of having to be able to guess the ability of their respondents in advance, so that they can choose a test of appropriate difficulty! Even so, the less able respondent is likely to find a constant stream of (for them) impossible items to be demotivating, whereas a highly able respondent may feel annoyed by being asked to answer what are (for them) insultingly easy items. Item response theory offers a much better alternative, known as 'adaptive testing'.

Suppose that a large number of items are given out to a large sample of people of widely varying abilities – it does not have to be a *random* sample. The item parameters are estimated by means of one of the programs mentioned above, perhaps using the two-parameter or three-parameter logistic models. Suppose, too, that the chosen model is found to provide a good overall fit to the data. We are now in a very powerful position, for it is a relatively simple matter to transfer the test items to a computer and write a computer program that will present the test items to an individual, one at a time.

We may first present an item of low to moderate difficulty. If a particular respondent fails to answer this item correctly, then we can choose another item that is slightly easier. If they answer this one correctly, the program can identify a somewhat more difficult item, using the item information function to determine which items will yield most information about the person's ability – until the program eventually determines precisely which items a person can just answer correctly, and which (more difficult) items they just fail. As more and more data are collected the computer program will be able to predict ever more accurately which as yet untaken items a person will be able to answer correctly, and which they will fail. This allows the person's ability to be established very rapidly. The experience of taking such tests is that the items are generally taxing but not impossible, and since no one is forced to plough through vast numbers of items that are either much too difficult or much too easy to yield any information about their ability, the whole testing process can be greatly shortened.

There are other advantages, too. As each person will probably see a completely different set of test items (since the choice of item to be presented at each stage depends upon the correctness of the respondent's answers to previous test items), test security becomes far less of a problem, particularly if the initial item is chosen more or less at random. Each person will sit their own, personally tailored, test. From what you already know about estimating ability from item parameters, it should be clear that it does not matter if different respondents have experienced quite different test items, since ability can be inferred from the performance on any set of items.

SUMMARY

There are basically two approaches that can be followed when constructing psychological tests. One is to apply a rather simple, robust model – that of classical test theory. Here the total score is taken as an estimate of ability, and the problems that arise through this being confounded by item difficulty are largely eliminated by the use of norms for the interpretation of test scores. It is a simple model that has served well for the past fifty years, although it has always struck me as strange that the classical model of test construction pays no heed whatsoever to the nature of the item difficulties, the item discriminations, or the respondents' attempts to guess the correct answer to multiple-choice tests. The item difficulties are never explicitly chosen in a test that is constructed through classical test theory. Items of extreme difficulty will tend not to correlate with others, and so will be eliminated through the process of item analysis. However, there is a kind of pious hope that the distribution of item difficulties and item discrimination indices for the remaining items will prove suitable for the population.

Item response theory (IRT) goes to the other extreme. It makes some rather strong assumptions about the relationship between ability and performance on individual test items, and (if these assumptions prove to be reasonable) it proves possible to separate the respondents' abilities from the difficulty of the test items. This has all kinds of advantages for computerised adaptive testing, and the technique may also be valuable in other applications, such as identifying bias in test items. However, what if one or more items do not seem to fit the test model? Should such items just be discarded, or should attempts be made to develop alternatives to the logistic models which might better fit such items?

There are several practical difficulties associated with test construction through IRT. The computing power needed to estimate item and person parameters for sensibly sized sets of data has been freely available only for the past ten years or so, and this may have hindered the development of such measures. There may be legal problems, as recent draft legislation in the USA has suggested that any individual taking a test must be able to work out their score, given that they know their responses. In practice, non-specialists would find that difficult. Moreover, as the underlying theory is very much more complicated than classical test theory, applied psychologists may be reluctant to invest time and effort in mastering its principles and (if my experience is typical) may be frankly sceptical of IRT's capacity to estimate ability independently of the characteristics of the individual test items. Psychometricians, too, have their concerns. As far as I am aware, there is no firm mathematical proof that the values of the item and person parameters are good, consistent estimates of their true values. The empirical evidence suggests that they may be, under certain conditions – but is this really enough? And how does the adequacy of model-fit affect the ability of IRT to disentangle person parameters from item parameters? It will be interesting to see whether in the twenty-first century psychological testing becomes synonymous with the administration of adaptive tests on portable microcomputers.

SUGGESTED ADDITIONAL READING

The obvious recommendation here is Hambleton *et al.* (1991). This is a simply written introduction to item response theory and adaptive testing, and it amplifies all of the points made above. Hambleton and Swaminathan (1985) go into slightly more detail, and Lord and Novick (1968) is *the* standard text for the mathematically sophisticated. The journal *Applied Psychological Measurement* publishes many papers on the theory and applications of item response theory.

ANSWERS TO SELF-ASSESSMENT QUESTIONS

SAQ 16.1
(a) 2, 1 – 0.8 = 0.2, 1 – 0.7 = 0.3, 1 – 1.7/2 = 0.15
(b) As the estimate of ability will depend on the response to just one item, luck in the choice of item content will affect both scores. If the test uses multiple-choice items, correct guessing will also affect the 'hardest item passed' estimate of ability.

SAQ 16.2
These can be estimated by measuring up from the point on the *x*-axis where ability = 1.0. There is a chance of approximately 0.85 that someone of this ability would answer an item that had a difficulty of 0 correctly, a chance of 0.15 that they would answer an item with a difficulty of 2.0 correctly, and a chance of 0.03 that they would answer an item of difficulty 3.0 correctly. The

probability of their answering an item with a difficulty of 1.0 correctly would be 0.5 – by definition, since the difficulty of an item is the point on the ability scale that is half-way up the slope of the graph, which in this case corresponds to a probability of 0.5.

SAQ 16.3

Item	Discrimination	Difficulty
A	0.5	0
B	1.0	0
C	2.0	1.0

17

Problems with tests

BACKGROUND

This chapter introduces some problems that can affect scores on tests of ability and personality – background, test-taking attitudes, and so on. In particular, it considers the claim that psychological tests are biased against members of minority groups, beginning with a look at the nature of test bias, and techniques for detecting it in tests.

Recommended prior reading

Chapters 11, 13 and 16.

INTRODUCTION

It is undeniable that psychological tests have a public-image problem, since grave doubts have been expressed in both the popular press and the psychological journals about the 'fairness' of various psychological tests. For example, Kamin (1974) draws our attention to the way in which some early ability tests were used to identify 'feeble-minded' immigrants to the USA during the 1920s. Rather than being tests of abstract reasoning, these tests included items assessing factual knowledge about the American culture (e.g. knowledge of past presidents). It is unsurprising that immigrants (many of whom could not even read or speak English, far less have a knowledge of the culture of a nation on the other side of the globe) failed to show their true ability on these tests. The tests were unfair to members of these cultures in that they grossly underestimated their true potential.

When tests systematically underestimate or overestimate the true scores of groups of individuals, they are said to be *biased* against (or in favour of) certain groups. Thus the IQ tests that Kamin cites were, without doubt, biased against all those who did not speak English fluently and/or had little knowledge of the American way of life. Members of these groups achieved scores on these tests that did not reflect their full potential. Note, however, that bias was found in this case *because of the way in which the test was used* –

someone, somewhere, selected an inappropriate test for this particular application. The test used in this example might have been perfectly adequate for other uses in school and occupational psychology, where language difficulty was not a problem. Hence it is important to appreciate that bias can creep into an assessment procedure because of a flawed choice of an otherwise perfectly satisfactory test, although tests themselves can also be at fault.

When we considered reliability theory in Chapter 13, each person's score on a test was assumed to have some measurement error associated with it. According to this model the square root of the reliability of the test is a close approximation to the correlation between an individual's score on the test and their 'true score' on the trait being assessed. The crucial assumption made there is that measurement error is essentially random. If an individual took several tests measuring the same trait, one might overestimate their scores slightly, another might underestimate their score slightly, but *on average* the tests would generally provide accurate estimates of the person's ability. In this chapter we shall instead consider systematic errors of measurement – the type of measurement error that will consistently overestimate some individuals' true scores, and underestimate the true scores of others. The immigration test will grossly underestimate the intellectual ability of certain well-defined groups of applicants (those who cannot read English and know nothing of American culture). It is not difficult to think of more subtle items that also show bias, particularly in knowledge-based tests, e.g. 'how many players are there in a netball team?', 'what is the ratio of flour to fat in shortcrust pastry?', 'what is the purpose of a camshaft?', and 'what is the ratio of cement to sand for bricklaying mortar?'.

It is not only trivial knowledge questions that can be affected by such forms of measurement error. When children are being assessed by educational psychologists, is it possible that the gender/age/race of the psychologist will affect their performance on the test? How about their motivation to perform well? It is clearly vital to ascertain whether any of these variables *can* influence children's performance, otherwise the abilities of some children may be over- or underestimated. The remainder of this chapter will mention some of these sources of measurement error, point to their implications, and suggest how they can be detected.

The finding that some groups achieve different scores on some psychological tests has serious implications for those who use such tests as part of a selection procedure. The use of these tests will clearly lead to group(s) with the lower mean scores on the test being under-represented in the work-force. This has led some bodies to abandon the use of psychological tests as part of a selection procedure, preferring instead to select suitably qualified individuals at random. Whilst random selection is likely to select individuals who are representative of all applicant groups, it is manifestly *unable* to choose the best person for the job. Since ability tests often have validity coefficients of the order of 0.4, this could imply that organisations will simply not employ the most able applicants.

It is therefore probably best not to discard psychological tests altogether, but to appreciate the (sometimes subtle) issues raised by group differences and test bias when using or interpreting the results of psychological tests, although some authors (e.g. Rust and Golombock, 1989) take a more pessimistic view.

It is not just membership of certain socio-cultural groups that can affect test scores. Several psychological or behavioural characteristics which are completely unrelated to what the test measures can also affect scores, particularly on personality tests. These are often known as 'response sets' or 'response biases', and efforts must be made to minimise their effects when designing or using tests.

EXTERNAL BIAS IN TESTS

What Kamin omits to mention in his discussion of ability tests is that the problems inherent in the tests would have been recognised if and when the tests had been validated. If scores on the tests had been correlated with subsequent criteria (e.g. annual income, school performance of children), it seems inevitable that the uselessness of the tests would quickly have become obvious. For example, follow-up studies might have shown a relationship such as that shown in Figure 17.1, which illustrates the (hypothetical) annual income of immigrants (denoted by circles) and second-generation Americans (denoted by crosses) 10 years after IQ testing, as a function of their scores on the IQ test.

In Figure 17.1 you will notice that most immigrants (circles) had very low scores on the IQ test – their scores are to the left of the graph. The crosses

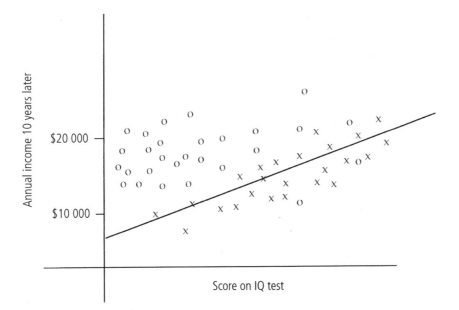

Figure 17.1 Hypothetical link between scores on an IQ test and income 10 years later for two groups of individuals.

represent the second-generation Americans, and it is clear that there is a substantial correlation between IQ test score and income for these individuals only. The figure shows the 'line of best fit' to the data for the second-generation Americans, calculated using a statistical technique called regression analysis. This allows one to predict subsequent income from the IQ test scores of the second-generation individuals. It is merely necessary to find the point on the *x*-axis that corresponds to a person's score on the IQ test and move vertically upwards until one meets this regression line. The individual's estimated income can then be read off the *y*-axis at this point.

If the test was fair to the immigrants, you might expect the same underlying relationship to apply. That is, if IQ is important in determining subsequent income (as seems to be the case in the second-generation group), then the low IQs of the immigrants would imply that they will subsequently earn relatively little. The immigrants' scores should lie close to the same regression line as the majority group's. You can see that this is far from being the case. Immigrants who have low scores on the IQ test tend to earn far more than would be expected on the basis of a regression analysis, and if you consider the immigrant group alone, you can see that there is virtually no correlation between their scores on the IQ test and their subsequent income – which is hardly surprising given that the IQ test is meaningless for members of this group.

SELF-ASSESSMENT QUESTION 17.1

Try to make up some data plotting income as a function of IQ for two groups of people where:

(a) there is the same substantial link between income and IQ for both the 'circles' and the 'crosses' but where the 'circles' tend to have both lower IQs and lower incomes.

(b) there is again a substantial link between income and IQ for the 'circles' and 'crosses', but the 'crosses' of all IQs have an income that is $2000 above that of the 'circles'.

The first graph produced in answer to SAQ 17.1 demonstrates a very important principle. Here there is a clear group difference in IQ scores (circles score lower), but members of this group also *earn* less. This suggests that there is a genuine difference in the IQ scores of the circles and the crosses, for whilst the circles achieve low scores on the IQ test, this graph (unlike Figure 17.1) shows that the IQ test does not appear to underestimate their potential.

The important lesson to learn from this is that *the presence of group differences does not necessarily imply that a test is biased*. This point cannot be made too strongly – it is fundamental and almost universally agreed by measurement specialists (e.g. Jensen, 1980; Berk, 1982; Reynolds, 1995). Test bias implies that test items are too difficult for members of certain groups *for reasons that are unrelated to the characteristic being assessed* – for example, because items in an IQ test require an ability to read and write English, or assume cultural knowledge that a recent immigrant simply will not possess. It is possible that there will be genuine differences between the abilities of different groups. For example, there is a substantial literature on sex differences in educational attainment.

If regression lines between test scores and criterion performance are the same for two groups, then it does not matter if there are differences in the mean scores of the groups.[17.1] Bias can be inferred when different groups follow different regression lies (differing in either slope or height), or when the scores of members of some groups fall further from the regression line than the scores of members of other groups (i.e. there is a lower correlation with the criterion). Using a test of low reliability automatically produces a larger spread of scores on either side of the regression line, so it is also sensible to check that the reliability of the test is similar in both groups.

Several psychologists are intensely interested in group differences (generally racial differences) in personality and ability, which some regard as genuine effects and not attributable to bias of any kind. Thus we read that the Japanese tend to have above-average spatial ability skills compared to Europeans, and that black Americans tend to have lower scores on IQ tests than white Americans. The lack of references to these papers is deliberate because, personally speaking, I cannot see the academic appeal of this area. Even if there *are* clear differences between groups, it is not entirely obvious why they have arisen. Do the Japanese have better skills because they eat more fish, because their educational system develops such skills more than in the West, because of genetic differences, or because they had to hunt for food during the ice age, and so there was natural selection for this characteristic (although, strangely, not for running fast)? All of these have been offered as explanations for the group differences, and it is not easy to test any of these hypotheses (particularly the last one).

It is also easy to become obsessed with group differences and to forget that individual differences *within* groups of people far outweigh the relatively small differences *between* groups of individuals. The political dangers of a doctrine of group differences, racial inferiority and the like can hardly be overlooked. Finally, there is the problem of how one should go about deciding which groups to compare, for each one of us is a member of a huge number of groups – we can be categorised by gender, age, religious background, social class, musical tastes, sexual orientation, hair colour, body-build, etc., and it would be quite possible to examine each of these for the presence of group differences. However, is it *useful* to do this? What does it *mean* if we find that gay red-headed females are more sociable than heterosexual red-headed females, for example? How does it drive psychological theorising forward? It seems to me to be just a fact of no great theoretical interest.

[17.1] Provided one assumes that the criterion is itself 'fair.' In the case of the immigrant example, we would have to assume that the immigrants were given as many opportunities as the other group to earn a good income.

Skin colour and gender nevertheless do appear to have a strange fascination for some psychologists. Applied psychologists also have to be aware of the implications of group differences in ability when using selection tests. For although I argued above that group differences need not necessarily imply that a test is biased, the legal system takes the opposite view and adopts what Kline (1993) calls the 'egalitarian fallacy'. It *assumes* that all ethnic and gender groups must have the same underlying levels of all abilities, and that if tests suggest otherwise then there must be something wrong with the tests. Those using tests for selection, guidance and placement are therefore obliged to ensure that their tests reflect few group differences.

SELF-ASSESSMENT QUESTION 17.2

Earlier in this chapter it was stressed that it is wrong to infer that a test is biased merely because it shows group differences. Suppose that you administer a test in order to select applicants for a particular job, find that a particular test predicts job performance quite well ($r = 0.3$), but discover that male applicants score appreciably lower than female applicants (e.g. half a standard deviation lower).

(a) What would happen if the test was used in its present form?

(b) What non-psychological factors might account for the observed difference in performance between the two genders?

(c) What steps might you take?

INTERNAL BIAS IN TESTS

The type of bias discussed above is known as 'external bias', since it examines the relationship between test scores and some external criterion. However, it is not necessary to have an external criterion to detect bias in a test, for it is possible that a test may contain just a few items that are demonstrably biased against one or more groups – that is, they are substantially more difficult for members of some groups than others. Several techniques have been developed to detect such 'internal bias', and Osterlind (1983) and Berk (1982) provide an excellent discussion of these issues. I shall only mention two approaches.

Suppose that many people complete an ability test, and that each response is scored as correct or incorrect. These individuals may be classified as members of one or more groups (e.g. according to gender and ethnic origin). To keep matters simple, we shall just concentrate on gender differences, and will assume that the test consists of 50 items. It is possible to perform a mixed-model (one-between-and-one-within) analysis of variance on the item scores, using 'gender' (two levels) as the between-subjects factor, and 'item' (30 levels) as the within-subjects factor. That is, we treat the responses to all 30 items in the test as different levels of a single within-subjects factor. The ANOVA table resulting from this analysis will show:

- the significance of the 'item' effect;
- the significance of the 'group' effect;
- the significance of the 'group × item interaction'.

The 'item' effect tests whether all of the items in the test have the same difficulty level. They will almost certainly not be equally difficult, so it can usually be guaranteed that this term will be very significant indeed. This term is of no interest whatsoever for detecting bias.

The 'group' effect tests whether males and females tend to have the same average score on the test items. This is of no great interest either, although the presence of substantial group differences will be a problem if one intends to use the test for selection or placement.

The 'group × item interaction' term is the really interesting one. If this effect is statistically significant, it implies that some items are easier for members of one group than for members of the other group – that is, some items are biased. It is possible to find out precisely which items are implicated by plotting the interaction, testing simple effects, etc. The items can then be removed from the test. Thus the presence of a significant group × item interaction can indicate that some test items are problematical.

One difficulty with this approach is, of course, that the statistical power of the procedure affects the significance of this interaction. In practice, this means that if the analysis is performed on a small sample of individuals, it is unlikely to detect subtle degrees of bias. However, if the analysis is performed on samples of many thousands of individuals, almost every item will be seen to show a statistically significant (albeit small) degree of bias. For the sake of completeness, I ought to acknowledge that there are known to be some problems with this approach, as has mentioned by Osterlind (1983) amongst others, although in my view (and experience) it can show up seriously biased items.

The second technique for discovering internal bias is based on the principles of item response theory discussed in Chapter 16. Suppose that the item parameters are estimated for each item separately for the male and female subjects, and plotted as an item characteristic curve (ICC). If the item showed no bias, the estimated ability, discrimination and guessing parameters would be virtually identical for the male and female samples – that is, the two item characteristic curves would lie exactly on top of each other. This is clearly *not* the case in Figure 17.2. Here the item appears to be considerably easier for females than for males, particularly in cases where the individual's ability is between about −1 and 3. Statistics such as the area between the two ICCs have been used to quantify the extent to which an item is biased. This is all a little more complex than it initially appears (since it is advisable to consider the accuracy with which the item parameters can be estimated, which will influence the certainty with which one can maintain that a particular item is

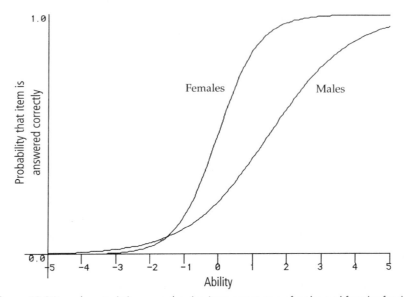

Figure 17.2 Item characteristic curves showing item parameters of males and females for the same test item.

biased). Another problem arises when the three-parameter model is used. The value of parameter 'c' (the 'guessing' or 'pseudo-chance' parameter which determines the value at which the graph levels off at the left-hand side) really needs to be the same for both groups – otherwise the area between the two graphs becomes infinite (Raju, 1988). The advantage of investigating bias in this way is that it is possible to detect quite subtle effects.

SELF-ASSESSMENT QUESTION 17.3

How would you interpret the pattern of bias shown in the item response curve of Figure 17.3?

I believe that it is advisable to consider internal (item) bias whenever developing or using a test. Suppose, for example, that a 40-item test consisted of 20 items that were much easier for females than for males, and 20 items that were much easier for males than females. If one merely looked for a significant difference in the total scores of the two groups, it is quite possible that none would be found, as the items that are difficult for men are easy for women, and vice versa. Thus it is quite possible for a test to be riddled with biased items, yet for the analysis of group differences or regression analyses of the type shown in Figure 17.1 to give the scale a clean bill of health. It is only by going down to the level of test items that one can really see what is going on, and identify items that could usefully be removed from the scale.

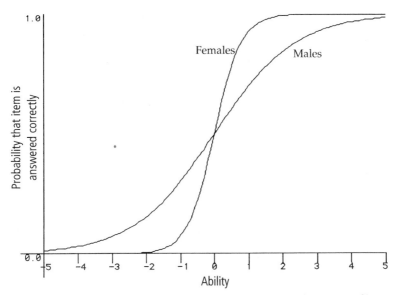

Figure 17.3 An item characteristic curve showing a rather more complex pattern of bias.

PERSONALITY TESTS

Whatever the test instructions may say, people do some rather strange things when completing personality tests, as you will be able to confirm if you have taken the Eysenck and Wilson scales. These characteristics are known as 'response biases' or 'response sets', since they describe the way in which individuals tend to use rating scales. For example, it is well known that individuals are more likely to agree with statements than to disagree with them – a tendency that is exploited to the full by unscrupulous market researchers. Suppose that you asked a carefully selected sample of the population 'do you intend to vote for the present government in the next election?' and found that 55 per cent said that they did. Then suppose you asked another sample of people 'do you intend to vote for one of the opposition parties in the next election?'. You might naively expect that, on the basis of the first survey, about 100 – 55 = 45 per cent of the population would answer 'yes'. In fact, the proportion is likely to be considerably higher, just because people seem to be more willing to say 'yes' than 'no' *whatever the question may be* (Cronbach, 1946). This is known as the response set of *acquiescence.*

This finding has some fairly unpleasant implications for personality testing. It means that any personality scale – a scale of anxiety, for example – whose items are all scored in the same direction (so that a response of 'yes' or 'strongly agree' to each item produces a high score on the test) will be influenced by acquiescence. Individuals' scores will be a little higher than they should be because of this tendency to agree with statements – everyone would appear to be a little more anxious than they actually are. This in itself may not appear to be too much of a problem. If it was possible to estimate that, on average, each person's score was two points higher than it should be because of this response set, then it would be a simple matter to deduct this amount from each individual's score. In practice, there would be no need to bother doing so, since the correlations between the test scores and other things would be unaffected by deducting a constant from each person's score. So what is the problem?

The real difficulties arise if there are individual differences in this response set of acquiescence. Perhaps some individuals have a strong tendency to agree with statements, whereas others are completely immune from doing so. This is what is so dangerous, since if individuals' scores on the anxiety test are influenced by both anxiety and their tendency to agree, it is clear that the test will overestimate the anxiety scores of the acquiescent individuals, whilst being completely accurate for low-acquiescent people. This is why most personality tests contain items that are scored in both directions. If about 50 per cent of the items are phrased so that agreeing with a statement implies a high score on the trait (e.g. 'I suffer from "nerves"') and the remainder are phrased the opposite way round (e.g. 'I am calm and relaxed most of the time'), then acquiescence will have little effect. When the test is scored, any tendency to acquiesce will cancel itself out. Tests that are *not* constructed in this way should be viewed with suspicion.

Social desirability is another 'response style' that can affect the way in which people answer test items. It is the tendency to show oneself in a good light, and to deny any behaviours or feelings that may be socially unacceptable. Items relating to swearing, being mean, being aggressive, having a sense of humour, being honest, being hard-working and being intelligent are among those that may be influenced by this response style. It is a particular problem when personality tests are used for personnel selection – anyone with a modicum of intelligence is likely to realise that it is probably not a good thing to admit to experiencing hallucinations, being dishonest or having a 'slapdash' attitude when filling in a personality questionnaire whilst applying for a job.

It is not difficult to measure social desirability. It is possible to ask raters to scrutinise items in personality questionnaires and to decide how much each item is affected by social desirability. Where there is good agreement between raters, then it is highly probable that social desirability will affect the way in which the item is answered. Edwards (1957) carried out this experiment, and observed that there was a substantial correlation between ratings of the social desirability of test items and the way in which they were answered. People tended to answer items in a socially desirable way.

As with acquiescence, this raises severe difficulties only if we assume that some people are more swayed by social desirability than others when filling in personality questionnaires. Unfortunately, it is rarely possible to use the same solution for social desirability (balancing the test items so that some socially desirable responses tend to increase the score on the trait, whilst others decrease it). Can you think of a test item that measures anxiety where the 'anxious' response is also more socially desirable than the 'low-anxiety' response? Instead, it is common practice to try to eliminate highly socially desirable items from personality questionnaires as they are being developed.

Individual differences in the tendency to give socially desirable responses can be measured using the Crowne–Marlow scale (Crowne and Marlowe, 1964), so a group of individuals can be given this questionnaire along with the questionnaire that is being developed *in the context in which it will be used*. If any items in the questionnaire are strongly influenced by social desirability, the responses to these questions will correlate substantially with individuals' scores on the Crowne–Marlow scale. If the items are little affected by social desirability, the correlations will be trivial. Thus it is possible to identify which items are strongly affected by social desirability, and so consider eliminating or rephrasing them during the process of test construction.

The way in which people use Likert scales can also be influenced by other features of their make-up. A typical Likert scale might invite someone to circle one of the numbers from 1 to 5, where a rating of 1 implies that they 'strongly disagree' with a statement, and a rating of 5 that they 'strongly agree' with it. Some years ago, Paul Kline, Jon May and I were interested in developing an 'objective test' to measure authoritarian attitudes. We suspected that authoritarian types tended to see the world in 'black and white' terms, free from any doubt or ambiguity. Therefore we postulated that when presented with a 5-point rating scale they would circle plenty of 1s and 5s, but rather few of the middle points compared to control groups, which is exactly what we observed (Cooper *et al.*, 1986). So here is another personality trait that influences the way in which people use any Likert scale.

SELF-ASSESSMENT QUESTION 17.4

Name some variables that may affect performance on personality tests.

FACTORS THAT AFFECT PERFORMANCE ON ABILITY TESTS

It should go without saying that the conditions under which the test is administered are likely to have a massive effect on test performance, particularly in the case of ability tests. Testing large groups of nervous people in an overcrowded, stuffy room with a high level of background noise is a fairly obvious recipe for disaster, as is *any* deviation from the test instructions, practice examples or time limits. However, in this section we shall consider some other psychological characteristics of individuals that can also influence the way in which they approach ability tests.

A person's motivation with regard to any test is likely to have some effect on their performance. Encouraging even young children to perform well can lead to significant increases in their scores on ability tests compared to control groups (Brown and Walberg, 1993). Cultural factors have also been suggested as important influences in test performance. If a child believes that he or she is unlikely to perform well on a test, then it is possible that he or she *will* perform poorly so as to conform to a stereotype (e.g. Steele and Aronson, 1995). It has also been suggested that the social psychology of the testing situation is important, and that the age, sex, level of anxiety and level of warmth of the individual may influence their scores. However, as Cronbach (1994) concludes, there is remarkably little evidence of any *consistent* differences. Nor do black children perform better at ability tests when the psychologist is black rather than white (Jensen, 1980; Sattler and Gwynne, 1987).

There is also a truly massive literature on the psychology of test anxiety and its effect on performance, there is an international society for the study of the subject, and there have even been tests of anxiety designed for particular subject areas such as mathematics or sport, as well as generalised test anxiety (Spielberger, 1980), although there is little convincing evidence (in my view) that test anxiety is really any different from 'normal' state or trait anxiety. High levels of anxiety do seem to be associated with lowered performance on many tests of ability or attainment (e.g. Schwarzer *et al.*, 1989), but arguing causality from this seems to be dangerous. It could be that high anxiety results from the (correct) appraisal that one is not going to perform at all well.

Practice effects and coaching can also improve test performance under some circumstances, but a distinction must be made between interventions that are designed to change the levels of the *trait*, and those that are specific to one particular *measuring instrument*, e.g. training for time-management and guessing strategies for the Scholastic Aptitude Test (SAT) (a test used for college admissions in the USA). Interventions designed to improve levels of traits pose no great ethical problems, yet attempts to improve performance on one particular test are undoubtedly unfair to candidates who lack the inside knowledge of how the test works that would enable them to choose appropriate strategies, or who lack the money to undertake coaching. Nor are the benefits enormous. In the case of the SAT, it is not entirely clear whether the time and energy devoted to learning the 'tricks of the test' would not be better spent taking a course to improve one's mathematical ability, or some other area of academic weakness (Evans and Pike, 1973). The fundamental point is surely that psychological tests should not be so well publicised that would-be candidates can gain useful knowledge in this way. All of the necessary information should surely be given to all candidates during the test instructions.

Those who argue that such problems mean that ability tests should be cast out into the psychological wilderness, along with phrenology and animal magnetism, overlook two points. First, if these effects were all-important, then ability tests would not be able to predict any criterion behaviours. As we have seen, the evidence suggests that, despite these issues, ability tests *can* make a useful contribution here. Second, they ignore guidelines for 'good practice' in test administration. The instructions for virtually all tests stress that the examiner should use his or her interpersonal skills to make participants feel as relaxed and unthreatened as possible, to motivate children to perform their very best, and so on. Moreover, virtually all tests include several test items that familiarise candidates with the types of problems to be presented, the use of the answer sheet, and so on. Thus, in practice, most candidates should be made to feel relaxed and motivated, and will get some practice prior to the main testing session.

In addition, several organisations now offer candidates the opportunity to pre-test themselves. For example, the Northern Ireland Civil Service runs an exemplary selection system that involves sending applicants a detailed sample of psychometric test items so that they can try these out for themselves before attending the psychometric assessment procedure (an additional benefit being that individuals who score very poorly on the self-administered tests may choose not to apply, thereby reducing costs).

SUMMARY

This chapter has considered some problems with psychometric testing, and in particular the concept of *bias* – which is poorly understood both within and without the psychological community. We have also briefly considered some other variables that can influence performance on tests of ability and personality, and commented on their importance and implications for testing practice.

SUGGESTED ADDITIONAL READING

Art Jensen's (1980) book *Bias in Mental Testing* is in my view one of the most interesting psychometrics books ever written. It contains excellent sections on the nature of test bias and its detection, and can be heartily recommended. Two elderly chapters by the late P. E. Vernon are still well worth reading – chapter 20 of Vernon (1979) and chapter 12 of Vernon (1963), and once again, Cronbach's and Anastasi's standard texts have thoughtful discussions of the influence of anxiety, motivation and the various response sets on performance, as do several occupational psychology texts.

ANSWERS TO SELF-ASSESSMENT QUESTIONS

SAQ 17.1

(a)

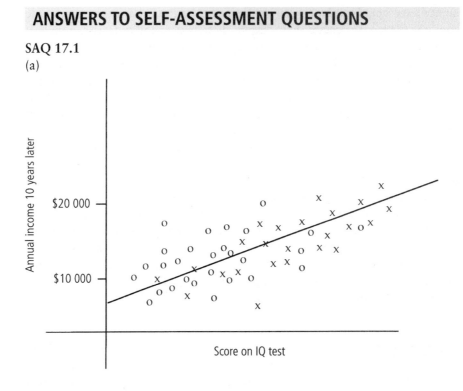

(b)

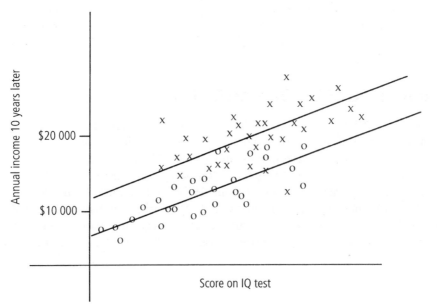

SAQ 17.2
(a) The test will select more females than males into the organisation.
(b) It is important to remember that applicants for a particular job do not form a random sample of the population. Factors such as geographical location of the business, the nature of competing businesses, *perceived* chances of employment, the structure of a divided education system, emigration, family traditions of employment, etc. can all interact with ability to produce rather distorted samples. For example, if there is a popular major employer in the same geographical area that takes large numbers of high-IQ female employees, other businesses may end up taking applicants who were rejected.
(c) Plot the graph of criterion performance vs. test performance for both groups, and check that the two lines have similar heights and slopes. Also check the reliability of the test within each group, and check for signs of internal bias. Remove biased items if any are found, and re-compute the validity coefficients. Consult the literature to discover whether others have reported similar results using the same test against similar criteria. If all else fails, consider trying another test.

SAQ 17.3
Low-ability females perform worse than low-ability males, but high-ability females outperform high-ability males on this test item. It shows substantial signs of bias, even though it is equally difficult for males and females.

SAQ 17.4
Apart from the personality trait that the test seeks to measure, responses will be influenced by social desirability, acquiescence and extreme-responding/conservatism, although other variables (such as the individual's perception of the *reason* for testing) might also be important.

18

Constructing a reliable test

BACKGROUND

This chapter is included for two reasons. First, it is possible that readers may at some stage want to develop their own scale and so it seems appropriate to offer some guidelines on how items may be constructed and assembled into a reliable scale, although I argue against this and explain why I think there are already far too many tests in psychology. Second, it shows why it is not possible to assemble a set of items and assume that they form a reliable and valid scale, and offers some insights as to how tests may be constructed without the use of factor analysis.

Recommended prior reading

Chapters 1, 11, 13 and 17.

INTRODUCTION

This chapter is included in case readers are either interested to learn how tests are constructed, or feel the urge to develop their own scale to measure some personality or ability trait. Please do not do so! In my experience, most students who decide to construct a scale do not appreciate how much work is involved in developing, refining and validating it.

Many readers will have encountered tests that are quite different from those that have been described in this text. Social psychologists, in particular, measure several dimensions of personality that seem to be quite different from the traits that were discussed in Chapters 5, 6 and 8, and readers may wonder why I have not yet discussed locus of control, self-esteem and the like. The problem is that most of these tests are simply not very satisfactory. Some (e.g. measures of locus of control) do not appear to measure a trait at all, but are situation specific (Coombs and Schroeder, 1988). Worse still, when the items are factored, they rarely form a single scale. Many (if not most) of these tests measure *mixtures* of several distinct personality traits, which, as we saw in Chapter 13, makes their interpretation almost impossible.

In the unlikely event of my becoming a dictator, my first edict would be as follows: '*It is a penal offence for any psychologist to publish any scale if more than 70 per cent of the reliable variance of that scale can be predicted by existing tests.*' In other words, I feel strongly that any new test must be shown to tap some aspects of personality or ability that are really rather different from any combination of traits that we already know and understand. Otherwise, tests will simply proliferate. One scale will measure two parts extraversion and one part neuroticism, while another will measure two parts extraversion and one part psychoticism. Enormous theories will be built up around these personality dimensions, and then someone will have the bright idea of correlating the two tests together and (because they both measure extraversion to some extent) the correlation will be large and positive. Ripples of excitement will run through the journals, reputations will be made, and yet more complicated theories will spring up to explain what seems rather obvious to us simple-minded psychometricians.

However, there must be something wrong with this description since most psychologists take exactly the opposite view, and the proliferation of tests continues – even though the evidence often suggests that this is really not a good idea. Consider tests measuring self-esteem – a widely used concept in social psychology. There is evidence (summarised in Kline, 1993, chapter 20) that tests which claim to measure 'self-esteem' really just tap a mixture of anxiety (or neuroticism) and extraversion. Since it is difficult to imagine why any psychologist would want to measure a mixture of two quite distinct traits in a single test, the continued use of these scales has always rather baffled this author. It is quite permissible to combine scores from several different scales, e.g. by adding together individuals' standardised scores on tests measuring general ability and neuroticism if there is a need to identify intelligent neurotics. The point is that, by doing this, test users are forced to become aware of what traits are really being assessed, rather than building elaborate theories on what are wrongly believed to be entirely novel aspects of individual differences.

Tests also proliferate in occupational psychology, but for rather different reasons. Here supposedly 'new' scales can be sold for startlingly large amounts of money even before they have been properly validated. Once again, I cannot see why test users would want to use ability tests or personality tests that simply re-invent the wheel, or (worse) measure *mixtures* of well-understood traits. For, as was seen in Chapter 13, it is possible to interpret the meaning of individuals' scores on a psychological scale only if all of its items measure the same trait.

Despite these dire warnings, it is useful to know the merits (and drawbacks) of several techniques for developing scales, so that one can understand and evaluate the merit of published tests. All of these apply to tests that measure traits, and which are generously timed (so that each person has time to attempt all of the questions). This latter point is important, since if very restricted time limits are imposed, the last items will always appear to be difficult, solely because many candidates will not have attempted them.

WRITING TEST ITEMS

Obviously, writing the items is *the* crucial step in designing a test. If the items are poorly written, then no amount of psychometric wizardry will be able to produce a reliable and valid scale. Kline (1986) has given some common-sense 'rules of thumb' for writing and I shall draw on this work in the next three sections. You may well also like to re-examine your professional association's guidelines for the construction and use of psychological tests, which may resemble those shown in Appendix B. The main points to be kept in mind when writing items are as follows.

- The items should be properly sampled, and should tap every single aspect of the concept. An arithmetic test should not be based solely on 'addition' problems. A depression inventory should enquire about behaviours (e.g. disturbed sleep and eating habits) as well as feelings. It may be advisable to draw up a list of the main 'facets' of the phenomenon to be assessed, and write equal numbers of items to tap each facet. For example, a teacher may decide to assess arithmetical ability on the basis of ability to perform long division, long multiplication, geometry/trigonometry, solution of simul-taneous equations, finding roots of quadratic equations, differentiation and integration. Very often it will be necessary to conduct a literature search (or examine diagnostic manuals such as the *Diagnostic and Statistical Manual of Mental Disorders* (DSM-IV) to ensure that you have a full and complete understanding of the topic that is to be assessed.
- The test should be long enough to ensure that it covers all aspects of the topic, and is reliable. As a rule of thumb, you may wish to start with at least 30 items and reduce these down to a list of no fewer than 20 items, although if there are many facets you may well need more.
- Each item should assess only the trait that it is designed to measure, so responses to the item should not be affected by individual differences in vocabulary, by social desirability (or any other variables mentioned in Chapter 17), or by any other traits.
- The cultural appropriateness of each item should be carefully considered. This will typically include the implicit knowledge required to understand (or solve) the problem. In the arithmetic test example, the teacher assumes that all children will be able to add, subtract, multiply and divide, and to understand the order in which arithmetic operations are performed in equations, etc.
- It is important to ensure that the items are logically independent. In the case of personality tests, check that if a logically consistent person answers any item in a particular way, then this does not 'force' them to give any particular answer to any other item(s) – that is, no two items should mean

the same thing. In the case of ability tests you should never base one item on the answer to a previous item such as 'item 1: what is 2 + 3?', 'item 6: what is the answer to item 1 multiplied by 4?'.

- You may have gathered that the issue of semantic dependency of items in personality scales is one that interests me considerably. It is very easy to produce a scale with a high level of reliability by paraphrasing the same item several times, but this is artificial, since the items are not being properly sampled from the domain of interest. Therefore I would urge item writers to examine every possible pair of items and check that the way a person answers one item does not force him or her to answer any other item in a particular way, other than through the influence of the trait that the test is designed to measure.

Writing items for ability tests

Decide on the response format, e.g. free response (2 + 2 = ?) or multiple choice (2 + 2 = (a) 4, (b) 22, (c) 5, (d) 3) and, if a multiple-choice format is chosen, decide how many alternatives should be offered. There should be at least four alternatives in order to reduce the effects of 'lucky' guessing.

Write an equal number of items for each facet, taking care to construct good, plausible distractors (possibly based on an analysis of common errors from other tests) if using a multiple-choice format, and trying to ensure that the items in each facet span a similar and appropriate range of difficulty.

Make sure that you are not tempted to test the trivial just because it is easy to do so. For example, if you were designing a test to assess students' statistical ability, the easiest type of item to write would concern formulae and definitions, e.g. 'what is the equation for calculating the sample standard deviation from a set of data?'. The problem is, of course, that the instructor *should* be interested in testing how well students *understand* and can *apply* the concepts – repeating definitions parrot-fashion is rarely what is wanted. The driving test provides another good example. I can remember learning and reciting stopping distances, although the examiners never seemed to check that candidates knew what those distances actually looked like when they were driving.

Gulliksen (1986) is an excellent, non-technical paper on the assessment of abilities and attainment. It considers several other forms of test items, and makes vital reading for anyone who is interested in constructing tests in this general area.

Writing items for personality tests

The first step is to decide how you want respondents to answer your questions – there are several popular formats. The test may present statements with which people agree, are neutral or unsure, or disagree, e.g. 'I lie awake at night worrying about the day's events'. You might also consider adding 'strongly agree' and 'strongly disagree' to the list, but do not use any more than seven categories. If you are using this type of scale, *always* use words such as 'agree/?/disagree' on the questionnaire, and not just numbers. Statistical problems can arise if less than three categories are used. With this type of item try to keep to an odd number of choices, since this ensures that there is a central, neutral answer which test takers like. Alternatively, the test may give several possible answers, e.g. 'in the last week, my worries kept me from falling asleep immediately on (a) no days, (b) 1 or 2 days, (c) 3 or 4 days (d) 5 or more days'.

Try to write items that are clear, unambiguous and require as little self-insight as possible. Wherever possible you should refer to behaviours rather than to feelings, as in the second example in the previous paragraph.

Ensure that each item asks only one question. For example, do not use a statement such as 'I sometimes feel depressed and have attempted suicide', since extremely depressed people who have not (quite) got round to attempting suicide would have to disagree with it, which is presumably not what is intended.

Try to avoid negatively phrased items such as 'I dislike students: yes/?/no', since choosing 'no' requires the participant to interpret a double negative.

Try to avoid questions asking about frequency or amount. Instead, refer to specific rather than general behaviour. Instead of asking 'do you read a lot?', try asking 'how many books have you read for pleasure in the past month?' – or better still, 'list the books that you have read for pleasure in the past month' (which may reduce socially desirable responses).

Ensure that none of the words is ambiguous. For example, one personality questionnaire used to include the item 'do you enjoy gay parties?', at a time when 'gay' (only) meant lively.

Try to ensure that about 50 per cent of the items in each facet are keyed so that a 'yes/strongly agree' response indicates a high score on the trait, and the others are keyed in the opposite direction. For example, 'I generally fall asleep at night as soon as the light is turned off' would be scored so that 'strongly disagree' indicated anxiety.

If you *must* ask about something socially undesirable, consider phrasing the item from another person's point of view, e.g. 'some people might describe me as mean' rather than 'are you mean?'.

Finally, it is wise to ensure that the instructions ask respondents to give the first answer that springs naturally to mind, rather than looking for hidden meanings.

GENERAL PRINCIPLES OF ITEM ANALYSIS

Having compiled a draft test, it is necessary to ensure that all of the items measure the same construct before proceeding to check that the test is reliable and valid. In order to do this, the test should be administered to a large ($n > 200$) sample of people, similar in nature to the individuals who will ultimately use the test. For example, if a test is to be used to select graduate applicants for a particular organisation, it would be appropriate to try out the test with undergraduates, but not with 16-year-old pupils in a comprehensive school (because of their different academic background) or pensioners (because of their different age). The responses are then scored, and a total score is calculated for each individual.

The next stage is to examine the mean score for each of the items, together with its standard deviation. In the case of an ability test (where a correct answer is awarded one point and an incorrect answer is given zero points) the mean score indicates the difficulty of each item. A mean score of 0.95 would indicate that 95 per cent of the sample gave the correct response to an item. In the case of personality tests, the mean score shows the extent to which individuals tend to agree or disagree with statements. As a general rule of thumb, it would be undesirable to have *too* many very easy or very difficult items in the test, so if more than about 10 per cent of items have mean scores above 0.8 or below 0.2, it might be prudent to consider removing some of them.

SELF-ASSESSMENT QUESTION 18.1

Why is it not advisable to have too many very easy or very difficult items in a test?

The size of the standard deviation for each item shows the level of individual differences found in participants' responses to it. For example, if an item has a standard deviation of zero, everyone has answered it in the same way, and the item is therefore clearly not tapping any kind of individual differences, and should be removed from the scale. (When items are scored using a two-point scale, such as correct/incorrect, the standard deviation is linked directly to the mean, as readers who have studied the binomial theorem should be able to verify. This step should be skipped in such cases.)

Although checking the items' means and standard deviations is a necessary first step, this cannot reveal which questions in the test are flawed in content. For example, suppose that one item in a personality test used language that was too difficult for the participants to understand, so causing them all to guess an answer. Another item might be badly affected by 'social desirability'. We shall mention four techniques of *item analysis* for identifying items that, for whatever reason, simply do not measure the same thing as the other items in the test.

When using any of the four techniques described below to eliminate items from the test, it is important to try to ensure that the test retains approximately equal numbers of items in all of its facets (as described above). Suppose, for example, that a teacher started off by writing five items in each of seven facets of mathematical attainment: long division, long multiplication, geometry/trigonometry, solution of simultaneous equations, finding roots of quadratic equations, differentiation and integration. Item analysis will remove some of the 35 items (those that are too easy, too hard or which simply do not seem to work), but it would clearly be unfortunate if the analysis led to the removal of *all* of the long-division items and *all* of the long-multiplication items, since the teacher believes that these are two important components of the pupils' mathematical attainment. Item analysis is an art as well as a science, and when removing items it is important to try to ensure that approximately equal numbers are left in each of the facets.

CONSTRUCTING TESTS BY CRITERION KEYING

Suppose that we are asked to construct a psychological test to select aeroplane navigators – the goal is to develop a test whose total score will be able to predict the navigators' final score on their training course, and which may therefore be used to identify applicants who are likely to perform poorly on this course. Having no clear idea of what may be appropriate personality and ability characteristics for this application, we might put together a vast questionnaire consisting of 600 items that we hope will measure all of the main abilities and personality traits that can be assessed. But which ones actually predict navigator performance?

Suppose that the draft version of the scale has been administered to several hundred trainees. The most obvious way of identifying the good (i.e. predictive) items in the test is to validate each item directly against some criterion. For example, suppose that at the end of their training, each trainee-navigator is awarded a mark of between 0 and 100, indicating their overall level of performance in the navigator-training course. Surely the item analysis process would simply involve correlating the trainees' scores on each of the items in the test with their scores on the training course. Items that have substantial correlations would appear to be able to predict the criterion, and those that do not would be dropped from the test.

This procedure, which is known as *criterion keying*, has been used in the construction of several well-known scales, including the Minnesota Multiphasic Personality Inventory (MMPI and MMPI-2: Hathaway and McKinley, 1967; Graham, 1990) and the California Psychological Inventory (Gough, 1975), the scales of which can supposedly discriminate between various clinical groups. *Do not use this method of item analysis.* As Nunnally (1978) reminds us, it has several fatal flaws.

First, it is very likely to produce scales that have very low reliability – that is, scales containing items that measure a number of different things. For example, suppose that success in the navigator-training course depended on mathematical ability, mechanical ability, spatial ability, low neuroticism, and extraversion. If criterion keying were to be applied to a large sample of items, it would produce a scale that measured a mixture of all of these things. Second, it is rarely possible to identify a *single* criterion to be used when selecting items. For example, consider my post, which involves lecturing in individual differences and psychometrics, research, writing and editing books, writing research papers, taking tutorials, administration (e.g. planning courses), marking essays and examination papers, co-ordinating certain laboratory activities, supervising PhD students, and a host of other activities. Which one of these should be used as the criterion against which my performance should be judged? If they are to be averaged in some way, how many scientific papers or how much course-planning are equivalent to one book? If one criterion is used, one particular set of predictive items will be identified – if another criterion is chosen, the chances are that quite a different selection of items will be indicated. The third point is a little more statistical. In order to select the 'best' items by criterion keying, one correlates responses to particular items with the criterion – if the test consists of 400 or so items (as does the MMPI), then one calculates 400 correlations. Without going into details, if large numbers of correlations are being calculated, we would expect several of the correlations to be appreciably larger than their true (population) values. In other words, some of the items that we select by this procedure are unlikely to work for other groups of applicants. Finally, this procedure gives us no real understanding of *why* the test works – it is completely atheoretical. Without an understanding of what psychological constructs are being measured by the 'useful' items, it is impossible to tell whether the test is likely to be useful in other applications (e.g. for selecting pilots or air-traffic controllers), and it becomes very difficult to 'fix' the test if it suddenly stops predicting performance. For all of these reasons, criterion keying should be avoided.

CONSTRUCTING TESTS BY FACTOR-ANALYSING THEIR ITEMS

Psychologists such as Cattell advocate the use of factor analysis to construct tests, although others (e.g. Nunnally, 1978) have identified some problems with this approach. Here the correlations between the (scored) items are factor-analysed, and the factor(s) that emerge are tentatively identified on the basis of their loadings, as described in Chapters 14 and 15. When putting together a set of items to measure one particular construct, we would of course *hope* that just one factor will emerge, and that all of the variables will have large loadings on that factor. In practice, there may be more than one factor, and some variables may not have loadings above 0.4 on *any* factor. This method of constructing scales simply involves identifying and retaining those items that have a substantial loading on the main factor(s).

When carrying out an item analysis by *any* method, it is important to try to ensure that roughly equal numbers of items are removed from each facet of the test. As the following example will show, item analysis is an art as well as a science. Suppose that when the 35-item arithmetic test described above was factor-analysed, just one factor was found. Suppose, too, that the analysis showed that three of the five items measuring long division had a loading above 0.4, as did three of the five items in each of the following facets: long multiplication, geometry/trigonometry, solution of simultaneous equations and finding roots of quadratic equations. However, now suppose that only *one* of the differentiation items and *all five* of the integration items had loadings above 0.4. Blindly applying the 'loadings above 0.4' criterion would produce a test with different numbers of items in each facet. It would be more sensible to check whether any of the differentiation items had loadings that were only marginally below 0.4, and, if they did, to include two of these and eliminate the two lowest-loading integration items. This would produce a 21-item test with equal numbers of items in each facet.

Experiments would then need to be performed to check that these items actually appear to be measuring the trait that they are supposed to – that is, their validity must be established as discussed in Chapter 13.

Problems arise when developing ability scales that are designed to be used with very restricted time limits. Since some candidates may not reach the items at the end of the test, it is very difficult to estimate the difficulty of those items, which becomes confused with the candidates' speed of answering. It is better to administer the test with unlimited time at the development stage, and to impose time limits when putting together the final version.

CONSTRUCTING TESTS WITH ITEM RESPONSE THEORY

Suppose that item response theory is applied to a set of test items as described in Chapter 16. The programs used will select the item parameters that best describe how the probability that an individual will answer a particular item correctly depends on his or her level of the ability being measured by the items in the test. What if one test item measures something very different from the other items? For example, suppose that 24 items assess mechanical ability whilst one measures vocabulary (an easy item written in such convoluted language that hardly anyone understood what it meant). What might the item parameters for this item look like?

The probability of 'passing' the vocabulary item will probably not depend greatly on a person's level of mechanical ability. After all, we know that these are two quite distinct ability factors. So it seems probable that the ICC will be quite flat – almost horizontal, in fact. This is the case when an item has a low level of discrimination. Thus if items like this *are* found when examining ICCs, it may be worth checking the content of the item. It is also worth checking how closely a particular item response theory model fits a particular item. If an item has high 'residual variance' (that is, variance that cannot be explained by the three item parameters), this is often taken to imply that this item is measuring something rather different from the others, and that the possibility of eliminating it from the scale should be considered, although this procedure of eliminating items that do not fit the model is somewhat controversial – some would argue that one should use a more sophisticated item response theory model instead. Hambleton and Swaminathan (1985) have given a rather detailed account of these issues.

However, item response theory *assumes* that a set of items measures one particular construct, and so it is standard practice to perform a quick factor analysis to check that only one factor runs through the data before starting the time-consuming item response theory analyses. It seems sensible to remove 'rogue' (i.e. low-loading) items at this stage. If item response theory is applied to a set of items that measure several distinct factors, the whole procedure rapidly falls apart, as *none* of the items fits the model very well, and the parameter estimates can look extremely strange – if indeed the computer program is able to converge on a solution at all. Thus if one is determined to select items using item response theory and the whole analysis is going badly, it may be worth checking that the items are truly one-dimensional. The main drawbacks of item response theory are, of course, its theoretical complexity and the specialised software that it requires.

CLASSICAL ITEM ANALYSIS

We have left the easiest technique of item analysis until last. You will recall that high reliability is generally thought to be an excellent feature of a test. It therefore seems sensible to try to estimate the extent to which each of the items in a test correlates with individuals' 'true scores', which, you will recall, are the scores that each individual would have obtained if he or she had been administered all of the items that could possibly have been written to measure the topic. If we somehow identify items each of which has a substantial correlation with the true score, when we add up individuals' scores on these items, the total scores on the test are bound to show a substantial correlation with the true score. This is, of course, another way of saying that the test has high internal consistency reliability. Thus if it is possible to detect items that show appreciable correlations with the true score, it is also possible to choose those items that will produce a highly reliable test.

The problem is that we can never measure individuals' true scores. However, there is one piece of data that can be shown to approximate to this, namely the individual's total score on all of the items in the test. Thus classical item analysis simply correlates the total score on the test with the scores on each of the individual items. Consider, for example, the data shown in Table 18.1, which represent the responses of six people to a five-item test (where a correct answer was scored as 1 and an incorrect answer as 0), together with each person's total score on the test. The row marked '*r* with total' simply correlates the responses to each of the items with the total scores on the test. You may wish to check one or two of these so that you can see how they have been calculated.

The correlations between each item and the total score are as close as we can get to estimating the correlation between each item and the *true* score, so it seems sensible to drop those items that have low correlations with the total score – once again keeping a very careful eye on which facet of the trait is measured by a particular item, and ensuring that the items that are left contain approximately equal numbers of items from each of the facets. Thus whilst the item analysis procedure involves removing an item which has a low correlation

	Item 1	Item 2	Item 3	Item 4	Item 5	Total
Person 1	1	0	1	1	1	4
Person 2	0	1	1	1	0	3
Person 3	0	0	1	0	0	1
Person 4	0	0	1	0	0	1
Person 5	0	1	0	1	1	3
Person 6	1	0	1	1	0	3
r with total	0.63	0.32	−0.20	0.95	0.63	
Corrected r with total	0.11	0.22	−0.48	0.87	0.50	

Table 18.1 Hypothetical data for item analysis

with the total score at each stage, this will not always be the very lowest-correlating item.

There is one obvious problem associated with correlating items with total scores, and this is the fact that each item *contributes* to the total score, so we are to some extent correlating each item with itself. In order to circumvent this difficulty, we usually base the item analyses on 'corrected item–total correlations', or the 'Guilford-corrected item–total correlations', which are simply the correlations between each item and the sum of the *other* remaining items. In the present example, item 1 would be correlated with the sum of items 2, 3, 4 and 5. Item 2 would be correlated with the sum of items 1, 3, 4 and 5, and so on. Other techniques for performing such corrections have been proposed, but they present psychometric problems (Cooper, 1983).

Each time an item is eliminated, the test's reliability (alpha) should be calculated. As items that have low correlations with the total score are eliminated, the value of alpha will rise. As more and more items are removed, the value of alpha will eventually start to fall, since it depends on both the average correlation between the items and the number of items in the test. Of course, removing a 'poor' item boosts the average correlation between the remaining items – but it also shortens the test. Items are successively removed (on the basis of a consideration of their corrected item–total correlations and the facets from which they originate) until the test is short, well balanced and highly reliable.

One rather annoying feature of this method of analysis is that it is not possible simply to look at the table of corrected item–total correlations and decide from this precisely which items should be eliminated. This is because each person's total score will inevitably change each time an item is dropped, and consequently each of the correlations between the remaining items and the total score will also change. Therefore it is necessary to decide which item to drop, re-compute the total scores and re-compute all of the remaining item–total correlations, as well as re-computing alpha at each stage. This is tedious, to put it mildly. However, I have written a BASIC computer program (listed in Kline, 1986) which performs such analyses automatically. An updated version for the Apple Macintosh is available free via my home-page on the School of Psychology's server at the Queen's University of Belfast (http://www.psych.qub.ac.uk). Alternatively, such analyses can be performed relatively painlessly using the SPSS Reliability procedure.

SELF-ASSESSMENT QUESTION 18.2

(a) What can factor analysis alone reveal about the structure of a test?

(b) In classical item analysis, why is it necessary to re-compute all of the item–total correlations after removing an item?

(c) Name four problems associated with constructing tests by criterion keying.

NEXT STEPS

The test constructor's task is far from finished once the item analysis has been completed. Instructions (and possibly answer-sheets) should be refined and example items should be developed and checked before the revised (shorter and hopefully more reliable) test is given to another sample of about 200 individuals, and its reliability and factor structure re-checked. Its validity should also be established at this stage (e.g. by construct validation as described in Chapter 13). In the case of ability tests, the amount of time that individuals take to complete the test should be noted, and a decision taken as to what time limits (if any) should be imposed. A test manual should be prepared showing the results of these analyses, the administration instructions, the marking scheme, and as much evidence as possible that the test is reliable and valid.

SUMMARY

This chapter has covered some basic principles of item-writing for both ability tests and personality tests. Item analysis has been introduced as a procedure for detecting and eliminating items that are inappropriate and which detract from the test's reliability and/or validity. Four techniques for performing item analysis have been discussed, namely criterion keying, factor analysis, item response theory and classical item analysis. Major problems have been identified in the all-too-common technique of criterion keying, and item response theory requires specialist software, therefore factor analysis and/or classical item analysis are recommended for producing short, reliable and potentially valid scales.

SUGGESTED ADDITIONAL READING

Gulliksen (1986) is essential reading for anyone who is interested in the assessment of abilities or educational attainment. Kline's (1986) *Handbook of Test Construction* contains a lot of good, practical advice about the whole process of test development and validation, as do Moshe and Zeidner (1995) and Spector (1992). References to specific techniques for analysing responses to test items can be found in Chapters 14, 15 and 16 of this volume.

ANSWERS TO SELF-ASSESSMENT QUESTIONS

SAQ 18.1

If the test contains many very easy or very difficult items, you will not obtain very good discrimination between the individuals in the sample. The trait that the test supposedly measures is probably normally distributed (that is, the frequency diagram is bell-shaped). If your test contains many difficult items, then it is drawing fine distinctions between the high-ability participants (of whom there are relatively few in the sample). If it contains plenty of very easy items, then the test is drawing fine distinctions between the low-ability participants (but there are also few of them). You would normally want to discriminate between the great majority of individuals in the sample, and this implies having plenty of items that discriminate well in the $p = 0.2$ to $p = 0.8$ range, since these are the items that discriminate between most members of the sample.

SAQ 18.2

(a) Factor analysis can show how many distinct constructs are measured by a set of items – other techniques *assume* this is just one. Sometimes a set of items can measure two quite highly correlated but distinct abilities, e.g. fluid and crystallised ability, and indeed Cattell (1971) claims that these two factors can be found when factor analysis is used to examine tests that were constructed using classical item analysis.

(b) Every time an item is removed, each person's total score changes, and so all the other items' correlations with this total score will *also* change.

(c) The test will have a very low (probably zero) reliability, as it will almost certainly measure a mixture of traits. The arbitrary choice of which criterion to measure will greatly influence the items that make up the test. Because so many correlations are calculated between the test items and the criterion, some of these correlations will be seen as significant purely by chance. Likewise, some items that *should* be included will not be. It is also very atheoretical – having constructed the test, we have no real understanding of *why* it works or what it measures.

19

Measuring mood and motivation

BACKGROUND

Whilst Chapters 13, 14, 15, 16 and 18 have focused on the assessment of stable traits (such as general ability, or extraversion), so far there has been no mention of the assessment of states – moods and motivation. This turns out to be considerably more complex than most test designers seem to assume, so it is necessary to consider the basic measurement issues before moving on to discuss the theories of mood and motivation described in Chapter 10.

Recommended prior reading

Chapters 11, 14 and 15.

INTRODUCTION

This chapter is all about the measurement of *states*. Unlike traits, states are not stable, constant features of individuals like (for example) extraversion and verbal ability. Instead, states are highly volatile, changing from hour to hour or from minute to minute, often (although not necessarily) in response to life events. A fuller discussion of the exact nature of states is given in Chapter 10, but the essential point to bear in mind is that they fluctuate in intensity.

Two broad classes of states have been identified, namely mood states and motivational states. Moods are the familiar surges of emotions that we feel on the morning of an examination, on seeing a beautiful sunset, on viewing a moving performance on stage or screen, or after seeing our team win an important match. Some theorists draw distinctions between moods and emotions, but I have suggested elsewhere that this is a dangerous practice (Cooper, 1997). The second main class of states are *motivational states* – internal feelings that drive us to eat when hungry, to spend hours assuaging our social conscience through voluntary work, to spend time and money finding a partner, and so on. This chapter considers how these two types of states can be assessed, and how scales that purportedly measure these states can be evaluated.

Scales that measure states, just like those that assess traits, must be shown to be reliable and valid. How can the reliability of a mood scale be assessed? One property that it most certainly must *not* show is high temporal stability (test–retest reliability). Because moods change over time whilst traits do not, if individuals are found to have similar scores on two occasions this strongly suggests that the scale is measuring a trait of some kind, rather than a state. However, it is possible to calculate the internal-consistency reliability of a mood scale, and it should be clear from Chapter 13 that this is, in any case, the more theoretically useful measure of reliability. Thus the reliability of mood scales can be established by measuring their internal consistency, just as with scales measuring traits.

Assessing the *validity* of scales that measure states is rather more problematical, for as states (by definition) last only for a short time and are susceptible to environmental influences, it is necessary to measure the mood (or motivation) and to assess the criterion behaviour(s) at almost the same time. There would be little point in measuring mood (once) on Monday, and then correlating these scores with some criterion data on Friday, as the level of mood/motivation will almost certainly have changed.

The construct validity of mood scales could, perhaps, be assessed by correlating scores on once-measured moods or motivation with scores on other criterion measures, such as sexual behaviour, anxiety (as rated by an observer), and so on. However, there is a problem with this approach, since it may confuse the mood (or motivation) with personality. For example, suppose the sample contains some individuals who are *always* anxious (i.e. high on the trait of anxiety or neuroticism). Any significant correlations between self-reported anxiety (in a mood questionnaire) and rated anxiety might simply show that the items in the questionnaire measure trait anxiety. The same is true for sex. Some people may *always* show a stronger interest in sex, so the questionnaire may pick up this trait instead of the state.

For this reason, it is much better to perform longitudinal studies, and to see how mood or motivational state varies relative to each individual's own baseline. For example, scores on state questionnaires and certain criterion behaviours (or ratings) could be obtained from one person on many occasions, and intercorrelated in order to determine whether that person tends to *look* most anxious at roughly the same time that the questionnaire shows that they *feel* most anxious, without being concerned too much about their habitual level of (trait) anxiety.

It is also possible to establish the content validity of mood scales, since many intense moods have clinical overtones – anxiety, depression, etc. For example, it would be difficult to argue that a mood scale which asked about all of the symptoms of depression in DSM-IV was not valid. However, this is rather more difficult for motivational states.

It is also rather more difficult to establish the predictive validity of scales that measure motivation or mood, since prediction implies future behaviour, whilst by their very nature moods and motives are transient. Individuals' scores on scales that measure motivation or mood states should not be able to predict stable, future behaviours, such as occupational success or physical health. Any studies of predictive validity would need to be performed over a period of minutes (or at most hours), rather than months or years, and there are few such studies in the literature.

ASSESSING MOODS

A glance at any of the Buros Institute's publications will reveal that a quite bewildering range of tests has been developed to assess mood, in particular. Some of these have been designed to assess single moods (e.g. the State–Trait Anxiety Inventory and the Depression Adjective Checklist), whilst question-naires such as the Profile of Mood States (POMS) (Lorr and McNair, 1988), the Howarth Mood Adjective Checklist (HMACL-4) (Howarth, 1988), the Eight State Questionnaire (8SQ) (Curran and Cattell, 1976), the Differential Emotions Scale (DES-III) (Izard *et al.*, 1982), the Nowlis Mood Adjective Checklist (Nowlis and Nowlis, 1956), the UWIST Mood-Adjective Checklist (Matthews *et al.*, 1990) and the Clyde Mood Scale (Clyde, 1963) each claim to measure a number of distinct mood states. As is discussed in Chapter 10, there is good evidence that all of these multi-scale tests measure two broad dimensions of mood known as positive affect and negative affect (Zevon and Tellegen, 1982; Watson and Tellegen, 1985; Lorr and Wunderlich, 1988; Watson *et al.*, 1988; McConville and Cooper, 1992b). These scales are very widely used, POMS in particular having attracted widespread interest in the area of sports psychology.

FOUR PROBLEMS IN MEASURING MOOD

Most of the scales mentioned above were constructed by administering samples of adjectives to groups of volunteers, and asking them to rate how accurately each of the adjectives described how they felt or behaved *at that instant*, rather than how they usually felt or acted. Supporters of this approach to mood-scale construction believe that this is sufficient to guarantee that the scale measures a state rather than a personality trait.

However, there are problems with almost all of the scales mentioned above. First, it is generally not at all obvious how or why each scale selected those particular items for inclusion. There is no guarantee that the items are a random sample of potentially mood-describing adjectives, a point made by Howarth (1988), among others. Second, no attempt is made to eliminate synonyms – many of the scales may be highly reliable simply because all of the adjectives contained within them mean precisely the same thing. If someone claims that they feel 'uptight', they are *bound* also to say that they feel 'anxious', since the two words mean the same thing. You may recall that when we studied how factor analysis has been used to reveal the main dimensions of ability and personality, the key requirement was that factor analysis identified essentially *unexpected* correlations between groups of variables. For example, if we factor-analysed the responses to items enquiring about early waking, feelings of depression, changes in eating habits, degree of cognitive confusion, changes in sexual activity, and so on, we should find a factor loading all of these variables, since all of them can be symptoms of depression (the 'source trait'). However, logically speaking they need not group together. For example, there is no physiological, semantic or psychological reason why early waking *has* to be associated with changes in eating habits. The finding that a group of items *unexpectedly* vary together is what allows us to infer the presence of some 'source trait'. We should not (sensibly) infer the operation of some source trait where the items *have* to form a factor because they are just synonyms, but this does not stop most theorists from doing so.

The third problem is more obvious. This method of constructing mood scales (factoring correlations between items following a single administration of the test to a large group of people) is precisely the same technique that was used to find personality traits. So how can we ever be sure that these scales measure mood *states* at all? Piously hoping that one is measuring a 'state' just because the instructions ask individuals to describe how they feel 'at this moment' does not seem particularly scientific. In any case, there are much better ways of constructing mood scales, and these will be discussed in the next section.

My final concern is about the conditions under which the questionnaires are usually administered, and the effects of test length on performance. Moods are supposedly exquisitely sensitive to environmental conditions, so the setting in which people complete the questionnaires is likely to influence the scores that are obtained, and this will itself influence the number and nature of the mood factors that are derived. Asking undergraduates to complete mood questionnaires in a large group thus seems to be rather short-sighted – it is difficult to imagine how *anyone* could feel fearful, exuberant, zestful or excited (for example) when sitting in a lecture theatre ploughing through a questionnaire containing hundreds of items for the sake of course credit. Consequently few individual differences will be found in the way in which people answer such items, so the items will not form factors. However, if the test were administered in a more naturalistic setting, it is entirely possible that individual differences would be found in responses to items such as these, and that factors would emerge. It seems quite likely that administering questionnaires under such conditions will fail to reveal some important moods – moods that *would* perhaps emerge if the same questionnaire were to be completed on randomly selected occasions during individuals' everyday lives.

SELF-ASSESSMENT QUESTION 19.1

Identify four problems of conventional mood scales.

Discovering the main dimensions of mood is thus a tricky problem, and there is little firm evidence that we have arrived anywhere near a solution. Most attempts to solve the problem have fallen foul of one of the four problems mentioned above, and anomalies often arise when the scales are examined in detail. For example, Curran and Cattell's Eight State Questionnaire supposedly measures eight quite distinct moods, yet the correlation between some of the scales is of the order of 0.7 to 0.8, once their reliability is taken into account (Matthews, 1983). Much the same is true of Howarth's scale (Howarth and Young, 1986). This suggests that the convergent validity of some of the scales is rather dubious. There is not space here to examine the psychometric properties of all of these scales in detail, but a hard-nosed reading of the test manuals and published literature often fails to reveal much convincing evidence for their validity. However, in the next section we shall consider a method of scale construction which guarantees that a scale will measure a mood state, rather than a trait, so eliminating one of the major problems outlined above.

A METHOD FOR MEASURING MOODS

The key feature that distinguishes mood from personality traits is that moods vary over time, whereas personality traits remain more or less constant. This basic distinction can be used to construct scales that can be shown to measure mood rather than personality. Consider, for example, the five-item questionnaire shown in Table 19.1.

Suppose that just one person was asked to answer the questions shown in Table 19.1 on several occasions. For example, suppose that the person completed this four-item questionnaire at the same time of day on 20 consecutive days. It would be possible to show how the responses vary from day to day by drawing graphs rather like those shown in Figure 19.1. (I arbitrarily decided to plot the daily responses to items (a) and (b) on the first

	Strongly agree	Agree	Neutral	Disagree	Strongly disagree
(a) At the moment I feel quite cheerful	5	4	3	2	1
(b) It is easy for me to concentrate	5	4	3	2	1
(c) My heart is pounding	5	4	3	2	1
(d) I am worrying more than usual	5	4	3	2	1
(e) I generally prefer my own company to that of other people	5	4	3	2	1

Table 19.1 Five items from a hypothetical questionnaire

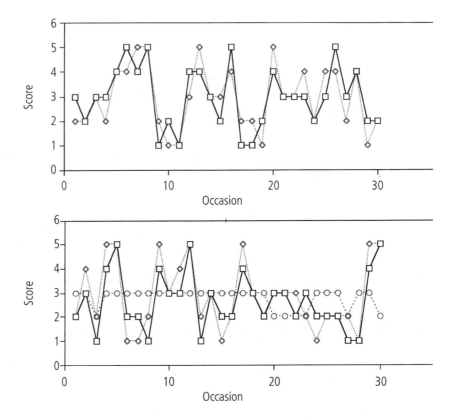

Figure 19.1 Daily responses of one person to the items shown in Table 19.1.

graph, and the daily responses to items (c), (d) and (e) on the second graph, since plotting all five items on the same graph appeared confusing.) It is possible to learn rather a lot about the structure of moods from graphs such as these.

For example, it is clear that items (a) and (b) tend to move up and down together – when one of them is high, so is the other. The same is true for items (c) and (d). Item (e) is quite interesting, since responses to this item vary relatively little from day to day, which is hardly surprising since the item appears to measure a personality trait rather than a state. (It asks the person how they *generally* feel, rather than how they feel *at this moment*.) Thus just by looking at this graph it is clear that the five items measure two distinct states plus one trait.

However, plotting graphs such as this is a time-consuming business, and interpreting the results is not particularly 'objective' – nor is it easy to see what is going on when the number of items becomes large. Fortunately, you already know how to analyse these data.

Suppose that we correlated together the person's scores on the five items in the questionnaire. This may seem rather odd – we have previously calculated correlations only for many people tested on one occasion, rather than for one person tested on many occasions. However, it is perfectly legitimate to perform such an analysis. One simply enters the data obtained on 30 occasions as if they had been obtained from 30 individuals, and uses the same statistical package as usual.

Factor analysis is the obvious tool to explore the structure of these correlations, and Table 19.2 shows the factor matrix that results from a principal-components/VARIMAX analysis of the correlation matrix, rotating two factors. This analysis can tell us how many groups of items tend to rise and fall together from day to day in a single individual. Items that do not vary much (or which do vary, but in a different way from any other items in the questionnaire) will not load on any of the factors, as you can see by looking at item (e) in Table 19.2. Thus this technique of factor analysis is able to distinguish traits from states, which is precisely what is required when developing a mood questionnaire.

This form of factor analysis, in which correlations between items are calculated after administering the items to one individual on many occasions, is known as P-technique, to distinguish it from the more usual method of factor analysis (which is sometimes referred to as R- or Regular technique).

Suppose that 10 people each completed the mood questionnaire on 30 occasions. Much the same technique can be used to analyse these data: the experimenter can either perform 10 separate analyses using P-technique (each based on 30 occasions), or else the 10 tables of data can be stacked one on top of each other, so that the computer program 'thinks' it is analysing the data from one individual on 300 occasions. This is sometimes known as 'Chain-P' technique. It can be very useful when the number of items to be analysed is large.[19.1] For example, if a questionnaire contains 100 items, it will be necessary

| Variable | Rotated factor matrix: | |
	Factor 1	Factor 2
V1	−0.33391	0.85188
V2	−0.32985	0.87516
V3	0.94627	−0.08151
V4	0.94616	−0.15725
V5	−0.16903	−0.34585

Table 19.2 Factor analysis of one person's responses to the five-item questionnaire administered on 30 occasions

[19.1] Although this is not mentioned in the textbooks, it might be prudent to standardise the scores on the mood-scales for each person (i.e. to transform the scores so that each person has a mean of 0 and a standard deviation of 1: z-scores) before 'stacking' the data and performing the P-factor analysis. This will guard against any contamination by traits, as you may care to verify using some made-up data.

to ask one person to complete it on more than 100 occasions in order to detect the states that run through it by P-technique, since there must be more occasions than items for P-technique to work, just as there must be more participants than items for R-technique to work. This would try any participant's patience to the limit. It is much more feasible to ask (for example) 20 people to complete the questionnaire on 10 occasions each, and then perform a Chain-P analysis.

It is also possible to administer questionnaires to large groups of people on two occasions, to calculate the difference between individuals' scores on each of the items on the two occasions, and factor-analyse these difference scores. This technique, too, will reveal any states that run through the questionnaire quite independently of any traits that might be present, and is sometimes known as dR (for 'differential-R') technique, since it is based on difference scores.

This paragraph has nothing to do with the psychology of mood or motivation. However, whilst we are dealing with the topic of cunning factor-analytical designs (such as P-technique), I should perhaps mention that there are several other factor-analytical designs that can be remarkably useful for analysing certain kinds of data. Some of them involve correlating *people* together on the basis of their response to items (rather than correlating items together on the basis of how people respond to them). Cattell (e.g. Cattell, 1973, 1978; Cattell and Kline, 1977) discusses them fully. They are under-used, and can be *very* useful.

SELF-ASSESSMENT QUESTION 19.2

(a) Why are P-, Chain-P and dR technique used when constructing mood scales?

(b) How might you discover the number and nature of the main dimensions of mood using P-technique?

This approach to developing mood scales by using P-technique, Chain-P technique or dR technique has been advocated by Cattell, and was used to develop the Eight State Questionnaire (Curran and Cattell, 1976). Unfortunately, however, when the correlations between the items in the test are factor-analysed, they simply fail to form the eight scales that Cattell predicted (e.g. Barton *et al.*, 1972) – a situation reminiscent of the 16PF, where a highly sophisticated methodology fails, for some reason, to produce a technically adequate test. There would seem to be plenty of scope for repeating this research, using P-technique, Chain-P technique or dR technique to discover the main mood factors that run through a carefully sampled set of items from which synonyms have been removed.

The experimental designs mentioned above also have clear implications for determining the validity of mood scales. For example, in dR technique, ratings of behaviour (e.g. trembling, if we are interested in assessing anxiety) could be obtained at the same time that the questionnaires are completed – the difference between individuals' rated behaviour on the two occasions could be correlated with their responses to items or factors. In P-technique, the individual's score on each of the factors on each occasion can be correlated with their levels of behaviour.

In summary, it is clearly essential to ensure that mood scales do indeed measure moods rather than personality traits. In order to ensure this, it is necessary to identify groups of items that rise and fall together when they are assessed on several occasions. Three techniques for achieving this (P-technique, Chain-P technique and dR technique) have been discussed.

MEASURING MOTIVATION

Measurement of motivation looks deceptively easy. It might appear that motivation is exactly the same as strength of interest or strength of attitudes, and so to tap motivation all that is necessary is to put together a few well-chosen test items (e.g. 'on a scale of 1 to 5 how important are (a) sex, (b) food (c) security ...?'), push them through some item analyses and factor analyses, and publish a motivation scale. This is in fact exactly what has been done. Several tests have been designed to measure specific aspects of motivation, e.g. 'achievement motivation' (McClelland, 1961), which supposedly measures why some individuals 'drive themselves hard' whilst others take a more relaxed approach to life. However, when this scale is factor-analysed with personality scales, it is found that it is a measure of personality, rather than of motivation, which is, after all, fairly obvious from the nature of the concept – it is not obvious how achievement motivation will rise and fall over time (which, as we saw earlier, is the hallmark of a motivational state). Exactly the same has been found for tests that were designed to measure the 'drives' postulated by McDougall (1932) and Murray (1938) (see Kline (1993) for further details). The problem is that such theorists have asked how keen people *usually* are about sex, security, working hard, making a good impression, and so on, which does not really sound like a motivational *state* at all.

The main criticisms levelled against mood questionnaires apply with equal force to questionnaires that claim to measure motivation. As mentioned above, many (perhaps all) questionnaires that supposedly assess motivation actually seem to show rather substantial correlations with the main personality factors – that is, they fail to measure mood states at all. Likewise, there is no guarantee either that the items in these scales are randomly sampled (e.g. from words in the dictionary that could possibly describe motivation) or that synonyms have been removed. The conditions under which the questionnaires are adminis-tered are as likely to influence motivation as they are to affect mood. Even if an individual entered the room with (for example) strong lustful feelings for the person sitting next to them (a high degree of sex drive), it seems likely that spending an hour answering a tedious motivation questionnaire would cause these feelings to decline.

There are also some other problems with the whole topic of motivation. So-called *instinct theories* were popular in the early part of the century as an explanation for motivation. For example, it was suggested that people are aggressive because they have an 'instinct' for aggression. However, this approach is clearly problematical, since the theories are *circular* – the term aggression is used both to describe and to explain the behaviour. The instinct 'aggression' is invoked to explain why people display aggressive behaviour, but the only evidence for this instinct of aggression is the aggressive behaviour itself. Moreover, there is potentially no limit to the number of instincts that can be identified. Is there an instinct for snarling at people who run over our feet with a supermarket trolley? Or an instinct for eating beans? The number of potential instincts is as large as the number of behaviours that can be observed, and such instincts in no way explain why the behaviours occur. Thus a better way of assessing motivation is needed.

Once again, Cattell offers some sound theoretical direction (e.g. Cattell and Child, 1975; Cattell and Kline, 1977) and argues that two basic issues need to be addressed. The basic assumptions are as follows.

- Our interests in objects or activities can shed light on what motivates us. It is possible that our degree of interest in an object or activity may manifest itself in many ways (e.g. by slips of the tongue, behaving irrationally, misperceptions such as misreading signs so as to 'see' the name of an object or person of interest, or mistaking a stranger for someone who is known to us), and so questionnaires may not be able to tap all aspects of interest strength.
- Each of these areas of interest can fulfil several basic needs. For example, playing football might provide an individual with company, an opportunity to behave aggressively (pugnaciously), as well as the intrinsic (physiological) pleasure afforded by the exercise.

First, it is necessary to be able to identify (and measure) precisely what we mean by 'interest strength', and then to look at the specific goals that are achieved, and emotions that are experienced, through following these interests. For example, suppose that research shows that aggression is a 'drive' that motivates many people. It is then necessary to explore why, precisely, some individuals engage in aggressive behaviour – what the goals of their action are, and what the emotional consequences may be.

Attitudes and interests are thought to provide the key to identifying the main dimensions of motivation, but Cattell is particularly critical of the narrow view of attitudes taken by social psychologists – with good reason, in my view. First, there is empirical evidence (mentioned above) which suggests that most 'motivation' questionnaires actually tap stable personality traits, and so tell us absolutely nothing about motivational states. The obvious way to check this would be to determine empirically whether the items in such questionnaires vary over time, using the P-, Chain-P or dR technique discussed above. Unfortunately, very few such analyses appear in the literature, and there is plenty of scope for research in this area.

Second, he argues that people may simply be *unaware* of their true feelings and behaviour, which will make self-reports of dubious value. Thus whilst social psychologists (and clinically based personality theorists such as Kelly and Rogers) build entire theories on attitude measurement, Cattell urges caution. Consider, for example, the item 'how religious are you?', to be answered on a scale of 1 (not at all) to 5 (very). One person may claim that they are highly religious because they are not usually the first person in the house to switch off religious programmes on the radio or television, or because they have some kind of strong unarticulated belief that people should be kind to one another, or they believe in some kind of deity or deities. Others may have a vast collection of images, take part regularly in organised religion, forgo food, wealth and marriage for the sake of their spiritual purity, be highly knowledgeable about the teachings of their religion, and so on – implications of the question that might never have been considered by the first group. Thus it may be more sensible to attempt to infer strength of interest from individuals' behaviour rather than relying on self-report.

Cattell and Child (1975, reprinted in Cattell and Kline, 1977) describe 68 'objective' ways of assessing strength of interest. These include preferences (e.g. expressed preference for praying over a number of other specified activities), reading preference (proportion of religious books), inability to see faults (e.g. being unable to list many disadvantages of the chosen form of religion), various physiological changes (e.g. increase in heart rate when shown a relevant religious symbol), proportion of time and money spent in religion-related activity, knowledge of religious facts (which is, of course, also likely to be influenced by intelligence), better memory for religious-related than for non-religious material in a laboratory-based test of memory, a belief that religious-related activities are in some way better than most other activities (e.g. 'it is better to spend a spare 10 minutes praying rather than talking to one's partner'), and so on.

Suppose that we ask a large group of individuals to identify some issues or activities in which people are likely to have varying degrees of interest (e.g. their job, football-playing, their religion, abortion, socialism and gastronomy), and we assess the strength of interest in each of these using some or all of the 68 techniques mentioned in the previous paragraph – the *interest measures*. The question is whether these all rise and fall together for each activity, or whether there are several distinct ways in which 'interest' can manifest itself. Cattell (1957) has reported just such a study. He found that, when the correlations between these various interest measures were factor-analysed, not one but *seven* factors emerged. This is important, for it suggests that measuring strength of interest by one method alone (e.g. by questionnaire) is likely to be inadequate, since strength of interest itself has several quite distinct aspects.

Alpha is the term given by Cattell to the component that reflects conscious wishes, including those that are illogical. Buying a dress despite the fact you know that you cannot afford it is a good example of the alpha component of your interest in clothes. Beta reflects conscious, rational preferences, of the type that will be expressed when responding to questionnaires that ask how much one likes or dislikes certain objects or activities. Buying a computer because you know that it is a useful tool to help your studies is an example of logical, conscious, beta-type motivation. Cattell and Child suggest that their third factor of motivation, gamma, is a form of motivation that arises because the individual feels that he or she *ought* to take an interest in something. Someone might feel pressured into listening to a particular piece of music or experimenting with drugs, not because they particularly want to do so, but because they feel that this is the kind of behaviour that is expected of their peer group. Delta is a purely physiological response to certain stimuli that (interestingly) appears to be quite distinct from the other aspects of interest – it seems that certain sights and sounds can lead directly to changes in activity of the autonomic nervous system. The nature of the remaining three factors is not as well understood, so I will not consider them here. Thus when psychologists ask why a person performs a particular activity, there will not be a single answer. Instead, up to seven main reasons need to be considered, at least one of which is purely physiological. Impulsive 'gut feeling', logical preference, a feeling of obligation and increased levels of physiological arousal may all play their part in directing our behaviour. Strength of interest in some object or activity can arise for a number of reasons.

SELF-ASSESSMENT QUESTION 19.3

(a) (i) A man's pulse races when he sees his next-door neighbour. (ii) When walking down the street he misreads a shop sign, thinking it shows the neighbour's name. When asked about the neighbour, he (iii) describes them as 'just a neighbour' and (iv) says that he feels that it would be wrong to feel any emotional attraction. Try to categorise this man as having low or high scores on components alpha to delta.

(b) Cattell claims that there is more than one factor of attitude strength, although this finding needs to be replicated. If it were to be replicated successfully, what would its implications be for social psychology?

(c) Can you detect any similarities to Freud's model of personality?

The second part of Cattell's theory tries to discover where these interests lead – that is, what the 'pay-offs' of these interests actually are. For example, if a person is found to have a strong alpha, beta, gamma and delta interest in vintage cars (thus indicating that cars are probably really rather important to them at a number of levels) it seems reasonable to ask what needs are met by this interest. Perhaps the local vintage car club provides company. The person may possibly like to bask in the interest awakened in onlookers when he or she drives around in it. The car may be seen as a financial investment, or perhaps the *real* reason is the pleasure inherent in fixing it when it breaks down –

having to manufacture parts from scratch. If psychologists can discover the ultimate reasons underlying such interests, they may claim to have understood motivation.

If someone is asked to give as many answers as possible to describe why they are performing a particular activity (e.g. 'why are you reading this book?') they will presumably answer 'to pass my exams', 'so that I don't look a fool in next week's tutorial', 'because it interests me', or something similar. The process can then be repeated (*why* is it important to pass one's examinations, or not to appear stupid in class?) time and time again until, eventually, the explanation cannot be taken any further. Eventually, something just *is* rewarding – 'because it interests me' is one example, 'to pass my exams → to get a good job → to provide for my family' may be another. So too might 'so as not to appear stupid in class → to maintain my self-respect'. This approach looks to me as if it is rather closely related to Hinkle's work with the repertory grid (discussed by Bannister and Fransella, 1971) although, so far as I am aware, no one has explored this. Hinkle's work may provide an appropriate methodological framework for studying this aspect of motivation.

These ultimate goals are known as ergs and sentiments in Cattell's model, and some of them are shown in Table 19.3. Ergs are thought to be direct biological drives whose fulfilment is intrinsically pleasurable (e.g. having sex, eating when hungry, protecting one's life, socialising, exploring, etc.). Sentiments are thought to be socially determined, and are likely to vary in strength from person to person and from culture to culture. If a person does not have parents/an interest in sport/a partner/a religious interest, then these clearly will not motivate that individual, and acquiring money *for its own sake* (rather than for what it can buy or do) may not be an important goal in some societies.

Cattell's theory of motivation thus suggests that the drives that are

Ergs	Sentiments
Hunger	Profession
Sex	Parents
Fear	Husband/wife/partner
Gregariousness	Superego (conscience)
Exploration	Religion
Self-assertion	Sport and fitness
Narcissism	Scientific interests
Pugnacity	Money
Acquisitiveness	Aesthetic interests

Table 19.3 Some ergs and sentiments from Cattell's theory of motivation (from Cattell and Child, 1975)

important for a person should be discovered by exploring the 'pay-offs' for a person's interests, and that these interests themselves should not be assessed merely by self-report questionnaire. The unfortunate fact is that very little work has been performed in this area, so we are still a long way from being able to measure interests, ergs or sentiments with any accuracy. Cattell has developed adult and children's versions of a test, known as the Motivation Analysis Test, which claims to measure the strength of the main ergs and sentiments (Cattell *et al.*, 1970b). Unfortunately, however, the adult version simply does not seem to form the factors that Cattell claims (Cooper and Kline, 1982), although Cattell disagrees with this view (Cattell, 1982). Nevertheless, I have discussed Cattell's theory in some depth because it does seem to be by far the most technically sophisticated approach to the measurement of motivation, and it raises several important issues (such as the inadequacy of assessing interest strength by means of self-report measures alone) that clearly deserve to be explored more thoroughly.

THE FUTURE

The obvious experiments that have yet to be performed include the following:

- checking whether responses to traditional mood and motivation check-lists do vary over time, using P-, Chain-P or dR techniques;
- replicating and extending Cattell's (1957) work on the measurement of interests, in order to discover all the ways in which interests can manifest themselves. This should result in a battery of questionnaires and objective tests that will allow the main dimensions of interest to be assessed;
- factor-analysing the correlations between a large number of interests in order to confirm Cattell's conclusions about the main drives – the 'ergs' and 'sentiments';
- identifying these factors by exploring the 'pay-offs' (the ultimate benefits to the individual) of each strongly held interest, and thereby being able to assess the importance of each of the ergs and sentiments for each individual;
- developing a test to measure individual differences in the strengths of these ergs and sentiments.

Much of Cattell's work requires independent replication, and until this is carried out, there really does not seem to be any satisfactory way of either conceptualising or assessing the main aspects of human emotion.

SUMMARY

This chapter has explored the nature and assessment of the major 'states' – moods and motives. I have suggested that there are four major flaws in the common practice of constructing mood scales in much the same way as personality scales are developed, and that Cattell's alternative methodologies are much to be preferred – even though the mood scale created by this technique does not appear to work very well. Finally, we have considered the topic of motivation, about which relatively little is known. I have suggested that motivation strength can be inferred by examining the benefits to the individual of performing various activities that interest them strongly, but I have pointed out that the assessment of strength of interest may require much more than the conventional attitude scales. Cattell's theory linking interests to ergs and sentiments has been discussed, but has not been evaluated in any detail because of the paucity of empirical evidence. Some suggestions have been made concerning future research.

ANSWERS TO SELF-ASSESSMENT QUESTIONS

SAQ 19.1
Most of these scales were constructed in the same way as scales measuring traits, so there is no guarantee that they assess mood at all. Most of them have no clear rationale for deciding whether items should be included in the analysis. Several items that mean the same thing may be included (synonyms), and any such items are bound to form a factor, but this factor is not necessarily of any psychological interest. Administering mood questionnaires under standard conditions is likely to make all participants feel bored and listless, and so prevent the research from detecting more 'positive' moods.

SAQ 19.2
(a) To ensure that a scale measures a state rather than a trait.
(b) Compile a questionnaire consisting of a broad range of mood items (but without synonyms). Ask a single person to complete this questionnaire on a very large number of occasions (ideally more than 100) whilst performing a number of different activities. Correlate the responses to the individual items together, and factor-analyse them in order to determine whether any particular groups of items tend to rise and fall together.

SAQ 19.3
(a) High delta, high alpha, low beta, low gamma.
(b) It means that simply asking people about their attitudes is not sufficient, as individuals may not even be *aware* of all of their attitudes. Thus theories (e.g. attribution theory) that are based on simple self-report measures of attitudes may have severe limitations.
(c) Cattell and Kline (1977) suggest that the beta component resembles conscious, rational ego processes, the gamma component resembles the superego, and the alpha and delta components rather resemble the id (even though alpha is to a large extent conscious), although this is highly speculative!

20

Conclusions

This book has covered a wide range of theories and methodologies, from classical psychoanalysis to item response theory by way of the main trait theories of personality and ability – proof indeed of the wide range of skills necessary both to understand and to evaluate other people's research, and to begin to *use* the techniques in earnest. For I hope that by now some of the interesting issues in individual differences research will be obvious.

GENERALLY AGREED ISSUES

There is now fairly good agreement about the structure of personality, with extraversion, neuroticism and a choice between agreeableness/ conscientiousness and psychoticism. There is also a good level of agreement about the structure of ability *as it is traditionally visualised*, although Sternberg's widening of the concept needs to be taken into account.

Process models have, of course, had to wait for some consensus structural model to emerge – one can hardly investigate the processes that seem to underpin personality and ability if there is no general agreement about the precise nature of the main dimensions. Thus most process models are fairly rudimentary, and significant new developments are reported in the journals every month. The correlations between measures of ability and reaction-time measures, inspection time, etc. seem solid, although considerably smaller than was first claimed.

The evidence that both personality and ability have a substantial genetic basis is absolutely solid, and this work also shows that the influence of the shared environment on adult personality and general ability is very small indeed, a finding that seems to me to have some rather interesting implications for the validity of certain personality theories that stress the importance of the family for adult development. It is possible that some minor personality factors or abilities may be influenced by these, but g, E and N most certainly are not.

Although new techniques of exploratory factor analysis are still being developed, there is now some agreement that the technique can produce replicable factor structures, given decent-quality data, which was a matter of some debate in the 1970s. There is a need for better tests for the number of factors, and an even more urgent need for those tests that *do* exist to be incorporated into the main computer packages.

Item response theory (particularly the one- and two-parameter models) is generally accepted as a legitimate technique. Once again, the independent estimation of item and person parameters was a matter of some controversy in the 1970s.

Clinically oriented psychologists find that repertory grid techniques, Q-sorts, etc. are therapeutically useful, although it is sometimes difficult to see how the techniques can be validated. This is not the place to try to evaluate the success of the Rogerian and personal-construct schools of therapy!

There is general agreement that psychoanalysis is an ineffective form of therapy, and that some of Freud's theories are untestable.

Finally, there is good agreement about the way to construct (and validate) scales measuring traits.

CONTROVERSIAL ISSUES

Anything to do with psychoanalytical theory or unconscious mental processes is regarded as highly controversial, and it must be said that many attempts to validate aspects of Freud's theories do not provide strong, replicable results, possibly (but not necessarily) because psychoanalytical concepts are so very difficult to operationalise. Work on the unconscious processing of threat-related stimuli looks to be one of the least disappointing areas of research.

Findings with regard to the relationship between EEG/AEP (Electro-Encephalogram and Auditory Evoked Potential) measures and personality and general ability has been a disappointment, with results sometimes *suggesting* links in the postulated directions, but apparently being influenced by many other variables. The several failures to replicate the Hendricksons' results represent a rather severe blow to neural theories of ability, although quite why high temporal consistency of the AEP (which is, surely, what is implied by the 'string measure') was important in the first place seems to have been the subject of rather less attention than one would have expected.

The subject of test bias is widely misunderstood, even in the psychological community, with many colleagues inferring bias from the presence of group differences. Group differences in ability are highly controversial, the right-wing argument appearing to go along the following lines:

- some racial groups perform less well than others on ability tests;
- intelligence has a substantial genetic component;
- therefore some groups are genetically inferior to others.

and although the last statement does not follow from the first two (as the genetic influence on ability is generally estimated to be somewhere between 50 per cent and 60 per cent), some seem to assume that it does.

The Bell Curve (Herrnstein and Murray, 1994) created considerable controversy when it appeared, much of it ill-informed. However, there is some agreement that, whilst the *data* presented there (linking IQ to a variety of social behaviours) may be legitimate, some of the political and social recommendations may not be.

Mood variability remains an enigma, with very inconsistent patterns of correlations with other personality variables, and no real attempts (backed up with data) to explain the phenomenon in terms of neural or other regulatory processes.

Sternberg's triarchic theory of abilities and Gardner's theory of multiple intelligences are still being evaluated.

In item response theory there is still some debate about what to do when item(s) do not fit the model. One school holds that the offending items should just be discarded. The other is demanding more sophisticated models, including those that can take into account characteristics of the person other than their ability with regard to the trait in question.

UNDER-RESEARCHED ISSUES

The whole area of mood and motivation does seem rather neglected, and there is not even much consensus on the structure of mood. A *vast* number of variables seem to affect mood level (including cognitions, scanning, and the appraisal of stress), which means that experiments in this area will need to control for a large number of potentially confounding variables.

The finding that most 'motivation' states seem instead to measure personality is really rather a blow to this area, and it would seem that research into the nature and structure of interests and the 'pay-offs' of various interests in terms of goal fulfilment really would repay some serious attention, even if it only involved an attempted replication of some of Cattell's work in this field.

CONCLUSIONS

The scientific study of individual differences has changed enormously in the last twenty years. There is now some measure of agreement between researchers about the main dimensions of personality and ability, making the search for process models possible, and readers will gather that there is still much to do – psychometricians do not yet have the measure of man.

Appendix A

CORRELATIONS

See also Liebetrau, A.M. 1983: *Measures of association*. Newbury Park, CA: Sage.

Suppose that each person in a sample produces two scores, which might be scores on psychometric tests, test items, or whatever. We often want to know the extent to which the two scores are related. A correlation coefficient – sometimes known as the Pearson correlation coefficient after its inventor, Karl Pearson – is a number between −1.0 and 1.0 which indicates the extent to which these two variables overlap, and the direction of this relationship.

Correlations show how much two variables overlap. Hence a correlation of 0 indicates that a high score on one variable is associated equally often with high, medium and low scores on the other variable. A scatter diagram shows individuals' scores on one variable plotted as a function of their scores on the other variable. The following scatter diagram (Figure A-1) shows a correlation of approximately zero.

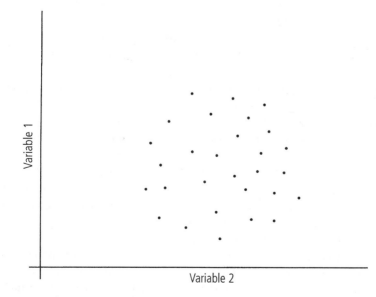

Figure A-1 Scatter diagram showing a correlation of 0.

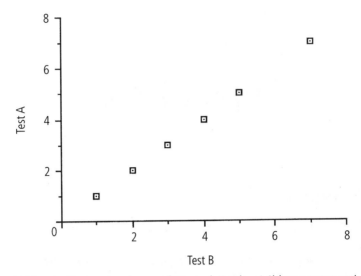

Figure A-2 Scatter diagram showing a perfect correlation ($r = 1.0$) between two variables.

A correlation of 1.0 or −1.0 would indicate that if one of each person's scores is known, it is possible to predict the other one exactly. Figure A-2 shows the scatter diagram for such a correlation.

This is an example of a perfect positive correlation, where 'perfect' means that all of the points lie *exactly* on a straight line, and 'positive' means that a person who has a high score on Test A also has a high score on Test B. A negative correlation would mean that a high score on Test A would be associated with a low score on Test B, so the points would lie on a line that slopes from top-left to bottom-right.

In this example, you can see that each person's score on Test A is exactly equal to their score on Test B. So if a person's score on one of these two tests were known, it would be a simple matter to work out what their score was on the other test. As the correlation is perfect (1.0), we would expect this prediction to be completely accurate.

Perfect correlations simply do not exist in real life. Even if the underlying relationship is 'perfect', each of the observed scores will be contaminated by measurement error, since no test has perfect reliability or validity. In the above example, imagine that each of the points was moved a small, arbitrary distance up/down (corresponding to measurement error on Test A) and left/right (corresponding to measurement error on Test B). The scatter diagram would then look something like that shown in Figure A-3.

Although there is still a strong tendency for high scores on Test A to be associated with high scores on Test B, this relationship is no longer perfect. So now knowing someone's score on one of the tests would only allow us to make a rough estimate of their scores on the other test, as the scores do not fall on a perfect straight line.

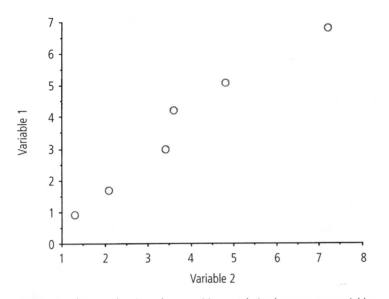

Figure A-3 Scatter diagram showing a large positive correlation between two variables.

QUESTION

To obtain a perfect positive correlation, is it necessary for one variable always to be equal to the other?

The answer is no, as shown in Figure A-4. Here you can see that there is again a perfect correlation between the two sets of variables. That is, they all lie exactly on a straight line. However, the variables most certainly are not

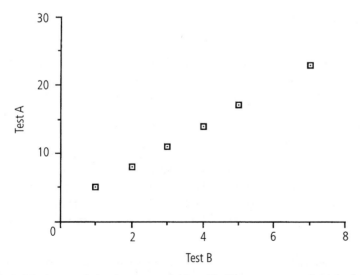

Figure A-4 Perfect correlation from two variables with different means and standard deviations.

equal (in fact, the equation linking them is 'Score on Test A = 3 × score on Test B + 2'). Thus a perfect correlation just shows that two variables are perfectly linearly related – not that they are identical.

EXERCISE

Suppose that when two tests, A and B, are given to a large sample of people, their scores on this test are found to have a correlation of 0.4. Try to work out whether this correlation would (a) rise, (b) fall, (c) change in some unpredictable way or (d) stay exactly the same if, instead of calculating the correlation from the raw data, you first:

(a) multiply each person's score on Test A by 6, leaving their score on Test B unaltered;
(b) subtract 20 from each person's score on Test A, leaving their score on Test B unaltered;
(c) multiply each person's score on Test A by 2, and subtract 9 from their score on Test B;
(d) square each of the values of Test A, leaving their score on test B unaltered.

If the answers are not obvious, you should try to settle this matter empirically. Using your favourite statistics package, define two variables, Test A and Test B. Then invent some scores on these two tests from half a dozen hypothetical students – just type in any numbers you like. Having done this, calculate the correlation between Test A and Test B, and then modify the values of Tests A and B as described above. Re-calculate the correlation at each step.

You should have found out that the correlation does not change at all when you:

- alter the mean level of either or both of the variables (by adding or subtracting a constant, e.g. 20, to either or both of the scores);
- alter the range (or more strictly, the standard deviation) of the scores on either of the variables (by multiplying or dividing test scores by a constant, e.g. 6).

However, when you perform any other operation (such as squaring, or taking logarithms) the correlation will change. It will *probably* decrease if there was a fairly linear relationship between the two untransformed variables.

The first two properties of the correlation (insensitivity to the mean or the standard deviation of either distribution of scores) are very necessary, since scores on tests:

- have an arbitrary zero-point. A raw score of 0 on a test of mechanical reasoning does not imply that a person has no mechanical reasoning ability whatsoever. If one person scores 20 on such a test, this does not imply that they have four times the ability of someone who scores 5. The scores form an *interval scale*, rather than a *ratio scale*;

- have an arbitrary scale of measurement. A scale having 20 items scored as 'number of items correctly answered' will produce scores that are about twice as high as a test consisting of 10 such items (assuming that each test contains items of similar difficulty). The correlation between the two tests logically should not be affected by the number of items in each test and/or the range of scores – and the exercise shows that this is indeed the case.

Thus correlations are very well suited for comparing scores on tests, as they are not affected by the mean or standard deviation of the scores on either of the scales.

QUESTION

Is the size of the correlation related to how steeply the line slopes? For example, which of the two graphs shown in Figure A-5 represents the larger correlation?

Both of these figures represent precisely the same correlation. As you discovered in the first part of the first exercise, the slope of the line merely reflects the scale on which one of the variables is measured, and this is arbitrary. What determines the correlation is how closely the points lie in relation to the line once both of the variables have been converted to 'standard

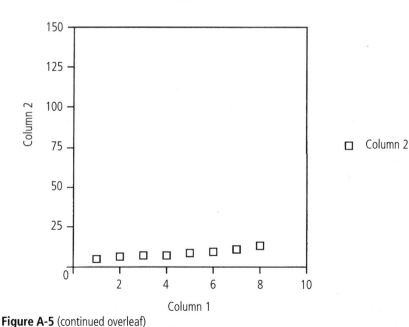

Figure A-5 (continued overleaf)

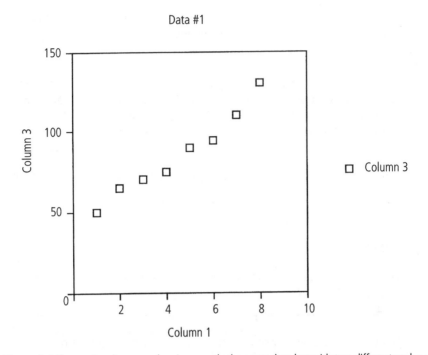

Figure A-5 Two scatter diagrams showing exactly the same data but with two different scales on the *y*-axis. This shows that the correlation is not related to the slope of the line of best fit.

scores'. This involves subtracting the mean from each score, and dividing this number by the standard deviation. Hence standard scores have a mean of zero and a standard deviation of 1.

It is possible to test whether a given correlation is significantly different from zero, from another value, or indeed from another correlation coefficient. We are usually interested in determining whether a correlation is significantly different from zero – that is, whether the data show that high scores on one variable tend to be associated with high (or low) scores on another variable. Any good statistics book will give details of how to do this.

THE IMPORTANCE OF r^2

Regardless of the number of cases, it is possible to calculate how accurate a prediction one can make about the likely value of one variable, given any value of the other, by considering the square of the correlation coefficient. r^2 is the percentage of the variance of one variable that can be predicted from the other. Thus if the correlation between two variables is 0.7, 49 per cent of the variance of one variable is predictable from a knowledge of the other. The remainder is due to other variables and/or random error.

SPECIAL CASES

There are a few special cases of the correlation coefficient of which you should be aware. One common case involves one variable which is continuous (e.g. a test score) and another which is dichotomous (i.e. which can only assume one of two values). Dichotomous variables are fairly common in psychology. Responses to test items may be coded as 'correct/incorrect', or responses such as 'true/false' or 'agree/disagree' may be correlated together. They will often be coded as 0/1, although in fact any two numbers can be used. When a dichotomous variable is correlated with a continuous variable, the correlation coefficient is often known as the point-biserial correlation. It is calculated in precisely the same way as the usual Pearson correlation – it just has a different name for historical reasons. (The biserial correlation is different, and best not used.) A common use of the point-biserial correlation is when correlating responses to individual test items with other variables – the test items being coded as correct (1) or incorrect (0).

When two dichotomous items are correlated together (again using the usual formula for a Pearson correlation), the correlation is sometimes known as the phi coefficient.

Both point-biserial and phi coefficients are problematical, the reason being that the correlations between variables can only be 1.0 under rather special circumstances. Instead of representing just the amount of overlap between two variables, the point-biserial and phi coefficients are also influenced by the difficulty levels of the two dichotomous items. An example will make this clear. Table A-1 shows individuals' responses on two dichotomous items, and the numbers denoted by a, b, c and d show the number of individuals falling into each of the cells of the table.

A perfect positive correlation will imply that $b = c = 0$ – that is, everyone who answers item 1 correctly also answers item 2 correctly, and everyone who fails item 1 also fails item 2. This is possible only when the proportion of individuals who answer item 1 correctly is exactly the same as the proportion

	Response to Item 1		
	Correct	Incorrect	Total
Response to Item 2			
Correct	a	b	a + b
Incorrect	c	d	c + d
Total	a + c	b + d	a + b + c + d

Table A-1 Responses to two two-valued (dichotomous) variables

who answer item 2 correctly, as you may care to verify. Phi can equal 1.0 only if the means of the two distributions are identical.

The same problem affects the point-biserial, only more so. It is mathematically impossible to obtain a point-biserial correlation larger than about 0.8, under the very best circumstances (which is when 50 per cent of the values of the dichotomous variable are 1 and the 50 per cent are 0). As this mean of the dichotomous variable shifts away from 0.5, the maximum possible point-biserial falls to 0.7 (mean = 0.2 or 0.8) and 0.6 (mean = 0.1 or 0.9). Nunnally (1978) has provided full diagrams showing this effect.

This creates problems when interpreting correlations. A small correlation could come from two variables that just happen not to be particularly strongly correlated together, or from two variables that have very different distributions and so *cannot* correlate substantially.

Appendix B

The Code of Fair Testing Practices in Education states the major obligations to test takers of professionals who develop or use educational tests. The Code is meant to apply broadly to the use of tests in education (admissions, educational assessment, educational diagnosis, and student placement). The Code is not designed to cover employment testing, licensure or certification testing, or other types of testing. Although the Code has relevance to many types of educational tests, it is directed primarily at professionally developed tests such as those sold by commercial test publishers or used in informally administered testing programmes. The Code is not intended to cover tests made by individual teachers for use in their own classrooms.

The Code addresses the roles of test developers and test users separately. Test users are people who select tests, commission test development services, or make decisions on the basis of test scores. Test developers are people who actually construct tests, as well as those who set policies for particular testing programmes. The roles may, of course, overlap, as when a state education agency commissions test development services, sets policies that control the test development process, and makes decisions on the basis of the test scores.

The Code has been developed by the Joint Committee on Testing Practices, a co-operative effort of several professional organisations, that has as its aim the advancement, in the public interest, of the quality of testing practices. The Joint Committee was initiated by the American Educational Research Association (AERA), the American Psychological Association (APA) and the National Council on Measurement in Education (NCME). In addition to these three groups, the American Association for Counselling and Development/Association for Measurement and Evaluation in Counselling and Development, and the American Speech-Language-Hearing Association are now also sponsors of the Joint Committee.

This is not copyrighted material. Reproduction and dissemination are encouraged. Please cite this document as follows.

Code of Fair Testing Practices in Education. (1988) Washington, DC: Joint

Committee on Testing Practices. (Mailing Address: Joint Committee on Testing Practices, American Psychological Association, 1200 17th Street, NW, Washington, DC 20036, USA.)

The Code presents standards for educational test developers and users in four areas:

A. Developing/selecting appropriate tests;
B. Interpreting scores;
C. Striving for fairness;
D. Informing test takers.

Organisations, institutions and individual professionals who endorse the Code commit themselves to safeguarding the rights of test takers by following the principles listed. The Code is intended to be consistent with the relevant parts of the Standards for Educational and Psychological Testing (AERA, APA, NCME, 1985). However, the Code differs from the Standards in both audience and purpose. The Code is meant to be understood by the general public, it is limited to educational tests, and the primary focus is on those issues that affect the proper use of tests. The Code is not meant to add new principles over and above those in the Standards, or to change the meaning of the Standards. The goal is rather to represent the spirit of a selected portion of the Standards in a way that is meaningful to test takers and/or their parents or guardians. It is the hope of the Joint Committee that the Code will also be judged to be consistent with existing codes of conduct and standards of other professional groups who use educational tests.

A. DEVELOPING/SELECTING APPROPRIATE TESTS[1]

Test developers should provide the information that test users need to select appropriate tests.

Test users should select tests that meet the purpose for which they are to be used, and that are appropriate for the intended test-taking populations.

TEST DEVELOPERS SHOULD:

1. Define what each test measures and what the test should be used for. Describe the population(s) for which the test is appropriate.

2. Accurately represent the characteristics, usefulness and limitations of the test for their intended purposes.

TEST USERS SHOULD:

1. First define the purpose for testing and the population to be tested. Then select a test for that purpose and that population based on a thorough review of the available information.

2. Investigate potentially useful sources of information, in addition to test scores, to corroborate the information provided by tests.

[1]Many of the statements in the Code refer to the selection of existing tests. However, in customised testing programmes, test developers are engaged to construct new tests. In those situations, the test development process should be designed to help ensure that the completed tests will be in compliance with this Code.

3. Explain relevant measurement concepts as necessary for clarity at the level of detail that is appropriate for the intended audience(s).

4. Describe the process of test development. Explain how the content and skills to be tested were selected.

5. Provide evidence that the test meets its intended purpose(s).

6. Provide either representative samples or complete copies of test questions, directions, answer sheets, manuals and score reports to qualified users.

7. Indicate the nature of evidence obtained concerning the appropriateness of each test for groups of different racial, ethnic, or linguistic backgrounds who are likely to be tested.

8. Identify and publish any specialised skills needed to administer each test and to interpret scores correctly.

3. Read the materials provided by test developers and avoid using tests for which unclear or incomplete information is provided.

4. Become familiar with how and when the test was developed and tried out.

5. Read independent evaluations of a test and of possible alternative measures. Look for evidence required to support the claims of test developers.

6. Examine specimen sets, disclosed tests or samples of questions, directions, answer sheets, manuals and score reports before selecting a test.

7. Ascertain whether the test content and norm group(s) or comparison group(s) are appropriate for the intended test takers.

8. Select and use only those tests for which the skills needed to administer the test and interpret scores correctly are available.

B. INTERPRETING SCORES

Test developers should help users to interpret scores correctly.

TEST DEVELOPERS SHOULD:

9. Provide timely and easily understood scores reports that describe test performance clearly and accurately, and also explain the meaning and limitations of reported scores.

10. Describe the population(s) represented by any norms or

Test users should interpret scores correctly.

TEST USERS SHOULD:

9. Obtain information about the scale used for reporting scores, the characteristics of any norms or comparison group(s), and the limitations of the scores.

10. Interpret scores, taking into account any major differences

comparison group(s), the dates the data were gathered and the process used to select the samples of test takers.

between the norms or comparison groups and the actual test takers. Also take into account any differences in test administration practices or familiarity with the specific questions in the test.

11. Warn users to avoid specific, reasonably anticipated misuses of test scores.

11. Avoid using tests for purposes not specifically recommended by the test developer, unless evidence is obtained to support the intended use.

12. Provide information that will help users to follow reasonable procedures for setting passing scores when it is appropriate to use such scores with the test.

12. Explain how any passing scores were set and gather evidence to support the appropriateness of the scores.

13. Provide information that will help users to gather evidence to show that the test is meeting its intended purpose(s).

13. Obtain evidence to help show that the test is meeting its intended purpose(s).

C. STRIVING FOR FAIRNESS

Test developers should strive to make tests that are as fair as possible for test takers of difference races, gender, ethnic backgrounds, or different handicapping conditions.

Test users should select tests that have been developed in ways that attempt to make them as fair as possible for test takers of different races, gender, ethnic backgrounds, or handicapping conditions.

TEST DEVELOPERS SHOULD:

TEST USERS SHOULD:

14. Review and revise test questions and related materials to avoid potentially insensitive content or language.

14. Evaluate the procedures used by test developers to avoid potentially insensitive content or language.

15. Investigate the performance of test takers of different races, gender and ethnic backgrounds when samples of sufficient size are available. Enact procedures that help to ensure that differences in performance are related primarily to the skills under assessment, rather than to irrelevant factors.

15. Review the performance of test takers of different races, gender and ethnic backgrounds when samples of sufficient size are available. Evaluate the extent to which performance differences may have been caused by the test.

16. When feasible, make appropriately modified forms of tests or administration procedures available for test takers with handicapping conditions. Warn test users of potential problems in using standard norms with modified tests or administration procedures that result in non-comparable scores.

16. When necessary and feasible, use appropriately modified forms or administration procedures for test takers with handicapping conditions. Interpret standard norms with care, in the light of the modifications that were made.

D. INFORMING TEST TAKERS

Under some circumstances, test developers have direct communication with test takers. Under other circumstances, test users communicate directly with test takers. Whichever group communicates directly with test takers should provide the information described below.

TEST DEVELOPERS OR TEST USERS SHOULD:

17. When a test is optional, provide test takers or their parents/guardians with information to help them to judge whether the test should be taken, or if an available alternative to the test should be used.

18. Provide test takers with the information they need to become familiar with the coverage of the test, the types of question formats, the directions, and appropriate test-taking strategies. Strive to make such information equally available to all test takers.

Under some circumstances, test developers have direct control of tests and test scores. Under other circumstances, test users have such control. Whichever group has direct control of tests and test scores should take the steps described below.

TEST DEVELOPERS OR TEST USERS SHOULD:

19. Provide test takers or their parents/guardians with information about rights test takers may have to obtain copies of tests and completed answer sheets, retake tests, have tests rescored, or cancel scores.

20. Tell test takers or their parents/guardians how long scores will be kept on file, and indicate to whom and under what circumstances test scores will or will not be released.

21. Describe the procedures that test takers or their parents/guardians may use to register complaints and have problems resolved.

Note: The membership of the Working Group that developed the Code of Fair Testing Practices in Education and of the Joint Committee on Testing Practices that guided the Working Group was as follows:

Additional copies of the Code may be obtained from the National Council on Measurement in Education, 1230 Seventeenth Street, NW, Washington, DC 20036, USA. Single copies are free of charge.

References

Abraham, K. 1952. The influence of oral eroticism on character formation. In *The selected papers of Karl Abraham*. London: Hogarth Press, 383–406.

Allport, G. W. and Odbert, H. S. 1936: Trait names: a psycho-lexical study. *Psychological Monographs*, Number 47.

Anastasi, A. 1961: *Psychological testing*. New York: Macmillan.

Anderson, M. 1992: *Intelligence and development*. Oxford: Blackwell.

Angleitner, A., Ostendorf, F. and John, O. P. 1990: Towards a taxonomy of personality descriptors in German: a psycholexical study. *European Journal of Personality* 4, 89–118.

Apter, M. A. 1975: *Experience and motivation*. London: Academic Press.

Assessment Systems Corporation 1989: *User's manual for the MicroCAT™ Testing System*. St Paul, MN: Assessment Systems Corporation.

Bachelor, A. 1988: How clients perceive therapist empathy: a content analysis of 'received' empathy. *Psychotherapy* 25, 227–40.

Bandura, A. 1986: *Social foundations of thought and action: a social cognitive theory*. Englewood-Cliffs, NJ: Prentice-Hall.

Bannister, D. and Mair, J. M. M. 1968: *The evaluation of personal constructs*. London: Academic Press.

Bannister, D. and Fransella, F. 1971: *Inquiring man: the theory of personal constructs*. London: Croom Helm.

Barrett, P. and Kline, P. 1981: The observation to variable ratio in factor analysis. *Personality Study and Group Behavior* 1, 23–33.

Barrett, P. and Kline, P. 1982a: An item and radial parcel factor analysis of the 16PF questionnaire. *Personality and Individual Differences* 3, 259–70.

Barrett, P. and Kline, P. 1982b: Personality factors in the Eysenck Personality Questionnaire. *Personality and Individual Differences* 1, 317–33.

Barrett, P. T. 1997: Process models in individual differences research. In Cooper, C. and Varma, V. (eds), *Processes in individual differences*. London: Routledge, 1–22.

Barrett, P. T. and Eysenck, H. J. 1992: Brain evoked potentials and intelligence: the Hendrickson paradigm. *Intelligence* 16, 361–81.

Barrett, P. T., Eysenck, H. J. and Lucking, S. 1986: Reaction time and intelligence – a replicated study. *Intelligence* 10, 9–40.

Bartlett, M. S. 1954: A note on multiplying factors for various chi-square approximations. *Journal of the Royal Statistical Society (Series B)* 16, 296–8.

Barton, K., Cattell, R. B. and Connor, D. V. 1972: The identification of state factors through P-technique factor analysis. *Journal of Clinical Psychology* 28, 459–63.

Bates, J. E. and Wachs, T. D. (eds) 1994: *Temperament: individual differences at the interface of biology and behavior*. Washington, DC: American Psychological Association.

Bates, T. and Eysenck, H. J. 1993: String length, attention and intelligence: focused attention reverses the string length/IQ relationship. *Personality and Individual Differences* 15, 363–71.

Bates, T., Stough, C., Mangan, G. and Pellett, O. 1995: Intelligence and the complexity of the averaged evoked potential: an attentional theory. *Intelligence* 20, 27–39.

Beck, A. T. and Emery, G. 1985: *Anxiety disorders and phobias: a cognitive perspective.* New York: Basic Books.

Benet, V. and Waller, N. 1995: The Big Seven model of personality description: evidence for its cross-cultural generality in a Spanish sample. *Journal of Personality and Social Psychology* 69, 701–18.

Bentler, P. M. 1989: *EQS structural equations program manual.* Los Angeles: BMDP Statistical Software Inc.

Benton, D. and Roberts, G. 1988: Effect of vitamin and mineral supplements on the intelligence of a sample of school children. *Lancet* No. 8578, 140–4.

Berk, R. A. (ed.) 1982: *Handbook of methods for detecting test bias.* Baltimore, MD: The Johns Hopkins University Press.

Bieri, J. 1966: Cognitive complexity and personality development. In Harvey, O. J. (ed.), *Experience, structure and adaptability.* New York: Springer, 178–208.

Block, J. 1961: *The Q-sort method in personality assessment and psychiatric research.* Springfield, IL: Thomas.

Block, J. 1971: *Lives through time.* Berkeley, CA: Bancroft Books.

Block, J. 1977: Advancing the psychology of personality: paradigmatic shift or improving the quality of research. In Magnusson, D. and Endler, N. (eds), *Personality at the crossroads.* Hillsdale, NJ: Lawrence Erlbaum, 37–64.

Block, J. 1995: A contrarian view of the five-factor approach to personality description. *Psychological Bulletin* 117, 187–215.

Boivin, D. B., Czeisler, C. A., Dijk, D.-J. *et al.* 1997: Complex interaction of the sleep–wake cycle and circadian phase modulates mood in healthy subjects. *Archives of General Psychiatry* (in press).

Bouchard, T. J. J. 1993: The genetic architecture of human intelligence. In Vernon, P. A. (ed.), *Biological approaches to the study of human intelligence.* New York: Ablex, 33–94.

Bouchard, T. J. J. 1995: Longitudinal studies of personality and intelligence: a behavior genetic and evolutionary psychology perspective. In Saklofske, D. H. and Zeidner, M. (eds), *International handbook of personality and intelligence.* New York: Plenum, 81–106.

Bouchard, T. J. J. and McGue, M. 1981: Familial studies of intelligence: a review. *Science* 212, 1055–8.

Bower, G. H. 1981: Mood and memory. *American Psychologist* 36, 129–48.

Bozarth, J. D. and Brodley, B. T. 1991: Actualization: a functional concept in client-centered therapy. *Journal of Social Behavior and Personality* 6, 45–59.

Brody, N. and Crowley, M. J. 1995: Environmental (and genetic) influences on personality and intelligence. In Saklofske, D. H. and Zeidner, M. (eds), *International handbook of personality and intelligence.* New York: Plenum, 59–80.

Brogden, H. E. 1969: Pattern, structure and the interpretation of factors. *Psychological Bulletin* 72, 375–8.

Brown, J. A. C. 1964: *Freud and the post-Freudians.* Harmondsworth: Penguin.

Brown, S. M. and Walberg, H. A. 1993: Motivational effects on test scores of elementary students. *Journal of Educational Research* 86, 133–6.

Brown, W. P. 1961: Conceptions of perceptual defence. *British Journal of Psychology Monograph Supplements*, No. 35.

Bruner, J. S. and Postman, L. 1947: Emotional selectivity in perception and reaction. *Journal of Personality* 16, 69–77.

Byravan, A. and Ramanaiah, N. V. 1995: Structure of the 16PF 5-ed from the perspective of the five-factor model. *Psychological Reports* 76, 555–60.

Byrne, D., Barry, J. and Nelson, D. 1963: Relation of the revised repression-sensitization scale to measures of self-description. *Psychological Reports* **13**, 323–34.

Caputi, P., Breiger, R. and Pattison, P. E. 1990: Analyzing implication grids using hierarchical models. *International Journal of Personal Construct Psychology* **3**, 77–90.

Carroll, J. B. 1980: *Report no. 163.* Chapel Hill, NC: The L. L. Thurstone Psychometric Laboratory.

Carroll, J. B. 1993: *Human cognitive abilities: a survey of factor-analytic studies.* Cambridge: Cambridge University Press.

Cattell, R. B. 1946: *Description and measurement of personality.* New York: World Book Company.

Cattell, R. B. 1952: *Factor analysis.* New York: Harper & Bros.

Cattell, R. B. 1957: *Personality and motivation structure and measurement.* New York: Harcourt, Brace & World.

Cattell, R. B. 1966: The scree test for the number of factors. *Multivariate Behavioral Research* **1**, 140–61.

Cattell, R. B. 1971: *Abilities, their structure, growth and action.* New York: Houghton Mifflin.

Cattell, R. B. 1973: *Personality and mood by questionnaire.* San Francisco: Jossey-Bass.

Cattell, R. B. 1978: *The scientific use of factor analysis in behavioral and life sciences.* New York: Plenum.

Cattell, R. B. 1982: The psychometry of objective motivation measurement. *British Journal of Educational Psychology* **52**, 234–41.

Cattell, R. B. 1986: The 16PF personality structure and Dr Eysenck. *Journal of Social Behavior and Personality* **1**, 153–60.

Cattell, R. B. and Warburton, F. W. 1967: *Objective personality and motivation tests: a theoretical foundation and practical compendium.* Urbana, IL: University of Illinois Press.

Cattell, R. B. and Child, D. 1975: *Motivation and dynamic structure.* London: Holt, Rinehart & Winston.

Cattell, R. B. and Kline, P. 1977: *The scientific analysis of personality and motivation.* London: Academic Press.

Cattell, R. B. and Vogelman, S. 1977: A comprehensive trial of the scree and KG criteria for determining the number of factors. *Journal of Educational Measurement* **14**, 289–325.

Cattell, R. B. and Schuerger, J. M. 1978: *Personality theory in action.* Champaign, IL: Institute for Personality and Ability Testing.

Cattell, R. B. and Krug, S. E. 1986: The number of factors in the 16PF: a review of the evidence with special emphasis on methodological problems. *Educational and Psychological Measurement* **46**, 509–22.

Cattell, R. B., Eber, H. W. and Tatsuoka, M. M. 1970a: *Handbook for the Sixteen Personality Factor Questionnaire.* Champaign, IL: Institute for Personality and Ability Testing.

Cattell, R. B., Horn, J. L. and Sweney, A. B. 1970b: *Manual for the Motivation Analysis Test.* Champaign, IL: Institute for Personality and Ability Testing.

Chambers, R. G. 1982: Correlation coefficients from 2 × 2 tables and from biserial data. *British Journal of Mathematical and Statistical Psychology* **35**, 216–27.

Cherny, S. S., Fulker, D. W. and Hewitt, J. K. 1996: Cognitive development from infancy to middle childhood. In Sternberg, R. J. and Grigoranko, E. (eds), *Intelligence: heredity and environment.* Cambridge: Cambridge University Press, 446–83.

Child, D. 1990: *The essentials of factor analysis*. London: Cassell.

Church, A. T., Katigbak, M. S. and Reyes, J. A. 1996: Towards a taxonomy of trait adjectives in Filipino: comparing personality lexicons across cultures. *European Journal of Psychology* 10, 3–24.

Claridge, G. S., Donald, J. R. and Birchall, P. M. 1981: Drug tolerance and personality: some implications for Eysenck's theory. *Personality and Individual Differences* 222, 153–66.

Clarkson, D. B. and Jennrich, R. I. 1988: Quartic rotation criteria and algorithms. *Psychometrika* 53, 251–9.

Clyde, D. J. 1963: *The Clyde Mood Scale*. Coral Gables, FL: Biometrics Laboratory, University of Miami.

Comrey, A. L. and Lee, H. B. 1992: *A first course in factor analysis*. Hillsdale, NJ: Lawrence Erlbaum Associates.

Conley, J. J. 1984: The hierarchy of consistency: a review and model of longitudinal findings on adult individual differences in intelligence, personality and self-opinion. *Personality and Individual Differences* 5, 11–25.

Coombs, W. N. and Schroeder, H. E. 1988: Generalised locus of control: an analysis of factor-analytic data. *Personality and Individual Differences* 9, 79–85.

Cooper, C. 1983: Correlation measures in item analysis. *British Journal of Mathematical and Statistical Psychology* 32, 102–5.

Cooper, C. 1988: The scientific status of the Defence Mechanism Test: a reply to Kline. *British Journal of Medical Psychology* 61, 381–4.

Cooper, C. 1995: Inside the WISC-III(UK). *Educational Psychology in Practice* 10, 215–19.

Cooper, C. 1997: Mood processes. In Cooper, C. and Varma, V. (eds), *Processes in individual differences*. London: Routledge, 89–107.

Cooper, C. (in press) Why many personality scales may be trivial. In Bermudez, J. C. (ed.), *Personality psychology in Europe*. Tilburg, The Netherlands: Tilburg University Press.

Cooper, C. and Kline, P. 1982: The internal structure of the Motivation Analysis Test. *British Journal of Educational Psychology* 52, 228–33.

Cooper, C. and Kline, P. 1986: An evaluation of the Defence Mechanism Test. *British Journal of Psychology* 77, 19–32.

Cooper, C. and Kline, P. 1989: A new objectively scored version of the Defence Mechanism Test. *Scandinavian Journal of Psychology* 30, 228–38.

Cooper, C. and McConville, C. 1989: The factorial equivalence of state anxiety/negative affect and state extraversion/positive affect. *Personality and Individual Differences* 10, 919–20.

Cooper, C., Kline, P. and May, J. 1986: The measurement of authoritarianism, psychoticism and other traits by objective tests: a cross-validation. *Personality and Individual Differences* 7, 15–21.

Coopersmith, S. 1967: *The antecedents of self-esteem*. San Francisco: Freeman.

Costa, P. T. J. and McCrae, R. R. 1976: Age differences in personality structure: a cluster-analytic approach. *Journal of Gerontology* 31, 564–70.

Costa, P. T. J. and McCrae, R. R. 1978: Objective personality assessment. In Storandt, M., Siegler, I. C. and Elias, M. F. (eds), *The clinical psychology of aging*. New York: Plenum, 59–92.

Costa, P. T. and McCrae, R. R. 1992a: *NEO-PI(R) professional manual*. Odessa, FL: Psychological Assessment Resources.

Costa, P. T. and McCrae, R. R. 1992b: 4 ways 5 factors are basic. *Personality and Individual Differences* 13, 653–65.

Cronbach, L. J. 1946: Response sets and test validity. *Educational and Psychological Measurement* 6, 475–94.

Cronbach, L. J. 1994: *Essentials of psychological testing*. New York: HarperCollins.

Cronbach, L. J., Gleser, G. C., Nanda, H. and Rajaratnam, N. 1972: *The dependability of behavioral measurements*. New York: Wiley.

Crowne, D. P. and Marlowe, D. 1964: *The approval motive*. New York: Wiley.

Curran, J. P. and Cattell, R. B. 1976: *Manual of the Eight State Questionnaire*. Champaign, IL: Institute for Personality and Ability Testing.

Deary, I. J. and Carryl, P. G. 1993: Intelligence, EEG and evoked potentials. In Vernon, P. A. (ed.), *Biological approaches to the study of human intelligence*. Norwood, NJ: Ablex, 259–316.

Deary, I. J. and Stough, C. 1996: Intelligence and inspection time: achievements, prospects and problems. *American Psychologist* **51**, 599–608.

Digman, J. M. 1990: Personality structure: the emergence of the five-factor model. *Annual Review of Psychology* **41**, 417–40.

Dixon, N. F. 1981: *Preconscious processing*. New York: Wiley.

Dobson, P. 1988: The correction of correlation coefficients for restriction of range when restriction results from the truncation of a normally distributed variable. *British Journal of Mathematical and Statistical Psychology* **41**, 227–34.

Eaves, L. J. and Yonng, P. A. 1981: Genetical theory and personality differences. In Lynn, R. (ed.), *Dimensions of personality*. Oxford: Pergamon, 127–79.

Eaves, L., Eysenck, H. J. and Martin, N. G. 1989: *Genes, culture and personality*. New York: Academic Press.

Ebmeier, K. P., Deary, I. J., O'Carroll, R. E., Prentice, N., Morfoot, A. P. R. and Goodwin, G. M. 1994: Personality associations with the uptake of the cerebral blood flow marker 99 m-Tc-Exametazime estimated with single photon emission tomography. *Personality and Individual Differences* **17**, 587–95.

Edwards, A. L. 1957: *The social desirability variable in personality research*. New York: Dryden Press.

Egan, V. and Deary, I. J. 1992: Are specific inspection time strategies prevented by concurrent tasks? *Intelligence* **16**, 151–68.

Ekstrom, R. B., French, J. W. and Harman, H. H. 1976: *Manual for the Kit of Factor-Referenced Cognitive Tests*. Princeton, NJ: Educational Testing Service.

Erdelyi, M. H. 1974: A new look at the New Look. *Psychological Review* **81**, 1–25.

Erdelyi, M. H. 1985: *Psychoanalysis: Freud's cognitive psychology*. New York: Freeman.

Ertl, J. P. and Schafer, E. W. P. 1969: Brain response correlates of psychometric intelligence. *Nature* **223**, 421–2.

Evans, F. R. and Pike, L. W. 1973: The effects of instruction for three mathematics item formats. *Journal of Educational Measurement* **10**, 257–72.

Eysenck, H. J. 1947: Dimensions of personality. New York: Praeger.

Eysenck, H. J. 1953: The logical basis of factor analysis. *American Psychologist* **8**, 105–14.

Eysenck, H. J. 1959: Review of the Rorschach inkblots. In Buros, O. K. (ed.), *Fifth Mental Measurement Yearbook*. New Jersey: Gryphon Press, 276–8.

Eysenck, H. J. 1962: *Know your own IQ*. Harmondsworth: Penguin.

Eysenck, H. J. 1967: *The biological basis of personality*. Springfield, IL: Charles C. Thomas.

Eysenck, H. J. 1973: Personality, learning and anxiety. In Eysenck, H. J. (ed.), *Handbook of abnormal psychology*. London: Pitman, 390–419.

Eysenck, H. J. 1982: Introduction. In Eysenck, H. J. (ed.), *A model for intelligence*. Berlin: Springer-Verlag, 1–12.

Eysenck, H. J. 1985: *The decline and fall of the Freudian empire*. Harmondsworth: Penguin.

Eysenck, H. J. 1986: The theory of intelligence and the neurophysiology of cognition. In Sternberg, R. J. (ed.), *Advances in the psychology of human intelligence*. Hillsdale, NJ: Erlbaum, 1–34.

Eysenck, H. J. 1992: 4 ways 5 factors are not basic. *Personality and Individual Differences* 13, 667–73.

Eysenck, H. J. 1994: Personality: biological foundations. In Vernon, P. A. (ed.), *The neuropsychology of individual differences*. San Diego, CA: Academic Press, 151–208.

Eysenck, H. J. 1997: Can the study of personality ever be objective? In Cooper, C. and Varma, V. (eds), *Processes in individual differences*. London: Routledge, 23–38.

Eysenck, H. J. and Levey, A. 1972: Conditioning, introversion-extroversion and the strength of the nervous system. In Nebylitsyn, V. D. and Gray, J. A. (eds), *Biological basis of individual behavior*. New York: Academic Press, 206–20.

Eysenck, H. J. and Wilson, G. D. 1976: *Know your own personality*. Harmondsworth: Penguin.

Eysenck, H. J. and Eysenck, M. W. 1985: *Personality and individual differences*. New York: Plenum Press.

Eysenck, M. W. 1992: *Anxiety: the cognitive perspective*. Hove: Lawrence Erlbaum Associates.

Eysenck, M. W. and Byrne, A. 1992: Anxiety and susceptibility to distraction. *Personality and Individual Differences* 13, 793–8.

Farrell, B. A. 1981: *The standing of psychoanalysis*. Oxford: Oxford University Press.

Feixas, G., Lopez-Moliner, J., Navarro-Montes, J. and Tudela-Mari, M. 1992: The stability of structural measures derived from repertory grids. *International Journal of Personal Construct Psychology* 5, 25–39.

Fenichel, O. 1946: *The psychoanalytic theory of neurosis*. London: Routledge & Kegan Paul.

Fisher, S. and Greenberg, R. P. 1996: *Freud scientifically appraised*. New York: John Wiley.

Floderus-Myrhed, B., Pedersen, N. and Rasmuson, I. 1980: Assessment of heritability for personality, based on a short form of the Eysenck Personality Inventory: a study of 12,898 twin pairs. *Brain Genetics* 10, 153–62.

Flynn, J. R. 1987: Massive IQ gains in 14 nations: what IQ tests really measure. *Psychological Bulletin* 101, 171–91.

Folkman, S. and Lazarus, R. S. 1980: An analysis of coping in a middle-aged community sample. *Journal of Health and Social Behavior* 21, 219–39.

Fransella, F. and Bannister, D. 1977: *A manual for repertory grid technique*. London: Academic Press.

Fransella, F. and Thomas, L. F. (eds) 1988: *Experimenting with personal construct psychology*. London: Routledge.

Freud, S. 1917/1964: *Introductory lectures on psychoanalysis*. Harmondsworth: Penguin.

Freud, S. 1920: Beyond the pleasure principle. In Strachey, J. (ed.), *Standard edition of the works of Sigmund Freud. Vol. XVIII*. London: Hogarth Press, 1–40.

Freud, S. 1923/1955: *Historical and expository works on psychoanalysis. Two encyclopedia articles: libido theory*. Harmondsworth: Penguin.

Freud, S. 1926/1955: *Inhibitions, symptoms and anxiety*. Harmondsworth: Penguin.

Freud, S. 1932: *New introductory lectures on psychoanalysis*. Harmondsworth: Penguin.

Freud, S. 1939: *An outline of psychoanalysis*. Harmondsworth: Penguin.

Freud, S. 1957: *Five lectures on psychoanalysis*. Harmondsworth: Penguin.

Freud, S. 1959: *An autobiographical study*. Harmondsworth: Penguin.

Freud, S. and Breuer, J. 1893/1964: *Studies in hysteria*. Harmondsworth: Penguin.

Gale, A. 1980: Naive parallelism: simply synchronise several simultaneous models. In Chapman, A. J. and Jones, D. M. (eds), *Models of man*. Leicester: British Psychological Society, 63–74.

Gale, A. 1983: Electroencephalographic studies of extraversion–introversion: a case study in the psychophysiology of individual differences. *Personality and Individual Differences* 4, 371–80.

Gale, A. and Eysenck, M. W. (eds) 1992: *Handbook of individual differences: biological perspectives*. Chichester: Wiley.

Galton, F. 1883: *Inquiries into human faculty and its development*. London: Macmillan.

Ghiselli, E. E. 1966: *The validity of occupational aptitude tests*. New York: Wiley.

Gilbert, D. G., Johnson, S., Gilbert, B. O. and McColloch, M. A. 1991: Event-related potential correlates of IQ. *Personality and Individual Differences* 12, 1183–4.

Goldberg, L. R. 1990: An alternative 'description of personality': the Big-Five structure. *Journal of Personality and Social Psychology* 59, 1216–29.

Gorsuch, R. L. 1983: *Factor analysis*. Hillsdale, NJ: Lawrence Erlbaum Associates.

Gough, H. G. 1975: *The California Personality Inventory*. Palo Alto, CA: Consulting Psychologists Press.

Graham, J. R. 1990: *MMPI-2: Assessing personality and psychopathology*. New York: Oxford University Press.

Gray, J. 1985: A whole and its parts: behaviour, the brain, cognition and emotion. *Bulletin of the British Psychological Society* 38, 99–112.

Gray, J. A. 1972: The psychophysiological nature of introversion–extraversion: a modification of Eysenck's theory. In Nebylitsyn, V. D. and Gray, J. A. (eds), *Biological bases of individual behaviour*. London: Academic Press, 151–88.

Gray, J. A. 1982: *The neuropsychology of anxiety*. Oxford: Clarendon Press.

Gruen, R. J., Folkman, S. H. and Lazarus, R. S. 1988: Centrality and individual differences in the meaning of daily hassles. *Journal of Personality* 56, 743–62.

Guadagnoli, E. and Velicer, W. F. 1988: Relation of sample size to the stability of component patterns. *Psychological Bulletin* 103, 265–75.

Guilford, J. P. 1967: *The nature of human intelligence*. New York: McGraw-Hill.

Guilford, J. P. and Fruchter, B. 1978: *Fundamental statistics in psychology and education*. Tokyo: McGraw-Hill Kogakusha.

Guilford, J. S., Zimmerman, W. S. and Guilford, J. P. 1976: *The Guilford–Zimmerman Temperament Survey handbook*. San Diego, CA: Edits.

Gulliksen, H. 1986: Perspective on educational measurement. *Applied Psychological Measurement* 10, 109–32.

Gustafsson, J.-E. 1981: A unifying model for the structure of intellectual abilities. *Intelligence* 8, 179–203.

Guttman, L. 1954: Some necessary and sufficient conditions for common factor analysis. *Psychometrika* 19, 149–61.

Haier, R. J., Sokolski, K., Katz, M. and Buchsbaum, M. S. 1987: The study of personality with positron emission tomography. In Strelau, J. and Eysenck, H. J. (eds), *Personality dimensions and arousal*. New York: Plenum, 251–67.

Hakstian, A. R. and Mueller, V. J. 1973: Some notes on the number of factors problem. *Multivariate Behavioral Research* 8, 461–75.

Hakstian, R. N. and Cattell, R. B. 1976: *Manual for the Comprehensive Ability Battery*. Champaign, IL: Institute for Personality and Ability Testing.

Hakstian, R. N. and Cattell, R. B. 1978: Higher stratum ability structure on a basis of 20 primary abilities. *Journal of Educational Psychology* 70, 657–9.

Hall, C. S. and van de Castle, R. L. 1963: An empirical investigation of the castration complex in dreams. *Journal of Personality* 33, 20–9.

Hall, D. P., Sing, H. C. and Romanowski, A. J. 1991: Identification and characterisation of greater mood variance in depression. *American Journal of Psychiatry* **148**, 1341–5.

Hambleton, R. K. and Swaminathan, H. 1985: *Item response theory: principles and applications.* Boston, MA: Kluwer-Nijhoff.

Hambleton, R. K., Swaminathan, H. and Rogers, H. J. 1991: *Fundamentals of item response theory.* Newbury Park, CA: Sage.

Hammer, E. F. 1953: An investigation of sexual symbolism: a study of HTPs of eugenically sterilised subjects. *Journal of Projective Techniques* **17**, 401–15.

Hampson, S. 1997: The social psychology of personality. In Cooper, C. and Varma, V. (eds), *Processes in individual differences.* London: Methuen, 73–88.

Harman, H. H. 1976: *Modern factor analysis.* Chicago: University of Chicago Press.

Harris, C. W. 1967: On factors and factor scores. *Psychometrika* **32**, 363–79.

Hathaway, S. R. and McKinley, J. C. 1967: *The Minnesota Multiphasic Personality Inventory Manual (revised).* New York: Psychological Corporation.

Hebb, D. O. 1949: *The organization of behavior.* New York: Wiley.

Hendrickson, D. E. 1972: An integrated molar/molecular model of the brain. *Psychological Reports* **30**, 343–68.

Hendrickson, D. E. 1982: The biological basis of intelligence. Part II. Measurement. In Eysenck, H. J. (ed.), *A model for intelligence.* Berlin: Springer-Verlag, 151–96.

Hendrickson, D. E. and Hendrickson, A. E. 1980: The biological basis of individual differences in intelligence. *Personality and Individual Differences* **1**, 3–33.

Hepburn, L. and Eysenck, M. W. 1989: Personality, average mood and mood variability. *Personality and Individual Differences* **10**, 975–83.

Herbart, J. F. 1824: *Psychologie als Wissenschaft.* Königsberg, Prussia: Unzev.

Herriott, P. 1989: *Assessment and selection in organisations.* Chichester: Wiley.

Herrnstein, R. J. and Murray, C. 1994: *The bell curve: intelligence and class structure in American life.* New York: The Free Press.

Holmstrom, R. W., Silber, D. E. and Karp, S. A. 1990: Development of the Apperceptive Personality Test. *Journal of Personality Assessment* **54**, 252–64.

Honess, T. 1979: Children's implicit theories of their peers: a developmental analysis. *British Journal of Psychology* **70**, 417–24.

Horn, J. L. and Cattell, R. B. 1966: Refinement and test of the theory of fluid and crystallised intelligence. *Journal of Educational Psychology* **57**, 253–70.

Howarth, E. 1988: Mood differences between the four Galen types. *Personality and Individual Differences* **9**, 173–5.

Howarth, E. and Young, P. D. 1986: Patterns of mood change. *Personality and Individual Differences* **7**, 275–81.

Howe, M. J. A. 1988: Intelligence as explanation. *British Journal of Psychology* **79**, 349–60.

Howell, D. C. 1992: *Statistical methods for psychology.* Belmont, CA: Duxbury.

Hundleby, J. D. and Connor, W. H. 1968: Interrelationships between personality inventories: the 16PF, MMPI and MPI. *Journal of Consulting and Clinical Psychology* **32**, 152–7.

Hunt, E. B. 1978: The mechanics of verbal ability. *Psychological Review* **85**, 109–30.

Ililivich, D. and Glaser, G. C. 1986: *Measuring defenses with the Defense Mechanisms Inventory.* Owosso, MI: DMI Associates.

Isen, A. M. and Levin, P. F. 1972: The effect of feeling good on helping: cookies and kindness. *Journal of Personality and Social Psychology* **34**, 384–8.

Izard, C. E., Dougherty, F. E., Bloxom, B. M. and Kotsch, N. E. 1982: *The Differential Emotions Scale: a method of measuring the subjective experience of discrete emotions.* Nashville, TE: Department of Psychology, Vanderbilt University.

Jackson, D. N., Paunonen, S. V., Fraboni, M. and Goffin, R. D. 1995: A five-factor versus a six-factor model of personality structure. *Personality and Individual Differences* 20, 33–45.

Jennrich, R. I. and Sampson, P. F. 1966: Rotation for simple loadings. *Psychometrika* 31, 313–23.

Jensen, A. R. 1980: *Bias in mental testing*. New York: The Free Press.

Jensen, A. R. 1982: Reaction time and psychometric *g*. In Eysenck, H. J. (ed.), *A model for intelligence*. Berlin: Springer-Verlag, 93–132.

Jensen, A. R. 1997: The psychophysiology of *g*. In Cooper, C. and Varma, V. (eds), *Process models of individual differences*. London: Routledge, 108–25.

Jensen, A. R. and Munroe, E. 1974: Reaction time, movement time and intelligence. *Intelligence* 3, 121–6.

Jones, E. 1953: *The life and work of Sigmund Freud*. Harmondsworth: Penguin.

Joy, V. L. 1963: Repression-sensitisation personality and interpersonal behavior. Unpublished PhD thesis, University of Texas, Austin, TX.

Kaiser, H. 1958: The VARIMAX criterion for analytic rotation in factor analysis. *Psychometrika* 23, 187–200.

Kaiser, H. F. 1960: The application of electronic computers in factor analysis. *Educational and Psychological Measurement* 20, 141–51.

Kaiser, H. F. 1990: On Guttman's proof that squared multiple correlations are lower bounds for communalities. *Psychological Reports* 67, 1004–6.

Kamin, L. J. 1974: *The science and politics of IQ*. Harmondsworth: Penguin.

Kanfer, P. L., Ackerman, Y. M. and Goff, M. 1995: Personality and intelligence in industrial and organizational psychology. In Saklofske, D. H. and Zeidner, M. (eds), *International handbook of personality and intelligence*. New York: Plenum, 577–602.

Kelly, G. A. 1955: *The psychology of personal constructs*. New York: Norton.

Kelly, G. A. 1963: *The autobiography of a theory*. Columbus, OH: Ohio State University.

Kline, P. 1967: Obsessional traits, obsessional symptoms and general emotionality in a normal population. *British Journal of Medical Psychology* 40, 153–7.

Kline, P. 1968: Obsessional traits, obsessional symptoms and anal erotism. *British Journal of Medical Psychology* 41, 299–305.

Kline, P. 1969: The anal character: a cross-cultural study in Ghana. *British Journal of Social and Clinical Psychology* 8, 201–10.

Kline, P. 1981: *Fact and fantasy in Freudian theory*. London: Methuen.

Kline, P. 1984: *Personality and Freudian theory*. London: Methuen.

Kline, P. 1986: *A handbook of test construction*. London: Methuen.

Kline, P. 1991: *Intelligence: the psychometric view*. London: Routledge.

Kline, P. 1993: *The handbook of psychological testing*. London: Routledge.

Kline, P. 1994: *An easy guide to factor analysis*. London: Routledge.

Kline, P. and Storey, R. 1977: A factor-analytic study of the oral character. *British Journal of Social and Clinical Psychology* 16, 317–28.

Kline, P. and Cooper, C. 1984a: A construct validation of the Objective-Analytic Test Battery (OATB). *Personality and Individual Differences* 5, 323–37.

Kline, P. and Cooper, C. 1984b: The factor structure of the Comprehensive Ability Battery. *British Journal of Educational Psychology* 54, 106–10.

Kragh, U. 1955: *The actual-genetic model of perception-personality*. Lund: Gleerup.

Kragh, U. 1962: Prediction of success in Danish attack divers by the Defense Mechanism Test (DMT). *Perceptual and Motor Skills* 15, 103–6.

Kragh, U. 1983: Studying effects of psychotherapy by the Defense Mechanism Test: two case illustrations. *Archiv für Psychologie* 135, 73–82.

Kuhn, M. H. and McPartland, T. S. 1954: An empirical investigation of self-attitudes. *American Sociological Review* 19, 68–76.

2

LaBuda, M. C., deFries, J. C. and Julker, D. W. 1987: Genetic and environmental covariance structures among WISC-R subtests: a twin study. *Intelligence* 11, 233–44.

Lacey, J. I. and Lacey, B. C. 1970: *Physiological correlates of emotion.* New York: Academic Press.

Larsen, R. J. and Kasimatis, M. 1990: Individual differences in entrainment of mood to the weekly calendar. *Personality and Individual Differences* 58, 164–71.

Lazarus, R. S. 1991: *Emotion and adaptation.* Oxford: Oxford University Press.

Lesch, K.-P., Bengel, D., Heils, A. *et al.* 1996: Association of anxiety-related traits with a polymorphism in the serotonin transporter gene regulatory region. *Science* 274, 1527–31.

Loehlin, J. C. 1987: *Latent variable models: an introduction to factor, path and structural analysis.* Hillsdale, NJ: Lawrence Erlbaum Associates.

Loehlin, J. C. 1992: *Genes and environment in personality development.* Newbury Park, CA: Sage.

Loehlin, J. C. and Nichols, R. C. 1976: *Heredity, environment and personality.* Austin, TX: University of Texas Press.

Long, J. S. 1983: *Confirmatory factor analysis: a preface to LISREL.* Beverly Hills, CA: Sage.

Longstreth, L. E. 1984: Jensen's reaction time investigations: a critique. *Intelligence* 8, 139–60.

Lord, F. M. and Novick, M. R. 1968: *Statistical theory of mental test scores.* New York: Addison-Wesley.

Lorr, M. and McNair, D. M. 1988: *Manual, Profile of Mood States, Bipolar Form.* San Diego, CA: Educational and Industrial Testing Service.

Lorr, M. and Wunderlich, R. A. 1988: Self-esteem and negative affect. *Journal of Clinical Psychology* 44, 36–9.

Lynn, R. 1993: Nutrition and intelligence. In Vernon, P. A. (ed.), *Biological approaches to the study of human intelligence.* Norwood, NJ: Ablex, 243–58.

McClelland, D. C. 1961: *Achieving society.* Princeton, NJ: Van Nostrand.

McConville, C. 1992: Personality, motivational and situational influences on mood variability. Unpublished PhD thesis, University of Ulster, Coleraine, County Londonderry.

McConville, C. and Cooper, C. 1992a: Mood variability and personality. *Personality and Individual Differences* 13, 1213–21.

McConville, C. and Cooper, C. 1992b: The structure of moods. *Personality and Individual Differences* 13, 909–19.

McConville, C. and Cooper, C. 1996: Mood variability and depression. *Current Psychology* 14, 329–38.

McDonald, R. P. and Burr, E. J. 1967: A comparison of four methods of constructing factor scores. *Psychometrika* 32, 381–401.

McDougall, W. 1932: *The energies of men.* London: Methuen.

McGue, M., Bouchard, T. J. Jr, Iacono, W. G. and Lykken, D. T. 1993: Behavioral genetics of cognitive ability: a life-span perspective. In Plomin, R. and McClearn, G. E. (eds), *Nature, nurture and psychology.* Washington, DC: American Psychological Association, 59–76.

Mackenzie, B. and Bingham, E. 1985: IQ, inspection time and response strategies in a university population. *Australian Journal of Psychology* 37, 257–68.

Martin, M. 1990: On the induction of moods. *Clinical Psychology Review* 10, 669–97.

Mathew, R. J., Weinman, M. L. and Barr, D. L. 1984: Personality and regional cerebral blood flow. *British Journal of Psychiatry* 144, 529–32.

Matthews, G. 1983: Personality, arousal states and intellectual performance. Unpublished PhD thesis, University of Cambridge, Cambridge.

Matthews, G. 1989: The factor structure of the 16PF: 12 primary and 3 secondary factors. *Personality and Individual Differences* 10, 931–40.

Matthews, G. and Dorn, L. 1989: IQ and choice reaction time: an information processing analysis. *Intelligence* 13, 299–317.

Matthews, G. and Amelang, M. 1993: Extraversion, arousal theory and performance: a study of individual differences. *Personality and Individual Differences* 14, 347–63.

Matthews, G., Jones, G. and Chamberlain, A. G. 1990: Refining the measurement of mood: the UWIST Mood Adjective Checklist. *British Journal of Psychology* 81, 17–42.

May, J., Cooper, C. and Kline, P. 1986: The reliability of reaction times in some elementary cognitive tasks: a brief research note. *Personality and Individual Differences* 7, 893–5.

May, J., Kline, P. and Cooper, C. 1987: A brief computerized form of a schematic analogy task. *British Journal of Psychology* 78, 29–36.

Meissner, W. W. 1958: Affective response to death symbols. *Journal of Abnormal and Social Psychology* 56, 295–9.

Minturn, L. 1965: A cross-cultural linguistic analysis of Freudian symbols. *Ethnology* 4, 336–42.

Mischel, W. 1968: *Personality and assessment*. New York: Wiley.

Mischel, W. 1986: *Introduction to personality*. New York: CBS College Publishing.

Mogg, K., Mathews, A. and Weinman, J. 1987: Memory bias in clinical anxiety. *Journal of Abnormal Psychology* 96, 94–8.

Morris, W. N. 1985: *Mood: the frame of mind*. New York: Springer-Verlag.

Moshe, R. B. and Zeidner, M. 1995: Constructing personality and intelligence instruments: methods and issues. In Saklofske, D. H. and Zeidner, M. (eds), *International handbook of personality and intelligence*. New York: Plenum, 475–504.

Mulhern, G. A. 1997: Intelligence and cognitive processing. In Cooper, C. and Varma, V. (eds), *Processes in individual differences*. London: Routledge, 149–63.

Murray, H. A. 1938: *Explorations in personality*. New York: Oxford University Press.

Neimeyer, G. J. and Neimeyer, R. A. (eds) 1990: *Advances in personal construct psychology: a research annual*. Greenwich, CT: JAI Press.

Neimeyer, R. A. 1985: *The development of personal construct psychology*. Lincoln: University of Nebraska Press.

Neimeyer, R. A. and Neimeyer, G. J. (eds) 1992: *Advances in personal construct psychology*. Greenwich, CT: JAI Press.

Neubauer, A. C. 1991: Intelligence and RT: a modified Hick paradigm and a new RT paradigm. *Intelligence* 15, 175–92.

Neuman, T. 1971: Perceptual defence organisation as a predictor of the pilot's adaptive behaviour in military flying. In Anderson, J. D. (ed.), *Reports of the Ninth Conference for Aviation Psychology*. Brussels: Western European Association for Aviation Psychology, 17–25.

Neuman, T. 1978: *Dimensioning and validation of percept-genetic defence mechanisms. FOA Report C-55020–H6* (in Swedish). Stockholm: Research Establishment of the Swedish Ministry of Defence, Central Department 5.

Norman, W. T. 1967: *2800 personality trait descriptors: normative operating characteristics for a university population*. Ann Arbor: Department of Psychological Sciences, University of Michigan.

Nowlis, J. and Nowlis, H. 1956: The description and analysis of mood. *Annals of the New York Academy of Science 55*, 345–55.

Nunnally, J. C. 1978: *Psychometric theory*. New York: McGraw-Hill.

O'Gorman, J. G. and Lloyd, J. E. M. 1987: Extraversion, impulsiveness and EEG alpha activity. *Personality and Individual Differences* 8, 257–318.

Olweus, D. 1980: The consistency issue in personality psychology revisited. *British Journal of Social and Clinical Psychology* **19**, 377–90.

Osterlind, S. J. 1983: *Test item bias*. Beverly Hills, CA: Sage Publications.

Parker, J. D., Bagby, R. M. and Summerfeldt, L. J. 1993: Confirmatory factor analysis of the revised NEO personality inventory. *Personality and Individual Differences* **15**, 463–6.

Pedersen, N. and Lichtenstein, P. 1997: Biometric analyses of human abilities. In Cooper, C. and Varma, V. (eds), *Processes in individual differences*. London: Routledge, 126–48.

Pederson, N. L., Plomin, R., McClearn, G. E. and Friberg, L. 1988: Neuroticism, extraversion and related traits in adult twins reared apart and reared together. *Journal of Personality and Social Psychology* **55**, 950–7.

Pennebaker, J. W. 1982: *The psychology of physical symptoms*. New York: Springer.

Plomin, R. 1988: The nature and nurture of cognitive abilities. In Sternberg, R. J. (ed.), *Advances in the psychology of human intelligence*. Hillsdale, NJ: Erlbaum, 1–33.

Plomin, R. and Daniels, D. 1987: Why are children in the same family so different from one another? *Behavioral and Brain Science* **10**, 1–16.

Plomin, R. and Rende, R. 1991: Human behavior genetics. *Annual Review of Psychology* **42**, 181–90.

Plomin, R., Loehlin, J. C. and DeFries, J. C. 1985: Genetic and environmental components of 'environmental' influences. *Developmental Psychology* **21**, 391–402.

Rachman, S. and Wilson, G. T. 1980: *The effects of psychological therapy*. London: Pergamon Press.

Raju, N. 1988: The area between two item characteristic curves. *Psychometrika* **53**, 495–502.

Ramey, C. T. 1992: High risk children and IQ: altering intergenerational patterns. *Intelligence* **16**, 239–56.

Raskin, N. J. and Rogers, C. R. 1989: Person-centred therapy. In Corsini, R. J. and Wedding, D. (eds), *Current psychotherapies*. Itasca, IL: F. E. Peacock, 154–94.

Reed, T. E. 1984: Mechanism for the heritability of intelligence. *Nature* **311**, 417.

Reed, T. E. and Jensen, A. R. 1991: Arm nerve conduction velocity (NCV), brain NCV, reaction time and intelligence. *Intelligence* **15**, 33–47.

Revelle, W. 1995: Personality processes. *Annual Review of Psychology* **46**, 295–328.

Reynolds, C. R. 1995: Test bias and the assessment of intelligence and personality. In Saklofske, D. H. and Zeidner, M. (eds), *International handbook of personality and intelligence*. New York: Plenum, 545–76.

Rijsdijk, F. V., Boomsma, D. L. and Vernon, P. A. 1995: Genetic analysis of peripheral nerve conduction in twins. *Behavior Genetics* **25**, 341–8.

Rogers, C. R. 1951: *Client-centered therapy*. Boston, MA: Houghton Mifflin.

Rogers, C. R. 1959: A theory of therapy, personality and interpersonal relationships, as developed in the client-centered framework. In Koch, S. (ed.), *Psychology: a study of a science*. New York: McGraw-Hill, 184–256.

Rogers, C. R. 1967: *On becoming a person*. London: Constable.

Rogers, C. R. 1992a: The necessary and sufficient conditions of therapeutic personality change. *Journal of Consulting and Clinical Psychology* **60**, 827–32.

Rogers, C. R. 1992b: The processes of therapy. *Journal of Consulting and Clinical Psychology* **60**, 163–4.

Rogers, C. R., Kirschenbaum, H. and Henderson, V.-L. (eds) 1989: *The Carl Rogers reader*. Boston, MA: Houghton Mifflin.

Rose, R. J. 1988: Genetic and environmental variance in content dimensions of the MMPI. *Journal of Personality and Social Psychology* **55**, 302–11.

Rose, R. J., Koskenvuo, M., Kaprio, J., Sarna, S. and Langinvaino, H. 1988: Shared genes, shared experiences and similarity of personality-data from 14,288 adult Finnish co-twins. *Journal of Personality and Social Psychology* **54**, 161–71.

Rosenberg, M. 1965: *Society and the adolescent self-image.* Princeton, NJ: Princeton University Press.

Royce, J. M., Darlington, R. B. and Murray, H. W. 1983: Pooled analyses: findings across studies. In *As the twig is bent ... lasting effects of preschool programs.* Consortium for Longitudinal Studies. Hillsdale, NJ: Erlbaum, 411–59.

Rushton, J. P., Brainerd, C. J. and Preisley, M. 1983: Behavioral development and construct-validity: the principle of aggregation. *Psychological Bulletin* **94**, 18–38.

Rust, J. and Golombock, S. 1989: *Modern psychometrics.* London: Routledge.

Rykman, R. M. 1992: *Theories of personality.* Belmont, CA: Wadsworth.

Sattler, J. M. and Gwynne, J. 1987: White examiners generally do not impede the intelligence test performance of black children. *Journal of Consulting and Clinical Psychology* **50**, 196–208.

Schmid, J. and Leiman, J. M. 1957: The development of hierarchical factor solutions. *Psychometrika* **22**, 53–61.

Schnurr, P. P. 1989: Endogenous factors associated with mood. In Morris, W. N., *Mood: the frame of mind.* Berlin: Springer-Verlag, 35–69.

Schwarzer, R., van der Ploeg, H. M. and Spielberger, C. D. (eds) 1989: *Advances in test anxiety research. Vol. 6.* Amsterdam: Swets & Zeitlinger.

Shagass, C., Roemer, R. A. and Straumanis, J. J. 1981: Intelligence as a factor in evoked potential studies of psychopathology. II. Correlations between treatment-associate changes in IQ and evoked potentials. *Biological Psychiatry* **16**, 1031–40.

Snow, R. E. and Yalow, E. 1982: Education and intelligence. In Sternberg, R. J. (ed.), *Handbook of human intelligence.* Cambridge: Cambridge University Press, 493–585.

Snyderman, M. and Rothman, S. 1987: Survey of expert opinion on intelligence and aptitude testing. *American Psychologist* **42**, 137–44.

Spearman, C. 1904: General intelligence objectively determined and measured. *American Journal of Psychology* **15**, 201–93.

Spector, P. E. 1992: *Summated rating scale construction.* Newbury Park, CA: Sage.

Spielberger, C. D. 1980: *Preliminary professional manual for the Test Anxiety Inventory.* Palo Alto, CA: Consulting Psychologists Press.

Spielberger, C. D., Gorsuch, R. L. and Lushene, R. E. 1970: *STAI manual for the state trait inventory.* Palo Alto, CA: Consulting Psychologists Press.

Stafford-Clarke, D. 1965: *What Freud really said.* Harmondsworth: Penguin.

Stankov, L., Boyle, G. J. and Cattell, R. B. 1995: Models and paradigms in personality and intelligence research. In Saklofske, D. H. and Zeidner, M. (eds), *International handbook of personality and intelligence.* New York: Plenum, 15–44.

Steele, C. M. and Aronson, J. 1995: Stereotype threat and the intellectual test performance of African Americans. *Journal of Personality and Social Psychology* **69**, 797–811.

Stephenson, W. 1953: *The study of behavior.* Chicago: University of Chicago Press.

Sternberg, R. J. 1977: *Intelligence, information processing and analogical reasoning: the componential analysis of human abilities.* Hillsdale, NJ: Lawrence Erlbaum.

Sternberg, R. J. (ed.) 1982: *Handbook of human intelligence.* Cambridge: Cambridge University Press.

Sternberg, R. J. 1985: *Beyond IQ.* Cambridge: Cambridge University Press.

Sternberg, R. J. 1988: Explaining away intelligence: a reply to Howe. *British Journal of Psychology* **79**, 527–34.

Sternberg, R. J. 1994: Thinking styles. In Sternberg, R. J. and Ruzgis, P. (eds), *Personality and intelligence.* Cambridge: Cambridge University Press, 169–87.

Sternberg, S. 1969: High-speed scanning in human memory. *Science* **153**, 652–4.

Stevens, R. 1983: *Freud and psychoanalysis*. Milton Keynes: Open University Press.

Stevenson, J. 1997: The genetic basis of personality. In Cooper, C. and Varma, V. (eds), *Processes in individual differences*. London: Routledge, 39–58.

Storm, C. and Storm, T. 1987: A taxonomic study of the vocabulary of emotions. *Journal of Personality and Social Psychology* 53, 805–16.

Stough, C. K. K., Nettelbeck, T. and Cooper, C. J. 1990: Evoked brain potentials, string length and intelligence. *Personality and Individual Differences* 11, 401–6.

Suinn, R. M. and Geiger, J. 1965: Stress and the stability of self- and other attitudes. *Journal of General Psychology* 73, 177–80.

Sulloway, F. 1979: *Freud, biologist of the mind*. London: Burnett.

Swaminathan, H. and Gifford, J. A. 1983: Estimation of parameters in the three-parameter latent trait model. In Weiss, D. (ed.), *New horizons in testing*. New York: Academic Press, 14–32.

Sweetland, R. C. and Keyser, D. J. (eds) 1991: *Tests*, 3rd edn. Austin, TX: Pro-Ed.

Tabatchnick, B. G. and Fidell, L. S. 1989: *Using multivariate statistics*. New York: Harper & Row.

Tellegen, A., Lykken, D. T., Bouchard, T. J., Wilcox, K., Segal, N. and Rich, A. 1988: Personality similarity in twins reared together and apart. *Journal of Personality and Social Psychology* 54, 1031–9.

Thompson, L. A. 1993: Genetic contributions to intellectual development in infancy and childhood. In Vernon, P. A. (ed.), *Biological approaches to the study of human intelligence*. Norwood, NJ: Ablex, 95–138.

Thurstone, L. L. 1938: *Primary mental abilities*. Chicago: University of Chicago Press.

Thurstone, L. L. 1947: *Multiple factor analysis: a development and expansion of the vectors of mind*. Chicago: University of Chicago Press.

Truax, C. B. and Mitchell, K. M. 1971: Research on certain therapist interpersonal skills in relation to process and outcome. In Bergin, A. E. and Garfield, S. L. (eds), *Handbook of psychotherapy and behaviour change*. New York: Wiley, 299–344.

Tryon, R. C. 1940: Genetic differences in maze-learning ability in rats. *Yearbook of the National Society of Student Education* 39, 111–19.

Tupes, E. C. and Christal, R. E. 1961: *United States Air Force ASD Technical Report No. 61–97*. San Antonio, TX: Lackland Air Force Base.

Tupes, E. C. and Christal, R. E. 1992: Recurrent personality factors based on trait ratings. *Journal of Personality* 60, 225–51.

Undheim, J. O. 1981: On intelligence. I. Broad ability factors in 15-year-old children and Cattell's theory of fluid and crystallised intelligence. *Scandinavian Journal of Psychology* 22, 171–9.

Vegelius, J. 1976: On various G index generalizations and their applicability within the clinical domain. *Studia Psychologica Upsaliensia, Number 4*. Uppsala: Acta Universitatis Upsaliensis.

Velicer, W. F. 1976: Determining the number of components from the matrix of partial correlations. *Psychometrika* 41, 321–7.

Velicer, W. F. and Jackson, D. N. 1990: Component analysis versus common factor analysis: some issues in selecting an appropriate procedure. *Multivariate Behavioral Research* 25, 1–28.

Velten, E. J. 1968: A laboratory task for the induction of mood states. *Behavior Research and Therapy* 6, 473–82.

Vernon, P. A. and Mori, M. 1992: Intelligence, reaction times and peripheral nerve conduction velocity. *Intelligence* 16, 273–88.

Vernon, P. E. 1950: *Structure of human abilities*. London: Methuen.

Vernon, P. E. 1963: *Personality assessment: a critical survey*. London: Methuen.

Vernon, P. E. 1979: *Intelligence, heredity and environment*. San Francisco: W. J. Freeman & Co.

Vickers, D., Nettelbeck, T. and Willson, R. J. 1972: Perceptual indices of performance: the measurement of 'inspection time' and 'noise' in the visual system. *Perception* 1, 263–95.

Wainer, H. 1987: *The first four millennia of mental testing: from ancient China to the computer age*. Research Report No. RR-87–34. Princeton, NJ: Educational and Testing Service.

Wallace, G. and Worthington, A. G. 1970: The dark adaptation index of perceptual defence: a procedural improvement. *Australian Journal of Psychology* 22, 41–6.

Watson, D. and Tellegen, A. 1985: Towards a consensual structure of mood. *Psychological Bulletin* 98, 219–35.

Watson, D., Clark, L. A. and Tellegen, A. 1988: Development and validation of a brief measure of positive and negative affect: the PANAS scales. *Journal of Personality and Social Psychology* 54, 1063–70.

Wessman, A. E. and Ricks, D. F. 1966: *Mood and personality*. New York: Holt, Rinehart & Winston.

Wickett, J. C. and Vernon, P. A. 1994: Peripheral nerve conduction velocity, reaction time, and intelligence: an attempt to replicate Vernon and Mori (1992). *Intelligence* 18, 127–31.

Wiggins, J. S. and Pincus, A. L. 1992: Personality: structure and assessment. *Annual Review of Psychology* 43, 473–504.

Wilson, R. C. 1983: The Louisville Twin Study: developmental synchronies in behavior. *Child Development* 54, 298–316.

Wingersky, M. S., Barton, M. A. and Lord, F. M. 1982: *LOGIST user's guide*. Princeton, NJ: Educational Testing Service.

Zajonc, R. B. 1980: Feeling and thinking: preferences need no inferences. *American Psychologist* 35, 151–75.

Zajonc, R. B. 1984: On the primacy of affect. *American Psychologist* 39, 117–23.

Zeidner, M. 1995: Personality trait correlations of intelligence. In Saklofske, D. H. and Zeidner, M. (eds), *International handbook of personality and intelligence*. New York: Plenum, 299–320.

Zevon, M. A. and Tellegen, A. 1982: The structure of mood change: an idiographic/nomothetic analysis. *Journal of Personality and Social Psychology* 43, 111–22.

Zuckerman, M. 1979: *Sensation seeking*. London: Wiley.

Zuckerman, M. 1991: *Psychobiology of personality*. Cambridge: Cambridge University Press.

Zuckerman, M. 1992: What is a basic factor and which factors are basic? Turtles all the way down. *Personality and Individual Differences* 13, 675–81.

Zuckerman, M. 1994: *Behavioral expressions and biosocial bases of sensation seeking*. Cambridge: Cambridge University Press.

Zuckerman, M., Kuhlman, D. M., Joireman, J., Teta, P. and Kraft, M. 1993: A comparison of three structural models for personality: the big three, the big five and the alternative five. *Journal of Personality and Social Psychology* 65, 757–68.

Zwick, W. R. and Velicer, W. F. 1986: Comparison of five rules for determining the number of components to retain. *Psychological Bulletin* 99, 432–42.

Subject index

Author index